Second Edition

SOCIOLOGY AS

for OCR

Stephen Moore Dave Aiken Steve Chapman

Collins

An imprint of HarperCollinsPublishers

William Collins' dream of knowledge for all began with the publication of his first book in 1819. A self-educated mill worker, he not only enriched millions of lives, but also founded a flourishing publishing house. Today, staying true to this spirit, Collins books are packed with inspiration, innovation and practical expertise. They place you at the centre of a world of possibility and give you exactly what you need to explore it.

Collins. Do more.

Published by Collins
An imprint of HarperCollins*Publishers* Limited
77–85 Fulham Palace Road
Hammersmith
London W6 8JB

Browse the complete Collins catalogue
at **www.collinseducation.com**

© HarperCollinsPublishers Limited 2005

Reprint 10 9 8 7 6 5 4 3 2 1

ISBN 0 00 719565 6

Commissioned by Thomas Allain-Chapman
Consultant editor Peter Langley
Reader Pam Law
Project managed by Hugh Hillyard-Parker
Production by Sarah Robinson
Edited by Ros Connelly
Cover design by Blue Pig Design
Internal design by Patricia Briggs
Typesetting by Hugh Hillyard-Parker
Photo research by Thelma Gilbert
Figures typeset by Liz Gordon
Cartoons by Oxford Designers and Illustrators
Index by Indexing Specialists (UK) Ltd, Hove, UK
Printed by Martins the Printers, Berwick-upon-Tweed, UK

Author acknowledgements

Stephen Moore would like to acknowledge the contribution of Claudia Moore in research and preparation.

Dave Aiken: Thanks again to Maggie for her unrelenting support – back on ironing duty I promise (and not just my own shirts, Ms Oakley). Love to the kids, Leo, Laurie and Amelia, who helped keep things in perspective, and to the Collins team for their patience. Also dedicated in loving memory of my mother (14/4/1930 to 12/6/2002), whose intelligence, sense of justice and love will always inspire me to make a positive contribution wherever I can.

Steve Chapman: For Fiona.

Sociology AS for OCR

UNIT 1 **The individual and society** **1**

Topic 1	Socialization, culture and identity	2
Topic 2	Consensus, culture and identity	6
Topic 3	Conflict, culture and identity	10
Topic 4	Social action, culture and identity	14
Topic 5	Postmodernism	20
Topic 6	Class and identity	24
Topic 7	Gender and identity	30
Topic 8	Ethnicity and identity	34
Topic 9	National identity	40
	Unit summary	46

UNIT 2 **Family** **48**

Topic 1	Defining the family	50
Topic 2	The family, morality and the state	56
Topic 3	Marriage and marital breakdown	62
Topic 4	Family diversity	68
Topic 5	Childhood	74
Topic 6	Power and control in the family	80
Topic 7	The dark side of family life	86
	Unit summary	92

UNIT 3 **Mass media** **94**

Topic 1	Ownership and control of the mass media	96
Topic 2	Public service broadcasting	102
Topic 3	The content of the mass media: making the news	106
Topic 4	How do the media affect people?	112
Topic 5	Is there too much violence in the media?	116
Topic 6	Gender and the media	122
Topic 7	Media representations	128
Topic 8	Postmodernism and the media	134
	Unit summary	138

UNIT 4 **Religion** **140**

Topic 1	Religion as a conservative influence on society	142
Topic 2	Religion as a force for social change	148
Topic 3	Organized religion and religious institutions	152
Topic 4	New religious and New Age movements	158
Topic 5	Gender, feminism and religion	164
Topic 6	Religion and ethnicity	170
Topic 7	The secularization debate	176
	Unit summary	182

UNIT 5 **Youth and culture** **184**

Topic 1	Youth culture	186
Topic 2	Functionalist and conflict theories of youth culture	192
Topic 3	Late-modern and postmodern theories of youth culture	198
Topic 4	Subcultural theories of youth offending	204
Topic 5	Gangs	210
Topic 6	Youth and schooling	216
	Unit summary	224

UNIT 6 **Sociological research skills** **226**

Topic 1	Researching social life	228
Topic 2	Methods, theories and ethics	234
Topic 3	Quantitative research: getting 'the truth'?	240
Topic 4	Understanding people: observation	246
Topic 5	Asking questions: questionnaires and interviews	252
Topic 6	Secondary sources of data	258
	Unit summary	264

UNIT 7 **Preparing for the AS exam** **266**

Topic 1	Preparing for the OCR AS-level exam	268

References	272
Index	276

ACKNOWLEDGEMENTS

The publishers would like to thank the following for permission to reproduce photographs. The page number is followed, where necessary, by T (top), B (bottom), L (left), R (right) or C (centre).

Alamy (1); Mary Evans Picture Library (2); Alamy (6); Science Photo Library (7); Alamy (14); Alamy (17L); Rex Features (17C); S&R Greenhill (17R); South American Picture Library (18); Mary Evans Picture Library (20L); Alamy (20R); Corbis (24TL); Alamy (24TR); Rex Features (24B); Empics (30L); Corbis (30CL&R); Alamy (30R); Rex Features (34TL&BR); Empics (34TR); Alamy (34BL); Empics (40 all); Getty-Images (49); Brian Jones (50); Ronald Grant Archive/Fox Television (51); Corbis (56TL&B); Network Photographers (56TR); Bubbles Photo Library (59, 60); Rex Features (62T); Getty-Images (62B); Getty-Images (65); Alamy (66); Photofusion (68 both); Bubbles Photo Library (69); Courtesy of NSPCC (74TL); Rex Features (74TR); Still Photos/Sebastian Bolesch (74BL); S&R Greenhill (74BR); S&R Greenhill (77); Bubbles Photo Library (80); Photofusion (83); Alamy (88); Rex Features (95); BBC/Dave Pickthorn (104); Associated Press (109); Corbis (112); Rex Features (116); Kobal Collection (118 both); Rex Features (119); Advertising Archives (122TL); Kobal Collection (122TR); BBC/Adam Pensotti (122 BL); Sky Sports (122 BR); Roger Scruton (125); Advertising Archives (128); Rex Features (130); PA/Empics (132, 135); Alamy (141); S&R Greenhill (142T); Panos (142C); Alamy (142B); Rex Features (144L); Alamy (144R); Rex Features (148 all); Empics (152L&R); Alamy (152C); Rex Features (154, 159); Alamy (161); Elvis (164); Rex Features (166); Alamy (172, 173); Rex Features (177T); Roger Scruton (177BL); Dave Aiken (177BR); Alamy (185); Rex Features (186 All); Alamy (188); Topfoto (189, 190R); Aquarius (190L); Alamy (192L); Rex Features (192R, 195, 198T&B); Alamy (198C, 201); S&R Greenhill (206); Alamy (210); Rex Features (213); Alamy (216); Getty-Images/Imagebank (227); Rex Features (228); Alamy (231); Photofusion (234); Topfoto (235); Rex Features (240); S&R Greenhill (241); Photofusion (244); Alamy (246); Getty-Images (249TL&TR); Getty-Images/ Imagebank (247BL); Empics (247BR); Rex Features (249); Alamy (255); Mary Evans Picture Library (258); Hugh Hillyard-Parker (260); S&R Greenhill (261); Science Photo Library (262); Corbis (267, 268).

Every effort has been made to contact copyright holders, but if any have been inadvertently overlooked, the publishers will be pleased to make the necessary arrangements at the first opportunity.

The organization of the book

The book is divided into a series of units, each linking into OCR AS-level modules. Each unit consists of a number of topics, which divide the unit into manageable parts. Each topic starts by building on your prior knowledge; it then goes on to provide all the knowledge you need, before giving you the chance to check your understanding and reinforce key concepts. There is then an opportunity to apply the knowledge, practise an exam-style question and build wider skills. Finally, there are research- and internet-based extension activities, creating opportunities to explore issues further.

Features of the textbook

Each topic contains a number of features designed to help you with learning, revision and exam-preparation. These are illustrated and described on the following two pages.

In addition to regular topic features, each unit ends with a Unit summary in the form of a 'spider diagram'. This provides an attractive visual overview of the whole unit and identifies important connections between the topics. This feature should prove particularly useful for revision. See, for example, pp. 46–7.

Sociology for AS Level: A guide for OCR candidates

The table below shows how the units in this book relate to the OCR AS-level specification. Turn to Unit 7: *Preparing for the AS exam* (pp. 266–71) for more detail and an explanation of the courses and their assessment.

How this textbook covers the OCR AS specification

Texbook unit	OCR AS
Unit 1 The individual and society	**AS module 2532:** The individual and society
Unit 2 Family	**AS module 2533** Culture and socialisation: Family option
Unit 3 Mass media	**AS module 2533** Culture and socialisation: Mass media option
Unit 4 Religion	**AS module 2533** Culture and socialisation: Religion option
Unit 5 Youth and culture	**AS module 2533** Culture and socialisation: Youth and culture option
Unit 6 Sociological research skills	**AS module 2534** Sociological research skills. Also provides the content for **module 2535**: Research report

GUIDED TOUR OF A TOPIC

Getting you thinking

The opening activity draws on your existing knowledge and experiences to lead in to some of the main issues of the topic. The questions are usually open and, although suitable for individual work, may be more effectively used in discussion in pairs or small groups, where experiences and ideas can be shared.

Main text

The important sociological concepts, debates and the latest research are all covered. A careful balance between depth and accessibility is maintained in every unit.

TOPIC 2

Functionalist and conflict theories of youth culture

getting you thinking

1. What names would you give to the youth cultural styles pictured here? When were they most popular? Are they still popular?
2. Identify as many youth cultures as you can.
3. Take one of these and try to work out what attracts young people to this particular style.
4. How many of your friends would identify with a particular youth cultural style?
5. To what extent do you think youth cultural styles are important to young people?

In Topic 1, we saw how youth culture developed in the 1950s as a result of a number of different social changes occurring together. However, sociologists are interested in looking beyond this to see if there are any general theoretical explanations for the development of youth culture.

Four major theoretical schools have provided competing overall explanations for the nature and existence of youth culture. These are:

- functionalist
- conflict
- late modern
- postmodern.

Because these approaches cover such wide ground, we have divided them into two topics. In this topic, we are going to explore functionalist and conflict (or Marxist-derived) approaches. In Topic 3, we move on to look at countercultures, late-modern and postmodern theories. In both topics, we will

choose various youth subcultural styles that sociologists have studied and use them as examples of the theories. We will also include discussion on 'race' and gender issues where they are relevant. However, you must remember that both topics are closely related and, in order to gain a full understanding, you need to combine the insights of both topics.

The functionalist approach: youth as transition

Functionalist theories are based on the idea that if something exists in society, then it must be there for a purpose. Their argument is simple: youth culture undoubtedly exists and it must, therefore, serve some purpose. This approach to understanding social phenomena has a long history in sociology. It can be traced back as early as the end of the 19th century in the work of Emile Durkheim and then, in a more

---

focus on research

Reynolds *et al.* (2003)
Caring and counting

The researchers interviewed 37 mothers and 30 fathers in couples who had at least one pre-school child (Reynolds *et al.* 2003). The mothers were working in a hospital or in an accountancy firm. All the mothers in the study had strong, traditional views about what being a 'good mother' and a 'good partner' was about. Employment did not necessarily lead to more egalitarian relationships with their partners.

In fact, most of the mothers and fathers interviewed subscribed to highly traditional and stereotypical views about the gendered division of labour within the

home. The mothers had primary responsibility for the home and the conduct of family life. Mothers who worked full time were just as concerned as those working part time to 'be there' for their children and to meet the needs of their children and their family. The researchers found no evidence of mothers becoming more 'work centred' at the expense of family life.

Apart from increasing the family income, mothers also felt their employment was helping them to meet their children's emotional and social development. Separate interviews with the women's partners revealed widespread agreement that the mother's work was having a positive impact on family relationships. Most fathers felt their children had benefited from their mothers' work, which provided a positive role model for their children.

Some mothers, nevertheless, expressed concern that their job had a negative impact on the family, particularly when they were overstretched at work, felt tired or had trouble 'switching off' from a bad day at work. A number of fathers also felt uneasy about the demands placed on their partners at work and the effect that work-related stress could have on their children and their relationship with each other.

Adapted from the website of the Joseph Rowntree Foundation (www.jrf.org.uk)

1. Comment on the sample used in the study.
2. How did parents feel that mothers' employment was having a positive effect on their families?
3. What concerns were expressed about mothers' employment?

Focus on research activities

A recent piece of interesting and relevant research is summarized, followed by questions that encourage you to evaluate the methods used as well as the conclusions drawn.

Check your understanding

These comprise a set of basic comprehension questions – all answers can be found in the preceding text.

Check your understanding

1 What do we mean by quantitative research?

2 Explain in your own words the importance of sampling.

3 Why are random samples not always representative?

4 What is 'quota' sampling? What is the main drawback of this method?

5 Identify and explain, in your own words, three types of random sampling.

6 In what situations might a sociologist use:
(a) snowball sampling?
(b) theoretical sampling?

7 Why don't sociologists use experiments?

8 What is a case study?

9 Give one example of a research project that has used the comparative method.

Key terms

There are simple definitions of important terms and concepts used in each topic, linked to the context in which the word or phrase occurs. Most key terms are sociological, but some of the more difficult but essential vocabulary is also included. Each key term is printed **in bold type** the first time it appears in the main text.

KEY TERMS

Familial ideology the view that a particular type of family (e.g. the nuclear family) and particular living arrangements (e.g. marriage, men as breadwinners, women as mothers and housewives, etc.) are the ideals that people should aspire to.

Idealized presented as an ideal.

Maternal deprivation the view that if a child is deprived of maternal love for any significant period of time, it will grow up to be psychologically damaged.

New Right a group of thinkers and commentators who believe very strongly in tradition. They tend to be against change and to support the Conservative Party.

Private institution something that occurs 'behind closed doors', with few links with the wider community.

Web tasks

Activities using the worldwide web to develop your understanding and analysis skills. This feature also serves to identify some of the key websites for each topic.

web.task

Go to the archive search at the website of the *Guardian* newspaper (www.guardianunlimited.co.uk) and key in the words 'government' and 'church'. What evidence can you find for the continuing influence of the church on politics in modern society?

research idea

- Interview (or conduct a focus group with) a small number of fellow students who attend religious events on a regular basis. Try to cover a range of religions. Ask them about their beliefs and their views about society.

  – Do they argue for social change or are they content with the way things are?

  – If they want change, what sort of changes are they looking for?

  – How do they think these might come about?

Research ideas

Suggestions for small-scale research which could be used as the basis for AS or A2 coursework, or for class or homework activities.

Exploring ...

Data response activities which follow the format of OCR AS-level exam papers. They reflect the structure of OCR questions for each module and can be used to assess your progress at the end of each topic, as well as providing regular exam practice.

exploring postmodernism and the media

Item A Use of new technology in the UK 1997 to 2004

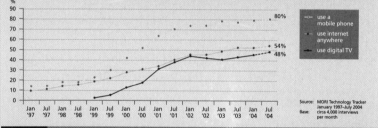

Source: MORI Technology Tracker January 1997–July 2004
Base: circa 4,000 interviews per month

Item B Class differences in the use of new technology

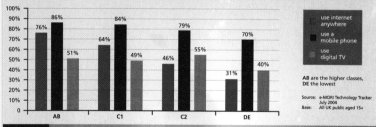

AB are the higher classes, DE the lowest

Source: e-MORI Technology Tracker July 2004
Base: All UK public aged 15+

Item C Cultural imperialism

In 1981, American films accounted for 94 per cent of foreign films broadcast on British TV, 80 per cent of those broadcast on French TV and 54 per cent on West German TV. In Western Europe as a whole, American imports represented 75 per cent of all imports. The share represented by US-originated programmes in other parts of the world is even greater. These media products depict Western (often idealized) lifestyles. This cultural imperialism is transnational. More recently, there has been some debate as to whether the US dominance is slipping, with increased competition at regional, national and local levels.

However, what has happened to replace American programming is in many cases a local adaptation of American television formats. Local cultures are re-presented in an Americanized form.

Adapted from Taylor, S. (2001) *Sociology: Issues and Debates*, London: Routledge

1 Explain in your own words what is meant by the term 'cultural imperialism' (Item C). (2 marks)

2 Identify and explain two ways in which the use of new technology is increasing (Item A). (4 marks)

3 Identify and explain three possible reasons for differences in the use of new technology according to social class (Item B). (9 marks)

4 Identify and explain two ways in which new technologies have had an impact on social life. (10 marks)

Exam practice

5 a Identify and explain two ways in which use of the media has changed in the last 20 years. (15 marks)

b Outline and discuss the view that we now live in a media-saturated society which defines our lifestyle and consumption patterns. (30 marks)

WHERE DO YOU BEGIN to look at a subject whose subject matter covers some of the most complicated and controversial issues facing humankind? Not an easy task. This unit begins by focusing on two key themes in the study of human societies. The first explains how societies are created and identifies some of the forces that bind people together into social groups.

Given the wide-ranging and controversial nature of the subject, it's not surprising that when sociologists look at societies they focus on different things. Some see shared values and agreement, while others see conflict and inequality for example. Topics 2 to 4 introduce you to some key sociological perspectives – perspectives that will reappear throughout your Sociology course. Topic 5 looks at recent social change in the context of a discussion of postmodernism.

The second half of this unit focuses on how members of society acquire their identity. Topics 6 to 9 focus on how our social class backgrounds, our gender, our ethnicity and our nationality impact on how we see ourselves and how others see us.

OCRspecification	topics	pages
Introducing the individual and society		
The role of values, norms and the agents of socialisation in the formation of culture	Covered in Topic 1	2–5
Learning social roles. How expected patterns of behaviour regulate social life	Covered in Topic 1	2–5
Culture and the formation of identities		
The meaning of 'gender identities'. The process of gender-role socialization.	Covered in Topic 7	30–33
The meaning of 'national' identities. The role of institutions in shaping and reinforcing national identity.	Covered in Topic 9	40–45
The meaning of 'ethnic identities'. Their impact on social behaviour.	Covered in Topic 8	34–39
The meaning of 'class identities'. Their impact on social behaviour.	Covered in Topic 6	24–29
Contemporary social change and the implications for gender, national, ethnic and class identities.	Recent social change is the subject of Topic 5. Changes in identities are covered as part of the discussion of particular identities in Topics 6, 7, 8 and 9.	20–23 24–45

The individual and society

TOPIC 1 Socialization, culture and identity **2**

TOPIC 2 Consensus, culture and identity **6**

TOPIC 3 Conflict, culture and identity **10**

TOPIC 4 Social action, culture and identity **14**

TOPIC 5 Postmodernism **20**

TOPIC 6 Class and identity **24**

TOPIC 7 Gender and identity **30**

TOPIC 8 Ethnicity and identity **34**

TOPIC 9 National identity **40**

UNIT SUMMARY **46**

Socialization, culture and identity

getting you thinking

Feral children

Feral or 'wild' children are those who, for whatever reason, are not brought up by humans. One famous example of feral children is that of two infant girls, Kamala and Amala, who were lost in the jungle in India in about 1918. The girls had been found living with wolves, in a cave-like den. The older girl was 6 or 7 years old and the other, who died a year later, perhaps a year younger.

When captured, the girls were like animals. They were naked and ran in a sort of stooped crouch.

Kamala, one of the 'wolf children', being taught to accept food and drink by hand

They were afraid of artificial light. They were afraid of humans and kept a good distance. They did not display any characteristically human qualities. For example, they did not use tools of any kind, not even a stick. They did not know how to make a shelter. They did not walk upright. They did not laugh. They did not sing. They did not show any affection or attraction or curiosity towards humans. But what is especially striking is that the girls used no language. They used no noises or gestures to communicate. They didn't point at things or directions, or nod their head in agreement or disagreement. They preferred to eat with the dogs in the compound, who seemed to accept them. They ate by pushing their faces into the food, the way dogs do, and they drank by lapping from a bowl.

Adapted from Singh, J.A. and Zingg, R.N. (1942) *Wolf Children and the Feral Man*, New York: Harper

Shirbit culture

The Shirbit culture believes that the human body is ugly and that its natural tendency is to feebleness and disease. The Shirbit therefore indulge in rituals and ceremonies designed to avoid this, and consequently every household has a shrine devoted to the body. The rituals associated with the shrine are private and secret. Adults never discuss the rituals and children are told only enough for them to be successfully initiated. The focal point of the shrine is a box built into the wall in which are kept charms and magical potions for the face and body. These are obtained from the medicine men who write down the ingredients in an ancient and secret language which is only understood by the herbalist who prepares the potion. These potions are kept in the charm-box for many years. Beneath the charm-box is a small font. Every day, twice a day, every member of the family enters the shrine room in succession and bows his or her head before the charm-box, mingles different sorts of holy water in the font and proceeds with a brief rite of ablution.

The Shirbit have an almost pathological horror of and fascination with the mouth, the condition of which is believed to have a supernatural influence on all social relationships. Were it not for the rituals of the mouth, they believe their teeth would fall out, their friends would desert them and their lovers would reject them. Finally, men and women indulge in barbaric acts of self-mutilation. Men engage in a daily body ritual of scraping and lacerating their faces with a sharp instrument, while women bake their heads in a small oven once a month.

Based on Levine, R. (1956) 'Body language of the Nacirema', *American Anthropologist*, 58

1 Make a list of the things that the feral girls could not do and compare them with what you were capable of at the age of 6 or 7 years.

2 In your opinion, what skills were the feral girls likely to have that you lack?

3 What does the first extract tell us about the behaviour of human beings?

4 What aspects of Shirbit cultural behaviour seem alien to you?

5 In what ways might Shirbit behaviour be thought to resemble British culture?

Defining culture

What would you be like if all human influences were removed from your life? Tragic stories of **feral children**, such as that described on the left, show us very clearly that being human is about contact with other people. Without that contact we are reduced to basic and **instinctive** behaviour. But when humans work together – as they usually do – they create **cultures** that are complex, fascinating and utterly different. Our own culture always appears to be the most 'normal', while other cultures may seem strange, different and even inferior in some cases (a view known as **ethnocentrism**). Did you notice that the odd culture of the 'Shirbit' (described on the left) was actually a description of 'British' behaviour, especially our obsession with cleanliness, as it might appear to someone from a very different culture? ('Shirbit' is an anagram of 'British'.)

The idea of 'culture' is very important for sociologists. Culture is commonly defined as the way of life of a social group. More specifically, the term refers to 'patterns of belief, **values**, attitudes, expectations, ways of thinking, feeling and so on' which people use to make sense of their social worlds (Billington *et al.* 1998).

Some sociologists argue that culture also consists of **customs** and rituals, **norms** of behaviour, **statuses** and **roles**, language, symbols, art and material goods – the entire way in which a **society** expresses itself. Culture brings people together because it is shared and taken for granted. The idea of culture helps us to understand how individuals come together in groups and identify themselves as similar to or different from others.

When societies become larger and more complex, different cultures may emerge in the same society. Think of Britain today, where there are cultures based on different ages, genders, classes, ethnic groups, regions and so on – a situation known as **cultural diversity**. Sociologists refer to these 'cultures within cultures' as **subcultures**. They share some aspects of what we think of as 'British culture' – maybe eating with a knife and fork and speaking English – but they also possess distinctive cultural features that are all their own, for example, ways of dressing, accents and attitudes to the family.

The formation of culture

Culture is made up of several different elements, including values, norms, customs, statuses and roles.

Values

Values are widely accepted beliefs that something is worthwhile and desirable. For example, most societies place a high value on human life – although during wartime this value may be suspended. Other examples of British values include fair play, democracy, free speech, achievement, tolerance, wealth, property, romantic love, marriage and family life.

Norms

Norms are values put into practice. They are specific rules of behaviour that relate to specific social situations, and they govern all aspects of human behaviour. For example, norms govern the way we prepare and eat food, our toilet behaviour and so on. Norms also govern how we are supposed to behave according to our gender – that is, there are rules governing what counts as masculine or feminine behaviour. These norms have changed in recent years – for example, only 40 years ago, women with young babies going out to work or wearing trousers to work would have met with social disapproval.

Customs

Customs are traditional and regular norms of behaviour associated with specific social situations, events and anniversaries which are often accompanied by rituals and ceremonies. For example, in Britain many people practise the custom of celebrating Bonfire Night on November 5th, and this usually involves the ritual of burning a Guy Fawkes effigy and setting off fireworks.

It is also the social custom to mourn for the dead at funerals, and this usually involves an elaborate set of ritualistic norms and a ceremony. For example, it is generally expected that people wear black at funerals in Britain. Turning up in a pink tuxedo would be regarded as **deviant**, or norm-breaking, behaviour.

Statuses

All members of society are given a social position or status by their culture. Sociologists distinguish between 'ascribed' statuses and 'achieved' statuses. Ascribed statuses are fixed at birth, usually by inheritance or biology. For example, gender and race are fixed characteristics (which may result in women and ethnic minorities occupying low-status roles in some societies). Achieved statuses are those over which individuals have control. In Western societies, such status is normally attained through education, jobs and sometimes marriage.

Roles

Society expects those of a certain status to behave in a particular way. A set of norms is imposed on the status. These are collectively known as a role. For example, the role of 'doctor' is accompanied by cultural expectations about patient confidentiality and professional behaviour.

Culture and biology

Some people, known as **sociobiologists**, believe that human behaviour is largely the product of nature, so we can learn much about humans by studying animals. Most sociologists reject this view. If human behaviour were biologically determined, they argue, we could expect to see little variation in how people behave, whereas human behaviour is actually richly diverse. For example, if we look at other societies, we can see very different values and norms relating to gender roles, marriage, family and bringing up children. If human behaviour is influenced by biology at all, it is only at the level of physiological need – for example, we all need to sleep, eat and go to the toilet. However, when you look more closely, you find that even these biological influences are shaped by culture. Cultural values and norms determine what we eat. For example, insects are not popular as a food in Britain, and cannibalism would be regarded with horror. Cultural norms also determine *how* we eat. For example, eating behaviour is accompanied by a set of cultural norms called 'table manners', while the binge eating associated with bulimia is normally conducted in secret because of cultural disapproval.

Socialization and the transmission of culture

At birth, we are faced with a social world that already exists. Joining this world involves rapidly learning 'how things are done' in it. Only by learning the cultural rules of a society can a human interact with other humans. Culture needs to be passed on from generation to generation in order to ensure that it is shared. Shared culture allows society's members to communicate and cooperate. The process of learning culture is known as **socialization**. This involves learning the norms and values of a culture so that ways of thinking, behaving and seeing things are taken for granted or **internalized**.

Primary socialization

The family, and specifically parents, are central to **primary socialization**, the first stage in a lifelong process. Children learn language and basic norms and values. These can be taught formally, but they are more likely to be picked up informally by children imitating their parents. Parents may use **sanctions** to reinforce approved behaviour and punish behaviour defined as unacceptable. Such processes develop children's roles within the family and society so that children

learn how they are expected to behave in a range and variety of social situations.

Feral children

We can illustrate the importance of primary socialization and contact with culture by examining feral children (children brought up in the wild by animals) to see what cultural characteristics they lack. If we consider the case of Kamala and Amala (see p. 2), we can see that they lacked toilet training, table manners and any sense of decorum. They had no sense of humour and consequently did not know how to laugh. They had no sense of music and could not sing. They did not know how to show affection. All of these things are cultural products which we pick up within the family.

Secondary socialization

Other institutions and groups also participate in the socialization of children. These are often referred to as agents of **secondary socialization**. Schools, religion and the mass media all play a role in teaching society's members how to behave in particular situations and how to interact with people of a different status.

Socialization in all its varied forms involves children interacting with others and becoming aware of themselves as individuals. It is the process through which children acquire both a personal and a social **identity**.

Culture, socialization and history

Norbert Elias (1978) argues that the process of socialization has grown more influential throughout history, so that culture exerts a greater civilizing influence over our behaviour now than in any other historical age. He points out that in the Middle Ages, there were fewer cultural constraints on individual behaviour. People ate with their fingers, urinated and defecated in public, and engaged in explicit sexual behaviour that today would be defined as indecent and obscene. Moreover, burping, breaking wind, spitting and picking one's nose in public were regarded as perfectly normal forms of behaviour.

KEY TERMS			
Cultural diversity describes a society in which many different cultures exist.	**Feral children** children brought up with limited contact with humans.	**Roles** positions in society such as 'mother' or 'police officer'. Roles are made up of norms.	**Society** a social system made up of social institutions such as the family, education, law, politics, the media, religion, peer groups, and so on.
Culture the way of life of a particular society or social group.	**Identity** the sense of who we are. **Instinct** a genetic or biological code in animals that largely determines their behaviour.	**Sanctions** actions that encourage or discourage particular behaviour, such as smiling or frowning at a young child.	**Sociobiology** the study of similarities between the natural and social worlds.
Customs traditional forms of behaviour associated with particular social occasions.	**Internalize** accept something so that it becomes 'taken for granted'.	**Secondary socialization** socialization that continues throughout life. Education, the media and religion are all important influences.	**Status** social position. **Subculture** a group within a larger culture that shares aspects of that culture but also has some of its own values, customs and so on.
Deviance rule-breaking behaviour.	**Norms** rules of behaviour in social situations.		
Ethnocentrism the belief that one culture is 'normal' and others inferior.	**Primary socialization** socialization in the very early years of life, normally through parents.	**Socialization** the process by which we learn acceptable cultural beliefs and behaviour.	**Values** widely accepted beliefs that something is worthwhile.

Culture and society

The concept of 'culture' is often used interchangeably with the concept of 'society', but it is important to understand that they do not mean exactly the same thing. Culture forms the connection between the individual and society – it tells the individual how to operate effectively within social institutions such as the family, marriage, education and so on. Zygmunt Bauman (1990) notes that socialization into culture is about introducing and maintaining social order in society. Individual behaviour that lies outside the cultural norm is perceived as dangerous and worth opposing because it threatens to destabilize society. Consequently, societies develop cultural mechanisms to control and repress such behaviour.

Culture and identity

Culture plays an important role in the construction of our identity. Identity is made up of two components – how we see ourselves and how others see us. It involves some choice on our part – that is, we often actively identify with aspects of our culture in regard to particular groups or activities, e.g. a football team, a friendship network, a fashion or trend. However, our identity is partly imposed on us by our culture. We are born into particular cultural positions or statuses – we do not choose our social class, gender, ethnic group, age, religion and nationality. Social forces like these shape our identity.

Check your understanding

1. Using examples, define what is meant by the terms 'values' and 'norms'.
2. Give an example of an ascribed status in Britain.
3. Why do sociologists believe that human behaviour is not biologically determined?
4. What is the difference between primary and secondary socialization?
5. What role does culture play in the construction of identity?

exploring culture and socialization

Item A Active socialization

Socialization is the process whereby the helpless infant gradually becomes a self-aware, knowledgeable person, skilled in the ways of the culture into which she or he is born. Children obviously learn a great deal from their parents but they also learn basic values, norms and language, from a range of people, including grandparents (especially grandmothers), childminders and babysitters, siblings and neighbours who act as 'aunts', etc. There are other secondary influences, such as playgroups and nurseries, as well as television, video and computer games and traditional media such as comics or storybooks. Children do not passively absorb these influences. They are from the very beginning active beings. They 'make sense' of their experience and decide for themselves how to react.

Adapted from Giddens, A. (1997) *Sociology* (3rd edn), Cambridge: Polity Press, p. 25 and Bernardes, J. (1997) *Family Studies: An Introduction*, London: Routledge, p. 112

a. Using Item A, identify and briefly explain two aspects of culture that children are socialized into by the family. (8 marks)

b. Identify and briefly explain the role in children's lives of the two secondary agents of socialization that are mentioned by Item A. (8 marks)

c. Outline and briefly evaluate two ways in which children may be influenced in terms of their behaviour by religion. (18 marks)

d. Discuss the view that without culture people are reduced to basic and instinctive behaviour. (26 marks)

research idea

- Draw up a questionnaire to give to other students which aims to find out the extent to which culture is shared. You might ask about aspects of culture such as mealtimes and food customs, leisure activities, values and beliefs, and taste in music. Carry out the survey and analyse your results.

web.task

Visit www.feralchildren.com

Choose a child and write a report on them detailing how the child differs from children who have experienced normal socialization.

Consensus, culture and identity

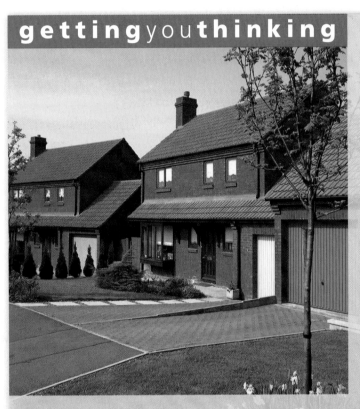

gettingyouthinking

<< Examining the homes in an English suburb, Nigel Barley noticed how organized they are. They begin with front gardens which must be kept in good order but never sat in; it is only permissible to sit in back gardens. Front doors, often elaborately furnished, open into a hall and various public rooms. Rooms are segregated according to functions relating to human bodily functions, such as eating, washing and defecating. Dinner, for example, will only be served in a bedroom if someone is ill. Access to rooms is regulated, so that access to the sitting room implies more formality than the kitchen, and lavatories can be used by visitors with permission. Bedrooms, where the most private undressing and sexual functions are performed, are considered to be the most personal rooms, and people knock on bedroom doors. The ideal is for each individual or sexual couple to have their own bedroom, and for new couples to have a new house. Bedrooms are individually furnished or decorated by their inhabitants, but it is never difficult to identify which member of the family owns a particular bedroom or their age or sex. >>

Billington, R. *et al.* (1998) *Exploring Self and Society*, Basingstoke: Macmillan, pp. 38–9

1 Can Barley's description of the suburban home be applied to your experience of home?

2 Do you think this description is typical of most homes in the UK?

3 Barley is describing a very ordered and structured world. What do you think is the reason for all this order and predictability? Where does it come from?

We learn from an early age to see our status as wrapped up with our home, and to see a happy family and home as important goals. In other words, there exists a great deal of agreement in society about how we ought to organize our daily lives. Sociologists refer to this agreement among members of society as **consensus**. This consensus means that we have a good idea of how we should behave in most situations. It also means that we can anticipate pretty accurately how other people are going to behave, just as we can guess the layout of their house or flat. Some sociologists see this order and predictability as the key to understanding society. If this order did not exist – if we were always confused and uncertain about our own and others' values and behaviour – then, they believe, chaos and anarchy would be the result. This theory of society is known as **functionalism** or consensus theory.

Functionalism

Functionalism is a **structuralist theory**. This means that it sees the individual as less important than the **social structure** or organization of society. It is a 'top-down' theory that looks at society rather than the individuals within it. Society is more important because the individual is produced by society. People are the product of all the social influences on them: their family, friends, educational and religious background, their experiences at work, in leisure, and their exposure to the media. All of these influences make them what they are. They are born into society, play their role in it and then die. But their deaths do not mean the end of society. Society continues long after they are gone.

Social order

Functionalists study the role of different parts of society – social institutions – in bringing about the patterns of shared and stable behaviour that they refer to as **social order**. They might study, for example, how families teach children the difference between right and wrong, or how education provides people with the skills and qualifications needed in the world of work. For functionalists, society is a complex system made up of parts that all work together to keep the whole system going. The economic system (work), the political system, family and kinship, and the cultural system (education, mass media, religion and youth culture) all have their part to play in maintaining a stable society from generation to generation.

A major function of social institutions is to socialize every individual into a system of norms and values that will guide their future behaviour and thinking. People need to be taught the core values of their society and to internalize them, so that they become shared and 'taken for granted'. The end result of this process is **value consensus** – members of society agree on what counts as important values and standards of behaviour. Such consensus produces a sense of **social solidarity**, i.e. we feel a sense of belonging to a group that has something in common. We feel a sense of common **identity**.

Another important foundation stone of social order in modern societies is the specialized division of labour. This refers to the organization of jobs and skills in a society. All members of society are dependent upon this division of labour, which supplies a vast and invisible army of workers to maintain the standard of living we take for granted. For example, hundreds of unskilled and skilled manual workers, professionals and managers are involved in supplying us with essential services such as electricity, gas, water, sewage systems, transport, food in supermarkets, and so on. The fact that you are able to sit in a classroom and read this book is also the product of hundreds of workers you will never see or meet. For example, someone has decided that your area needs a school or college, somebody has hired a caretaker to open and maintain the building, cleaners to clean, secretaries to run the office, teachers to teach and managers to decide to put on AS Sociology. The presence of this book in front of you required an author, editors, proofreaders, graphic designers, picture researchers, illustrators, a publisher, printers, people involved in the production of paper and ink, lorry drivers to transport the finished product to warehouses and bookshops, and someone behind the counter or a computer to sell it on to schools, teachers and students. Note, too, that you are already part of this division of labour. Without students, educational institutions would be pointless. The list of people we are dependent upon is endless. Think about how your life would change if all electricity workers were abducted by aliens overnight!

The specialized division of labour, therefore, is crucial because without it, society would soon descend into chaos. Consequently, another function of **social institutions** is to prepare young people to take their place in the division of labour by transmitting the idea that education, qualifications, working hard and a career are all worthwhile things. This ensures that young people will eventually come to replace workers who have retired or died, and so social order is maintained.

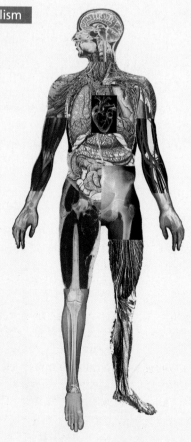

Figure 1.1 Understanding functionalism

Functionalism looks at society as though it were a living thing like a human being.

How is society like a human body?

The body

Every part of the body has a function which helps to keep it alive and healthy.

- The human body grows and develops.
- All of the parts of the body link together into one big system.
- The body fights disease.

Society

Every part of society helps to keep society going – for example, the family helps by bringing up the next generation.

- Societies gradually develop and change.
- All of the parts of society work together and depend on each other – they are interdependent.
- Society has mechanisms to deal with problems when they occur, such as the police and the legal system.

Talcott Parsons

Talcott Parsons (1902–79) was a key functionalist thinker. He argued that socialization is the key to understanding human behaviour patterns. The role of social institutions, such as the family, education, religion and the media, is to ensure the passing on, or reproduction, of socially acceptable patterns of behaviour. Social institutions do this in a number of ways:

- They socialize people into key values of society, such as the importance of nuclear family life, achievement, respect for authority and hierarchy, and so on. The result is that most members of our society share common values and norms of behaviour (value consensus), and consequently, we can predict how people are going to behave in the vast majority of social situations. The family, education and the mass media are primarily responsible for this function.
- They give some values and norms a sacred quality, so that they become powerful formal and informal moral codes governing social behaviour. These moral codes underpin our definitions of criminal, deviant and immoral behaviour. An example of a formal moral code is 'do not steal', because it is embodied in the law, while examples of more informal moral codes are 'do not lie' or 'do not commit adultery'. The social institutions of religion and the law are primarily responsible for the transmission of these codes, although media reporting of crime and deviance also contributes by reminding members of society about what counts as normality and deviance, and publicizing the punishments handed out to those who indulge in behaviour that lies outside the consensus.
- They encourage social solidarity (a sense of community) and **social integration** (a sense of belonging). For example, the teaching of history is an important means of achieving this goal, because it reminds members of society about their shared culture.

So, our behaviour is controlled by the rules of the society into which we are born. The result is that we don't have to be told that what we are doing is socially unacceptable. We will probably feel inhibited from indulging in such behaviour in the first place because we are so successfully immersed in the common values of society by our experience of socialization.

Identity

Identity is the way we feel about ourselves, which is partly shaped by how others view us. People's identity as fathers, mothers and children, for example, is controlled by a value consensus. This defines and therefore largely determines what roles each status has to adopt if it is to fit successfully into society. In other words, there is a clear set of expectations about what makes a 'good' mother or father, son or daughter. For example, people defined as 'normal' parents will engage in socially approved behaviour – they will protect their children from harm rather than neglect them or inflict excessive physical punishment on them; they will give them unconditional love; they will support them economically, and so on. Note that these expectations may change according to gender – hence the commonly held belief that working mothers, rather than working fathers, may be a cause of psychological damage in children. Functionalists point out that our experience of socialization and social control ensures that most of us will attempt to live up to those social and cultural expectations without question.

Criticisms of functionalism

Functionalism is far less popular in sociology today than it was in the 1950s. Part of its decline in popularity is probably linked to the problems it had attempting to explain all the diversity and conflict that existed in society from the 1960s onwards. Criticism of functionalism has therefore been widespread:

- Functionalism has been criticized for overemphasizing consensus and order, and failing to explain the social conflicts that characterize the modern world. We see clear differences in behaviour all around us every day, and there may be clear cultural differences present in the same society. For example, behaviours on which most of society might have been agreed 50 years ago, such as women with young children going out to work, cohabitation, abortion or homosexuality (which were all regarded as wrong), now attract a range of differing opinions. Some functionalists have attempted to explain this by reference to subculture. This can be defined as a way of life subscribed to by a significant minority who may share some general values and norms with the larger culture, but who may be in opposition to others. For example, in a

---

KEY TERMS

Consensus a general agreement.

Functionalism a sociological perspective that focuses on understanding how the different parts of society work together to keep it running smoothly.

Identity the way we feel about ourselves.

Social institution a part of society such as education or the family.

Social integration a sense of belonging to society.

Social order patterns of shared and predictable behaviour.

Social solidarity a sense of community.

Social structure an alternative term for the social organization of society.

Structuralist theory a theory that believes that human behaviour is influenced by the organization of society.

Value, or moral, consensus an agreement among a majority of members of society that something is good and worthwhile.

multicultural society like the UK, some minority ethnic groups may retain very traditional ideas about women's roles, marriage, homosexuality, etc.

- Functionalism has also been accused of ignoring the freedom of choice enjoyed by individuals. People choose what to do – they do what makes sense to them. Their behaviour and ideas are not imposed on them by structural factors beyond their control. In this sense, functionalism may present 'an oversocialized' picture of human beings.
- There may also be problems in the way functionalists view socialization as a positive process that never fails. If this were the case, then delinquency, child abuse and illegal drug-taking would not be the social problems they are.
- Finally, functionalism has been accused by Marxists of ignoring the fact that power is not equally distributed in society. Some groups have more wealth and power than others and may be able to impose their norms and values on less powerful groups. The next few topics focus on this process.

Check your understanding

1. Using your own words, explain what is meant by value consensus.

2. What are the key values of society according to Parsons, and what agencies are mainly responsible for their transmission?

3. What agencies are responsible for turning key values into powerful moral codes that guide our most basic behaviour?

4. Why do social agencies such as the law and the media need to regulate our behaviour?

5. How might the teaching of British history encourage a sense of community and integration in British schools?

exploring consensus, culture and identity

Item A Key social institutions

Durkheim believed that the function of social institutions was to promote and maintain social cohesion and unity. The family is one of the key institutions binding the individual into the fabric of social life. It provides society with an orderly means of reproduction and provides physical and economic support for children during the early years of dependence. The child learns the essential ideas and values, patterns of behaviour and social roles (such as gender roles) required for adult life. Education develops both values and the intellectual skills needed by children to perform the role in the specialized division of labour and society to which they are allocated. The discipline structure and socialization of children in schools function to maintain consensus and ensure that society operates smoothly. Religion provides a set of moral beliefs and practices which socially integrates people into a common identity and community.

Adapted from Chapman, K. (1986) *The Sociology of Schools*, London: Routledge, p. 38; Thompson, I. (1986) *Religion*, London: Longman, pp. 4–5; and Wilson, A. (1991) *Family*, London: Longman, pp. 9–10

a Using Item A, identify and briefly explain two functions of the family. (8 marks)

b Identify and briefly explain two ways in which socialization into gender roles contributes to an ordered and predictable society. (8 marks)

c Outline and briefly evaluate two ways in which children are socialized into a value consensus. (18 marks)

d Discuss the view that there exists a great deal of consensus in terms of values and norms in modern British society. (26 marks)

research idea

- Interview a sample of people of different ages and genders about their values. To what extent do they share similar values?

web.task

Search for the website 'Dead Sociologists' Society'. Use it to find out about the ideas of the founding father of functionalism, Emile Durkheim.

Conflict, culture and identity

gettingyouthinking

Imagine that we could illustrate the distribution of income in the UK by getting the population to take part in a parade that will take an hour to pass by. Imagine, too, that we can somehow magically alter the height of individuals in the parade so that it reflects how much money they have. Those with an average income will have a height of 5ft 8in. Our parade begins with those with the lowest incomes – in other words, the shortest people – and ends with those with the highest incomes – in other words, the tallest people.

The first people to pass by are tiny. For example, after three minutes, an unemployed single mother living on welfare goes by. She is about 1ft 10in high. Six minutes later a single male pensioner, owning his own home and claiming income support, passes by. He is about 2ft 6in high. After 21 minutes, semi-skilled manual workers start to pass by – they are 3ft 9in high. After 30 minutes, there is still no sign of the people

earning average incomes. We don't see these until 62 per cent of the population have gone by. After about 45 minutes skilled technicians pass – they are 6ft 10in tall. With ten minutes to go, heights really start to grow. Middle-class professionals pass by – they are 11 feet high. However, the real giants only appear in the last minute of the parade. Chief executives of companies over 60 feet high. In the last seconds, there are amazing increases in height. Suddenly, the scene is dominated by colossal figures, people as high as tower blocks. Most of them are businessmen, owners of companies, film stars and a few members of the Royal Family. Robbie Williams and Prince Charles are nearly a mile high. Britain's richest man is the last in the parade, measuring four miles high.

Adapted from Penn, J., quoted in Donaldson, P. (1973) *A Guide to the British Economy*, Harmondsworth: Penguin

1 What does this parade tell us about the way income is divided in the UK?

2 Give examples of how long it took for people on different incomes to appear in the parade.

3 Does the parade surprise you in any way? Is Britain more, or less, unequal than you thought?

Lots of students have part-time jobs. Perhaps you have. If so, you sell your time and your ability to work to an employer who, in return, gives you money. But is this a fair exchange? Think about why they employ you. It's not to do you a favour, but because they benefit: the work you do is worth more to them than the amount they pay you. They would benefit even more if they paid you less for the same work or got you to do more

work for the same pay. Of course, it would be better for you if you were paid more for the same work or worked less for the same pay. To put it another way, what is good for your boss is bad for you, and vice versa. There's a very basic conflict of interest between you and your employer. This conflict occurs not because you are unreasonable or your boss is money-grabbing. It occurs simply because the system works that way.

Marxism

This is the starting point for **Marxism**, a sociological perspective based on the ideas of Karl Marx (1818–83). For Marxists, the system we live in (which he called **capitalism**) divides everyone up into two basic classes: bosses and workers. Marx called the bosses the **bourgeoisie** or ruling class (because they controlled society), and the workers he called the **proletariat**. The ruling class benefit in every way from how society operates, while the workers get far less than they deserve.

Like functionalism, Marxism is a structuralist theory – that is, it sees the individual as less important than the social structure of society. In particular, Marxism sees the economic organization of societies as responsible for the behaviour of individuals. This is because Marxism claims that individuals are the products of the class relationships that characterize economic life.

Society is based on an exploitative and unequal relationship between two economic classes. The bourgeoisie are the economically dominant class (the ruling class) who own the **means of production** (machinery, factories, land, etc.). The proletariat or working class, on the other hand, own only their ability to work. They sell this to the bourgeoisie in return for a wage. However, the relationship between these two classes is unequal and based on conflict because the bourgeoisie aim to extract the maximum labour from workers at the lowest possible cost.

According to Marxists, the result is that the bourgeoisie exploit the labour of the working class. The difference between the value of the goods and services produced by the worker and the wages paid is pocketed by the capitalist class and lies at the heart of the vast profits made by many employers. These profits fuel the great inequalities in wealth and income between the ruling class and the working class. For example, according to the Inland Revenue, in 1994, 53 per cent of financial wealth in the UK was owned by 5 per cent of the population. Even if we add property ownership to financial wealth, the least wealthy 50 per cent of the population only own about 10 per cent of all wealth in the UK. These figures are also likely to be underestimates, because people generally do not declare the full sum of their wealth to the tax authorities – for instance, they may keep wealth abroad.

If society is so unfair, how come the working class go along with it? Why aren't there riots, strikes and political rebellion? Why does society actually appear quite stable, with most people pretty content with their position?

Ideology

Marxists argue that the working class rarely challenge capitalism because those who control the economy also control the family, education, media, religion – in fact, all the cultural institutions that are responsible for socializing individuals. Louis Althusser (1971) argued that the function of those cultural institutions is to maintain and **legitimate** class inequality. The family, education, the mass media and religion pass off ruling-class norms and values as 'normal' and 'natural'. Marxists refer to these ruling-class ideas as **ideology**.

Socialization is an ideological process in that its main aim is to transmit the ruling-class idea that capitalist society is **meritocratic** – that is, if you work hard enough, you can get on – despite the fact that the evidence rarely supports this view. This ideological device is so successful that the majority of the working class are convinced that their position is deserved. In other words, they are persuaded to accept their lot and may even be convinced that capitalism has provided them with a decent standard of living.

Marxists argue that capitalist ideology shapes the way of life of a society – its culture. A good example of this, say Marxists, is the way that the mass media convince us through advertising and popular culture – television, cinema, pop music, tabloid newspapers, etc. – that our priority should be to buy more and more material goods (see Figure 1.2 below). We want to be rich so that we can buy more and more and more, and, somehow, this will make us happy. What is more, while we are all watching soap operas and reading the latest celebrity gossip, we're not noticing the inequalities and exploitation of the capitalist system.

This means that most of us are not aware of our 'real' identity as exploited and oppressed workers. We experience what Marxists describe as **false class consciousness**. Eventually though, Marxists believe, we will learn the real truth of our situation and rebel against the capitalist system.

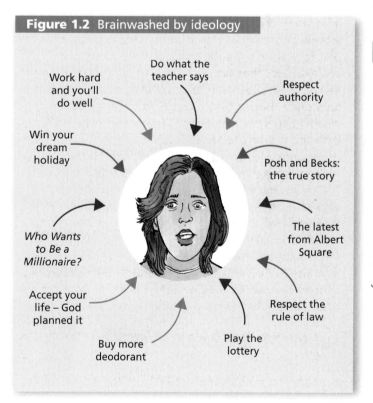

Figure 1.2 Brainwashed by ideology

- Do what the teacher says
- Work hard and you'll do well
- Respect authority
- Win your dream holiday
- Posh and Becks: the true story
- Who Wants to Be a Millionaire?
- The latest from Albert Square
- Accept your life – God planned it
- Respect the rule of law
- Buy more deodorant
- Play the lottery

Criticisms of Marxism

- The notion of 'false class consciousness' has been undermined by surveys such as those conducted by Marshall *et al.* (1988) and the government in the form of the British Social Attitudes survey (Jowell, *et al.* 1995). The British Social Attitudes survey found that 69 per cent of people thought their opportunities were influenced by their social class 'a great deal' or 'quite a lot'. Marshall argued that over 70 per cent of his survey sample believed that social class was an inevitable feature of British society and over 50 per cent felt that class conflict existed in the UK between a ruling class that monopolized economic and political power and a lower class that could do little to change its position. Marshall noted that most people were aware of social injustices, especially relating to inequalities in the distribution of wealth and income, but felt there was little they could do practically to bring about more equality. However, in support of the concept of ideology, Charlesworth's (1999) study of working-class people in Rotherham blames the educational system for this indifference and cynicism. He argues that the working-class experience of education results in them devaluing themselves and restricting their ambitions to 'being disappointed' in life.

- Like functionalism, Marxism has been accused of ignoring the freedom of choice enjoyed by individuals. People choose what to do and think – they are not 'brainwashed' by ideology. In this sense, Marxism too may present an 'oversocialized' picture of human beings.
- This criticism is not true of all Marxists. Some have argued that **oppositional subcultures** can exist within the capitalist system. For example, Hall and Jefferson (1976) argued that youth subcultures are often a means by which young people can express dissatisfaction with the capitalist system. They argued that the value systems, dress codes and behaviour of groups such as mods, skinheads and punks are a form of symbolic and temporary resistance to society. Their resistance is symbolic in that their behaviour often shocks society, but temporary in that they eventually become passive adults.
- Marxism may put too much emphasis on conflict. After all, despite all its inequalities, capitalism has managed to improve most people's standard of living. Perhaps Marxism also ignores common interests that employers and workers have. If workers work well, then the business does well and employers can afford to increase wages.
- Marxism, in general, has been criticized for claiming that all cultural activity is geared to class interests. Consequently, Marxists neglect the fact that culture may reflect religious, patriarchal, nationalistic and ethnic interests.

The work of Max Weber

Another sociologist who took a conflict perspective was Max Weber (1864–1920). He agreed with Marx that social class was an important source of inequality but argued that inequality could also be rooted in influences that have nothing to do with economics. Weber stressed the concept of 'status differences' as being at the heart of inequality – class was only one form of status. For example, Weber pointed out that in many societies, power is acquired from being born into a particular tribe or ethnic group. Inequality between Blacks and Whites in apartheid South Africa in the period 1950 to 1990 stemmed from status rather than social class, in that even the poorest White was regarded as having more status and power than educated and economically successful Black people.

In Hindu India, the **caste** system (even though illegal) still exerts a strong influence on inequality. In this system, every person is born into one of four closed status groups or, situated below these, the non-caste group known as 'untouchables'. This system of status differences is based upon religious purity – the better the life you lead, the more likely you will be reborn (reincarnated) as a member of a higher caste. Meanwhile, you cannot work your way out of your caste, your job is determined by it and you must marry within it.

Feminism

Feminists argue that another important status difference and source of inequality and conflict is gender. They point out that the UK is a patriarchal or male-dominated society – that is, men generally have more power and prestige than women across a range of social institutions. Women generally have less economic power than men. In 2003, women working full time earned on average 18 per cent less than men working full time and they were more likely to be in poverty. Natasha Walter, in *The New Feminism* (1999), notes that women do not enjoy equality of access to jobs, especially the top jobs in the city. Males still monopolize professional and managerial positions – for example, in 2000, only 18 per cent of hospital consultants, 7 per cent of university professors and 4.5 per cent of company directors were women. Moreover, women are still expected to be predominantly responsible for the upkeep of the home and child-rearing – surveys continue to indicate that family life is not yet characterized by equality between the sexes in terms of household labour.

Feminists believe that sexual discrimination is still a problem today and Walter argues that women still need to achieve financial, educational, domestic and legal equality with men.

KEY TERMS

Bourgeoisie (or **capitalists**) the owners of businesses, and the dominant class in capitalist societies.

Capitalism an economic system associated with modern societies, based on private ownership of businesses.

False class consciousness the state of not being aware of our true identity as exploited workers.

Ideology the norms and values that justify the capitalist system.

Legitimate make something appear fair and reasonable.

Marxism a sociological perspective based on the writings of Karl Marx. It believes that societies are unequal and unfair.

Means of production the land, factories, machines, science and technology, and labour power required to produce goods.

Meritocratic based on ability and effort.

Oppositional subcultures social groups whose value systems and behaviour challenge the dominant capitalist value system.

Proletariat the working class in capitalist societies.

Liberal feminists are optimistic that this will eventually happen. They believe that there has been a steady improvement in the position of women, as old-fashioned attitudes break down, more girls do well in education and more women have successful careers.

Other types of feminists are not so hopeful. Marxist-feminists argue that patriarchy suits the capitalist system as well as men, because women are unpaid domestic labourers who service the male labour force, making them fit and healthy for work, and who produce and rear the future workforce. True equality between the sexes can only occur when the capitalist system is dismantled.

Radical feminists believe that the patriarchal oppression and exploitation of women is built into every aspect of the way society is organized. In particular, the family is identified as the social institution in which patriarchy is rooted. Radical feminists argue that, through gender-role socialization, women are socialized into accepting female subordination and into seeing motherhood as their main goal in life. Moreover, radical feminists argue that men aggressively exercise their physical, economic and cultural power to dominate women in all areas of social life, and particularly in personal relationships, such as marriage, domestic labour, childcare and sex. All men benefit from this inequality – there are no good guys!

research idea

- Conduct a small survey to see how aware people are of (a) their social class and (b) inequalities in income and wealth in the UK.

Check your understanding

1 What is the relationship between the bourgeoisie and the proletariat?

2 What is the function of ideology?

3 Describe two important criticisms of Marxism.

4 What is the purpose of socialization according to Marxists?

5 How do youth subcultures challenge capitalism?

6 What other sources of inequality exist, apart from social class, according to Weber and feminist sociologists?

web.tasks

1 Using the website of the Office for National Statistics at www.statistics.gov.uk, try to find statistics that give an indication of the extent of inequality in Britain. You might look for figures on income, wealth, education and health.

2 Search for the website 'Dead Sociologists' Society'. Use it to find out about the ideas of Karl Marx.

exploring conflict, culture and identity

Item A Transmitting capitalist values

Marxists believe that social institutions such as the education system, the media, the legal system and religion are agents of capitalism which transmit ruling-class ideology. For example, the education system socializes the working class into believing that their educational failure is due to lack of ability and effort, when, in reality, the capitalist system deliberately fails them so that they will continue to be factory workers. Television socializes the working class into believing that consensus is the norm and that serious protest about the way society is organized is 'extremist'. The law socializes the working class into believing that the law is on their side when, in reality, it mainly supports and enforces the values and institutions of the capitalist ruling class.

Adapted from Brown, C. (1979) *Understanding Society: An Introduction to Sociological Theory*, London: John Murray, p. 75; and Moore, S. (1987) *Sociology Alive*, Cheltenham: Stanley Thornes, p. 274

a Using Item A, identify and briefly explain two ways in which the mass media socializes the working class into ruling-class ideology. (8 marks)

b Identify and briefly explain two means, other than the mass media, by which capitalism shapes working-class identity, according to Marxists. (8 marks)

c Outline and briefly evaluate two ways in which youth identity may challenge dominant capitalist values and norms. (18 marks)

d Discuss the view that identity is the product of the class relationships that characterize British economic and social life. (26 marks)

Social action, culture and identity

DRIVING LICENCE   A030019

1 Surname
PAYNE MR
2 Other names
JAMES   Town of birth
3 Date of birth   Worcester
24 03 1988
4 Permanent Address
14 Roseacre Drive
Worcester WR8 9LA
5 Issued by DVLA SWANSEA

6 Valid from   Valid until
17 09 2005   23 03 2058
7 No
PAYN 785288 B87VU

Signature
James Payne

EUROPEAN UNION

UNITED KINGDOM OF
GREAT BRITAIN
AND NORTHERN IRELAND

DIEU ET MON DROIT

PASSPORT

I have known Rachael for four years. She is a mature young woman who takes her responsibilities seriously. Consequently, she has a conscientious and industrious approach to her academic studies and can be trusted to work independently and with initiative. She also works well as a member of a team and is well liked and respected by both her peers and teachers. I have no doubt that you will find Rachael to be a thoroughly honest and reliable person. I was always impressed by her enthusiasm, persistence, motivation and ability to work under pressure. I have no hesitation in recommending her to your institution.

My mother loves me.
I feel good.
I feel good because she loves me.

I am good because I feel good
I feel good because I am good
My mother loves me because I am good.

My mother does not love me.
I feel bad.
I feel bad because she does not love me
I am bad because I feel bad
I feel bad because I am bad
I am bad because she does not love me
She does not love me because I am bad.

R.D. Laing (1970) *Knots*,
Harmondsworth: Penguin

1 What do these documents tell us about a person? What do they not tell us?

2 What does the reference tell us about Rachael's identity? What doesn't it tell us?

3 What does the poem tell us about this person's identity?

4 How does the self-identity apparent in the poem contrast with the picture of the individual in the reference?

Official documents tell us about the identity we present to the world – our date and place of birth, age, nationality, address, marital status and so on. References, like the example on the left, give us some insight into **social identity** – how well we perform our social roles, such as our jobs. However, poems, like the one on the left, can tell us about the way we see ourselves – our **self-identity** – and how this is often the result of how we interpret other people's reactions to us.

Think about a small child. Children try out different sorts of behaviour and then watch other people react. By doing this, they learn about themselves and about what is acceptable and unacceptable. In other words, people find out about themselves through the reactions of others.

Social action theory

What has just been described is the view of **social action** or **interactionist** sociologists. They reject the structuralist assumption that social behaviour is determined, constrained and even made predictable by the organization of society. They see people as having a much more positive and active role in shaping social life. If structuralist theory is a 'top-down' theory, then social action theory is 'bottom-up', as it starts with people rather than society.

Social action theorists reject the view that people's behaviour is the product of external forces over which they have little control. Most people do not feel themselves to be puppets of society. Rather, as Chris Brown (1979) notes:

≪*They feel they are living their own lives, making their own decisions and engaging, for the most part, in voluntary behaviour. There may be things they have to do which they resent, but resentment is, of course, tangible evidence of an independent self, forced to comply, but unwillingly and under protest.*≫

However, although we operate as individuals, we are aware of other people around us. Social action theorists argue that the attitudes and actions of those other people influence the way we think and behave – that society is the product of people coming together in social groups and trying to make sense of their own and each other's behaviour.

People are able to work out what is happening in any given situation because they bring a set of **interpretations** to every interaction and use them to make sense of social behaviour. In particular, we apply meanings to symbolic behaviour. For example, gestures are symbols – putting up two fingers in a V-sign may be interpreted as insulting, because it has an obscene meaning. When we are interacting with others, we are constantly on the lookout for symbols, because these give us clues as to how the other person is interpreting our behaviour – for instance, if they are smiling, we might interpret this as social approval, and if they maintain prolonged, intense eye contact, we might interpret this as a 'come-on'.

Our experience of this 'symbolic interaction' means we acquire a stock of knowledge about what is appropriate behaviour in particular situations. We learn that particular contexts demand particular social responses. For example,

I might interpret drinking and dancing at a party as appropriate, yet the same behaviour at a funeral as inappropriate. It is likely that other people will share my interpretations and so it is unlikely that the behaviour described would occur at the funeral.

Socialization and identity

Socialization involves learning a stock of shared interpretations and meanings for most given social interactions. Families, for example, teach us how to interact with and interpret the actions of others; education brings us into contact with a greater range of social groups and teaches us how to interpret social action in a broader range of social contexts. The result of such socialization is that children acquire an identity.

Social action theorists suggest that identity has three components:

1 Personal identity refers to aspects of individuality that identify people as unique and distinct from others. These include personal name, nickname, signature, photograph, address, National Insurance number, etc.
2 Social identity refers to the personality characteristics and qualities that particular cultures associate with certain social roles or groups. For example, in our culture, mothers are supposed to be loving, nurturing and selfless. Therefore, women who are mothers will attempt to live up to this description and hence acquire that social identity. As children grow up, they too will acquire a range of social identities, such as brother, sister, best friend, student. Socialization and interaction with others will make it clear to them what our culture expects of these roles in terms of obligations, duties and behaviour.
3 The individual has a **subjective** (internal) sense of their own uniqueness and identity. Sociologists call this the 'self'. It is partly the product of what others think is expected of a person's social identity. For example, a mother may see herself as a good mother because she achieves society's standards in that respect. However, 'self' is also the product of how the individual interprets their experience and life history. For example, some women may have, in their own mind, serious misgivings about their role as mother. The self, then, is the link between what society expects from a particular role and the individual's interpretation of whether they are living up to that role successfully.

The concept of self has been explored extensively by social action sociologists. Some have suggested that the self has two components – the 'I' and the 'me'. The 'I' is the private inner self, whereas the 'me' is the social self that participates in everyday interaction. When a person plays a social role as a teacher or student, it is the 'me' that is in action. The 'me' is shaped by the reactions of others – that is, we act in ways that we think are socially desirable. However, the 'I' supplies the confidence or self-esteem to play the role successfully.

Goffman (1961) argues that interaction is essentially about successful role-playing. He suggests that we are all social actors engaged in the drama of everyday life. Stage directions are symbolized by the social and cultural context in which the action takes place. For example, the classroom as a stage symbolizes particular rules that must be followed if the interaction is to be successful, e.g. students sit at desks while teachers can move around the room freely. Sometimes the script is already in place, e.g. we adhere to cultural rules about greeting people – 'Good morning, how are you?' – although often the script has to be improvised. Goffman argues that the public or social identity we present to the world is often simply a performance designed to create a particular impression. This makes sense if we think about how we behave in particular contexts or company, e.g. your behaviour in front of your grandparents is likely to be very different compared with your behaviour in front of friends. Therefore, you have a catalogue of different identities you can adopt.

Goffman invents a number of concepts that he claims people as social actors use in everyday action to assist in the management of other people's impression of them. Some people will use 'front' to manage an interaction. This refers to items of physical or body equipment that a social actor uses to enhance their performance – for example, teachers who want to convey authority may wear formal clothing to distance themselves from students. Another concept is 'region' – the classroom is the front region where the teacher 'performs', while the staffroom is where the teacher relaxes and becomes another person, such as the colleague or friend.

Labelling theory

Labelling theory is closely linked to the social action approach and helps us to understand how some parts of society may be responsible for socializing some people into identities that may have negative consequences. Take education as an example.

Interactionists believe that the social identity of pupils may be dependent on how they interact with teachers. If teachers act in such a way that pupils feel negatively labelled – as 'lazy' or 'thick', for example – then this will seriously affect their behaviour and progress.

Howard Becker (1963) pointed out that labels often have the power of a **master status**. For example, the master status of 'criminal' can override all other statuses, such as father, son or husband. In other words, deviant labels can radically alter a person's social identity. For example, someone labelled as 'criminal' may be discriminated against and find it difficult to get employment, make new friends and be accepted into their community. They may end up seeking others with similar identities and values, and form deviant subcultures. A **self-fulfilling prophecy** is the result, as the reaction to the label makes it come true.

Think about how the experience of streaming or setting may affect the self-esteem of a pupil. How do pupils who are placed in low streams or sets feel? They may well accept a view of themselves as 'failures' and stop trying – after all, what's the point if you're 'thick'? Or what if a pupil feels labelled as a 'troublemaker' because they are Black? The negative label may be internalized (accepted) and a self-fulfilling prophecy may occur. The self sees itself as a 'failure' or as 'deviant' and reacts accordingly. The label becomes true (see Figure 1.3 below).

Goffman (1961) illustrated the power of such labelling in his ethnographic study of inmates in a mental hospital in the USA. Goffman refers to such hospitals as 'total institutions' because they attempt to shape all aspects of their inmates lives, e.g. by organizing their routine. Goffman argues that total institutions deliberately break down a person's sense of self through a process he calls 'mortification' – they are stripped, given a common uniform to wear and referred to by a serial number.

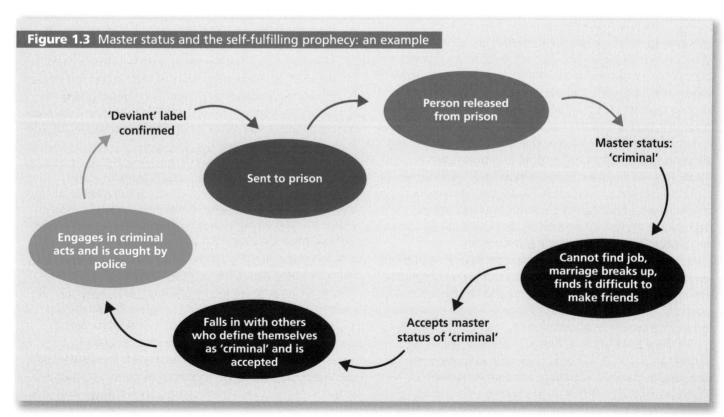

Figure 1.3 Master status and the self-fulfilling prophecy: an example

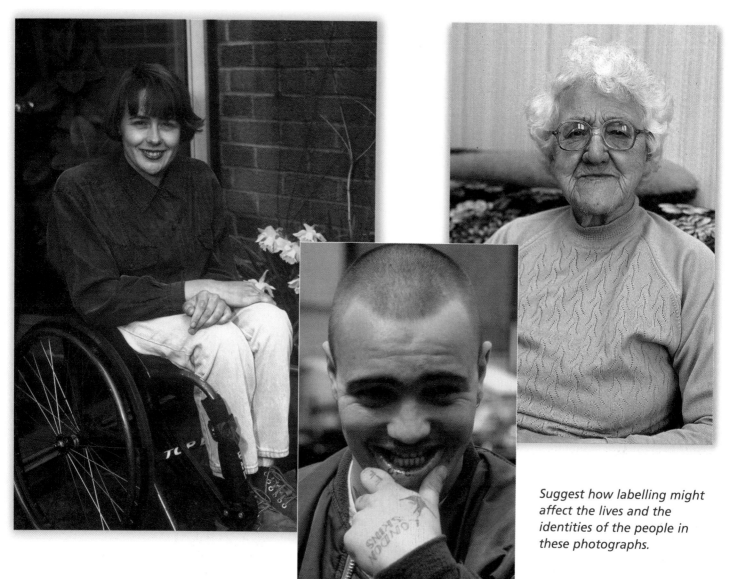

Suggest how labelling might affect the lives and the identities of the people in these photographs.

In other words, the institution sets about destroying individuality. The institution then attempts to rebuild the self in its own collective image. However, Goffman notes that the inmates he studied reacted in various ways to this process. Some conformed to the institution's demands; some even became institutionalized – they became so completely dependent on the institution that they could no longer survive in the outside world. Some, however, hung on to their individuality by giving the impression that they were conforming, while others openly opposed the system. What Goffman's work indicates is that the self and self-esteem can be very resilient and that labelling does not always have to be such a destructive process. Those who have been labelled can actually resist the definitions of the powerful.

Recent studies in a social action context have focused on how we interpret our bodies. It is argued that the way people view themselves and others is shaped by the dominant cultural ideas and images about ageing, body shape, weight and beauty that we see in media products such as magazines, advertisements, television and films. It is argued by feminist commentators that British culture sees the slim or thin female form as the ideal goal, with the result that young girls are socialized into seeing the slim figure as a source of status and success, while 'too much' weight is unattractive and socially inadequate. It is suggested that eating disorders, such as anorexia and bulimia, may be the outcome of these dominant cultural ideas, as female identity is often bound up with how women perceive their bodies. Research on female eating disorders suggests that those with the disorders often have low self-esteem and often subscribe to distorted images about their weight and attractiveness.

A recent symbolic interactionist study focused on shyness. Scott (2003) carried out in-depth interviews with 16 'shy' individuals in the South Wales area who volunteered after responding to an advertisement. She also set up a website about 'shyness and society' that included an email distribution list. Over a period of nine months, a virtual community composed of 42 individuals was created which exchanged ideas and discussed online the social aspects of shyness.

Scott found evidence of the notion of an 'I' and a 'me', in that shyness was often experienced as a conflict between a desire to be part of a social scene and the fear of being negatively judged or criticized. The shy 'I' was often beset by feelings of 'anxiety, uncertainty and inhibition', while the shy 'me' was concerned about how other people would view them – that is, they were afraid of making a fool of themselves or not

Douglas Yu
The Matsigenka

Douglas Yu (1998) carried out a study with the Matsigenka tribe, who lived in a remote area of South-Eastern Peru and had not been exposed to television and advertising. He showed male members of the tribe pictures of females with different body shapes. He found that the Matsigenka men favoured more 'rounded' female shapes, i.e. plump women. They often remarked that the slim-waisted females looked skinny or pallid – and were perhaps recovering from a bout of diarrhoea. The researchers then tested the perceptions of men who used to live in the same area but had since moved to towns, where advertising and television were more common. These males when shown the same images preferred the slimmer forms.

Adapted from Senior, M. (1999) 'With the body in mind', *Sociology Review*, 8(4)

1 What was the main cause of the difference in male perception in your view?

2 What do you think is the ideal body image, according to Matsigenka women?

3 What might be the effect on the Matsigenka women's body image and identity when television finally comes to that part of Peru?

fitting in. Many participants felt plagued by 'what if' feelings, such as 'what if they don't like me?'. Scott's sample often felt shy in particular social contexts in which the reactions of others were perceived as important. Scott notes that shyness is often seen as a 'deviant' activity, although society is likely to interpret it as 'normal' in particular social groups, such as among girls. She argues that there is a lot of moral pressure put on shy people to overcome their 'problem' through the use self-help books, miracle drugs and shyness clinics.

Criticisms of social action theory

Social action theories have been criticized because they tend to be very vague in explaining who is responsible for defining acceptable norms of behaviour. They do not explain who is responsible for making the rules that so-called deviant groups break. In this sense, they fail to explore the origin of power and neglect potential sources such as social class, gender and ethnicity. For example, Marxists argue that the capitalist ruling class define how social institutions such as education and the law operate. In other words, social action theories tend to be descriptive rather than explanatory.

Check your understanding

1 How is society formed, according to social action theorists?

2 From an interactionist perspective, what is the function of socialization?

3 What is meant by 'social identity'?

4 Explain the meaning of 'self'.

5 What causes a 'self-fulfilling prophecy'?

6 What is the result of deviant labels becoming master statuses?

KEY TERMS

Interpretations the meanings that we attach to particular objects or situations, e.g. we usually interpret classrooms as learning environments and act accordingly.

Labelling theory the idea that categorizing or stereotyping individuals or groups can seriously affect their behaviour. Used especially in the fields of education and deviance.

Master status a label or status that can override all others (e.g. criminal, child abuser).

Self-identity refers to how we see ourselves, usually in reaction to how we think others see us.

Self-fulfilling prophecy a prediction that makes itself become true.

Social action theory or **interactionism** a sociological perspective that focuses on the ways in which people give meaning to their own and others' actions.

Social identity refers to how society sees us, in terms of whether we live up to the cultural expectations attached to the social roles we play.

Subjective personal, based on your own view.

Item A 'All the world's a stage'

Individuals, like actors, are performing for an audience. Speech, acts and gestures all require someone else to be watching or listening. Our identities, therefore, are the product of how we present ourselves and how others perceive us. For example, you have to persuade your tutor that you have seriously adopted the identity and role of student. Your tutor may respond by according you an 'ideal' student label or identity. If you fail to convince, you may be labelled as a 'deviant' student, i.e. as idle or troublesome. This 'deviant' label is a 'master status' which overshadows other aspects of identity. Often, people who are considered deviant in one respect are assumed to be deviant in other respects. For example, other teachers may judge you negatively in staffroom discussions.

Those labelled as 'deviants' often experience stigma – people behaving differently towards them. In reaction, those labelled may pursue a deviant career by adopting a lifestyle which confirms their deviant status. In other words, a self-fulfilling prophecy results.

Adapted from Woodward, K. (ed.) (2000) *Questioning Identity: Gender, Class, Nation*, London: Routledge, pp. 14–15 and Croall, H. (1998) *Crime and Society in Britain*, Harlow: Longman pp. 61–2

a Using Item A, identify and briefly explain two ways in which a self-fulfilling prophecy might come about for a student in a school or college. (8 marks)

b Identify and briefly explain two criticisms of the concept of labelling. (8 marks)

c Outline and briefly evaluate two ways in which our identity in terms of body image may be affected by the interpretations of others. (18 marks)

d Discuss the view that social identity is largely the product of interaction with others. (26 marks)

research ideas

- Observe an everyday situation involving interaction between people. It could be in a library, at a bus stop, in a common room or a pub.
  - What is going on?
  - Does everyone share the same interpretation of the situation?
  - How do people try to manage the impression they give of themselves?

- Find two groups of students: one group who have experience of being placed in a high stream, and one group who have experience of being placed in a low stream. Give a questionnaire to, or interview, each group in order to find out how streaming affected their self-image, motivation and progress. Compare the responses of the two samples.

web.task

Visit the following websites on shyness and write a brief report detailing how it may affect a person's self-esteem and identity:

- **Susie Scott's 'Shyness and Society' website at www.cf.ac.uk/socsi/shyness**

- **The Shyness Institute, a major shyness research centre at www.shyness.com/shyness-institute.html**

- **The Shyness Home Page detailing the work of the American sociologists, L. Henderson and P.G. Zimbardo, at www.shyness.com**

Postmodernism

gettingyouthinking

Try to imagine the life ahead for the woman from the 1930s in the first photograph.

1 **What sort of family life do you think she would have had?**

2 **Might she have had paid employment? What problems might she have faced in pursuing a career?**

3 **What about the roles played by her and her husband?**

Now think about the future for the young woman of today.

4 **What sort of family life do you think she is likely to have?**

5 **Is she likely to have paid employment?**

6 **What about her relationship with her husband?**

You may well have found it fairly straightforward to plot out the future for the young woman of 70 years ago. Attempting the same task for a woman today is much more difficult. Maybe she will choose not to marry or live in a family. Maybe she won't have children. Alternatively, she could devote her life to a family, but then again she might decide to focus on following a career – or she could do both. The choices appear endless. Being a woman today seems much more flexible and uncertain – and less predictable – than in the past.

Sociologists have watched recent social changes with great interest. Some have reached the conclusion that society has experienced such major upheavals that the old ways of explaining it just won't work any more. They believe that we are

entering a new sort of society, which they refer to as the postmodern world or **postmodernity**. But before we can consider this, we need to head back to the beginnings of sociology.

Have you ever wondered why sociology came about? History tells us that sociology developed in order to explain the rapid social changes associated with **industrialization** and **urbanization** during the 19th century. Lives changed so drastically during this period that, not surprisingly, people began to look for theories and explanations that would help make sense of the bewildering changes taking place. Families left the rural communities where they had lived for centuries, to find work in the new cities. They had to adjust to a different lifestyle, different work, different bosses and different kinds of relationships with family and community.

On the whole, early sociologists approved of these changes and the kind of society they created – now commonly referred to as **modernity** or the modern world. They set out to document the key features of what they saw as an exciting new order.

The nature of the modern world

Sociologists have identified four major characteristics of the modern world:

1 *Industrialization* – Production is industrial and economic relationships are capitalist. Factories produce goods, bosses own factories, and workers sell their labour to bosses. Social class is therefore the basic source of difference and identity in modern societies.
2 *Urbanization* – Early modernity was associated with great population movement to the cities, known as urbanization. Twentieth-century theories of modernity have tended to celebrate the bright lights and innovation of the city while ridiculing rural culture as living in the past.
3 *Centralized government* – Government is characterized by a **bureaucratic** state that takes a great deal of responsibility both for the economy and for the welfare of its citizens.
4 *Rational, scientific thinking* – What really made modern society stand apart from premodern societies was the revolution in the way people thought about the world. Before industrialization, tradition, religion and superstition had provided the basis for views of the world. The modern world adopted a new way of thinking, shaped by science and reason.

New ideas and theories (referred to by postmodernists as '**big stories**' or **meta-narratives**) competed with each other to explain this constantly changing modern world and these theories frequently called for more social progress. Some of these theories were political (e.g. socialism), while others were cultural (e.g. the ideas of feminism). To paraphrase Marx, one of the leading modernist thinkers, their job was not just to explain the world – the point was to change it.

Sociology and the modern world

Sociologists were caught up in this excitement about modernity, and attempted to create scientific theories that would explain the transition from the traditional to the modern. One of the founding fathers of sociology, Auguste Comte, believed that sociology was the science of society. This **positivist** view argued that sociological research based upon scientific **rationality** could rid the world of social problems such as crime.

Marx, too, celebrated modernity, despite his criticism of its economic relationships, because he believed that science had given people the power to change the world. Sociological theories, therefore, also developed into meta-narratives as they attempted to provide us with knowledge or 'truth' about the nature of modernity.

The postmodern world

In the past 20 years or so, some sociologists have identified trends and developments which, they claim, show that modernity is fragmenting or dissolving. They argue that it is being replaced by a postmodern world in which many sociological ideas and concepts are becoming irrelevant.

Characteristics of postmodernity have been identified in aspects of work, culture, identity, globalization and knowledge.

Work

The nature of work and economic life has changed. Work is no longer dominated by mass factory production in which thousands of people work alongside each other. Work today is mainly located within the **service sector**, and is dominated either by jobs that mainly involve the processing of information (e.g. the financial sector), or by jobs that involve the servicing of **consumption** (e.g. working in a shop).

Our ideas about work have also changed. People today are less likely to expect a job for life, and are more willing to accept a range of flexible working practices, such as part-time work, working from home and job-sharing.

Culture

As our society has grown wealthier, so the media and other cultural industries – such as fashion, film, advertising and music – have become increasingly central to how we organize our lives. It is suggested that we are a 'media-saturated' society in which media advice is available on how we can 'make over' our homes, gardens, partners and even ourselves. Look, for example, at the lifestyle magazines ranged on the shelves of bookshops and newsagents, advising you on skin care, body size and shape, hair colour and type, fitness, cosmetic surgery and so on. What these trends tell us is that consumption is now a central defining feature in our lives.

Postmodern culture is also about mixing and matching seemingly contradictory styles. Think about the way in which different music from different times and different styles is 'sampled', for example.

Identity

Our identities are now likely to be influenced by mainstream popular culture which celebrates **diversity**, consumerism and choice. In other words, the old 'me' was about where I came from in terms of my family and class background, the area I lived in and so on. The new postmodern 'me', however, is about designer labels, being seen in the right places, the car I drive, listening to the right music and buying the right clothes. Style has become more important than substance. As Steve Taylor (1999) argues, society has been transformed into:

>> *something resembling an endless shopping mall where people now have much greater choice about how they look, what they consume and what they believe in.*>>

Globalization

The global expansion of **transnational companies** – such as McDonald's, Sony, Coca-Cola and Nike – and the global marketing of cultural forms – such as cinema, music and computer games – have contributed to this emphasis on consumption. Such globalization has resulted in symbols that are recognized and consumed across the world. Images of Britney Spears and Eminem are just as likely to be found adorning the walls of a village hut in the interior of New Guinea as they are a bedroom wall in Croydon. Brands like Nike and Coca-Cola use global events like the World Cup and the Olympic Games to beam themselves into millions of homes across the world.

It is therefore no wonder that this global culture is seen to be challenging the importance of national and local cultures, and challenging **nationalism** as a source of identity. Information technology and electronic communication such as email and the internet have also been seen as part of this process.

Knowledge

In the postmodern world, people no longer have any faith in great truths. In particular, people have become sceptical, even cynical, about the power of science to change the world, because many of the world's problems have been brought about by technology. In the political world, ideologies such as **socialism** – which claimed they were the best way of transforming the world – have been discredited in many people's eyes, with the collapse of communism in Eastern Europe. Postmodernists insist that truth is both unattainable and irrelevant in the postmodern world. Instead, they stress the **relativity** of knowledge, ideas and lifestyles, such that many different yet equally authentic values are possible.

Postmodernism and sociology

Steve Taylor argues that these developments have three main consequences for sociology:

1 Most sociology is concerned with explaining the nature and organization of modern societies and social institutions. However, the key relationships that underpin such societies – class, family, gender – are no longer relevant.
2 Sociologists can no longer claim to produce expert knowledge about society, because in postmodern societies, relativity and uncertainty have replaced absolute judgements about what is or should be. As Swingewood (2000) argues, in postmodern societies 'knowledge is always incomplete, there are no universal standards, only differences and **ambiguity**'. The big sociological stories, such as functionalism and Marxism, have become redundant, because 'knowledge' is now judged in terms of its usefulness rather than its claim to be a universal 'truth'.
3 Sociologists can no longer make judgements or claim that they know what is best for societies. Sociology is only one set of ideas competing with others. All have something relevant to offer. If people want to listen to sociologists and act upon their findings, it is up to them. It is equally relevant not to do so.

Endless choice in the postmodern world

Criticisms of postmodernism

Critics of postmodernism suggest that it is guilty of making too much of recent social changes. Evidence suggests that aspects of the postmodernist argument – especially the decline of social class, ethnicity and nationalism as sources of identity – are exaggerated. For example, surveys indicate that people still see social class as a strong influence in their lives, and use aspects of it to judge their success and status and that of others. There is no doubting that consumption has increased in importance, especially among young people, but it is pointed out that consumption does not exist in a vacuum. The nature of your consumption – what and how much you consume – still very much depends upon your income, which is generally determined by your occupation and social class. Similarly, our ability to make choices is still also constrained by our gender and ethnicity, because of the influence of patriarchy and institutional racism.

Check your understanding

1 **What term is used by postmodernists to describe theories of society?**
2 **What was the role of sociology, according to Auguste Comte?**
3 **Identify two social changes that have led some sociologists to argue that we are entering a postmodern world.**
4 **How do the media contribute to our sense of identity?**
5 **What is the relationship between globalization and postmodernism?**
6 **How did the collapse of communism in Eastern Europe contribute to people's cynicism about meta-narratives?**
7 **What is the role of the internet in postmodern society?**

KEY TERMS

Ambiguity the state of being open to a range of interpretations – the meaning is not clear.

Bureaucratic based on rules and procedures.

Consumption the use of goods and services, especially as part of forming an identity.

Diversity variety.

Industrialization the transformation of societies from being agricultural to industrial, which took place in the 18th and 19th centuries.

Meta-narratives or **'big stories'** the postmodernist term for theories like Marxism and functionalism, which aim to explain how societies work.

Modernity period of time starting with the industrial revolution, associated with industrial production, urban living, rational thinking and strong central government.

Nationalism belief system or political view that stresses shared geographical location, history and culture.

Positivism the view that sociological research based upon scientific principles could rid the world of social problems such as crime.

Postmodernity term used by postmodernists to describe the contemporary period, which is characterized by uncertainty, media-saturation and globalization.

Rationality actions decided by logical thought.

Relativity the idea that no one example of something (e.g. political view, sociological theory, lifestyle, moral) is better than any other.

Service sector a group of economic activities loosely organized around finance, retail and personal care.

Socialism a political belief system based on the idea of collective ownership and equal rights for all.

Transnational companies companies that produce and market goods on a global scale.

Urbanization the trend towards living in towns and cities rather than in rural areas.

exploring postmodernism

Item A An endless shopping mall

A good deal of postmodern theory in sociology (and popular culture) is an attempt to come to terms with some of the effects of living in a media-saturated society. Postmodernists argue, in opposition to most sociological theories of the media, that the 'information explosion' of the last two or three decades has not led to increasing conformity and acceptance of 'dominant values', but rather, has led to greater choice and diversity. We are now bombarded with a mass of different media images.

The effect of this, according to postmodern theorists, has been to transform society into something resembling an endless shopping mall where people now have much greater choice about how they look, what they consume and what they believe in.

A consequence of this, postmodernists argue, is that what most sociologists call societies, or social structures, have become fragmented and have become much less important in influencing how people think and act.

For postmodernists, our sense of identity – that is, our ideas of who we are – comes less from things like where we live, our family, our class and our gender, and much more from the images we consume via the media. In a postmodern world, people define themselves much more in terms of the choices they make about their clothes, cars, football teams and so on.

Adapted from Taylor, S. (1999) 'Postmodernism: a challenge to sociology', 'S' Magazine, 4, p. 14

a Using Item A, identify and briefly explain two consequences of the 'information explosion'. (8 marks)

b Identify and briefly explain two sources of identity in modern societies. (8 marks)

c Outline and briefly evaluate two characteristics of postmodern society. (18 marks)

d Discuss the view that identity in the postmodern world is the product of increasing diversity and choice. (26 marks)

web.task

Use the world wide web to search for information on:

- **postmodernism – find out about its influence on art, architecture and literature**
- **Jean Baudrillard, a key postmodern thinker.**

research idea

- Interview a sample of 16- to 19-year-olds about their expectations of the future (jobs, relationships, family, etc.). To what extent are they uncertain or clear about their future?

Class and identity

gettingyouthinking

1 Examine the photographs above. Place the people doing each activity in a social class of your choice.

2 What differences do you think might exist between these individuals, in terms of values, standard of living and lifestyle, political attitudes and leisure activities?

Let's face it: class exists. You were probably able to identify quite different characteristics for the people in the photographs on the left. Wealth, income and status matter. They influence our educational achievement, our chances of good health or an early death – even our choice of leisure pursuits (how many working-class people go fox-hunting?). So what classes exist, and how does class affect the way we feel about ourselves and the world around us?

The working class

Traditional working-class identity

An important factor influencing people's identity is the workplace. 'Work' and 'going to work' play a crucial part in defining a person's identity and giving them status.

Those engaged in traditional manual work, especially in industries such as mining and factory work, typically possessed a very strong sense of their economic or social-class position. This awareness was the primary factor shaping a traditional working-class identity that was dominant for most of the 20th century and which is still influential in some parts of the UK. It was reinforced daily by the nature of working-class communities (manual workers tended to live in urban clusters close to their place of work), membership of trade unions, leisure time spent in working-men's clubs, reading working-class newspapers and identifying with the political party they saw as representing their class interests, i.e. the Labour Party. For example, studies of mining communities show how this dangerous and demanding work produced 'a male culture of mutual dependence which continued outside working hours into leisure and other activities' (Billington *et al.* 1998). Table 1.1 summarizes the different influences that help to shape working-class identity.

The 'new' working class

However, more recently, some researchers have claimed that the notion of a working-class identity is less important, particularly because of the decline in manual work in the last 30 years. The numbers employed in traditional heavy industries, such as mining and shipbuilding, have dropped rapidly since the 1970s and 1980s. Manual workers now make up considerably less than half of the total workforce and, as a result, the economic basis for class identity and solidarity has weakened.

Table 1.1 The traditional working-class: agents of socialization	
Sphere of influence	**Importance in shaping working-class identity**
The workplace	Manual workers identified very strongly with each other. This was partly due to the dangerous nature of some manual jobs (such as mining), but was also due to the collective nature of their jobs – factories were often made up of thousands of workers controlled by a minority of supervisors. This led to a strong sense that the world was divided into 'them', i.e. the bosses (capital), who were only interested in exploiting the workers and making profit out of them, and 'us'. Many workers belonged to trade unions which represented workers' interests and engaged in industrial action when it was thought that such interests were being threatened by management.
The extended family	Studies of traditional working-class family life suggest that it was important to a working man's identity that he provided for both his wife and children. The male was clearly the head of the household. Children were often brought up to have very limited aspirations. Although some working-class children benefited from education, most left school at 15/16 to go to work. For example, in mining communities, 'boys were destined to become miners and girls to be the wives of miners' (Billington *et al.* 1998). There is some evidence that extended kinship networks were important. Adult children often lived close to their parents and saw them on a regular basis. Mutual support was offered by a range of relatives, especially in terms of childcare, financial help and finding work.
The Labour Party	There is evidence that the traditional working class had a strong political identity and saw the Labour party as representing its natural interests against those of the employers. Consequently, at general elections until the 1970s, the Labour Party could count on the loyal support of about 80 per cent of the working-class electorate. Trade union support for Labour reinforced this political allegiance.
The mass media	Newspapers in the UK openly take a political position and target particular socio-economic groups. For example, the *Daily Mirror* successfully portrayed itself as the newspaper which best represented the political and social interests of the traditional working class until the 1970s. Some media commentators have suggested that the editors of such influential newspapers are able to 'set an agenda', i.e. to select the issues which they want their working-class audience to think about and to act upon.

Research has also identified a new instrumental sort of working-class identity: one which is 'instrumental', seeing work as a means to an end, rather than as a source of community and status. Traditional hostility towards capitalism is being abandoned, as capitalism is seen by workers to be effective in raising living standards. The new working class, therefore, have no heightened sense of class injustice or political loyalty. They believe in individualism (putting themselves and their immediate families first), rather than collective or community action. They define themselves through their families and their lifestyle and standard of living, rather than through their work. They vote for whichever political party furthers their individual interests. These alleged changes in working-class identity have led to politicians such as Tony Blair claiming that we are all middle class now. He claimed that 'a middle class that included millions of people who traditionally may see themselves as working class but whose ambitions were far broader than those of their parents and grandparents' had emerged in the last 25 years.

There are a number of reasons offered by sociologists for the emergence of this 'instrumental', 'individualized' and affluent working class:

- The decline of traditional industries and consequently working-class communities – Work and workplace were no longer the great social integrators of the past.
- The expansion of education – This meant that working-class children could aspire to white-collar and professional jobs.
- The feminization of the economy and the accompanying 'genderquake' in women's attitudes – This meant that traditional male assumptions about work, identity and power were challenged.
- Fundamental changes in political ideology – After the election of Mrs Thatcher in 1979, it became widely acceptable to pursue self-interest, and working-class people were strongly encouraged to invest in share ownership, private education, home ownership and private health care.
- The role of the media – They played a key role in suggesting that lifestyle, in the form of consumerism and materialism, was more important in shaping domestic and family life than social class.

Does the working class exist?

Pete Saunders (1990) sees the old class divisions based on work as becoming less and less relevant. For Saunders, what you do with your money is more significant than how you get it. He believes that society is now characterized by a major **'consumption cleavage'** (a split based on what people do with their money). In particular, Saunders argues that home ownership has encouraged the more well-off members of the working class to focus their attention on their homes and family lives. This has loosened their ties with other members of the working class. These workers are less likely to see their identity as 'working class'.

However, surveys such as that carried out by Marshall *et al.* (1988) indicate that manual workers are still aware of class-based issues. Many believe that the distribution of wealth and income is grossly unfair. Importantly, in the survey, most workers

identified themselves as working class. Marshall concludes that working-class identity is still distinctive, but is more **fragmented** than in the past. For example, divisions exist within the working class based on gender and ethnicity. Female and ethnic-minority manual workers earn less than White male manual workers and enjoy less job security.

The 'underclass'

In recent years, a number of commentators, most notably Murray (1990) and Mount (2004), have identified a supposed 'new' form of identity organized around dependency upon state benefits – this is the so-called 'urban **underclass**' found on run-down council estates and in the depressed inner cities. This group allegedly consists of individuals who are likely to be unemployed and single parents as well as drug addicts, criminals, etc. Murray suggests that the culture and identity of this underclass revolve around being workshy, feckless, anti-authority, anti-education, immoral and welfare dependent. It is suggested, too, that the children of the underclass are being socialized by their inadequate parents into a culture of idleness, failure and criminality.

The right-wing commentator, Ferdinand Mount (2004) argues that the working class in the UK have been transformed into a tribe he calls the 'Downers'. He argues that they spend most of their time drunk and disorderly, and that they are foul-mouthed. He suggests that:

>> *The women are slags, either scrawny with straggly blonde hair, or grotesquely fat and bulging out of their track suit bottoms. The children are surly, whining, spoilt, wolfing down their junk food with no concept of manners and not much grasp of their native language. The men – in the regulation T shirt, earring, shaven heads – are equally surly and incoherent, callous and faithless to their women.* >> (quoted in Pritchard 2005)

This picture is not dissimilar to that painted of the working class by the media commentator, Tony Parsons, when he claimed in 1992:

>> *Something has died in the working class: a sense of grace, feelings of community, their intelligence, decency and wit. The salt of the earth have become the scum of the earth, a huge tribe of tattooed White trash. Today the working class are peasants.* >> (quoted in Jones and Jones 1999)

Similar observations are being made about the 'chav' culture that emerged in 2004.

Unsurprisingly, not everyone agrees with these controversial views. Studies of the poor and long-term unemployed, such as that of Jordan (1992), suggest that those living in poverty have the same ideas about work and family as everyone else. Surveys of the poor indicate that they often feel shame about getting into debt, guilt about having to ask others for help, insecurity and lack of dignity.

Simon Charlesworth's (1999) study of working-class people in Rotherham suggests that the working class are often misunderstood by other social classes because they experience negative self-identity and low self-esteem. Charlesworth argues that working-class males compensate for feelings of insecurity and helplessness by exaggerating working-class culture which routinely involves the 'piss-take', and also a self-consciously 'bad' attitude, things which are utterly alien and confusing to more middle-class observers (Pritchard 2005). He blames the educational system for this indifference and cynicism. He argues that the working-class experience of education results in them devaluing themselves and restricting their ambitions to 'being disappointed' in life.

The middle class

Savage's research (1995) describes four types of middle-class identity:

1 *Professionals* – such as doctors and lawyers – tend to adopt an intellectual identity gained from a long and successful education. They value cultural assets such as knowledge, qualifications, lifestyle and values, and feel it is important to pass these on to their children. Such **cultural capital** is crucial in contributing to the success of children from this background.
2 *Managers in private businesses* define success in terms of their standard of living and leisure pursuits. However, despite high pay and status, they are aware that their jobs are more insecure than those of professionals such as doctors and lawyers. A takeover or reorganization of the business can mean the disappearance of their job. Consequently, they encourage their children to make the most of education in order to follow professional rather than managerial careers.
3 *Self-employed owners of small businesses* have traditionally operated as individuals. However, the insecurity brought about by economic recession has recently led to collective action such as the blockading of fuel depots by farmers and hauliers.
4 The ***entrepreneurial*** group works mainly in the City or in the media. This group has an identity that revolves around the consumption of a mixture of high and popular culture –

they may go to the Royal Opera House as well as going to Premier League football matches or spending a night 'clubbing'.

White-collar or clerical workers – clerks and secretaries, for example – have traditionally been seen as having a middle-class identity. However, some sociologists have suggested that their skills are less important today because of the introduction of technology such as computers. As a result, their pay and status are in decline, and they now have more in common with the working class. However, surveys of clerical workers indicate that they still see themselves as middle class. They rarely mix with manual workers, and spend their leisure time and money in quite different ways.

Most sociologists argue that the key to understanding middle-class identity is home ownership. Although owning your home is increasingly common for working-class people, for much of the 20th century, it was dominated by the middle classes, who bought houses in the suburbs of towns and cities and became a commuting class. The result was the development of a suburban lifestyle or subculture that still has a profound effect on middle-class identity today. It shapes social rules, norms and values, especially the view that being middle-class is about respectability, decency and self-control. A summary of resulting, so-called 'middle-class values' is given in Figure 1.4 below.

The key agents of socialization in this middle-class world are undoubtedly the family and the education system. King and Raynor (1981) suggest that **child-centredness** is a distinctive feature of the middle-class family, especially in terms of passing on the educational opportunities and attitudes required for educational success. Some sociologists claim, controversially, that socialization in middle-class homes is superior to that in working-class homes. Douglas (1964) claimed that middle-class parents take more interest in their children's education; Newson and Newson (1963, 1965) claimed that middle-class parents were more skilled in child-rearing practices, whilst Bernstein (1961, 1964, 1966) suggested that the language codes taught by middle-class parents contributed to educational success. King and Raynor concluded:

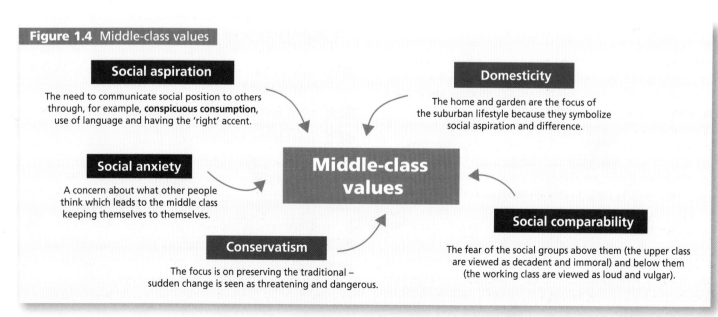

Figure 1.4 Middle-class values

Social aspiration

The need to communicate social position to others through, for example, **conspicuous consumption**, use of language and having the 'right' accent.

Social anxiety

A concern about what other people think which leads to the middle class keeping themselves to themselves.

Conservatism

The focus is on preserving the traditional – sudden change is seen as threatening and dangerous.

Middle-class values

Domesticity

The home and garden are the focus of the suburban lifestyle because they symbolize social aspiration and difference.

Social comparability

The fear of the social groups above them (the upper class are viewed as decadent and immoral) and below them (the working class are viewed as loud and vulgar).

≪*The picture that emerges of the child in the middle-class family is fairly consistent. The home provides material, intellectual and motivational resources deliberately provided by parents to further the development of the child, which grows up with a belief in its own potency, a positive attitude towards school and the expectation of educational and occupational success.*≫

There is also considerable evidence that education benefits middle-class pupils, perhaps at the expense of working-class pupils. The Marxist, Pierre Bourdieu suggests that schools are essentially middle-class institutions run by middle-class teachers for the benefit of middle-class pupils (Bourdieu and Passeron 1977). He argues that what goes on in schools in terms of what is regarded as acceptable knowledge, language and behaviour is defined by middle-class professionals. The home experience of middle-class children equips them with the 'right' values, ways of speaking, knowledge, etc., for interacting with middle-class teachers. Bourdieu refers to this middle-class advantage as 'cultural capital' and notes that it is supplemented by economic capital (i.e. middle-class parents are more likely to send their children to private nurseries and schools and to invest in private tutoring, computers, etc.) and social capital (middle-class parents may use their knowledge and contacts to further the interests of their children, e.g. in terms of work experience).

Religion and the media are also important as agencies of socialization. The middle class are more likely to attend established churches than the working class. Newspapers such as the *Daily Mail* and *Daily Express* target a middle-class market and generally tend to reinforce their conservative value system.

The upper class

There has been limited research into the identity of the upper class. Mackintosh and Mooney (2000) point out that 'wealth and privilege are not very visible. The wealthy can withdraw into a private world of fee-paying schooling, private transport and health care, and social networks that are largely invisible to the non-wealthy.'

However, it is likely that their sense of identity is powerful for four reasons:

- The concentration of wealth in their hands (e.g. in 1994, 53 per cent of all financial wealth in the UK was owned by 5 per cent of the population) is a tremendous source of opportunity, privilege and power over others. Clearly, this is something they see as worth reproducing and protecting.
- The upper class shares a common background – it is mainly made up of a fairly small number of wealthy extended families often interconnected by marriage. In other words, the upper class is a self-selecting and exclusive elite that is closed to outsiders, i.e. this is known as **social closure**. This is reinforced by parents encouraging their children to choose partners from other upper-class families as well as immersing children in a culture of privilege which reinforces the children's awareness that they are 'superior' to other social groups. This culture of privilege is expressed through taking for granted the presence of servants and nannies, a concern

with etiquette or social conventions (e.g. addressing people in the correct fashion), socialization into 'high' culture (e.g. classical music and opera), participation in blood sports, etc.

- The upper class share a common background in terms of education at public schools and Oxbridge. 'Such schools socialize upper-class pupils into a common culture which promotes the values of conservatism and especially respect for tradition, nationalism, acceptance of authority and hierarchy as natural outcomes of superior breeding and upbringing and hostility towards socialist ideals. Public schoolboys are encouraged to see themselves as the elite' (Chapman 2001).
- The public school and Oxbridge experience leads to 'old-boy' or 'old school-tie' networks made up of people who share the same cultural values and assets, and who use these contacts to further each other's careers and influence.

Children born into the upper class, therefore, learn distinct ways of speaking, mannerisms, attitudes, values and ways of seeing the world that clearly distinguish them from other groups.

Class today

In recent years, some sociologists have argued that class has ceased to be the main factor in creating identity. Postmodernists argue that class identity has fragmented into numerous separate identities. Gender, ethnicity, age, region and family role interact with consumption and media images to make up our sense of identity today.

But are postmodern ideas exaggerated? Marshall *et al.*'s (1988) research does indicate that social class is still a significant source of identity for many. Members of a range of classes are aware of class differences and are happy to identify themselves using class categories.

Postmodernists also ignore the fact that, for many, consumption depends on having a job and an income. For some, poverty is going to limit any desire to pursue a postmodern lifestyle. In other words, consumption – what we buy – depends on social class.

Check your understanding

1. Identify two reasons for the decline in working-class identity.
2. What motivates the 'new' working class?
3. What is the 'underclass'?
4. In what ways could it be argued that the working class is fragmented?
5. What different kinds of middle-class identity exist?
6. Which social class practises social closure? How?
7. Why might postmodern views of class be 'exaggerated'?

KEY TERMS

Child-centredness prioritizing your children's needs and placing them at the centre of social and domestic life.

Conspicuous consumption buying luxury items in order to acquire status.

Consumption cleavage the idea that society is now stratified by spending patterns and habits rather than social class.

Cultural capital the cultural advantages passed down from middle- and upper-class parents to their children.

Entrepreneurial a term used to describe people in business who are willing to take risks to make gains.

Fragmented broken up.

Social closure the practice of preventing 'outsiders' from joining a group.

Underclass a subculture that exists outside mainstream culture, supposedly characterized by welfare dependency, criminal tendencies and single parents.

White-collar, or **clerical**, **workers** people in lower-level office work.

exploring class and identity

Item A A divided society

Social class provides us with a sense of belonging and identity; it can tell us who 'we' are and who 'they' are and, hence, how to relate to the world around us. Many people see the UK as a society sharply divided by class divisions and inequalities. In a 1996 survey, two-thirds of those interviewed agreed that 'there is one law for the rich and one for the poor' and that 'ordinary people do not get their fair share of the nation's wealth'. However, despite this 'class consciousness', individuals may not have a strongly developed sense of class identity any more because of changing patterns of occupation, income, lifestyle and authority. The old labels 'working class' and 'middle class' may be less relevant today because most manual workers now lead a middle-class consumer lifestyle, as statistics on everything from videos and home ownership to foreign holidays and school staying-on rates tell us. However, despite these trends, it can be argued that we are a more, not less, divided society. Accents, houses, cars, schools, sports, food, fashion, drink, smoking, supermarkets, soap operas, holiday destinations, even training shoes: virtually everything in life is graded with subtle or unsubtle class tags attached. Snobbery is the religion of England.

Adapted from Woodward, K. (ed.) (2000) *Questioning Identity: Gender, class, nation,* London: Routledge, pp. 95–6, and Adonis, A. and Pollard, S. (1997) *A Class Act: The myth of Britain's classless society,* Harmondsworth: Penguin, p. 10

a Using examples from Item A, identify and briefly explain two ways in which social class may provide people with a sense of belonging and identity. (8 marks)

b Identify and briefly explain two changes which may mean that class labels are less important today. (8 marks)

c Outline and briefly evaluate two ways in which the children of the upper class are socialized into a 'culture of privilege'. (18 marks)

d Discuss the view that social class is still important as a source of identity in Britain today. (26 marks)

research idea

- Conduct a survey to find out the extent of class identity among a sample of young people. What classes do they think exist? Do they believe that class is still important? Do they feel that they belong to any particular class?

web.task

Find the website of the polling organization MORI (Market and Opinion Research International). Use their 'search' facility to find the results of any surveys they have conducted about any aspect of social class. What research has taken place and what are the key findings?

Gender and identity

≪A visit to Isabella Mackay's home is like a walk through the pages of *Little Women*. She opens the door wearing a pretty pink blouse, children hiding in her flowing skirt. Isabella has some interesting ideas about motherhood. She says 'I could no more go out to work, abandon my children or disobey my husband than I could grow an extra head. I don't have any of the modern woman's confusion about her role in life. From the day I was born I knew I was destined to be a wife and mother. By the age of 16, 1 knew that all I really wanted from life was to get married, have children and make a lovely home. That was my ambition.'

She not only believes that a mother's place is in the home, but that the feminist movement is a 'dangerous cancer and perversion'. The world, she says, would be a better place if the Equal Opportunities Commission was shut down and workplace crèches were scrapped. The rape-within-marriage law should be abolished too. She says 'in the rare event of a wife refusing sex with her husband he has every right, perhaps even a duty, to take her as gently as possible. Once a woman is married she loses the right to say no to her husband's advances. The female role is a submissive one. The male role is assertive and aggressive.' ≫

Adapted from *Woman* magazine (1994)

1 List the stereotypical and non-stereotypical masculine and feminine characteristics that come to mind on first seeing the images above.

2 What aspects of Isabella Mackay's view of femininity do you agree or disagree with?

The exercise above should have shown you that our gender identities are strongly influenced by stereotypical ideas about what is masculine or feminine. However, the exercise should also have shown you that there are different types of men and women. Some men may have some typically feminine characteristics, whilst some women may exhibit masculine tendencies.

The Isabella Mackay exercise may have provoked a more emotional response, especially from female students! I suspect that many readers reacted strongly to her ideas. However, only 30 years ago such ideas were very common, and they probably still have some credibility with an older generation of women. Ideas about femininity have certainly changed. One of the reasons for these changes has been the growth of **feminism**. Feminist views are summarized in Topic 3 – review pp. 12–13

now before reading on. A key term for most feminists is gender. What exactly do they mean by this?

Gender identity

Sociologists often distinguish between 'sex' and 'gender':

● **Sex** refers to the biological differences between males and females, for example in chromosomes, hormones and genitals. These biological differences are not necessarily permanent. Women's body shape, for example, has historically shifted with fashion. The 'beautiful' women in previous centuries were often far larger than 'beautiful' women today.

- **Gender** refers to the expectations society places on males and females. Gender expectations are transmitted to the next generation through gender-role socialization. Because gender differences are the result of society's expectations, they are often described as **socially constructed**, as opposed to being **biologically determined**.

Gender-role socialization

From an early age, people are trained to conform to social expectations about their gender. Much of this training goes on in the family during primary socialization. For example, people use gender-based terms of endearment when talking to children, they dress boys and girls differently, and sex-typed toys are often chosen as presents. Oakley (1982) identifies two processes central to the construction of gender identity:

- **Manipulation** refers to the way in which parents encourage or discourage behaviour on the basis of appropriateness for the child's sex.
- **Canalization** refers to the way in which parents channel children's interests into toys and activities that are seen as 'normal for that sex'.

These types of gender reinforcement are extremely powerful. Statham (1986) studied parents who deliberately tried to avoid gender-stereotyping of their children. She found that it was almost impossible for parents to overcome the cultural pressure for their children to behave in gender-stereotyped ways.

There is some evidence that once a child has worked out the socially appropriate identity for their gender, they will work quite hard in constructing and maintaining it. Francis' research (1997, 1998) into children aged between 7 and 11, found that in role-play situations, boys often took on high-status positions and naturally saw themselves in positions of power and domination. In contrast, females took on roles in which they could express selfless and mature behaviour.

Other agencies of socialization are also involved in gender-role socialization. Schools, children's books and the mass media all have a significant role to play. Until the 1980s, education was seen as a major source of gender inequality. Many females consequently saw the educational aspect of their identity as unimportant and often left school at 16. For example, Sue Sharpe's (1976) survey of working-class girls in the early 1970s found that such experiences meant that female identity revolved around 'love, marriage, husbands, children, jobs and careers, more or less in that order'.

Today, female achievement at all levels of the examination system outstrips that of males (although a significant number of working-class females continue to underachieve). There are many explanations for this dramatic change in fortune. Certainly, educational changes have played a part, especially the introduction of girl-friendly modes of teaching, such as coursework and a national curriculum aimed at preventing the gender stereotyping of subject choice. Changes in the economy and labour market which have seen the decline of traditional industries (which mainly employed men) and the rise of the service sector of the economy (in which most new jobs were for women) have also contributed to changes in women's attitudes.

However, we must be careful not to overdo the positive here. There is considerable evidence that experience of schooling may still have a negative impact on feminine identity. Research by Murphy and Elwood (1998) concludes that boys and girls arrive at school with 'gendered interests and behaviours' that are the product of family experiences. These have a profound effect upon school behaviours and experiences. Both boys and girls see 'creative' and 'discursive' activities as feminine, whilst 'constructional' and 'rational' activities are viewed as masculine. Teachers tend to reinforce such gender stereotyping, for example by making negative judgements about female confidence in subjects such as mathematics. It is argued that these gender processes have a profound influence on subject choice, particularly at A-Level and in higher education and future careers. Arts and social science subjects are dominated by females whilst the 'hard' sciences, mathematics, IT and engineering are dominated by males.

Billington *et al.* (1998) point out that masculine identity is centrally linked for many men with being workers. However, despite the fact that so many women are in paid work, female identity is more often shaped by women's role as domestic labourers. Females are encouraged from a very early age to see nurturing as an essential part of 'being feminine' (think about the role of dolls and toys in this process). The mass media reinforces this process by endowing television commercials for household items such as detergents with emotional overtones – the implication being if you use a particular product, you are a more effective carer of your family.

Moreover, Billington and colleagues argue that women's identity is also defined by their ability to be 'naturally feminine and attractive'. They point out that there is a whole media industry devoted to encouraging women to perfect their figure, make-up and sexual desirability. The male equivalent of such media does not exist to the same degree. The way sexual identity is defined in modern societies may mean that women's social identity is dependent upon being seen as physically attractive by men. Their social identity may have little to do with being educated and intelligent. Rather, it may depend on how well they conform to society's definition of women as sex objects.

Some feminist sociologists have suggested that these types of media representations of femininity may be responsible for eating disorders in modern societies. There is no doubt that a range of media products encourage the view that the ideal feminine form is slim and thin. As Hunt (2001) notes, 'the media recognizes society's obsession with looking slim and perpetuate the idea that slimness equals success, health, happiness and popularity'.

Other studies of gender identity have focused on the assumption that males and females have different sexual identities. Males are supposed to be promiscuous predators (wanting sex with as many women as possible), whereas females are supposed to be passive and more interested in love than sex. Because of this, gender identity for women carries risks. Their identity may be subjected to being labelled a 'slag' or a 'slapper' if they appear to behave in similar ways to men. Lees (1986) found that females in her study conformed to gender expectations in order to protect their reputation.

Criticisms of the idea of gender-role socialization

The idea of gender-role socialization has been criticized on a number of counts:

- The experiences of men and women vary greatly, depending on ethnicity (race), area, class and age. Most accounts of gender socialization ignore these differences.
- It assumes that women passively accept the gender identity imposed on them. It neglects the choice we have in developing an identity and the fact that many women and men resist attempts to make them conform to stereotypes.

Postmodernism and gender

Postmodernists argue that changes in gender roles are having a positive effect on female identity. It is suggested that the increasing participation and success of women in the world of paid work mean that traditional notions of female identity are being abandoned. For example, Sharpe's study (1994) suggests that young females are becoming more assertive about their rights, ranking education and career above marriage and family as priorities in their lives. Moreover, there are signs that women are now more willing to use divorce to escape husbands who insist on their wives playing a subordinate domestic role.

Helen Wilkinson (1994) argues that there has been a fundamental shift in values amongst women aged under 35. She argues that this shift is so dramatic that it is a 'genderquake' and has led to a profound change in the distribution of power between men and women. She argues that the feminization of the workplace has led to a revolution in women's ambitions. Family commitments no longer have priority in women's lives. Work and career are now the defining feature of young women's identity and self-esteem.

What is more, increasing economic independence means that women are now viewed as significant consumers. There are signs that mass media products are increasingly being targeted at single women. This means that women are more likely to see consumption and leisure as the key factors in their identity. Being a good mother and housewife – the traditional domestic role – is becoming less significant in terms of female identity.

Criticisms of postmodernism

Some feminists reject this view. They point out that there is little evidence that men and women are sharing equally in the consumption of goods and services. For example, most media and cultural products are still aimed at men. Consumption in the form of clubbing, buying CDs, etc., may only be a temporary phase that young single women go through before setting out on the well-trodden paths of marriage and motherhood.

Masculinity

Connell (1995) argues that, until recently, most British men were socialized into what he calls 'hegemonic masculinity'. They expected to be financial providers and authority figures in the home, dispensing wisdom and firm discipline to their wives and children. Men were expected to be individualistic, aggressive, risk-taking and ambitious. They were not expected to participate in domestic work or to express their emotions. This type of masculinity was also responsible for defining what counted as 'feminine'. Ideas about female beauty, 'sexiness', ideal shape and behaviour were all shaped by men; women were either sex objects or mother/housewife figures. Connell acknowledges that masculinity today is experiencing change. He documents the emergence of three other forms of masculinity:

1 **Complicit masculinity** refers to those men who believe that men and women should share roles within families. Such men still benefit from what he calls 'the **patriarchal** dividend', because even in these households women perform the majority of housework and especially childcare. Some sociologists have even gone as far as suggesting that a '**new man**' has emerged who is more in touch with his feminine and emotional feelings. Others have suggested that this is merely a creation of the advertising industry.

2 **Subordinate masculinity** refers to homosexual men. Although there is greater tolerance and acceptance of homosexuality in society today, it still generally remains a subordinate and stigmatized identity.

3 **Marginalized masculinity** is a response to the fact that the traditional masculine identity of male protector/breadwinner

---

KEY TERMS

Biologically determined fixed by our physical make-up.

Canalization the channelling of children's interests into toys and activities traditionally associated with their sex.

Complicit masculinity refers to those men who believe that roles within families should be shared.

Crisis in masculinity the view that men who have been socialized into hegemonic forms of masculinity are experiencing anxiety and uncertainty because

their patriarchal authority is being challenged by economically successful women.

Feminism the belief that women are treated unfairly and that society should be changed to create equality between the sexes.

Gender refers to the expectations society places on men and women.

Gender-role socialization the process by which boys and girls are socialized (by the family and by secondary agents of socialization such as education

and the mass media) into masculine and feminine modes of behaviour.

Hegemonic masculinity traditional ideas about the role of men as breadwinners and authority figures.

Manipulation the way in which parents encourage or discourage behaviour on the basis of appropriateness for the child's sex.

Marginalized masculinity refers to the decline of traditional masculinity.

'**New man**' a type of masculinity that is keen to explore its feminine and sensitive side. Many sociologists believe it to be mostly a media creation.

Patriarchy a social system in which men oppress and exploit women and children.

Sex refers to the biological differences between men and women.

Socially constructed produced by society.

Subordinate masculinity homosexuality.

may be changing. Working-class men in particular can see that economic recession has led to the decline of manual work and to large-scale unemployment. They can see that women are taking many of the new jobs.

Mac an Ghaill (1996) talks about how this is leading to a '**crisis in masculinity**'. If work is the defining feature of masculinity, then unemployment leads to loss of self-esteem and status, as well as a loss of identification with others. Older men may feel threatened as their wives become the main breadwinners and they are expected to take on more domestic responsibilities. Domestic violence and even suicide may result. Younger males may see their futures as bleak and, therefore, view schooling and qualifications as irrelevant to their needs. There is evidence that many working-class boys fail to identify with schooling and learning because they associate it with femininity. They may seek alternative sources of status in activities in which they can stress their masculinity, such as delinquency.

The changing nature of masculinity in modern society can be seen in Gary Whannel's (2002) study of David Beckham. Whannel notes that 'pictures of David Beckham have both expressed and challenged some of the dominant assumptions of masculinity and identity'. Whannel points out that Beckham embodies both traditional assumptions of masculinity via his tattoos, and his leadership and aggression on the football pitch, and a feminized masculinity via his love of his children and the sexualization of his image in advertising, e.g. Beckham is also a gay icon. As Whannel notes, Beckham 'changes appearance more often than football clubs change their away-strip, moving effortlessly from being a fop to a family man to a hard man'.

Check your understanding

1. How are the views of liberal and radical feminists different (See Topic 3, pp. 12–13)?

2. Explain in your own words the meaning of 'patriarchy' (See Topic 3, pp. 12–13).

3. What is the difference between the two concepts 'sex' and 'gender'?

4. Explain in your own words what is meant by 'gender-role socialization'.

5. Why does gender identity carry risks for females?

6. Identify three important agencies of secondary socialization and illustrate how these may reinforce gender roles.

7. Explain in your own words the meaning of 'hegemonic masculinity'.

8. In what ways has masculinity changed in the past 20 years?

research idea

- Get hold of at least two catalogues that include toys. Analyse any links between gender and the presentation of the catalogues. Are girls or boys pictured playing with toys? Do the pictures reflect or challenge typical gender roles? Are some toys targeted more at girls and others more at boys? Which are targeted at which? How can you tell?

web.task

Find the website www.feminist.com

What issues are covered and what information is available? Look around the site and identify the key issues that concern feminists today.

exploring gender identity

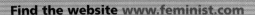

Item A Changes in male identity

Frank Mort argues that there were significant changes in male identity in the mid-1980s, reflected in the portrayal of men and masculinity in the media and through the marketing and consumption of large quantities of toiletries, such as aftershave, other perfumes and hair gel. However, Sean Nixon points to a backlash against the 'new man' phenomenon in the early 1990s with what is popularly termed 'new laddism'. Nixon suggests there has been another shift in cultural norms as young men revert to sexist type as reflected in magazines such as *Loaded* and *Maxim*.

Adapted from Abbott, D. (2000) 'Identity and new masculinities', *Sociology Review*, 10(1), pp. 5–6

a Using Item A, identify and briefly explain two ways in which changes in male identity in the mid-1980s were expressed. (8 marks)

b Identify and briefly explain two ways in which families socialize children into gender roles. (8 marks)

c Outline and briefly evaluate two ways that sociologists distinguish between 'sex' and 'gender'. (18 marks)

d Discuss the view that there are a variety of feminine and masculine identities in modern society. (26 marks)

Ethnicity and identity

gettingyou**thinking**

1 What characteristics do you generally attach to these members of minority ethnic groups?

2 Are these characteristics justified or are they stereotypes?

3 What do you think is the role of religion in shaping the identity of these people?

4 What problems are people from these groups likely to face in their interaction with the White majority?

Some people may have attached negative characteristics to most of the people pictured above. For example, some may think of Abu Hamza as a terrorist or as someone who holds fanatical beliefs which many find threatening. Some readers might also look at pictures of the female Muslim and think that she has been forced to wear her religious outfit and she's likely to be forced into a marriage against her will. However, I imagine that most of you recognized Lenny Henry and that you didn't attach negative characteristics to him. This is not surprising: he is a popular celebrity and people generally identify him as a comedian and entertainer rather than as a person of African-Caribbean heritage with a distinctive ethnic identity.

Interestingly, many of his characters and routines do in fact celebrate aspects of African-Caribbean culture. You will also have worked out that religion is an important part of much of ethnic identity in the UK. This is difficult for many White British people to understand because religion does not play a major role in most White people's lives. Finally, you will have no doubt recognized that the relationship between ethnic minority groups and the White majority in the UK is not characterized by consensus and harmony. Rather prejudice and discrimination are part and parcel of White treatment of ethnic minorities and this has had a profound effect upon ethnic minority identity and culture in the UK.

What is ethnic identity?

Ethnic identity – or **ethnicity** – refers to the fact that people recognize that they share a cultural distinctiveness within a group based on various factors. These include:

- Common descent – This could be represented by colour, race or other physical characteristics, e.g. for some people of African-Caribbean descent, being Black is their prime source of identity.
- Geographical origins – Links with a country of origin are important, e.g. ethnic identity may involve seeing oneself as 'Pakistani' or 'Indian' or 'Irish' first and foremost.
- History – Members of ethnic cultures may share a sense of struggle and oppression which originates in a particular historical context, such as slavery, colonialism or persecution. For example, Jewish identity may be partially shaped by events like the Holocaust.
- Language – As well as speaking English, members of particular groups may speak the language(s) of their country of origin at home, e.g. older generation Chinese people may speak in Cantonese.
- Religion – For some minority ethnic groups, this is the most important influence on their daily lives, e.g. some Pakistanis will see themselves as Muslim first and foremost.
- Traditions and rituals – These are normally cultural or religious events, ceremonies and celebrations that reinforce a sense of ethnic community and therefore identity, e.g. the Notting Hill Carnival held annually in London.

People recognize themselves as part of ethnic groups and feel positively about others who share the same culture. It is important to understand that ethnic identity often overlaps with national identity. For example, White Scottish people have their own unique Scottish ethnic identity, i.e. they share cultural characteristics which distinguish them from Welsh or English people, for example, the identification with clans or the wearing of kilts. This cultural distinctiveness also underpins their national identity as a country distinct from Wales and England. Scottish football fans may deliberately stress their national identity by wearing kilts and painting saltires (the cross of St Andrew) on their faces. Note too that **second-** or **third-generation** Scottish Asians may subscribe to a distinctly Asian or even Muslim ethnic identity, but also tap into Scottish national identity in their support of the Scotland football team.

However, ethnic identity can also be negative as well as positive. Mason (2000) points out that many British White people tend to see ethnicity as something other groups have. This leads to the use of 'they' statements made up of imagined and prejudicial assumptions about minority ethnic groups. For example, according to Said (1985), Whites tend to see Islamic identity as extreme and fanatical. Such views undermine the relationship between Islam and Western culture and create mutual suspicion and hostility. For example, many Whites view Islam as oppressive in its treatment of women despite evidence to the contrary. Some commentators have suggested that **Islamophobia** has become a norm in the UK since 9/11 because the media has done little to challenge mistaken assumptions about what being a Muslim in the UK involves.

Ethnic minorities

In Britain, ethnicity is mainly associated with minority groups from the former British colonies on the Indian subcontinent, in the Caribbean and in Africa. This kind of categorization is a problem because it emphasizes skin colour rather than common cultural characteristics. In doing so, it ignores significant White minority ethnic groups resident in the UK, such as Greek Cypriots, Jews, gypsies and Irish people. It also means that differences between minority groups such as Asians and African-Caribbeans, and the majority White population are exaggerated, whilst differences between ethnic minorities such as Bangladeshis and Pakistanis are neglected.

The ability of ethnic minorities in Britain to shape their self-identity is also limited by the way in which they are seen and treated by powerful groups. Racial prejudice and discrimination practised by the majority White group may make it difficult for ethnic minorities to express their cultural identity fully. Discrimination can take a number of different forms. There is some evidence of **institutional racism** within the educational system. For example, it is argued that some White teachers are unable to cope with the way African-Caribbean boys express their ethnic identity at school and this is the explanation why these boys are more likely than any other type to be excluded from school.

Another, perhaps more contentious, form of discrimination in education can be seen in the case of a Muslim student, Shabina Begum (see photograph left). In March 2005, Shabina won a high court case against her secondary school for refusing to teach her because she had flouted the dress rules. The school, which is made up of mainly Muslim students had a dress code which permitted the wearing of the shalwar kameez (trousers and tunic). Shabina had worn this outfit until September 2002 but switched to a full length gown called a jilbab which leaves only the hands and face exposed. She was sent home and subsequently transferred to another school which accepts this form of dress. Upon her legal victory, she was quoted as saying the case was 'a victory for Muslims who wanted to preserve their identity and values, despite prejudice and bigotry'.

Other discriminatory practices have been identified in policing. The MacPherson Report into the death of the Black teenager, Stephen Lawrence, accused the London Metropolitan Police of institutional racism, especially against African-Caribbean people. This is defined as 'unwitting prejudice, ignorance, thoughtlessness and racial stereotyping which disadvantages minority groups'. Some commentators have seen the fact that the police stop and search Black youth far more than any other ethnic group as a symptom of such racism. Evidence suggests that the cultural identity of African-Caribbean youth is often based on resentment of such treatment and is consequently anti-authority and antipolice.

It is important to understand that racism and hostility are not confined to Whites. There is evidence of tensions between the African-Caribbean and Asian communities in some urban areas in the UK. Moreover, it is a mistake to assume that there is one Asian ethnic identity. The Asian community is divided along a number of lines, including country of origin, region within the country of origin and religion. Moreover, even within particular groups, such as Sikhs and Hindus, there are differences along **caste** lines. These divisions too can lead to tension, hostility and even conflict. Some of this is fairly obvious – in some areas, there are gang fights between Sikhs and Muslims, and between Hindus and Muslims. Sometimes these differences are very subtle and certainly invisible to many Whites. For example, Modood (1997) found that Asian ethnic identity is very specific in terms of differences in religion, language, dress codes, jewellery and diet. In this study, a Gujerati Hindu was quoted as saying: 'there is a great deal of difference between a Gujerati and, say, a Punjabi. Their clothing is more expensive. They wear more jewellery. I cannot find many similarities between our cultures'. There may even be subtle differences in the ethnic identity of groups who share the same religion, for example between Shia and Sunni Muslims.

Ethnic identities as resistance

Sometimes ethnic identity is used as a means of resisting racism, as the following examples demonstrate:

- Skin colour is an important source of identity to many African-Caribbeans, according to Modood's research. Black identity and pride may be celebrated as a response to Black people's perceptions of racial exclusion and stereotyping by White people, especially symbols of White authority such as teachers and the police.
- Jacobson (1997) argues that many young Pakistanis are adopting an Islamic identity in terms of diet, dress and everyday routines and practices. She suggests that this is essentially a defensive identity that has developed as a response to racism and social exclusion. Islamic identity compensates for such marginalization because it stresses the exclusion of the White excluders by the excluded.
- There is some evidence that Black-led evangelical churches and the Rastafarian movement may provide similar sources of identity for African-Caribbeans.
- Gilroy (1993) notes that young African-Caribbeans often adopt identities based on ethnic history and popular culture to challenge racism and exclusion. He notes that African-Caribbean youth identity often utilizes gangsta rap and hip-hop to symbolize their feelings about what they perceive as White oppression.

Ethnic identity and the family

Butler (1995) observes that Asian newcomers to the UK in the 1960s and 1970s were concerned to maintain traditional Asian culture. She notes that Muslim migrants sought to maintain close links with one another in order to provide not only security and support, but also to safeguard traditional cultural values and ethnic identity. The first generation was concerned that their children would not have a particularly strong sense of ethnic identity and, as a result, might become Westernized and abandon both their culture and religion.

Ghuman (1999) outlines some of the socialization practices of the first generation of Asian parents:

- Children were brought up to be obedient, loyal to and respectful of their elders and community around them. Social conformity was demanded and children learned to be interdependent rather than individualistic, which was seen as a threat to the authority of the head of the family.
- The choice of education was to be left in the hands of their parents, who were thought to know best the interests of their children and their future.
- The choice of marriage partner was thought to be best left to parents, and children were taught the drawbacks of dating and courting, the dangers of premarital and promiscuous sex, and the perceived disadvantages of love marriages.
- Religious training was considered to be very important because it reinforced the values described above and stressed humility rather than self-pride and assertiveness.
- The role of the mother tongue is seen as crucial in maintaining links between generations and in the transmission of religious values. Children therefore tend to be bilingual, and are often able to use both the mother language, e.g. Urdu, Punjabi, Gujerati or Hindi, and English interchangeably.

Many of these family socialization practices continued into the second generation of Asian immigrants. For example, Anwar's research (1981) found that Asian families – regardless of whether they are Hindu, Muslim or Sikh – socialize children into a pattern of obligation, loyalty and religious commitment, which, in most cases, they accept. However, Ghuman notes that some Asian commentators have expressed concern about the parenting practices of second-generation Asians and what is seen as a generation gap opening up between parents and children, especially as the latter get caught 'between two cultures'. Anwar (1981) identified three issues which were seen to be causing tensions between Pakistani parents and children in regard to their cultural identity:

- Western clothes, especially for girls
- arranged marriages
- the question of freedom.

Anwar suggests that the family can be a site of conflict between grandparents, parents and children, especially as the first generation often come from rural cultures which are very different to Western culture. The younger generation has mixed with people with very different values and attitudes from their own families, and this has resulted in the younger generation holding values and ideas which their parents regard as alien. This is particularly the case in regard to young females. Muslim families tend to stress the control of females because it is believed the future of the community depends on them becoming wives and mothers and socializing the next generation into key Muslim values. There is also some evidence of patriarchal values underpinning Pakistani and Bangladeshi culture and identity, in that men are accorded more freedom because women are perceived as subordinate to men. Moreover, reputation and honour are extremely important and, consequently, the reputation of daughters and wives must be protected at all costs. Many parents may, therefore, come into conflict with their daughters over issues such as continuing in education and the free mixing of the sexes, especially in Westernized contexts. The experience of school and college, and the peer relationships established with their White or African-Caribbean peers may result in Pakistani and Bangladeshi girls challenging the notion that they should play a lesser role in their communities.

A good example of such conflict involves dating, which is disapproved of by the older Asian generation. However, Drury (1991) found that one fifth of girls in her Asian sample were secretly dating boys. Moreover, some were going to pubs and drinking alcohol without the knowledge and consent of their parents. Such practices can cause great anguish as the following quote from a Sikh girl indicates:

≪I would like to have a boyfriend and I would like to have a love marriage, but the consequences are too great. Gossip spreads and you can lose everything. Everyone in the family can be hurt and nobody will want to marry my sister… I think that Sikh boys in England are given too much freedom. They can go out with White girls yet they are expected to marry an innocent Indian girl.≫ (Drury 1991, p. 396)

There is also evidence that Asian girls have strong feelings about the freedom given to their male siblings and the fact that they are expected to take on domestic responsibilities, i.e. to help with housework and childcare, when their brothers are not.

Ethnic identity and the peer group

Tony Sewell (2004) argues that peer-group pressure is extremely influential in shaping ethnic identity among disaffected African-Caribbean youth in British inner cities. He believes this is probably partly responsible for educational underachievement and the high levels of exclusion found in this group. He argues that African-Caribbean male identity is focused on being a 'hyper-male' and 'gangsta' in the eyes of their peers, and that this often compensates for the lack of a father figure in the lives of many of these teenagers. Furthermore, Sewell notes that this street identity is partly shaped by media agencies, such as advertising and MTV, which encourage young African-Caribbean males to subscribe to a consumer culture that views material things such as clothing and trainers as more important than education.

Sewell argues that the identity of Black youth is the result of a 'triple quandary':

1 They feel that they do not fit into the dominant mainstream culture. They feel rejected by it.
2 They become anxious about how they are perceived by society, and especially by their Black peers. They therefore seek to position themselves in a positive way by constructing a deviant and highly masculine identity.

3 Many aspects of this identity are taken from media culture, particularly the emphasis on designer labels and the imitation of male role models, e.g. rap stars, in terms of macho attitudes and forms of behaviour.

This culture of masculinity is valued as a comfort zone – that is, their peer group's acceptance of this identity compensates for the strong sense of rejection that they feel by their fathers, the education system, White society, and so on.

Ethnic identity and religion

Religion has a profound influence in shaping the ethnic identity of young Asians. It seems to have less influence in the shaping of African-Caribbean culture and identity, although African-Caribbean youth are more likely to be practising Christians (especially born-again Christians) than White youth, and are especially likely to be involved in sects and cults such as **Rastafarianism** and the Seventh-day Adventists.

Modood (1997) questioned two generations of Asians, African-Caribbeans and Whites on the statement: 'Religion is very important to how I live my life'. They found that those most in favour of religion were the Pakistani and Bangladeshi samples. They found that 82 per cent of the 50+ sample and 67 per cent of those aged 16 to 34 valued the importance of Islam in their lives. About one third of young Indians saw their religion as important. The lowest figure was for young Whites – only 5 per cent saw religion as important, compared with 18 per cent of young African-Caribbeans. In all ethnic groups, the older generation saw religion as more important than the younger generation, although the gap was lowest among the Muslim sample.

Drury's **ethnographic** research found that 42 per cent of the Sikh girls in her sample went regularly to the temple, whilst 44 per cent said they hardly ever attended. Research by Stopes-Roe and Cochrane (1990) on young Asian people aged 18 to 21 found that 85 per cent thought the teaching of religion to be very important or important. Interestingly, these ideas seemed to be higher for Pakistani and Bangladeshi youth – among Indian youth, religion was less likely to shape their way of life or world view. They were much more likely to challenge the myths and superstitions surrounding their faiths, although many still celebrated traditional rituals and festivals.

Modood (2001) notes that the centrality of religion in Asian communities – and therefore in shaping their ethnic identity – can be illustrated in the fact that very few Asians marry across religious or caste lines, and that most of their children will be socialized into a religious value system.

Ethnic identity and education

As we saw earlier, some problems may emerge out of the interaction between the education system and ethnic minority culture and identity, especially if educational policy makers, headteachers and teachers make no allowances for ethnic minority values and norms. Moreover, as we have already seen, there may be some scope for generational conflict as some

Asian females acquire educational and career aspirations which conflict with their parents' desire that they settle down into a domestic role.

Ghuman notes that the mosque is the centre for the religious, educational and political activities of Muslim communities and these religious institutions often exert a strong influence on the way parents rear and educate their children. Many Muslim parents send their children to mosques for the teaching of the Koran. Ghuman notes that many Muslim parents would prefer separate schools (faith schools), particularly for their girls. Muslims have expressed concern at the curriculum of the comprehensive sector, especially with regard to religious education, the teaching of physical education, music and drama. For example, Ghuman points out that teachers encourage an inquiring and critical attitude in their students, which can conflict with Muslim religious traditions and undermine respect for the values of their elders, especially in the area of arranged marriages. In contrast, research suggests that Hindu and Sikh parental attitudes towards female education are extremely positive and may partly account for the success of Indian girls at both further and higher education levels of British education.

Modern ethnic identities

There is some evidence that ethnic identities are evolving and modern **hybrid** forms are now developing among Britain's younger minority ethnic citizens. Charlotte Butler (1995) studied third-generation young Muslim women ('third-generation' means that their parents were born in the UK, but their grandparents migrated to the UK). She found that they choose from a variety of possible identities. Some will choose to reflect their ascribed position through the wearing of traditional dress, while others may take a more 'negotiated' position. This may mean adopting Western ideas about education and careers, whilst retaining some respect for traditional religious ideas about the role of women. Some young Islamic women may adopt quite different identities compared with their mothers on issues such as equality, domestic roles, fashion and marriage.

Johal (1998) focused on second- and third-generation British Asians. He found that they have a dual identity, in that they inherit an Asian identity and adopt a British one. This results in Asian youth adopting a 'White mask' in order to interact with White peers at school or college, but emphasizing their cultural difference whenever they feel it is necessary. He notes that many British-Asians adopt 'hybrid identities'; Jill Swale (2001) defines this as a 'pick-and-mix approach to cultural behaviour patterns found in postmodern societies', which involves the young selecting aspects of British, Asian and international culture relating to fashion, music and food. For example, many young British-Asians like Bhangra music – a mixture of Punjabi music married to Western rhythms.

Ghuman suggests that Hindu and Sikh girls use '**compartmentalism**' to cope with the twin pressures of parental restriction and racial prejudice. He notes: 'On the one hand, South Asian girls learn to think and behave as obedient and respectful daughters wearing salwar kameez and speaking in Punjabi/Hindi at home. On the other, they wear European-style uniform and speak English at school and are engaging and assertive like their English peers.'

However, he also notes that some Asian girls have to give up their hope of a career and accept an arranged marriage because of parental pressure. These girls probably redefine their ethnic identity in terms of conforming to their parents' culture by becoming a 'good' wife and mother.

Recently, sociologists have observed that intermarriage, especially between White females and African-Caribbean males has risen considerably. Consequently, more mixed-race children are being produced. These children may have a unique problem of self-identification compared with other ethnic minority identities. Tizard and Phoenix (1993) found that 60 per cent of the mixed-race children in their sample were proud of their mixed parentage but they noted that 'it is still not an easy ride to be of mixed Black and White parentage in our society', because of racism from both White and Black populations.

Finally, whilst acknowledging the appearance of new ethnic cultural identities, Modood (2001) notes how important traditional values, customs and rituals still are in shaping ethnic identity today. He points out that nearly all Asians, whether they be Pakistani, Bangladeshi or Indian, can understand a community language and two-thirds use it with other family members younger than themselves. Moreover, more than half of married 16- to 34-year-old Pakistanis and Bangladeshis have had their spouse chosen by their parents. He concludes that, although there has been some decline in belief in traditional values and practices across the younger generation, this does not mean that the traditional exercises a weak influence. In fact, he notes that in some cultures, the traditional is the main shaper of ethnic identity – Modood notes that Muslim traditional values and practices are experiencing a political and religious revival among Pakistani young men in the early 21st century.

Check your understanding

1. Define in your own words what is meant by 'ethnicity'?

2. Why is it problematic to associate ethnicity only with racial characteristics such as skin colour?

3. How do religion, ethnicity and racism affect young Pakistanis' sense of identity?

4. What do Butler and Johal conclude about the relationships between second- and third-generation young Asians, their parents' generation, and their White peers?

5. What sorts of factors are shaping African-Caribbean ethnic identity compared with the sorts of factors shaping Asian identity?

6. Why is it important to be careful when discussing the concept of Asian ethnic identity and culture?

KEY TERMS

Caste traditional Hindu social divisions.

Compartmentalism dividing your life up into sections so conflicting pressures can be managed.

Ethnicity a shared identity based on common cultural and religious factors.

Ethnographic type of research based on qualitative methods which aims to study social life as 'naturally' as possible.

Hybrid identity a new form of identity resulting from a mixture of two or more influences.

Institutional racism racism that is built into the 'taken-for-granted', everyday life of an organisation.

Islamophobia fear or hatred of Islam.

Rastafarianism a religion originating in Jamaica and associated with reggae music.

Second generation the children of those who migrated to Britain.

Third generation group whose parents were born in the UK, but whose grandparents migrated to the UK.

exploring ethnicity and identity

Item A Muslim women

«It is important to point out that although all of the Muslim women interviewed considered their Muslim identity to be most important to them, the majority also identified with being Asian. Young Asians are constantly aware of being 'different' and of being treated as inferiors because of the colour of their skin. Such racial hostility plays a major role in causing young people to reassert or hold fast to their ethnic identity.

Gender is also an important factor in the identity formation of second-generation Asian Muslim women, for, as several of the women interviewed believed, all cultures are predominantly 'man-made' phenomenon employed by men to sustain their own position in society. Thus, many felt it was not the laws of Islam that were responsible for confining the lives of Asian Muslim women, but culture. The women interviewed pointed out that it was not Islam but traditional customs that confined women to the home and discouraged them from seeking employment or going on to further and higher education. Furthermore, it was customs that encouraged women to be obedient to their husbands and not to show disrespect.»

Butler, C. (1995) 'Religion and gender: young Muslim women in Britain', *Sociology Review*, 4(3), February 1995

a Using Item A, identify and briefly explain two ways in which traditional customs reduced the opportunities of Asian Muslim women. (8 marks)

b Identify and briefly explain two ways in which female Asian identity might be shaped both by traditional and western culture. (8 marks)

c Outline and briefly evaluate two factors that shape the African-Caribbean identity of young Black males. (18 marks)

d Discuss the view that the family and religion are the most important agents of socialization in regard to ethnic minority identity. (26 marks)

research idea

● Conduct semi-structured interviews with a small sample of students from various minority ethnic groups. To what extent do they possess 'hybrid identities'?

web.task

The Institute of Race Relations (www.irr.org.uk) has excellent information, especially on current issues and statistics. Test your knowledge about migration by trying the quiz at www.irr.org.uk/quiz/index.htm

National identity

gettingyouthinking

1. Look closely at the flags – what do these symbolize for you?

2. Kelly Holmes won Olympic gold for Great Britain in Athens in 2004. What qualities does she have that make her British? Would all British people accept her as British?

3. What role do you think sport plays in national identity?

4. How does the monarchy contribute to people's sense of Britishness?

Photos clockwise from top: Orangemen marching in Northern Ireland; Prince Charles in traditional Scottish dress; the Welsh Rugby Union team celebrating after winning the 2005 Six Nations Grand Slam; Dame Kelly Homes receiving one of her two Olympic gold medals

Flags are important symbols of national identity. If you look at images of the World Cup Final in 1966 between England and West Germany, you will notice that the Union Jack is the most common symbol being waved by the crowd. By the 1996 European Championship, England fans had largely abandoned the British flag, while flags and face paints of the St George Cross dominated. The Five Nations Rugby Union Championship saw the Welsh dragon being used in a similar way. Sport, then, is an important aspect of national identity. During the 2000 soccer World Cup, a survey of Scottish football fans suggested that most would support any team but England. This begs the question: what is it about Englishness that the Scots so dislike? And did the Scots antipathy extend to the English athlete, Kelly Holmes? It is unlikely – surveys suggest that the people most likely to object to Kelly were 'little Englanders' – a group so sensitive to their Englishness that they generally subscribe to racist views that involve the rejection of immigration and mixed-race marriages. Such Englishness usually involves reverence for English institutions such as the monarchy, despite that institution's attempt to stress its Scottish and Welsh connections (as in the photo of Prince Charles in a kilt).

National identity

National identity can be defined as 'the feeling of being part of a larger community in the form of a nation, which gives a sense of purpose and meaning to people's lives as well as a sense of belonging'. Note how the following extract from Billington et al. (1998) illustrates this definition.

>> *When I go away for holidays to Europe, I am conscious of 'being abroad', of being a foreigner. My passport cover bears the legends 'European Community' and 'United Kingdom of Great Britain and Northern Ireland'. Inside it states that I am a 'British Citizen'. While abroad, despite being dressed in what appears to be the inconspicuous clothes of a middle-aged, middle-class woman, I notice that people frequently address me in English, even before I have spoken. During a stay in the USA which, despite the dominance of the English language, felt 'foreign' to me, I was approached in shops and other places by people who noted my English accent, welcomed me to America, told me about their trips to England and, sometimes, their English ancestors. Formally asked my nationality, I usually reply 'British'. Asked to describe myself to people of other nationalities, I say I am English. If asked to write an autobiographical piece, I probably would not include either of these two identities.* >> (pp. 166–7)

Billington and colleagues note that most of the time we take our national identity for granted. It is only when our attention is drawn to how other cultures view us, through the actual experience of 'being abroad' and especially the experience of 'other' cultural practices and customs, that we think about our own national identity. Our perception of this may also be provoked by the 'British' stereotypes found in Hollywood films such as *Mary Poppins* and television series such as *Friends*. What we learn from these experiences is that national identity involves a range of distinct and subtle differences that mark out cultural distinctions between 'them' and 'us'. Such distinctions are reinforced by the mass media. As Billington notes:

>> *When there is an air or rail crash or other disaster involving people from a range of countries, the news media announce the number of British dead or injured, the implication being that it is our own compatriots, those who 'belong' to us, who are our main concern.* >> (p.168)

There is a negative side to this identification, too, in that it can often lead to fears about foreigners, which may be expressed in **xenophobia** and racism.

National identity is not necessarily the same thing as '**nationality**'. The latter concept is a formal, legal category which derives from belonging to a '**nation state**', a country recognized by other countries as exercising authority and power over a geographical territory. Nationality is symbolized by legal rights, such as being able to carry a passport, being legally able to marry or vote at a particular age, etc. It also involves certain duties, such as obeying the law of the land. The crime of 'treason', i.e. betraying one's country, is seen as one of the most appalling crimes one can commit.

It is important to recognize that the legal status of being British, i.e. formal nationality, does not necessarily mean that people will subscribe to a British identity. Many citizens of the United Kingdom, defined as British in the law, identify with 'nations within the nation', that is they see themselves primarily as English, Scottish, Welsh or Irish. Moreover, many British subjects may see their national identity as primarily tied up with their country or region of origin and hence see themselves as African-Caribbean, Punjabi, Bengali, Pakistani, etc. Others may subscribe first and foremost to identities deriving from their religious affiliations, such as Muslim or Jewish.

British national identity

The British are a 'mongrel nation', a mix of social and immigrant groups that have settled in Britain since Roman times. As Guibernau and Goldblatt (2000) note, no case can be made for a single, original, authentic group of Britons. They note that up to the 1707 Act of Union that linked Scotland to England and Wales, there was no such thing as a British national identity. People identified more with the regions in which they lived than with a loyalty to the British nation state. However, they note that over the following 200 years, a sense of British identity was gradually created around the following five key themes.

Geography

The fact that the UK is made up of islands gave it a clear sense of boundaries that made it distinct from Europe. It can be argued that although the UK is physically, politically and legally part of Europe, British identity has rarely extended to feeling 'European' because of our island status. Our immediate European neighbours – the French – have attracted the bulk of our anti-European feeling.

Religion

Despite the presence of Catholic religious communities and practices, Protestantism in its various forms (the Church of England, Presbyterianism, Methodism, etc.) is the dominant religious identity of Great Britain. Despite **secularization**, it can be argued that religion still symbolizes national identity for many in the UK. People who do not attend church on a regular basis still identify themselves as, for example, Church of England or Church of Scotland. In times of national celebration, such as royal weddings, or disaster and remembrance of the war dead, religion plays a central role in the proceedings. In the courts, most people still swear to tell the truth using the bible and the national anthem asks God to look after the Queen, the ultimate symbol of the British nation.

War

Wars against the French in the 17th and 18th centuries, as well as the two World Wars of the 20th century, reinforced the sense of 'them' versus 'us', and especially the uniquely British themes of self-sacrifice, perseverance, fair play, heroism and putting up with exceptional hardship. Think about the sense of Britishness associated with historical events such as the London Blitz and Dunkirk, and figures such as Winston Churchill and Ellen MacArthur. Public ceremonies and celebrations marking events such as the end of the Second World War symbolize both individual sacrifice for the nation and the preservation of the British way of life – in other words, British identity.

The British Empire

Britain's success as an imperial power in the 18th and 19th centuries brought economic success for the country's elite, and a sense of pride and achievement in what was perceived as British superiority over other cultures and races. Some commentators today would argue that these attitudes underpin the racism and anti-European feeling present in the UK today.

Monarchy

From the middle of the 18th century, the monarchy deliberately set out to win popularity with the mass of the people. The cultural symbols of British nationality, in particular, the song 'God Save the Queen' and the Union Jack were created in order to place the monarchy at the heart of British identity. Billig (1992) notes that, today, people identify with the Royal Family despite having cynical feelings about them because the Royals have managed to represent themselves as an ordinary family doing an extraordinary job very well. In 1977, the punk rock band the Sex Pistols caused huge outrage with their song 'God Save the Queen' because its lyrics were deemed insulting to the monarchy – 'it's a fascist regime' – whilst the cover of the single shocked with its image of the Queen with a safety pin through her nose.

The death of Diana, Princess of Wales, illustrated very clearly how deeply the British feel about such symbols. Billington and colleagues note:

≪At a national level, the Princess's death has been emphasized and perceived by the media, in particular, as a national calamity and loss, because she was both the mother of the future monarch and an effective worker for charity.≫ (p.181)

At a more personal level, people felt grief, despite some criticisms of her personal life, because she reminded people of their own complicated lives. In this sense they were able to identify with her as a human being, as well as a member of the Royal Family.

National identity and socialization

Schudsen (1994) points out that the British people are socialized into a British identity through various factors, especially the following.

A common language

In the UK, this is obviously English. Language is central to our sense of identity because we use it to express ourselves and communicate with others. It is seen as central to our cultural identity and we often refer to it as the 'mother tongue'. (Note how many ethnic minority groups stress their identity by speaking both English and the language of their country or region of origin at home.) Some commentators have suggested that one aspect of British identity is our reluctance to learn foreign languages – we assume that foreigners will speak English because it is the universal and dominant language of business, etc.

Education

The teaching of history, English literature and religion in British schools tends to promote national identity. For example, Shakespeare is often promoted as the world's greatest playwright, while traditional history teaching often focused on Britain's positive achievements at the expense of such negative British activities as slavery, massacres and exploitation. The Education Reform Act (1988) stresses Christian worship in schools, despite the fact that the UK is a **multicultural society**.

National rituals

Guibernau and Goldblatt note that 'national identities need to be upheld and reaffirmed at regular intervals'. In particular, royal and state occasions are used to reinforce the British way of life and the public are invited to take part, usually via television. Guibernau and Goldblatt observe that Remembrance Sunday 'is not just about remembering the past, it creates one view of the nation in the present and makes the experience of war part of British identity'. In other words, rituals unite us in Britishness. Think about how other uniquely British rituals do this, such as the changing of the guard, the State opening of Parliament, royal weddings and funerals, the Queen's televised Christmas speech and even Bonfire Night.

Symbols

Guibernau and Goldblatt argue that symbols are powerful indicators of national identity. These might include styles of dress, uniforms, passports, styles of music, national anthems, and, particularly, flags. The Union Jack is symbolic of Britishness, especially of the British Empire, the Queen and Parliament. It often indicates tradition and patriotism, especially during wartime or at sporting events. Young people, too, have been encouraged to take pride in this symbol, most recently, through its association with Cool Britannia and Britpop.

The mass media

On the whole, television, magazines and newspapers encourage people to identify with national symbols such as the Royal Family by taking a keen interest in their activities. Members of the Royal Family are treated as celebrities and their lives are closely scrutinized. Despite some periods in which media coverage is negative (such as immediately following the death of the Princess of Wales), the mass media generally approve of and defer to the monarchy and are critical of the notion of republicanism. Moreover, the media play a key role in reinforcing our sense of national identity. The tabloid media are particularly notorious in their anti-European sentiments and are consequently keen to talk up British successes. A good example of this in 2005 was Ellen McArthur's achievement in setting a new world record in sailing 'around' the world. The crucial aspect of this story for many British journalists was the fact that the record had been previously held by Britain's 'old enemy', the French. In times of war, the media focus on 'our boys', while sporting events such as the Olympic Games are reported almost as quasi-wars against other nations. Our athletes win or lose battles, and often, the greatest compliment a foreign athlete can receive is that they displayed the 'British' virtues of fair play and sportsmanship.

The mass production of fashion and taste

Britishness can also be embodied in particular foods (e.g. fish and chips), consumer goods (e.g. the Rolls-Royce car) and retail outlets (such as Marks and Spencer). People often think that the British way of life is in jeopardy if any of these things are threatened or changed. Recently Nestlé caused a great national controversy by changing the packaging of the very British chocolate bar, the Kit-Kat. It was even suggested by one tabloid newspaper that this sort of underhand behaviour was typical of a foreign company!

The decline of British identity

Some sociologists have suggested that the concept of British identity is misleading because 'Britishness' is really 'Englishness', in that the English have always dominated the union with the Scots, Irish and Welsh. A good example of this can be seen in the recent BBC poll of Great Britons – nine of the top ten were English. However, despite this dominance, Waters (1995)

suggests that British or English identity may be under threat in the 21st century for a number of reasons.

Celtic identity

Celtic identity has always been a powerful source of identity, especially in Wales and Scotland. It has recently been given political and legal legitimacy in Scotland and Wales in the form of the Scottish Parliament and Welsh Assembly, which have the power to introduce legislation on a wide range of issues.

There is evidence that people in Wales are more likely to stress Welsh identity at the expense of Britishness, which historically has been associated with Englishness. For example, a Labour Force Survey in 2001 found that 87 per cent of people born in Wales saw themselves as Welsh only. This powerful sense of national identity has been assisted by legislation aimed at protecting the Welsh language and culture, especially in the education system. The Welsh language is compulsory in Welsh schools up to year 11, despite the fact that it is only spoken by a minority of the Welsh population. Language seems to be crucial to Welsh identity. The Labour Force survey found that 89 per cent of Welsh speakers saw themselves as Welsh, compared with only 59 per cent of those who did not speak the language. There is a 'Welsh dimension' to all subjects in secondary school. History, for example, partly focuses on Welsh resistance to English occupation. Literature focuses on Welsh poets and novelists. Finally, Welsh schools are encouraged to organize their own Eisteddfford, a cultural celebration involving Welsh songs, poetry and literature, in addition to celebrating St David's Day. Welsh identity is also reinforced by two Welsh TV channels, as well as strong cultural traditions in fields such as opera and choral singing. Sport in the form of rugby union is an important source of national pride too, especially if this involves beating England.

Globalization

The boundaries between nation states are becoming less significant as **transnational companies** and international financial markets increasingly dominate world trade. British identity may be diluted as British companies and products are taken over by foreign companies and British companies close down their factories in this country and move production to the cheaper developing countries. There are also concerns that American culture is taking over the British high street as companies such as McDonalds, Starbucks and Borders expand their British operations. Moreover, television programmes, films and music are increasingly being produced for the international market. There are fears that these largely American products may erode Britishness and create a single commercialized culture offering superficial mass entertainment.

Multicultural nature of society

The multicultural nature of British society seems to be having an effect on our sense of British or national identity. Many members of Britain's ethnic minority communities experience a sense of exclusion from the identity 'British'. Modood's survey (1997) of ethnic minority groups found that most of his second-generation sample thought of themselves as mostly, but not entirely, culturally and socially British. There was evidence of a rejection of British national identity from over a quarter of British-born Caribbeans and Asians. There is little evidence of improvement, as a survey conducted in March 2005 by ICM found that only 39 per cent of minorities saw themselves as 'fully British'. Modood found that Asians and African-Caribbeans did not feel comfortable with a 'British' identity because they felt that the majority of White people did not accept them as British because of their colour and cultural background. Members of ethnic minority groups, then, are more likely to see their identity in ethnic or religious terms – as Indians, Sikhs, Muslims, etc. (see Topic 8 for examples) – although there is some evidence that an increasing number of third-generation young Asians, particularly Indians, are using terms like British-Asians or Indo-British to describe themselves today as they tap into and are influenced by Western culture. Interestingly, in Scotland, young Asians tend to see themselves as Scottish rather than British.

Nature of English identity

Concerns have been expressed about English identity. It has been suggested that, whilst groups such as the Welsh and Scots have developed a strong sense of identity underpinned by language, history, education, government and media, the English are undergoing an identity crisis. It is argued that many intellectuals have been unwilling to adopt the symbols of English identity such as the St George's Cross because of its long association with racist political parties and football hooliganism. Williams (1996) has even argued that football hooliganism, which is seen as the '**English disease**' abroad, may even be a form of **defensive patriotism**, a way of asserting English identity in the face of Britain's international political and economic decline.

Denscombe (2001) notes that:

≪*English identity tends to be defined by what it is not, rather than what it is; who the English are not, rather than who they are. Those with the strongest sense of English identity are characterized by suspicion of the outsider, the foreigner and those of other races.*≫ (p. 20).

These are the 'Little Englanders'. Research by Curtice and Heath (2000) suggests that this group who identify themselves as 'English' rather than 'British' has increased from 7 per cent of the population to 17 per cent in 1999 (i.e. more than 6 million adults). Of this total, 37 per cent openly admitted to being racially prejudiced. Nearly half thought that measures to achieve equal opportunities for Asians and Blacks in Britain 'had gone too far', while 70 per cent felt that immigrants take jobs away from Whites. Many are convinced that the European Union is plotting to abolish Britishness, e.g. by replacing the pound with the euro.

Research from Urban (1999) confirms that people's sense of English identity differs according to factors such as region,

ethnicity and age. He showed two videos of national images to focus groups around the country. Both focused on British themes; one on the traditional defiance of outsiders, the other on love of personal freedom. The 'traditional' video contained shots of war, the monarchy and emphasized teamwork. This video drew a very positive response from older audiences especially those outside London. The 'liberal' tape featured images of innovation, freedom and tolerance, along with pictures of Shakespeare, the Notting Hill Carnival, great British inventions and Lenny Henry. Many people in London identified with these images, but people in the provinces were less convinced that these images represented Englishness and were less likely to identify with the images of race and multiculturalism.

Despite these negative trends, there are positive signs that a new sense of 'Britishness' is slowly emerging in the field of popular culture, especially in the worlds of food, fashion and music. It is well illustrated by the news that chicken tikka masala, a hybrid of Indian spices and English gravy has now replaced fish and chips as the UK's most popular food. In other words, a new form of Britishness may be emerging shaped both by 'traditional' British values and institutions, and by values and institutions which originate in the increasingly multicultural and globalized nature of UK society.

Check your understanding

1 What is the difference between national identity and nationality?

2 Identify three symbols associated by foreigners with Britishness.

3 What is the role of the mass media in transmitting ideas about British national identity?

4 What institutions are responsible for maintaining Welsh identity in Wales?

5 In what ways do the sports of football, rugby union and cricket influence national and ethnic identities in the UK?

6 How does the monarchy unite the people in a national identity?

7 In what ways do transnational corporations dilute national identity?

8 Identify two negative effects of the rise of the 'little Englander' sense of national identity.

9 What is 'the English disease'?

10 In what sense might ethnic identity interact with national identity to create multiple or hybrid identities?

Celtic a term used to describe the origins and culture of the Welsh, Irish and Scots.

Defensive patriotism aggression caused by the need to assert one's Britishness abroad in order to counter the view that British dominance is on the decline.

English disease football hooliganism and aggression in general.

Globalization the process whereby national boundaries become increasingly irrelevant.

Multicultural society a society characterized by a diversity of ethnic groups.

Nationality the legal status that derives from being a citizen of a particular country.

Nation state a country recognized by others as exerting power and authority over a given territory.

Secularization the decline of religion.

Transnational (or multinational) companies companies that have offices or factories in different countries.

Xenophobia fear or hatred of foreigners.

exploring national identity

Item A Ethnic minorities and British identity

Subscribing to a British identity is not the first priority for most young Muslim women born and brought up in Britain. They often do not want to abandon their parents' way of life in favour of British culture. Most wish to maintain a distinct Muslim identity. Being British is not considered as important as Islam which, contrary to popular media stereotypes, promotes the rights of women and gives Muslim women the right to study and work. In terms of feeling British, other ethnic-minority groups experience similar feelings.

Surveys of British-born African-Caribbeans suggest they find it difficult to see themselves as 'British' as they feel that the majority of White people do not accept them as British because of their race or cultural background. They feel that their claim to be British is all too often denied by hurtful jokes, harassment, discrimination and violence.

Miri Song's research into the Chinese in Britain found that second-generation Chinese see themselves as influenced by both Chinese and British cultures. They aspire to British cultural goals, such as educational achievement and careers outside the family business, and consequently their cultural identity is less influenced by Chinese culture.

Adapted from Butler, C. (1995) 'Religion and gender: young Muslim women in Britain', *Sociology Review*, 4(3), February 1995, pp. 21–2; Modood, T., quoted in Abercrombie, N. and Warde, A. (2000) *Contemporary British Society*, Cambridge: Polity Press, p. 238; and Abbott, D. (1998) *Culture and Identity*, London: Hodder & Stoughton, p. 113

a Identify and briefly explain two ways in which Item A challenges the idea of a single British national identity. (8 marks)

b Identify and briefly explain two reasons why people from ethnic-minority backgrounds may be reluctant to adopt fully a British identity. (8 marks)

c Outline and briefly evaluate two ways in which British identity is transmitted by the mass media. (18 marks)

d Discuss the view that there is no such thing as a British identity shared by all those who live in the UK. (26 marks)

research idea

- Put together two collections of photographs that illustrate a 'traditional' and 'liberal' view of 'Britishness' (see Urban's research on p. 44). Show them to a sample of students within your college or community to discover views about what constitutes 'Britishness' in your area.

web.task

List 10 characteristics, images, symbols, etc., that constitute Scottish and Irish identities. Visit the tourist board websites of these respective countries or look at holiday brochures for clues.

The individual and society

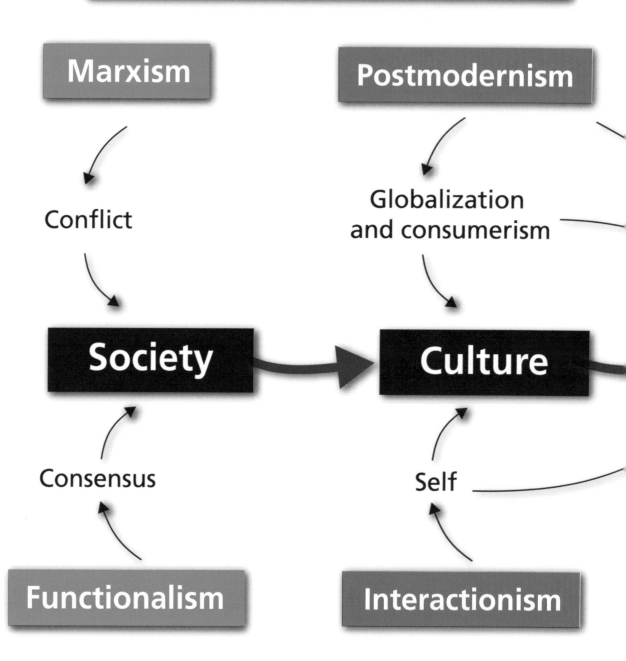

Marxism

Conflict

Postmodernism

Globalization
and consumerism

Society → **Culture**

Consensus

Self

Functionalism

Interactionism

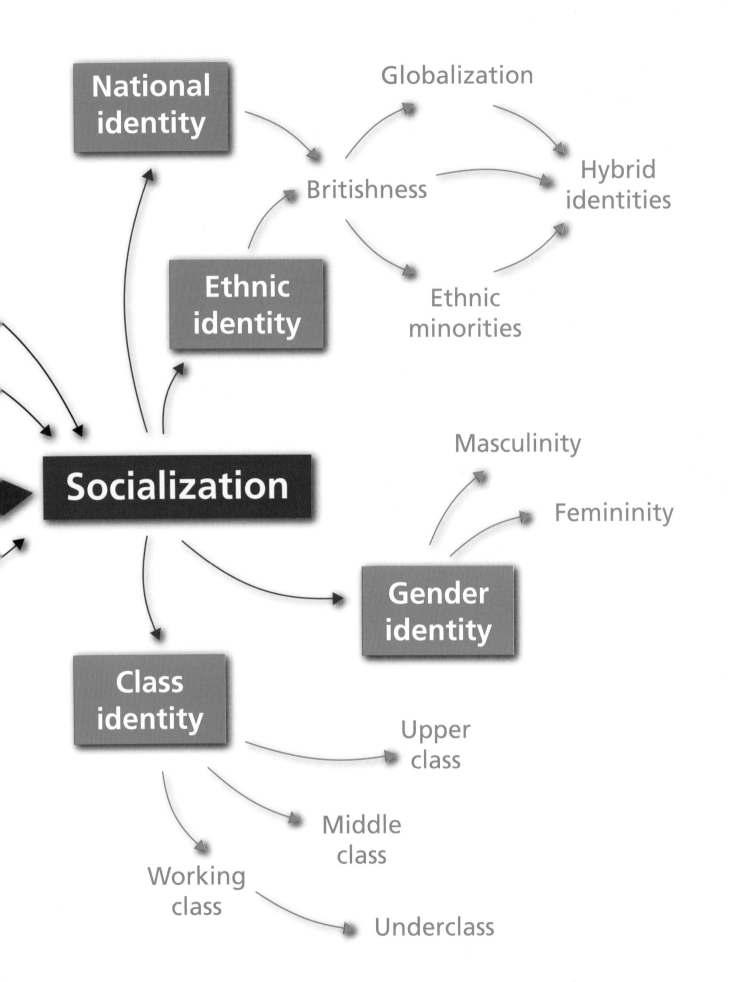

EVERYONE THINKS THEY KNOW SOMETHING ABOUT FAMILIES AND HOUSEHOLDS. This is not surprising, as virtually all of us will live in a family at some point in our lives. We often assume that most people share our experience of family life and that most families are organized along the lines of our own. Also, because family life is often intense and emotional, we often feel strongly about the family setup and find it difficult to understand why other people don't do things as we do. The study of families and households can sometimes be difficult because we find it hard to set aside our own experiences. However, as you study this unit, you must try to be objective and impartial – a good sociologist puts aside their own prejudices and emotions, and makes judgements purely on the basis of evidence.

This is particularly important with regard to Topic 1, in which we examine what is meant by the 'family' and how definitions of what constitutes 'proper' or 'ideal' family life have been dominated by particular perspectives.

In Topic 2, we examine the view that the modern family is under attack and in decline, and that the state is partially responsible for this situation. In Topic 3, this theme is continued through an examination of a range of family changes that are seen by New Right commentators as responsible for a so-called 'crisis in family life'. This crisis has supposedly led to a number of social problems, including a rise in crime, male underachievement at schools and teenage pregnancy. We look at the evidence with regard to marriage, cohabitation and divorce.

Topic 4 continues on this trail because family traditionalists also argue that the appearance of alternative types of families in recent years is yet more evidence of family decline. This section, therefore, examines the facts about one-parent families, reconstituted families, ethnic minority families and other forms of diversity. Some sociological theories argue that such family diversity is actually healthy for society and individuals.

Topic 5 deals with childhood, which many people assume is a biological state of age. However, this topic will show that childhood is, in fact, socially constructed, as experiences of it differ from society to society, as well as *within* societies. How we treat children is yet another concern of those who believe that society is in moral decline.

Topic 6 focuses on power and control in the family, and critically examines the view that relationships between men and women in families have become more equal. It looks at a range of different aspects of family life including domestic labour, emotional labour, fathering and domestic violence, in order to work out the degree of change in family relationships. Finally, Topic 7 deals with the difficult issue of violence and abuse in the family – sometimes referred to as the 'dark side' of family life.

OCR specification	topics	pages
The family and recent social change		
Family concepts and definitions: kinship and households, nuclear and extended families	Key concepts about the family and a discussion of the difficulties in defining the family are contained in Topic 1.	50–55
Recent demographic change: divorce, births, ageing population	Trends in births, marriages and divorce are covered in Topic 3.	62–67
Social policy and the family: family values debates. Policy towards families and children	Social policy is the focus of Topic 2 but is also discussed in relation to divorce in Topic 3 and childhood in Topic 5.	56–61 62–67 74–79
Diversity in families and households		
Recent trends in family life; cohabitation, one-parent families, reconstituted families, dual career families, single-person households	Trends in partnership formation and childbirth are covered in Topic 3. Trends in household formation more generally in Topic 4.	62–67 68–73
Dimensions of diversity; class, gender, ethnicity, life-cycle and location	Family diversity is the focus of Topic 4.	68–73
Explanations of family diversification, changing economic and domestic roles of men and women, changes in family obligations	Some explanations of diversification as well as coverage of changes in family obligations can be found in Topic 4. The changing roles of men and women are discussed in Topic 6.	68–73 80–85
Power, inequality and family policy		
The distribution of power between men and women in the family. Patriarchy, the domestic division of labour, decision-making	Topic 6 concentrates on the distribution of power in the family.	80–85
The relationship between parents and children; changing conceptions of childhood, the legal status of children	Covered in Topic 5.	74–79
The dark side of family life: violence, child abuse and social policy	Covered in Topic 7.	86–91

Family

TOPIC 1 Defining the family **50**

TOPIC 2 The family, morality and the state **56**

TOPIC 3 Marriage and marital breakdown **62**

TOPIC 4 Family diversity **68**

TOPIC 5 Childhood **74**

TOPIC 6 Power and control in the family **80**

TOPIC 7 The dark side of family life **86**

UNIT SUMMARY **92**

Defining the family

gettingyouthinking

Left: an Ik village clings to the hillside

Below: an Ik child called Lokiira

The family does not feature heavily in the culture of the Ik of Northern Uganda. In fact, as far as the Ik are concerned, the family means very little. This is because the Ik face a daily struggle to survive in the face of drought, famine and starvation. Anyone who cannot take care of him- or herself is regarded as a useless burden by the Ik and a hazard to the survival of the others. Families mean dependants such as children who need to be fed and protected. So close to the verge of starvation, family, sentiment and love are regarded as luxuries that can mean death. Children are regarded as useless appendages, like old people, because they use up precious resources. So the old are abandoned to die. Sick and disabled children too are abandoned. The Ik attitude is that, as long as you keep the breeding group alive, you can always get more children.

Ik mothers throw their children out of the village compound when they are 3 years old, to fend for themselves. I imagine children must be rather relieved to be thrown out, for in the process of being cared for he or she is grudgingly carried about in a hide sling wherever the mother goes. Whenever the mother is in her field, she loosens the sling and lets the baby to the ground none too slowly, and laughs if it is hurt. Then she goes about her business, leaving the child there, almost hoping that some predator will come along and carry it off. This sometimes happens. Such behaviour does not endear children to their parents or parents to their children.

Adapted from Turnbull, C. (1994) *The Mountain People*, London: Pimlico

1 How do the Ik define the family?

2 Given your own experience of family life, think of three features of the family that you would expect to find in all families, wherever they are. How do these three features differ from the Ik?

3 In what ways might some British families share some of the characteristics of the Ik?

You probably reacted to the description of the Ik with horror. It is tempting to conclude that these people are primitive, savage and inhuman, and that their concept of the 'family' is deeply wrong. However, sociologists argue that it is wrong simply to judge such societies and their family arrangements as unnatural and deviant. We need to understand that such arrangements may have positive functions. In the case of the Ik, with the exceptional circumstances they find themselves in – drought and famine – their family arrangements help ensure the survival of the tribe. Moreover, you may have concluded that family life in the UK and for the Ik have some things in common. British family life is not universally experienced as positive for all family members. For some members – young and old alike – family life may be characterized by violence, abuse and isolation.

The problem with studying the family is that we all think we are experts. This is not surprising, given that most of us are born into families and socialized into family roles and responsibilities. It is an institution most of us feel very comfortable with and regard as 'natural'. For many of us, it is the cornerstone of our social world, a place to which we can retreat and where we can take refuge from the stresses of the outside world. It is the place in which we are loved for who we are, rather than what we are. Family living and family events are probably the most important aspects of our lives. It is no wonder then that we tend to hold very fierce, emotional, and perhaps irrational, views about family life and how it ought to be organized. Such 'taken-for-granted' views make it very difficult for us to examine objectively family arrangements that deviate from our own experience – such as those of the Ik – without making critical judgements.

Defining 'the family'

The experiences of the Ik suggest that family life across the world is characterized by tremendous variation and diversity. However, we can see that, until fairly recently, popular definitions of 'the family' in modern UK society were dominated by a traditional view that the **nuclear family** was the ideal type of family to which people should aspire. It was generally accepted that this family, which was the statistical norm until the 1980s, should have the following characteristics:

● It should be small and compact in structure, composed of a mother, father and usually two or three children who are biologically related.
● The relationship between the adults should be **heterosexual** and based on romantic love. Children are seen as the outcome of that love.
● The relationship between the adults should be reinforced by marriage, which, it is assumed, encourages **fidelity** and therefore family stability.
● Marriage should be companionate, i.e. based on husband and wives being partners. There is an overlap between male and female responsibilities as men get more involved in childcare and housework. However, some 'natural' differences persist. It is taken for granted that women want to have children and that they should be primarily responsible for **nurturing** and childcare. The male role is usually defined as the main economic breadwinner and head of the household.

51

Unit 2 Family

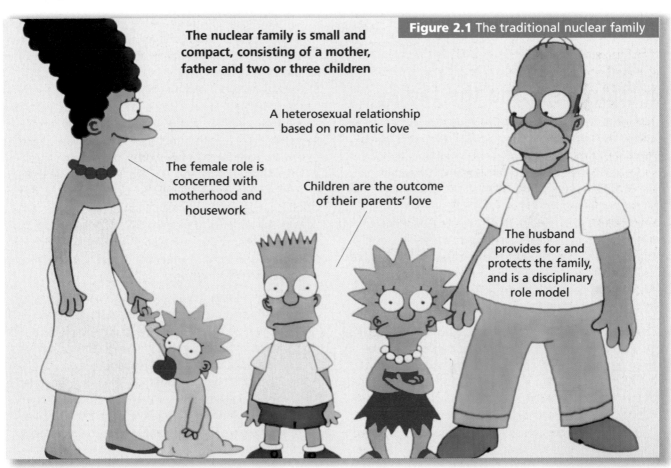

The nuclear family is small and compact, consisting of a mother, father and two or three children

Figure 2.1 The traditional nuclear family

A heterosexual relationship based on romantic love

The female role is concerned with motherhood and housework

Children are the outcome of their parents' love

The husband provides for and protects the family, and is a disciplinary role model

The influence of the traditional view of the family

Despite recent changes in the structure of families, and the liberalization of attitudes towards family life, we can still see the influence of traditional beliefs about family life in the UK. It can be argued that they constitute a powerful 'ideology' about what families should look like and how family members should behave. For example, the belief that the main responsibility for parenting lies with mothers is still very influential.

We can see this dominant set of ideas about family life reflected in government **social policy** – for example, in the assumption that there is no need for state provision of free childcare because women are happy to give up work to look after children. Traditional beliefs are also reflected in the pronouncements of religious leaders, politicians and editors of newspapers, which regularly state that certain types of relationships (e.g. homosexual ones) and certain types of living arrangements (e.g. lone parents and **cohabitation**) are not worthy of being called families. We can even see such views reflected in our own everyday behaviour and attitudes, as Jon Bernardes argues:

<< *It is not just that many people think of women as the most appropriate carers of children but rather that we all act on this belief in our daily lives. Men may hesitate or not know how to engage in certain tasks or, in public, men may be discouraged from comforting a lost child whilst a woman may 'naturally' take up this role. Examples of family ideology can be found in a wide range of everyday practices, from images on supermarket products to who picks up dirty laundry (or who drops it in the first place).* >>

Bernardes, J. (1997) *Family Studies: An Introduction*,
London: Routledge, p. 31

Functionalism and the family

For many years, the sociology of the family was dominated by the theory of functionalism. Functionalist sociologists see the family as one of the most important social institutions. In particular, functionalists see the family as the cornerstone of society because it is functional or beneficial both for the individual and for society. It meets the needs of individuals for emotional satisfaction, social support, personal development, identity and security. It meets the needs of society for social order and stability. It plays a key role in making individuals feel part of society.

Functionalists have identified a number of functions of the family that contribute to the well-being of society:

1 The family is the *primary agent of socialization* – It socializes new generations into the culture of society by teaching them common values, norms, traditions and roles. For example, children learn the patterns of behaviour expected of their gender, i.e. what is regarded as appropriate masculine and feminine behaviour. Parsons (1955) argued that families are 'personality factories', producing children who are committed to shared norms and values and who have a strong sense of belonging to society. In these ways, the family is central to the creation of value consensus, **social integration** and, therefore, social order.

2 *The family is an important agent of social control* – It polices society's members on a daily basis, in order to maintain the consensus and social order brought about by socialization. For example, the family defines what is socially acceptable behaviour with regard to sex and regulates behaviour such as dating, pre-marital sex, marital sex and extra-marital sex. These family controls prevent the potential anarchy and disorder that might result if people were allowed to engage in unregulated sex. Furthermore, marriage results in emotional stability for the couple. As regards children, primary socialization involves the development of a conscience that allows the individual to know the difference between 'right' and 'wrong'. This is backed up through parental use of positive sanctions (e.g. rewards) and negative sanctions (e.g. punishments).

3 *Marriage* is regarded as *the most appropriate setting for* **procreation** – In fact, children are seen as the natural outcome of romantic love. Reproduction is an essential function because the family provides new members of society to replace those who have died.

4 The family also has a number of *economic functions* – It provides children with economic support, not only during their early years of dependence, but often well after they have flown the family nest, e.g. to go on to university or to set up homes of their own. The family also provides the economy with workers. The family, along with education, functions to ensure that its members are willing to take on occupational duties and obligations. Families also play a central role as consumers of the material goods and services produced by the economy. An examination of television advertising reveals the family to be the central unit of economic consumption.

5 Parsons argued that the *family functions to relieve the stress of modern-day living* – He claimed that family life 'stabilizes' adult personalities. This is sometimes referred to as the 'warm bath' theory, in that the family provides a relaxing environment for the male worker to immerse himself in after a hard day at work (see Fig. 2.2 above right). Romantic love and the unconditional love parents have for their children provide family members with the means to cope with the anxieties of modern life. In this sense, the family is 'home sweet home', a 'haven in a heartless world'.

6 Families also perform a number of *miscellaneous functions to support their members*:

– The economic, social and educational resources the family offers us give us our social status in the eyes of other members of society, e.g. our social-class position. These resources can determine whether or not we experience upward social mobility.

– Family members are often cared for and supported by other family members if they are ill, disabled or in poverty. The family, therefore, plays important health and welfare functions, and works alongside social institutions such as the National Health Service.

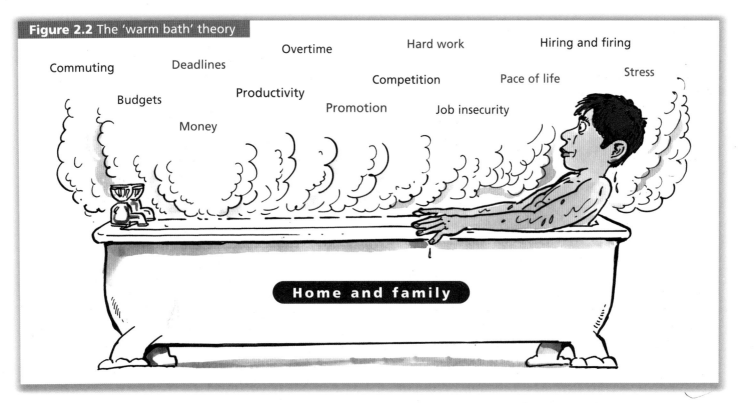

Figure 2.2 The 'warm bath' theory

Commuting · Deadlines · Overtime · Hard work · Hiring and firing · Budgets · Productivity · Competition · Pace of life · Stress · Money · Promotion · Job insecurity

Home and family

- Most children are taught to read and write by family members before they go to school. The family also often provides children with a number of cultural and material supports throughout their educational careers.
- Other sociologists point out that the family is important for both political and religious socialization. Many of our beliefs, prejudices and anxieties may be rooted in the strong emotional bonds we forge with our parents.
- The family is often an important site of leisure and recreation for its members.

Functionalists, therefore, see the family as a crucial social institution functioning positively to bring about healthy societies and individuals. Murdock (1949) went as far as to claim that the nuclear family is a biological necessity because it is universal, i.e. it can be found in all human societies.

Criticisms of functionalist views of the family

- The idea that families benefit all the individuals in them has been strongly attacked, especially by feminist sociologists, who argue that the family serves only to exploit and oppress women. Moreover, the rosy and harmonious picture of family life painted by functionalists ignores social problems such as increases in the divorce rate, child abuse and domestic violence.
- Functionalist analyses of the nuclear family tend to be based on middle-class and American versions of family life and, as a result, neglect other influences such as ethnicity, social class and religion. For example, Parsons does not consider the fact that wealth or poverty may determine whether or not women stay at home to look after children.

Since Parsons wrote in the 1950s, many Western societies, including the UK, have become multicultural. Religious and cultural differences may mean that Parsons' version of the family is no longer relevant in contemporary society.

- Functionalists also tend to see socialization as a one-way process, with children as passive recipients of culture. However, this view underestimates the role of children in families – they may have more choice in accepting or rejecting the attempts to mould their personalities than functionalists give them credit for.
- Functionalist thinking on the family suggests that the domestic **division of labour** is both 'natural' and unchangeable because it is based on biological differences. However, there is a lack of scientific evidence to support this view.
- Finally, social and cultural changes may mean that some of the functions of the family have been modified or even abandoned altogether, as demonstrated in Table 2.1 on the following page.

KEY TERMS

Cohabitation unmarried couples living together as man and wife.

Division of labour the organization of work.

Extended kin relations beyond the nuclear family, such as aunts, uncles and grandparents.

Fidelity faithfulness.

Heterosexual attracted to the opposite sex.

Nuclear family a family consisting of two parents and their children.

Nurturing caring for and looking after.

Procreation having children.

Social policy the measures the government takes to address social issues.

Social integration the sense of belonging to society.

Table 2.1 Changes in the functions of the family

Family function	Recent social trends – have these undermined or supported family functions?
Procreation	The size of families has declined as people choose lifestyle over the expense of having children. Many women prefer to pursue careers and are making the decision not to have children. The UK birth rate has consequently fallen.
Regulating sex	Sex outside marriage is now the norm. Alternative sexualities, e.g. homosexuality, are becoming more socially acceptable.
Stabilizing personalities	A high percentage of marriages end in divorce. However, some argue that divorce and remarriage rates are high because people continue to search for emotional security.
Economic	Although welfare benefits are seen by some as undermining family economic responsibilities, the family is still a crucial agency of economic support, especially as the housing market becomes more expensive for first-time buyers, and young people spend longer periods in education with the prospect of debt through student loans.
Welfare	A decline in state funding of welfare in the 1980s led to the encouragement of 'community care', in which the family – and especially women – became responsible for the care of the elderly, the long-term sick and the disabled.
Socialization	This is still rooted in the family, although there are concerns that the mass media and the peer group have become more influential, with the result that children are growing up faster.
Social control	Power has shifted between parents and children as children acquire more rights. This trend, alongside attempts to ban smacking in England and Wales, is thought by some sociologists to undermine parental discipline. Some sociologists argue that families need fathers and see the absence of fathers in one-parent families as a major cause of delinquency.

Check your understanding

1 Identify four features of the traditional family.

2 How influential is biology in shaping the traditional family?

3 What has been the impact of the traditional model of the family on popular thinking?

4 What is the 'warm bath' theory?

5 How have functionalist views of the family been criticized by feminists?

research ideas

- Conduct a survey amongst your classmates to find out about other families and their lifestyles. Focus particularly on size of family, whether parents work, who takes responsibility for domestic duties in the home, contact with **extended kin** such as grandparents and cousins, the role and responsibilities of children, and so on. How much do their accounts differ from your own experience of family life?

- Make a list of the functions that your family performs. Think about how family functions change according to how old you are and what gender you are. For example, think about how the family functioned for you as a baby. Compare that with how you think the family will function for you when you are 20.

web.task

Visit websites dedicated to the family such as www.familyeducation.com and www.familiesonline.co.uk

Look at the content of these sites in terms of advice, news and letters from parents. What functions should families be performing according to these sites? Do such functions support the functionalist theory of the family?

Item A Traditional ideas about the nuclear family

There are five sentiments that underpin traditional ideas about the nuclear family. First, marriage is regarded as the climax of romantic love, and children are seen as symbolic of the couple's commitment to each other. Second, it is assumed that the ultimate goal of women is to have children, stay at home and gain satisfaction through the socialisation of their children. Women who choose not to have children may be viewed as 'unnatural'. Third, it is assumed that the family is a positive and beneficial institution in which family members receive nurturing, care and love. Fourth, the male is expected to be head of the household and to provide for the family. Finally, it is assumed that the immediate family comes first and all other obligations and relationships come second.

Adapted from Chapman, S. and Aiken, D. (2000) 'Towards a new sociology of families', *Sociology Review*, 9(3)

Item B Questioning the functionalist view

The existence of 'the family' has been taken for granted by many sociologists. For functionalist sociologists, in particular, any query over the use of 'the family' appears trivial and tends to be dismissed. The failure by functionalists to question the idea of 'the family' has allowed all sorts of mistaken ideas to persist, such as the naturalness of monogamy (whereas many societies permit more than one marriage), the inevitability of female inferiority (which many feminists dispute), the right of men to control and abuse women (which many women dispute), and the right of parents to smack children (which is banned in some European countries, including Scotland).

Adapted from Bernardes, J. (1997) *Family Studies: An Introduction*, London: Routledge, pp. 4–5

Item C Essential and non-essential functions of the family

Ronald Fletcher distinguishes between 'essential' and 'non-essential' functions of the family. He argues that, while other agencies have become responsible for six 'non-essential' functions, the family still performs three 'essential' functions that only it can perform. These are the stable satisfaction of sexual needs, the production and rearing of children, and the provision of a home. Fletcher argues that the state actually supports the family in fulfilling these essential functions through the provision of health care, child benefit, council housing, etc. Fletcher argues that the family is no longer primarily responsible for production of housing, clothing and food for its own needs, education, recreation, religion, health and welfare, although he stresses that the family still continues to play an important role in most of these areas of social life.

Adapted from Steel, E. and Kidd, W. (2001) *The Family*, London: Palgrave

1 Explain what is meant by 'monogamy' (Item B). (2 marks)

2 Suggest two ways in which the traditional family is supposed to benefit adults, according to Item A. (4 marks)

3 Identify three functions associated with the traditional family by functionalist sociologists (Items A and C). (9 marks)

4 Identify and briefly describe two 'mistaken ideas' that have arisen out of the failure to question the idea of the family, according to Bernardes in Item B. (10 marks)

Exam practice

5 a Identify and explain two ways in which definitions of 'family' are dominated by traditional views about how family life ought to be lived. (15 marks)

b Outline and discuss the view that the functions of the family are increasingly irrelevant in contemporary Britain. (30 marks)

The family, morality and the state

Valerie Riches, the founder president of a body called Family and Youth Concern, is a woman of conviction. She is convinced, for instance, that sex education harms the young and undermines the family. She is clear that sending childless housewives out to work means that men's 'masculine role as the provider and father' is being obliterated. She has also criticized the decision of a gay couple to have a child by a surrogate mother. 'It's against the natural order of things', she says. Interestingly, although Ms Riches is second to none in her opposition to single-parent families, she is none the less firmly opposed to the introduction of emergency contraception – the morning-after pill – which might reduce the creation of more such faulty units. 'Taking a morning-after pill will encourage girls to be easy and carefree', she says.

Adapted from Bennett, C. (2000) 'Valerie's moral lead', *Guardian*, 14 December

1 Look carefully at the images above. How might some people see them as threatening the traditional family?

2 In the article, five things are identified that Valerie Riches thinks are undermining the family. What are they? Do you agree that these things are harming the family unit?

3 Think of any ways in which the government influences your family life. In your opinion, should it play a greater or a lesser role? What role, if any, should it play?

In the UK over the last 50 years, public debate about the family has focused on the changing nature of family life and its impact on society. This debate has often been dominated by those who, like Valerie Riches, take the view that the traditional nuclear family and the moral character of the young are under attack from a number of 'threats', including sex education, contraception, working mothers, homosexuality, divorce and single-parent families. Moreover, the state is accused of not doing enough to protect the traditional family. In fact, some commentators have suggested that liberal state policies, especially those introduced in the 1960s, are responsible for starting the perceived decline in traditional family values.

The golden age of family life

Those who claim that the family is in decline can be grouped under the label '**New Right**', in that they are usually conservative thinkers and politicians who believe very strongly in tradition. These commentators often assume that there was once a 'golden age' of the family, in which husbands and wives were strongly committed to each other for life, and children were brought up to respect their parents and social institutions such as the law.

Many New Right thinkers see the 1960s and early 1970s as the beginning of a sustained attack on traditional family values, particularly by the state. They point to social policies, such as the legalization of abortion in the 1960s and the NHS making the contraceptive pill available on prescription, as marking the beginning of family decline. The sexual freedom that women experienced as a result of these changes supposedly lessened their commitment to the family. At the same time, equal opportunities and equal pay legislation distracted women from their 'natural' careers as mothers. The 1969 Divorce Reform Act was seen as undermining commitment to marriage. The decriminalization of homosexuality and the lowering of the homosexual age of consent have been interpreted as particularly important symbols of moral decline, because the New Right see homosexuality as 'unnatural' and deviant.

Familial ideology

New Right views on the family reflect a **familial ideology** – a set of ideas about what constitutes an 'ideal' family. Their preferred model is the traditional nuclear family with a clear sexual division of labour, as described in 1 (see p. 53). This ideology is transmitted by sections of the media and advertising, politicians, religious leaders, and pressure groups such as 'Family and Youth Concern'.

Family decline and the 'New Right'

This familial ideology also makes a number of assumptions about how not to organize family life. In particular, it sees the declining popularity of marriage, the increase in cohabitation, the number of births outside marriage, and teenage pregnancy as symptoms of the decline in family morality. Homosexuality, single parenthood, liberal sex education, abortion and working mothers are all seen as threats, both to family stability and to the wellbeing of society itself.

A good example of the New Right approach to the family can be seen in the view that there exists an underclass of criminals, unmarried mothers and idle young men who are responsible for rising crime. It is argued that this underclass is welfare-dependent, and that teenage girls are deliberately getting pregnant in order to obtain council housing or state benefits. To make things worse, this underclass is socialising its children into a culture revolving around crime and delinquency, and anti-authority, antiwork and antifamily values.

State policy and the family

Britain, unlike other European countries, does not have a separate minister for family affairs. However, three broad trends can be seen in state policy which suggest that the ideology of the traditional nuclear family has had, despite New Right misgivings, some positive influence on government thinking:

1 Tax and welfare policies have generally favoured and encouraged the heterosexual married couple rather than cohabiting couples, single parents and same-sex couples. Graham Allan (1985) goes as far as to suggest that these policies have actively discouraged cohabitation and one-parent families.

2 Policies such as the payment of child benefit to the mother, and the government's reluctance to fund free universal nursery provision, have reinforced the idea that women should take prime responsibility for children.

3 The lack of a coordinated set of family policies may reflect the fact that the state has tended to see the family as a **private institution** and is therefore reluctant to interfere in its internal organization. Despite being accused of being a 'nanny state' by its critics, the Labour government of Tony Blair has generally not directly intervened with legislation in family affairs. For example, in 2004, the state shied away from making the smacking of children by parents illegal.

Nevertheless, New Right thinkers still believe that grave damage has been inflicted on the nuclear family ideal by misguided government policy. For example, they claim that governments have encouraged mothers to return to work and, consequently, generations of children have been 'damaged' by **maternal deprivation**. There have been few tax or benefit policies aimed at encouraging mothers to stay at home with their children. The New Right argue that commitment to marriage has been weakened by governments making divorce too easy to obtain. Morgan (2000) even suggests that the government is 'antimarriage'. The New Right also claim that 'deviant' family types such as single-parent families have been encouraged by welfare policies.

Criticisms of the New Right

Government policy has generally been aimed at ensuring that the family unit does not overwhelm the rights of the individuals within it. Therefore, legislation has focused on improving the social and economic position of women. For example, the Conservative government made marital rape illegal in 1991. The Labour government introduced the 'New Deal' in April 1998, which aimed to encourage single mothers back to work. The same government also instructed police forces to get tough on domestic violence. The rights of children have also been enhanced through successive Children's Acts. There is no doubt that such legislation has undermined traditional male dominance in families, but many people believe that improved rights for women and children strengthen the family rather than weaken it.

The traditional nuclear family is still central to state policy. Feminist sociologists and other radical critics argue that the state generally supports familial ideology, as can be seen in Table 2.2 below.

There is also evidence that the Labour Government supports the familial ideology. Despite recognition of other family types, especially single-parent families, and sympathetic noises about improving the rights of gay people, cabinet ministers have regularly stated that married parents create the best environment for bringing up children.

Evaluating familial ideology

Feminists have claimed that familial ideology is merely patriarchal ideology – a set of ideas deliberately encouraged by men that ensure male dominance in the workplace. For example, Oakley (1986) points out that if society subscribes to the view that women have a maternal instinct, it follows on that society will believe that women who elect not to have children are somehow deviant, that 'real' women are committed to giving up jobs to bring up children, and that working mothers are somehow 'damaging' their children. Oakley argues that this aspect of familial ideology benefits men because it results in women withdrawing from the labour market – they do not compete with men for jobs which results in men enjoying advantages in promotion and pay. This ideology ties women to men, marriage, the home, children and, for a while, economic dependence. Moreover, such family ideology permeates gender-role socialization – girls are taught from infancy that motherhood is their ultimate goal.

Other sociologists have argued that familial ideology has led to the nuclear family being over**idealized**. It fails to acknowledge that divorce and one-parent families might be 'lesser evils' than domestic violence and emotional unhappiness. The ideology also neglects key cultural changes, such as the changing roles of men and women and, especially, cultural and ethnic diversity, as well as social and economic problems such as poverty, homelessness, racism, etc.

The view that the family is a private institution has led to the general neglect of severe social problems, such as child abuse and domestic violence. Until the late 1980s, for example, only as a very last resort would social workers break up families in which they suspected abuse. It took a series of abuse-related child deaths to change this policy.

A similar theme suggests that the ideology results in the worsening of family problems, such as domestic violence, because women believe that their husbands 'punish' them for being 'bad' wives and mothers. They therefore see themselves as deserving of punishment and believe that they should stick

Table 2.2 State policy and familial ideology

	State policy	Familial ideology
Care in the community	The state has encouraged families to take responsibility for the elderly and long-term sick and disabled. Female members of the family often carry the burden of this care, which means they are less likely to work full time and are more likely to be economically dependent upon a male.	The traditional sexual division of labour is reinforced; women as emotional and physical caretakers, and men as breadwinners.
Housing Policy	Fox Harding (1996) argues that the best council housing is often allocated to married couples with children and the worst housing on problem estates is allocated to one-parent families. Housing in the UK is overwhelmingly designed for the nuclear family.	The traditional nuclear family is clearly the dominant family type. Other types of family are 'punished' or discouraged.
Parenting	Fathers have only two days paid leave from work on the birth of a child – they have no legal rights for paid or unpaid leave for longer periods. The Child Support Agency (CSA) was set up to pursue absent fathers in order that they take financial responsibility for their children. Mothers are often awarded custody of children after divorce and fathers are often denied access to children by the law. Unmarried fathers have few legal rights over their children compared with married men.	It is assumed that women's primary role is motherhood and childcare rather than paid work. It is implied that men have no childcare skills. The function of the CSA is to ensure women's continuing economic dependence on men. Marriage is seen as superior to cohabitation.

by their man through thick and thin. This theme is explored further in Topic 7.

Barrett and McIntosh (1982) argue that familial ideology is antisocial because it dismisses alternative family types as irrelevant, inferior and deviant. For example, as a result of the emphasis on the nuclear family ideal and the view that families need fathers, one-parent families are seen as the cause of social problems, such as rising crime rates and disrespect for authority. This theme will be further explored in Topic 4.

The family: in decline or just changing?

New Right politicians strongly believe that the family – and therefore family ideology – is in decline, and that this is the source of all our social problems. However, it may simply be that family ideology is evolving rather than deteriorating, as we realize that the traditional family denies women and children the same rights as men. People today may be less willing to tolerate these forms of inequality and the violence and abuse that often accompany them. Increasing acceptance and tolerance of a range of family types may be healthy for society, rather than a symptom of moral decay.

focus on research

Reynolds *et al.* (2003)
Caring and counting

The researchers interviewed 37 mothers and 30 fathers in couples who had at least one pre-school child (Reynolds *et al.* 2003). The mothers were working in a hospital or in an accountancy firm. All the mothers in the study had strong, traditional views about what being a 'good mother' and a 'good partner' was about. Employment did not necessarily lead to more egalitarian relationships with their partners.

In fact, most of the mothers and fathers interviewed subscribed to highly traditional and stereotypical views about the gendered division of labour within the home. The mothers had primary responsibility for the home and the conduct of family life. Mothers who worked full time were just as concerned as those working part time to 'be there' for their children and to meet the needs of their children and their family. The researchers found no evidence of mothers becoming more 'work centred' at the expense of family life.

Apart from increasing the family income, mothers also felt their employment was helping them to meet their children's emotional and social development. Separate interviews with the women's partners revealed widespread agreement that the mother's work was having a positive impact on family relationships. Most fathers felt their children had benefited from their mothers' work, which provided a positive role model for their children.

Some mothers, nevertheless, expressed concern that their job had a negative impact on the family, particularly when they were overstretched at work, felt tired or had trouble 'switching off' from a bad day at work. A number of fathers also felt uneasy about the demands placed on their partners at work and the effect that work-related stress could have on their children and their relationship with each other.

Adapted from the website of the Joseph Rowntree Foundation (www.jrf.org.uk)

1 Comment on the sample used in the study.

2 How did parents feel that mothers' employment was having a positive effect on their families?

3 What concerns were expressed about mothers' employment?

Jonathan Gershuny (2000)
Standards of parenting

A major theme of those who believe that the family is in decline is working parents and particularly working mothers. However, research illustrates the complexity of the debate about whether standards of parenting have fallen. In 2000, Jonathan Gershuny, using data from the diaries of 3000 parents, suggested that the quality of parenting had significantly improved compared with the past. He noted that the time British parents spent playing with and reading to their children had increased fourfold and this was the case for both working and non-working parents.

1 How could the use of diaries in Gershuny's research be criticized?

Check your understanding

1 What legislation introduced in the 1960s and 1970s is seen as damaging to the family, according to New Right commentators?

2 What is the attitude of the Labour government towards the family?

3 What are the main symptoms of the decline in family morality, according to the New Right?

4 In what ways has familial ideology had an impact on state policy?

5 In what ways has state policy been good for family members?

research ideas

● Conduct a mini-survey of teenagers and old-age pensioners to see whether there is any major difference in how they perceive family life and so-called 'threats' to it, such as homosexuality, cohabitation and illegitimacy.

● Observe the media and other institutions for signs of familial ideology. You could, for example:
  – study television commercials at different times of the day
  – examine the content of specific types of programmes, such as soap operas or situation comedies
  – analyse the content of women's magazines
  – stroll through family-orientated stores, such as Mothercare, Boots and BHS, to see whether familial ideology is apparent in their organization, packaging, marketing, etc.

web.tasks

1 Visit the websites of organizations dedicated to protecting family life, such as the Family Matters Institute at www.familymatters.org.uk and Family and Youth Concern at www.famyouth.org.uk and make a list of the family issues they consider to be important. In what ways do these issues support familial ideology?

2 Visit the websites of the major political parties and find out what their policies are towards the family.

exploring the family, morality and the state

Item A Conservative views of the family

Conservative thinkers have tended to define what the traditional family should be in terms of a heterosexual conjugal unit based on marriage and co-residence. A clear segregation of tasks based on sexual differences is seen as the 'traditional', 'natural' and 'God-given' way of ordering our lives. It is assumed that the man is the 'natural' head of the family. The family's key tasks are the reproduction of the next generation, the protection of dependent children and the inculcation of proper moral values in children. The family also disciplines men and women in economic and sexual terms: it keeps us in our proper place. Order, hierarchy and stability are seen as the key features of the 'healthy' family and the 'healthy' society. However, conservative commentators see this traditional family as under threat and in decline. This is seen as one of the main causes of the claimed wider moral decay in society.

Adapted from Sherratt, N. and Hughes, G. (2000) 'Family: from tradition to diversity?' in G. Hughes and R. Fergusson (eds) *Ordering Lives: Family, Work and Welfare*, London: Routledge, p. 60

Item B State intervention in the family

<< The state has intervened significantly in families for a considerable length of time, whether by providing support (such as family income credits for those earning low wages and with dependent children) or in overseeing the bringing up of children (if social workers think this is not being done properly, then children may be put temporarily or more permanently into the care of the local authority). This interference has not lessened – indeed, as politicians and the media have come together to discuss what they see as the decline of the family, so the extent of that interference has increased. However, conservative thinkers tend to believe that there has not been enough state input into protecting the traditional family, or that state interference has actually contributed to its decline by encouraging the development of 'deviant' living arrangements.>>

Abercrombie, N. and Warde, A. (2000) *Contemporary British Society* (3rd edn), Cambridge: Polity Press, pp. 287–8

Item C Same-sex couples are families too

The House of Lords has ruled that a homosexual couple in a stable relationship can be defined as a family. One of the law lords, Lord Nicholls defined a family as follows: 'The concept underlying membership of a family is the sharing of lives together in a single family unit living in one house. It seems to me that the bond must be one of love and affection, not of a casual nature, but in a relationship which is permanent, or at least intended to be so. As a result of that permanent attachment, other characteristics will follow, such as a readiness to support each other emotionally and financially, to care for and look after each other in times of need, and to provide a companionship in which mutual interests and activities can be shared'. Dr. Adrian Rogers of the pressure group, Family Focus, deplored the ruling and said 'homosexual couples cannot be defined as families – the basis of true love is the ability to procreate and have children'.

Adapted from the *Guardian*, 29 October 1999.

1 Explain what is meant by the phrase 'the traditional family' (Item A). (2 marks)
2 Suggest two living arrangements that conservative commentators might consider 'deviant' (Item B). (4 marks)
3 Identify and explain three ways in which the state intervenes in family life (Item B). (9 marks)
4 Identify and briefly explain two problems that may be caused by the overidealization of the nuclear family. (10 marks)

Exam practice

5 a Identify and explain two reasons why the traditional family unit is seen by the New Right as being in decline. (15 marks)

b Outline and discuss the view that government policy has done little to support the traditional nuclear family. (30 marks)

Marriage and marital breakdown

gettingyouthinking

A summary of changes over time
Marital status and cohabitation

Living in Britain
The 2002 General
Household Survey

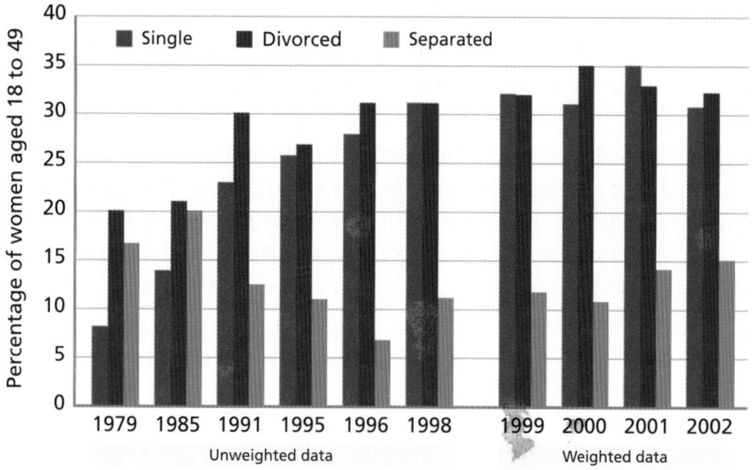

Percentage of women aged 18 to 49 (bar chart, values 0–40)

Legend: Single | Divorced | Separated

Years shown: 1979, 1985, 1991, 1995, 1996, 1998 (Unweighted data) | 1999, 2000, 2001, 2002 (Weighted data)

Percentage of single, divorced and separated women aged 18 to 49
cohabiting, by legal marital status: Great Britain, 1979 to 2002
Widows have not been included because their numbers are so small.

Divorces

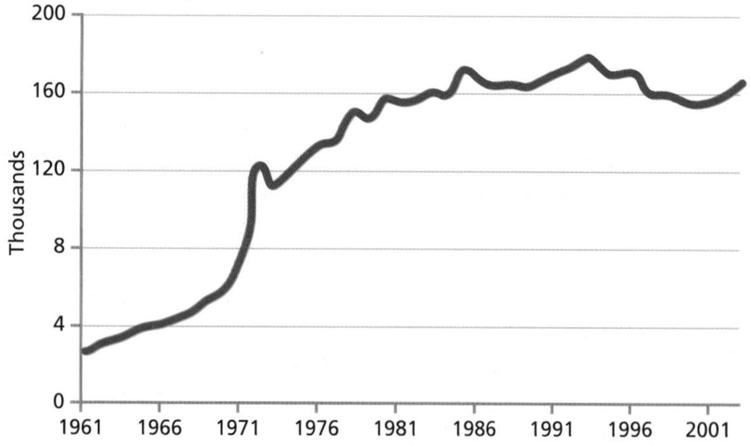

United Kingdom (line chart, Thousands, 0–200)

Years: 1961, 1966, 1971, 1976, 1981, 1986, 1991, 1996, 2001

Divorces
Includes annulments. Data for 1961 to 1970 are GB only.

*Above: Marriage in the 21st century?
A couple on the escalator on their way to
tying the knot in the clothing department
at the supermarket where they work*

*Below: Is marriage still a lifelong
commitment?*

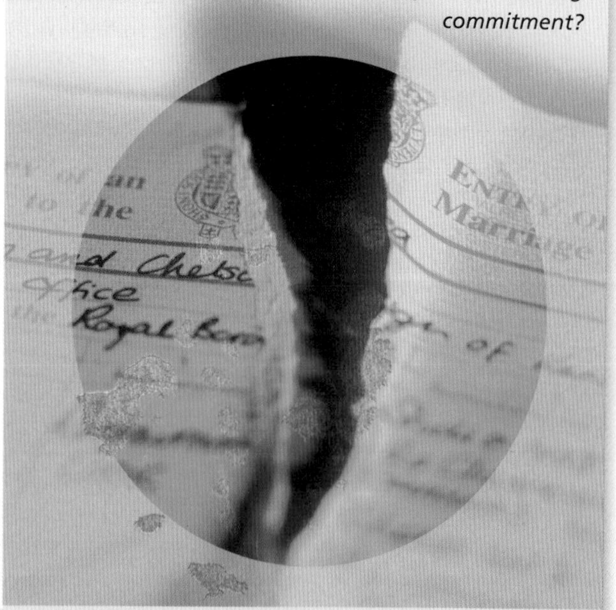

1 **What has been the general trend for divorce since 1961?**

2 **What does the bar chart tell us about the marital status of cohabiting women since 1979?**

3 **Suggest possible explanations for the trends illustrated above.**

4 **Why might the images above and the statistical trends be alarming for supporters of the traditional family?**

It is not difficult to see why supporters of the traditional family, such as the New Right, are so alarmed by figures and images such as those on the left. They believe that they indicate a crisis in the family, which will inevitably result in increasing antisocial behaviour and moral breakdown. Many postmodernists and feminists look at the figures and images in a very different way – they see them as indicators of greater personal choice in our private lives, and as evidence of a rejection of patriarchal family arrangements. So who is right?

Marriage

The latest statistics indicate that fewer people are getting married than at any other time in the last century. There were just fewer than 250 000 weddings in 2001, compared with 426 000 in 1972, although this improved to 254 000 in 2002. Only 34 per cent of marriages involved a religious ceremony in 2002 compared with 51 per cent in 1991.

In 1996, only one third of all British women in their late twenties were married with children, compared with two thirds in 1973. Berthoud (2000) has observed ethnic differences in the marriage statistics. For example, he notes that about three quarters of Pakistani and Bangladeshi women are married by the age of 25, while Black British people are the group least likely to get married.

These figures have recently provoked a keen debate between New Right commentators and feminists. New Right commentators express concerns about the decline in marriage. Patricia Morgan (2000) argues that marriage involves unique 'attachments and obligations' that regulate people's behaviour. For example, she claims that married men are more likely to be employed than unmarried or cohabiting men and earn more (i.e. 10 to 20 per cent more in 2001) because they work harder than any other male group. Furthermore, married people live longer than single people.

However, fears about what these statistics reveal are probably exaggerated for three reasons:

1 People are delaying marriage rather than rejecting it. Most people will marry at some point in their lives. However, people are now marrying later in life, probably after a period of cohabitation. The average age for first-time brides in 2001 was 28.4 years and for all grooms 30.6 years, compared with 22 for women and 24 for men in 1971. Women may delay marriage because they want to develop their careers and enjoy a period of independence.
2 British Social Attitude Surveys indicate that most people, whether single, **divorced** or cohabiting, still see marriage as a desirable life-goal. People also generally believe that having children is best done in the context of marriage. Few people believe that the freedom associated with living alone is better than being married to someone.
3 More than 40 per cent of all marriages are remarriages (in which one or both partners have been divorced). These people are obviously committed to the institution of marriage despite their previous negative experience of it. An interesting new trend is the number of young men – aged under 25 – who are marrying women significantly older than them, i.e. 'toy-boy' marriages. One in three of first-time grooms are younger than their brides, more than double what it was in 1963.

Wilkinson (1994) notes that female attitudes towards marriage and family life have undergone a radical change or 'genderquake'. She argues that young females no longer prioritize marriage and children, as their mothers and grandmothers did. Educational opportunities and the feminization of the economy have resulted in young women weighing up the costs of marriage and having children against the benefits of a career and economic independence. The result of this is that many females, particularly middle-class graduates, are opting out of marriage and family life altogether.

Other feminist sociologists are sceptical about the value of marriage. Smith (2001) argues that marriage creates unrealistic expectations about **monogamy** and faithfulness in a world characterized by sexual freedom. She argues that at different points in people's life cycles, people need different things which often can only be gained from a new partner. Campbell (2000) suggests that marriage is promoted because of fears about lack of discipline among young people. Moreover, she suggests that marriage benefits men more than it does women.

Cohabitation

A constant source of concern to the New Right has been the significant rise in the number of couples cohabiting during the last decade. In 1998, 28 per cent of men and 26 per cent of women living in Britain, aged between 25 and 29, cohabited. New Right commentators claim that cohabitation is less stable than marriage. A report by the Institute for the Study of Civil Society (Morgan 2000) claimed that cohabiting couples were less happy and less fulfilled than married couples, and more likely to be abusive, unfaithful, stressed and depressed.

However, surveys indicate that few people see cohabitation as an alternative to marriage. Rather, it is merely seen as a prelude to marriage, i.e. as a test of compatibility, and consequently tends to be a temporary phase, lasting on average about five years, before approximately 60 per cent of cohabiting couples eventually marry – usually some time after the first child is born. Although cohabitation marks a dramatic change in how adults live together – it was met with extreme moral disapproval as recently as the 1960s – cohabiting couples with and without children only account for 6 per cent of all households. Cohabitation is also linked to the rising divorce rate, i.e. a significant number of people live together quite simply because they are waiting for a divorce.

Births outside marriage

New Right commentators have been especially disturbed by the fact that one in three babies is now born outside marriage. In particular, media **moral panics** have focused on the fact that the UK has the highest rate of teenage pregnancy in Europe.

For example, in 2002, there were 44 100 pregnancies in the 16-to-18 age group and 7875 among the under 16s.

However, according to the National Council for One Parent Families, the under-16 conception rate has fallen considerably, compared with the 1960s, and it has fallen slightly over the last ten years to approximately 8 per 1000 girls. Only 3 per cent of unmarried mothers are teenagers, and most of them live at home with their parents. Experts are generally sceptical that such teenagers are deliberately getting pregnant in order to claim state housing and benefits. Moreover, four out of five births outside marriage are registered to both parents, and three-quarters of these are living at the same address. Most births outside marriage, therefore, are to cohabiting couples. It should also be pointed out that a significant number of marriages break up in the first year after having a child, which suggests that marriage is not always the stable institution for procreation that the New Right claim it is.

Some sociologists argue that we should be more concerned about the trend towards childlessness that has appeared in recent years. The Family Policy Studies Centre estimates that one woman in five will choose to remain childless, and this figure is expected to double in the next 20 years (McAllister 1998). In 2000, one in five women aged 40 had not had children compared with one in ten in 1980, and this figure is expected to rise to one in four by 2018. There is no doubt that fewer children are being born. Current fertility patterns suggest that women today have an average of 1.7 children each. This is not sufficient to replace the population lost due to death and emigration. Moreover, women are having children later in life, e.g. births to women aged between 35 and 39 have dramatically increased in the last 20 years.

Marital breakdown

Types of marital breakdown

Marital breakdown can take three different forms: divorce, separation and **empty-shell marriages**:

- *Divorce* refers to the legal ending of a marriage. Since the Divorce Reform Act of 1969, divorce has been granted on the basis of '**irretrievable** breakdown' and, since 1984, couples have been able to petition for divorce after the first anniversary of their marriage. 'Quickie' divorces are also available, in which one partner has to prove the 'fault' or 'guilt' of the other, for matrimonial 'crimes' such as adultery, although these tend to be costly.
- *Separation* is where couples agree to live apart after the breakdown of a marriage. In the past, when divorce was difficult to obtain or too expensive, separation was often the only solution.
- *Empty-shell marriages* are those in which husband and wife stay together in name only. There may no longer be any love or intimacy between them. Today, such marriages are likely to end in separation or divorce, although this type of relationship may persist for the sake of children or for religious reasons.

The divorce rate

Britain's divorce rate is high, compared with other industrial societies. Within Europe, only Denmark has a higher rate. In 1938, 6000 divorces were granted in the UK. This figure had increased tenfold by 1970, and in 1993, it peaked at 165 000 but fell thereafter. However, in 2002, divorce rose for the first time in seven years to 148 000. People who had been divorced before constituted about 20 per cent of this total. There are now nearly half as many divorces as marriages.

By the late 1980s, almost 25 per cent of all women who had married when under 20 years of age were separated after only five years of marriage. If present trends continue, about 40 per cent of current marriages will end in divorce.

New Right sociologists argue that such divorce statistics are a symptom of a serious crisis in the family. They suggest that, because of the easy availability of divorce, people are no longer as committed to the family as they were in the past. This view was partly responsible for the government abandoning the section of the Family Law Act (1996) that intended to replace existing divorce procedures with a single ground for divorce. Under this new legislation, divorce would have been granted to couples with children after a compulsory cooling-off period of 18 months, if both parties agreed after counselling that their marriage had ended. However, fears that this was an easier way out of marriage than the present system prompted the Labour government to abandon the proposal in 2001.

Why is the divorce rate increasing?

Changes in divorce law have generally made it easier and cheaper to end marriages, but this is not necessarily the cause of the rising divorce rate. Legal changes reflect other changes in society, especially changes in attitudes. In particular, sociologists argue that social expectations about marriage have changed. Functionalist sociologists even argue that high divorce rates are evidence that marriage is increasingly valued and that people are demanding higher standards from their partners. Couples are no longer prepared to put up with unhappy, 'empty-shell' marriages. People want emotional and sexual compatibility and equality, as well as companionship. Some are willing to go through a number of partners to achieve these goals.

Feminists note that women's expectations of marriage have radically changed, compared with previous generations. In the 1990s, most **divorce petitions** were initiated by women. This may support Thornes and Collard's (1979) view that women expect far more from marriage than men and, in particular, that they value friendship and emotional gratification more than men do. If husbands fail to live up to these expectations, women may feel the need to look elsewhere.

Women's expectations have probably changed as a result of the improved educational and career opportunities they have experienced since the 1980s. Women no longer have to be unhappily married because they are financially dependent upon their husbands. Moreover, Hart (1976) notes that divorce may be a reaction to the frustration that many working wives may feel if they are responsible for the bulk of housework and childcare. Similarly, it may also be the outcome of tensions produced by women taking over the traditional male role of breadwinner in some households, especially where the male is unemployed and the 'crisis of masculinity' might result from the male feeling that his role has been usurped.

Divorce is no longer associated with stigma and shame. This may be partly due to a general decline in religious practices. The social controls, such as extended families and **close-knit communities**, that exerted pressure on couples to stay together and that labelled divorce as 'wicked' and 'shameful', are also in decline. Consequently, in a society dominated by **privatized nuclear families**, the view that divorce can lead to greater happiness for the individual is more acceptable. It is even more so if divorce involves escaping from an abusive relationship or if an unhappy marriage is causing emotional damage to children. However, it is important to recognize that such attitudes are not necessarily a sign of a casual attitude towards divorce. Most people experience divorce as an emotional and traumatic experience, equivalent to bereavement. They are usually also aware of the severe impact it may have on children.

Beck and Beck-Gernsheim (1995) argue that rising divorce rates are the product of a rapidly changing world in which the traditional rules, rituals and traditions of love, romance and relationships no longer apply. In particular, they point out that the modern world is characterized by individualization, choice and conflict.

- *Individualization* – We are under less pressure to conform to traditional collective goals set by our extended family, religion or culture. We now have the freedom to pursue individual goals.

- *Choice* – Cultural and economic changes mean that we have a greater range of choices available to us in terms of lifestyle and living arrangements.
- *Conflict* – There is now more potential for antagonism between men and women because there is a natural clash of interest between the selfishness encouraged by individualization and the selflessness required by relationships, marriage and family life.

Beck and Beck-Gernsheim argue that these characteristics of the modern world have led to personal relationships between men and women becoming a battleground (they call it the 'chaos of love') as evidenced by rising divorce rates. However, Beck and Beck-Gernsheim are positive about the future because they note that people still generally want to find love with another in order to help them cope with a risky, rapidly changing world. In particular, love helps compensate for the stress and, particularly, the impersonal and uncertain nature of the modern world. Love is the one thing people feel is real and that they can be sure of. Divorce and remarriage may simply be signs that people still have faith that they will one day find the true love they need to help them cope with the complexity of modern life.

Divorce trends suggest that monogamy (one partner for life) will eventually be replaced by **serial monogamy** (a series of long-term relationships resulting in cohabitation and/or marriage). However, the New Right panic about divorce is probably exaggerated. It is important to remember that although four out of ten marriages may end in divorce, six out of ten succeed. Over 75 per cent of children are living with both natural parents who are legally married. These figures suggest that society still places a high value on marriage and the family.

Figure 2.3 Reasons for increasing divorce rate

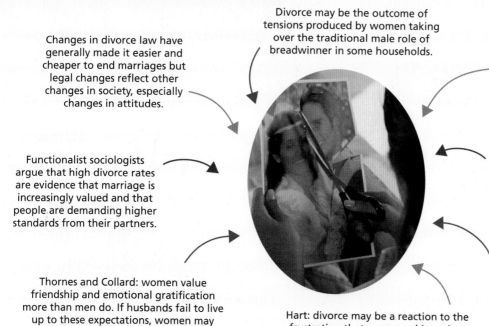

Changes in divorce law have generally made it easier and cheaper to end marriages but legal changes reflect other changes in society, especially changes in attitudes.

Divorce may be the outcome of tensions produced by women taking over the traditional male role of breadwinner in some households.

Divorce is no longer associated with stigma and shame. The view that divorce can lead to greater happiness for the individual is more acceptable.

Functionalist sociologists argue that high divorce rates are evidence that marriage is increasingly valued and that people are demanding higher standards from their partners.

Beck and Beck-Gernsheim (1995): rising divorce rates are the product of a rapidly changing world in which the traditional rules, rituals and traditions of love, romance and relationships no longer apply.

Thornes and Collard: women value friendship and emotional gratification more than men do. If husbands fail to live up to these expectations, women may feel the need to look elsewhere.

Hart: divorce may be a reaction to the frustration that many working wives may feel if they are responsible for the bulk of housework and childcare.

Women's improved educational and career opportunities mean that they no longer have to be unhappily married because they are financially dependent upon their husbands.

Smart and Stevens (2000)
Cohabitation: testing the water?

Smart and Stevens (2000) carried out interviews with 20 mothers and 20 fathers who were separated from cohabiting partners with whom they had had a child. They found that most of the sample were either indifferent to marriage or had been unsure about marrying the person with whom they had lived. Many of the female respondents had wanted their partners to become more 'marriage-worthy', especially in terms of expressing emotional commitment and helping more with the children. Cohabitation, then, was generally a test of their own and their partner's commitment. Many felt that their level of commitment to each other was the same as married couples but they believed it was easier to leave a cohabiting relationship than it was to leave a marriage.

1 What does this research tell us about the meaning of cohabitation?

2 What effect might the choice of sample have had on the findings?

KEY TERMS

Close-knit community a community in which there are close relationships between people (everyone knows everyone else).

Divorce the legal ending of a marriage.

Divorce petition a legal request for a divorce.

Empty-shell marriage a marriage in which the partners no longer love each other but stay together, usually for the sake of the children.

Irretrievable unable to be recovered. Broken down for ever.

Monogamy the practice of having only one partner.

Moral panic public concern over some aspect of behaviour, created and reinforced in large part by sensational media coverage.

Privatized nuclear family a home-centred family that has little contact with extended kin or neighbours.

Serial monogamy a series of long-term relationships.

web.tasks

1 **Use the archives of either the *Guardian* or the *Daily Telegraph* websites to research the debate about divorce. The latter is excellent for links to relevant sites such as www.divorceon-line.com, the family law consortium and the Lord Chancellor's Department.**

2 **Visit the websites of the following organizations and work out whether they support familial ideology:**

- **www.themothersunion.org**

- **www.civitas.org.uk – this site has a collection of interesting fact sheets on the family plus excellent links to traditionalist family sites**

- **www.oneplusone.org.uk**

Check your understanding

1 Why have marriage rates declined in recent years?

2 What has been the trend in the number of births outside marriage?

3 Why are teenage mothers not the problem the media make them out to be?

4 Why is cohabitation not a threat to marriage?

5 Why are women more likely to initiate divorce proceedings than men?

research ideas

- Carry out a mini-survey across three different age groups (e.g. 15 to 20, 25 to 30, and 35 to 40), investigating attitudes towards marriage, cohabitation, childlessness, births outside marriage, etc.

- Interview two males and two females to find out what characteristics they are looking for in a future partner. Do your findings support the view that females set higher standards in relationships?

Item A The changing family

The family seems to be dwindling as a social institution. The stark figures would suggest that British society has turned its back on those things normally associated with the idea of 'the family'. Within one generation, we have seen the following changes: only half as many people are getting married, lone-parent families have increased threefold, children born outside marriage have quadrupled in number, and the number of divorces has trebled. However, there is strong evidence that these things indicate a change in the nature of the family, rather than its death. The family remains a cornerstone of British society in terms of people's lives and their sense of identity. Families are still a crucial source of care and support for the elderly and the disabled. Nearly two in three working mothers turn to relatives for help with childcare. Most people are in regular contact with relatives and see them at least once a month. At Christmas, more than four in five people join in some form of family gathering.

Adapted from Denscombe, M. (1998) *Sociology Update*, Leicester: Olympus Books, p. 20

Item B Deferring motherhood

Marriage is a normal and expected part of women's lives in Western society. However, although the vast majority of women will expect to marry at some time and at least once, in recent years there has been some decline in the popularity of marriage. In 1971, only 4 per cent of women remained unmarried by the age of 50, but by 1987, the proportion had grown to 17 per cent. Women today are marrying older and marrying less. The Family Policy Studies Centre estimates that one in five young women will remain childless. Typically, those who defer motherhood are educated women. A recent study showed that women who have qualifications are twice as likely as those with no qualifications to say they expect to have no children.

Adapted from Chandler, J. (1993) 'Women outside marriage', *Sociology Review*, 2(4), and Jorgensen, N. et al. (1997) *Sociology: An Interactive Approach*, London: Collins Educational, pp. 100–1

Item C The conventional family

Despite all the arguments about the decline of marriage, the increase in illegitimacy and so on, it continues to be the case that most people in Britain grow up, get married and form a nuclear family for part of their adult life. Nine out of ten people get married at some time in their lives; 90 per cent of women are married by the age of 30 and over 90 per cent of men before the age of 40. Most couples who get married (or have stable cohabitation relationships) have children. Thus nine out of ten married women have children, and four out of five children live with their two natural parents. Seventy-nine per cent of families with children are headed by a married couple.

Adapted from Abbott, P. and Wallace, C. (1997) *An Introduction to Sociology: Feminist Perspectives* (2nd edn), London: Routledge

1 Explain in your own words what is meant by the term 'serial monogamy'. (2 marks)

2 Identify two trends that suggest that the family remains a 'cornerstone of society' (Item A). (4 marks)

3 Suggest three reasons why some women are choosing voluntary childlessness (Item B). (9 marks)

4 Identify and explain two reasons why cohabitation may not be a threat to the family. (10 marks)

Exam practice

5 a Identify and explain two reasons why women are 'marrying older and marrying less' (Item B). (15 marks)

   b Using information from the Items and elsewhere, outline and assess the view that the increase in divorce is due to its easy availability. (30 marks)

Family diversity

gettingyouthinking

© Posy Simmonds (from *The Observer*, 25 October 1998)

1. **Examine the Posy Simmonds cartoon above – which of these family setups fit the traditional view of the family?**

2. **Which family setups are furthest from the ideal? Explain why.**

3. **In what way do the photos of family life above support the view that familial ideology is out of touch with reality?**

The nuclear family is by no means the only way to organize living arrangements. Rapoport *et al.* (1982) are very critical of the functionalist and New Right view that the typical family is nuclear. They point out that even back in 1978, only 20 per cent of families fitted this ideal. Rapoport and colleagues argue that family life in Britain is actually characterized by **diversity**. A range of family types exist, with diverse internal setups reflecting the changing nature of British society.

Organizational or structural diversity

In 1999, only 23 per cent of households were made up of couples with dependent children. In other words, the nuclear unit seems to be in the minority. However, household statistics give us only a static picture of family life. Other categories, such as married-couple and single-person households, may have evolved out of nuclear units, or may evolve into nuclear units in the near future. It is important, therefore, not to dismiss the nuclear unit as irrelevant. If we look at the statistics in another way, a different picture emerges – for example, two-parent families make up 74 per cent of all families. However, there is no doubt that other family structures – such as cohabiting couples with children, one-parent families and reconstituted families – are growing in importance. Denscombe notes that 41 per cent of children live in a non-traditional family today in 2004.

One-parent families

The number of one-parent families with dependent children tripled from 2 per cent of UK households in 1961 to 7 per cent in 2003. There are now approximately 1.75 million lone-parent families in Britain, making up about 25 per cent of all families. About 26 per cent of people under the age of 19 live in a one-parent family.

Ninety per cent of single-parent families are headed by women. Most of these are ex-married (divorced, separated or widowed) or ex-cohabitees. The fastest growing group of single parents is made up of those who have never married or cohabited. Haskey estimated this group to be 26 per cent of all single mothers in 2002. Contrary to popular opinion, most single mothers are not teenagers – teenage mothers make up just 3 per cent of lone parents. The average age of a lone parent is actually 34.

Ford and Millar (1998) note that lone parenthood is seen by some as an inherently second-rate and imperfect family type, reflecting the selfish choices of adults against the interests of children. For example, New Right thinkers see a connection between one-parent families, educational underachievement and delinquency. They believe that children from one-parent families lack self-discipline and can be emotionally disturbed, because of the lack of a firm father figure in their lives. In addition, New Right thinkers are concerned about the cost of one-parent families to the state. Public expenditure on such families increased fourfold in the 1990s. It is suggested that the state offers 'perverse incentives', such as council housing and benefits, to young females to get pregnant.

Ford and Millar note that the 'perverse incentives' argument is flawed when the quality of life of lone parents is examined. Many experience poverty, debt and material hardship, and try to protect their children from poverty by spending less on themselves. Ford and Millar also suggest that poverty may be partly responsible for lone parenthood. Single women from poor socio-economic backgrounds living on council estates with higher than average rates of unemployment are more likely than others to become solo mothers. Motherhood is regarded as a desired and valued goal by these women and may be a rational response to their poor economic prospects. Surveys of such women suggest that children are a great source of love and pride, and most lone parents put family life at the top of things they see as important.

Feminist sociologists maintain that familial ideology causes problems for the one-parent family because it emphasizes the nuclear family ideal. This ideal leads to the **negative labelling** of one-parent families by teachers, social workers, housing departments, police and the courts. Single parents may be **scapegoated** for inner-city crime and educational underachievement, when these problems are actually the result of factors such as unemployment and poverty. The New Right also rarely consider that single parenthood may be preferable to the domestic violence that is inflicted by some husbands on

focus on research

Burghes and Brown (1995)
Teenage single mothers

A qualitative study using unstructured interviews with 31 mothers who were teenagers at conception and who have never been married was carried out by Burghes and Brown in 1995. They found that most of the pregnancies were unintended. However, nearly all the respondents expressed strong anti-abortion views and adoption was rarely considered. Most of the mothers reported that their experience of lone motherhood was a mixture of hard work and enormous joy. For the most part, the mothers interviewed preferred to be at home caring for their children. All the mothers intended to resume training or employment once their children were in school. Marriage was also a long-term goal.

1 How does this research challenge stereotypes about teenage mothers?

their wives and children – or that the majority of one-parent families bring up their children successfully.

Reconstituted families

The **reconstituted** or stepfamily is made up of divorced or widowed people who have remarried, and their children from the previous marriage (or cohabitation). Such families are on the increase because of the rise in divorce. In 2003, it was estimated that 726 000 children were living in this type of family.

Reconstituted families are unique because children are also likely to have close ties with their other natural parent. An increasing number of children experience co-parenting, where they spend half their week with their mother and stepfather and spend the other half with their father. Some family experts see co-parenting as a characteristic of binuclear families – two separate post-divorce or separation households are really one family system as far as children are concerned.

De'Ath and Slater's (1992) study of step-parenting identified a number of challenges facing reconstituted families. Children may find themselves pulled in two directions, especially if the relationship between their natural parents continues to be strained. They may have tense relationships with their step-parents, and conflict may arise around the extent to which the step-parent and stepchild accept each other, especially with regard to whether the child accepts the newcomer as a 'mother' or 'father'. Strained relations between step-parents and children may test the loyalty of the natural parent and strain the new marriage. These families may be further complicated if the new couple decide to have children of their own, which may create the potential for envy and conflict among existing children.

Kinship diversity

There is evidence that the **classic working-class extended family** continues to exist. The study *Villains*, by Janet Foster (1990) – of an East End London community – found that adults were happy to live only a few streets away from their parents and close relatives, and visited them regularly. Ties between mothers and children were particularly strong, and contacts between mothers and married daughters were frequent. Close kinship ties also formed the major support network, providing both emotional and material support.

Brannen (2003) notes the recent emergence of four-generation families – families that include great-grandchildren – because of increasing life expectancy. However she points out that as people are having smaller families because of divorce or women pursuing careers, we are less likely to experience horizontal intragenerational ties, i.e. we have fewer aunts, uncles and cousins. Brannen argues that we are now more likely to experience vertical intergenerational ties, i.e. closer ties with grandparents and great-grandparents. Brannen calls such family setups 'beanpole families'. She argues that the 'pivot generation', i.e. that sandwiched between older and younger family generations is increasingly in demand to provide for the needs of both elderly parents and grandchildren. For example, 20 per cent of people in their fifties and sixties currently care for an elderly person, while 10 per cent care for both an elderly person and a grandchild. Such services are based on the assumption of 'reciprocity', i.e. the provision of babysitting services is repaid by the assumption that daughters will assist mothers in their old age.

There is also evidence that extended kinship ties are important to the upper class, in their attempt to maintain wealth and privilege. The economic and political **elite** may use marriage and family connections to ensure 'social closure' – that is, to keep those who do not share their culture from becoming part of the elite.

Cultural diversity

There are differences in the lifestyles of families with different ethnic origins and religious beliefs. Research carried out at Essex University in 2000 indicates that only 39 per cent of British-born African-Caribbean adults under the age of 60 are in a formal marriage, compared with 60 per cent of White adults (Berthoud 2000). Moreover, this group is more likely than

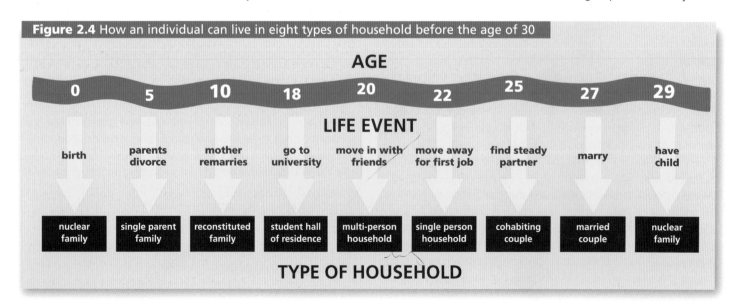

Figure 2.4 How an individual can live in eight types of household before the age of 30

AGE

| 0 | 5 | 10 | 18 | 20 | 22 | 25 | 27 | 29 |

LIFE EVENT

| birth | parents divorce | mother remarries | go to university | move in with friends | move away for first job | find steady partner | marry | have child |

| nuclear family | single parent family | reconstituted family | student hall of residence | multi-person household | single person household | cohabiting couple | married couple | nuclear family |

TYPE OF HOUSEHOLD

any other group to intermarry. The number of mixed-race partnerships means that very few African-Caribbean men and women are married to fellow African-Caribbeans and only one-quarter of African-Caribbean children live with two Black parents. Ali (2002) notes that such marriages result in interethnic families and mixed-race (sometimes called 'dual heritage') children. Some sociologists have suggested that these types of families have their own unique problems, such as facing prejudice and discrimination from both White and Black communities. Children too may feel confused about their identity in the light of such hostility.

There is evidence that African-Caribbean families have a different structure to White families. African-Caribbean communities have a higher proportion of one-parent families compared with White communities – over 50 per cent of African-Caribbean families with children are one-parent families. Rates of divorce are higher but there is also an increasing tradition in the African-Caribbean community of mothers choosing to live independently from their children's father. Berthoud notes two important and increasing trends:

- 66 per cent of 20-year-old African-Caribbean mothers remain single compared with 11 per cent of their White peers, while at 25 years, these figures are 48 per cent and 7 per cent respectively.
- At the age of 30, 60 per cent of African-Caribbean men are unattached, compared with 45 per cent of their White peers.

These trends indicate that African-Caribbean women are avoiding settling down with the African-Caribbean fathers of their children. Berthoud (2003) suggests that the attitudes of young African-Caribbean women are characterized by 'modern individualism' – they are choosing to bring up children alone for two reasons:

- African-Caribbean women are more likely to be employed than African-Caribbean men. Such women rationally weigh up the costs and benefits of living with the fathers of their children and conclude that African-Caribbean men are unreliable as a source of family income and are potentially a financial burden. Surveys indicate that such women prefer to be economically independent.
- Chamberlain and Goulbourne (1999) note that African-Caribbean single mothers are more likely to be supported by an extended kinship network in their upbringing of children – interestingly, African-Caribbean definitions of kinship often extends to including family friends and neighbours as 'aunts' and 'uncles'.

The Essex study also found that the Pakistani and Bangladeshi communities are most likely to live in old-fashioned nuclear families, although about 33 per cent of Asian families – mainly Sikhs and East African Asians – live in extended families. East African Asian extended families are likely to contain more than one generation, while Sikh extended units are organized around brothers and their wives and children.

Berthoud argues that South Asians tend to be more traditional in their family values than Whites. Marriage is highly valued and there is little divorce (although this may indicate empty-shell marriages). Marriage in Asian families – whether Muslim, Hindu or Sikh – is mainly arranged and there is little intermarriage with other religions or cultures. There is also evidence that Bangladeshi and Pakistani women have more children than Indian and White women, and at younger ages. Relationships between Asian parents and their children are also very different from those that characterize White families. Children tend to respect religious and cultural traditions, and they feel a strong sense of duty to their families, and especially to their elders. South Asian families, particularly, feel a strong sense of duty and obligation to assist extended kin in economic and social ways. This is important because Bangladeshi and Pakistani families in the UK are more likely to be in poverty compared with Indian and White families. Such obligations often extend to sending money to relatives abroad on a regular basis and travelling half way around the world to nurse sick or dying relatives.

Lone households

Berthoud and Gershuny (2000) identify a number of people who do not live with any member of their nuclear family, i.e. not with parents, spouse or children. This group is composed of elderly widows and young people in their twenties. For example, 9 per cent of adults aged 20 to 29 lived entirely alone in 1996, while 9 per cent lived with non-relatives (who were not a partner or spouse).

Class diversity

The Rapoports suggest that there may be differences between middle-class and working-class families in terms of the relationship between husband and wife and the way in which children are socialized and disciplined. Some sociologists argue that middle-class parents are more child-centred (see Topic 6) than working-class parents. They supposedly take a greater interest in their children's education, and consequently pass on cultural advantages in terms of attitudes, values and practices (i.e. cultural capital – see Unit 1, Topic 6) which assist their children through the educational system. However, critical sociologists argue that working-class parents are just as child-centred, but that material deprivation limits how much help they can give their children. Therefore, the working-class child's experience is likely to be less satisfactory – because of family poverty, poor schools, lack of material support, greater risks of accidents both in the home and in the street, and so on.

Sexual diversity

As discussed earlier in this unit, the New Right have expressed concern at the increasing number of same-sex couples who are cohabiting – and particularly the trend of such couples to have families through adoption, artificial insemination and surrogacy. In 1999, the law lords ruled that a homosexual couple can be legally defined as a family, and the Government is now looking to introduce legislation which will mean that long-term same-sex partners will have similar rights to heterosexual married couples with regard to inheritance (of property and pensions, for example) and next-of-kin status. New Right commentators have suggested that such family setups are 'unnatural' and that children will either be under pressure to experiment with the lifestyles of their parents or will be bullied at school because of the sexuality of their parents. In the courts, such fears have meant that in the past mothers who have come out as lesbians have lost custody of their children.

There have been a number of sociological studies of homosexual couples and children. Studies of couples suggest that relationships between partners are qualitatively different from heterosexual partners in terms of both domestic and emotional labour because they are not subject to gendered assumptions about which sex should be responsible for these tasks. There may, therefore, be more equality between partners. It is also suggested that same-sex couples work harder at relationships in terms of commitment because they face so many external pressures and criticisms, e.g. disapproval by other members of their family. However, recent research indicates that they may face the same sorts of problems as heterosexual couples in terms of problems such as domestic violence.

Studies of children brought up in single-sex families show no significant effects in terms of gender identification or sexual orientation. For example, Gottman (1990) found that adult daughters of lesbian mothers were just as likely to be of a heterosexual inclination as the daughters of heterosexual mothers. Dunne (1997) argues that children brought up by homosexuals are more likely to be tolerant and see sharing and equality as important features of their relationships with others.

Postmodernism and family diversity

Postmodernists argue that postmodern family life is characterized by diversity, variation and instability. For example, women no longer aspire exclusively to romantic love, marriage and children. Pre-marital sex, serial monogamy, cohabitation, economic independence, single-sex relationships and childlessness are now acceptable alternative lifestyles. Men's roles too are no longer clear cut in postmodern society, and the resulting 'crisis in masculinity' (see p. 88) has led to men redefining both their sexuality and family commitments. Beck and Beck-Gernsheim (1995) argue that such choice and diversity have led to the renegotiation of family relationships as people attempt to find a middle ground between individualization and commitment to another person and/or children. Others disagree with this view. They argue that family diversity is exaggerated, and that the basic features of family life have remained largely unchanged for the majority of the population since the 1950s.

There is no doubt that nuclear families are still very common, but the increasing number of other family types – especially single-parent families and reconstituted families – indicates a slow but steady drift away from the nuclear ideal.

(see p. 88)

Check your understanding

1. How might reconstituted family life differ from that experienced in nuclear families?

2. Why do feminist sociologists think that one-parent families are seen as a 'problem'?

3. In what sense might working-class and upper-class families be similar in terms of their contact with extended kin?

4. What differences might exist between working-class and middle-class families?

5. What types of families are African-Caribbeans and South Asians likely to be living in?

KEY TERMS

Classic working-class extended family a family in which sons and daughters live in the same neighbourhood as their parents, see each other on a regular basis and offer each other various supports.

Diversity difference, variation.

Elite the most powerful, rich or gifted members of a group.

Negative labelling treating something as being 'bad' or 'undesirable'.

Reconstituted families stepfamilies.

Scapegoated unfairly blamed.

research idea

- If you know people from ethnic or religious backgrounds different from your own, ask them if you can interview them about their experience of family life. Make sure your questionnaire is sensitive to their background and avoids offending them.

web.task

Use the web to research one-parent families. The following websites contain a range of useful data and information:

www.gingerbread.org.uk

www.opfs.org.uk

www.oneparentfamilies.org.uk

www.apsoc.ox.ac.uk/fpsc/

exploring family diversity

Item A Postmodern family life

Postmodern family life is clearly pluralistic, i.e. characterized by diversity, variation and instability rather than by some universal nuclear ideal. In the postmodern world, we can see such diversity in the fact that women no longer view romantic love and marriage as their primary goals. Premarital sex and serial monogamy are socially acceptable. More young women are electing not to have children in favour of having careers. Reproductive technology and developments in genetics mean that non-traditional women, e.g. lesbians, women in their sixties, etc., can have children. The increase in dual-career families means greater emphasis on fathering and the appearance of alternative masculinities symbolized by househusbands. In the past we set rules and limits for children. We are now more likely to set lists and schedules and to make deals with them as equals.

Adapted from Chapman, S. and Aiken, D. (2000) 'Towards a new sociology of families?', *Sociology Review*, 9(3)

Item B Is one type of family 'better' than others?

Fuelled by media moral panics about rising crime, low standards in education, the young lacking a work ethic, the rise of illegitimacy, divorce and single-parenthood, politicians and other 'opinion formers' appear to give support to the traditional nuclear family. Family diversity, from this view, is a 'social problem' to be solved. However, postmodernists suggest that we cannot say that one type of family is better than another because absolute meaning or truth has collapsed in social life. In postmodern societies, we are free to choose the lifestyles we wish, since this is the only way to search for meaning in a society that offers choice, fragmentation and diversity. Claims that some family forms are 'better' or more 'natural' or more 'normal' than others are a leftover from modernist thought, which attempted to establish truths about ideal family forms. In a postmodern society, we cannot even say what constitutes a 'family'.

Adapted from Kidd, W. (1999) 'Family diversity in an uncertain future', *Sociology Review*, 9(1)

Item C Children in lone-parent families

Controversy surrounds the issue of how children are affected by living in single-parent families. Poorer educational achievement and behavioural problems have been highlighted. However, only a minority of children in separated families experience such outcomes. Above all, such problems are caused by poverty and poor housing rather than inadequate socialization. In the absence of poverty, children from one-parent families fare no worse than children in other families. Ninety per cent of lone parents say they would like to work at some point, although many find it difficult to combine work with caring for children alone.

Adapted from *One Parent Families Today: The Facts*, National Council for One Parent Families, March 2000

---

1 Explain what is meant by 'househusbands' (Item A). (2 marks)

2 Suggest two ways in which family structures or relationships have changed according to postmodernist sociologists (Items A and B). (4 marks)

3 Identify and briefly explain three variations in family life which are the product of cultural differences. (9 marks)

4 Identify and briefly describe two problems faced by one-parent families (Item C). (10 marks)

Exam practice

5 a Identify and explain two examples of family diversity in the contemporary UK. (15 marks)

   b Outline and discuss the view that changes in family structures and lifestyles have been exaggerated. (30 marks)

gettingyou**thinking**

Image used in an NSPCC campaign against child abuse

Funeral of a Palestinian child killed in an Israeli attack

Gun-toting children in Sierra Leone

Friendship in childhood

Abused children can't speak up.

1 What does the cartoon on the right tell us about family life in the Middle Ages?

2 How does the experience of medieval childhood differ from that of today?

3 What do the images above tell us about the experience of childhood today?

Children dressed like their parents

In the MIddle Ages, young and old played together in games and festivals, as in this scene based on Brueghel's painting, the 'Battle between Carnival and Lent', where the children are depicted as small adults.

Everyone worked together

At 8 years, I was put out as an apprentice

So he could learn his trade from me.

Everyone was held responsible

Tudor law says a 7-year-old can be hanged for stealing

In many cases, houses were not split up into special rooms for eating, sleeping, working or cooking

So children could not escape from the adult world

What is a child? Innocent, cute, funny? That's certainly the popular image suggested by birthday cards, magazines and so on. However, the cartoon above and some of the images on the left give a different impression. We can see that ideas about childhood appear to vary between different societies and different historical periods. This means that childhood is a **social construction** – something created by society, rather than simply a biological stage.

Childhood in pre-industrial society

The social historian Philippe Aries (1962) suggested that what we experience today as childhood is a recent social invention. He claimed that, in pre-industrial society, childhood as we know it today did not exist. Children were 'little adults' who took part in the same work and play activities as adults. Toys and games specifically for children did not exist. Moreover, Aries argued

that children were regarded as an **economic asset** rather than as a symbol of people's love for one another. Investing emotionally in children was difficult when their death rate was so high.

Aries's evidence for this view of childhood has been questioned, but other historians agree that the pre-industrial family was a unit of production, working the land or engaged in crafts. Children were expected to help their parents from a very young age. Those who did not help with domestic production usually left home to become servants or apprentices.

Childhood and industrialization

After industrialization these attitudes continued, especially among the working classes, whose children were frequently found working in factories, mines and mills. Aries argued that middle-class attitudes towards children started to change during this period. There was a growth in marital and parental love in middle-class families as the **infant mortality rate** started to fall.

Social attitudes towards children really started to change in the middle of the 19th century. Children were excluded from the mines and factories where thousands of them had been killed or injured. Some working-class parents, however, resisted these moves, because they depended on their children's wages.

Many 19th-century campaigners were concerned about juvenile delinquency, beggars and child prostitution, and consequently wanted to get children off the streets. However, there is considerable evidence that children continued to be badly treated in this period, and child prostitution and abuse were common features of most cities. It was not until the turn of the 20th century that the age of sexual consent was raised to 16.

Childhood in the 20th century

The 20th century saw the emergence of a **child-centred** society. This was probably the result of improved standards of living and nutrition in the late 19th century, which led to a major decline in the infant mortality rate. The higher standard of living also meant that having children became more expensive. The increased availability and efficiency of contraception allowed people to choose to have fewer children. Consequently, parents were able to invest more in them in terms of love, socialisation and protection.

Childhood and adolescence were consequently seen as separate categories from adulthood. Children were seen as being in need of special attention and protection.

Children and the state

Concern over the rights of children can be seen in greater state involvement in protecting them. Parents' rearing of children is now monitored through various pieces of legislation, such as the 1989 Children Act. The role of social services and social workers is to police those families in which children are thought to be at risk. The state also supervises the socialization of children through compulsory education, which lasts 11 years. It also takes some economic responsibility by paying child benefit and children's tax credits to parents.

Increasingly, children have come to be seen as individuals with rights. The Child Support Act (1991) deals with the care, bringing up and protection of children. It protects children's welfare in the event of parental separation and divorce, emphasizing that the prime concern of the state should be the child, and what children themselves say about their experiences and needs. Some children have recently used the act to 'divorce' their parents, while others have used it to 'force' their separated/divorced parents to see them more regularly.

Theoretical approaches to childhood

The conventional approach

Many functionalists and New Right thinkers tend to subscribe to what has been termed a 'conventional' approach to childhood. This sees children as a vulnerable group – both under threat from and in need of protection from adult society. This approach suggests that successful child-rearing requires two parents of the opposite sex, and that there is a 'right' way to bring up a child. Such views often 'blame' working mothers or single mothers, and/or inadequate parents, for social problems such as delinquency. They also see children as in need of protection from 'threats' such as homosexuality and media violence.

Melanie Phillips' book *All Must Have Prizes* (1997) is typical of this conventional approach to childhood. She argues that the culture of parenting in the UK has broken down and the 'innocence' of childhood has been undermined by two trends:

1 The concept of parenting has been distorted by liberal ideas, which have given too many rights and powers to children. Phillips argues that children should be socialized into a healthy respect for parental authority. However, she argues that children's rights have undermined this process, and parents are increasingly criticized and penalized for resorting to sanctions such as smacking.

2 Phillips believes that the media and the peer group have become more influential than parents. She sees the media in the form of magazines aimed at young girls, pop music videos and television as a particular problem, because they encourage young girls to envisage themselves as sexual beings at a much younger age.

These trends mean that the period of childhood has been shortened – it is no longer a sacred and innocent period lasting up to 13 or 14 years. Phillips complains that adulthood encroaches upon the experiences of children a great deal earlier than in the past. She argues that many children do not have the emotional maturity to cope with the rights and choices that they have today. The result, she believes, is an increase in social problems such as suicide, eating disorders, self-harm, depression and drug/alcohol abuse.

The assumptions contained in conventional approaches to childhood have been very influential on social policy. For example, in family law and especially the divorce courts, children are portrayed as potential victims in need of protection from the law and the state. They tend not to be given any say in the decisions made by parents, judges and politicians. It is assumed that they lack the maturity and experience to contribute to the debate about their futures.

An alternative view

This conventional approach has been criticized by sociologists who have researched children's perspectives on society and family. They suggest that functionalist and New Right

Neil Postman (1982)

Is childhood disappearing?

Postman argues that childhood is disappearing. His view is based on two related ideas.

1 The growth of television means that there are no more secrets from children. Television gives them unlimited access to the adult world. They are exposed to the 'real world' of sex, disaster, death and suffering.

2 'Social blurring' has occurred so there is little distinction between adults and children. Children's games are disappearing and children seem less childlike today. They speak, dress and behave in more adult ways, while adults have enjoyed looking more like their kids and youth generally. Over time, nearly all the traditional features that mark the transition to adulthood – getting a job, religious confirmation, leaving home, getting married – no longer apply in any clear way.

Postman's analysis has been heavily criticized. His arguments do not appear to be based on solid evidence, while recent studies indicate that adults are actually taking more and more control of their children's lives. For example, David Brooks (2001) diagnoses parents today as obsessed with safety, and ever more concerned with defining boundaries for their kids and widening their control and safety net around them.

Perhaps it is children that are disappearing rather than childhood. Children are a smaller percentage of our overall population today and are diminishing in relative proportion to other age groups.

Adapted from Allen, D. (2001) 'Is childhood disappearing?', *Studies in Social and Political Thought,* 6(1), 2001

1 **What methods could be used to collect data about the impact of television on children?**

2 **To what extent do you believe that childhood is disappearing? What evidence can you use to support your view?**

arguments assume that children are simply empty vessels. Family life is presented as a one-way process in which parenting and socialization aim to transform children into good citizens. However, this view ignores the fact that children have their own unique interpretation of family life, which they actively employ in interaction with their parents. In other words, the relationship between parents and children is a two-way process in which the latter can and do influence the nature and quality of family life. For example, research by Morrow (1998) found that children can be constructive and reflective contributors to family life. Most of the children in Morrow's study had a pragmatic view of their family role – they did not want to make decisions for themselves but they did want a say in what happened to them.

Conventional approaches are also criticized because they tend to generalize about children and childhood. This is dangerous because, as we saw earlier, childhood is not a fixed, universal experience. Historical period, locality, culture, social class, gender and ethnicity all have an influence on the character and quality of childhood. This can be illustrated in a number of ways:

- In many less developed nations, the experience of childhood is extremely different from that in the industrialized world. Children in such countries are constantly at risk of early death because of poverty and lack of basic health care. They are unlikely to have access to education, and may find themselves occupying adult roles as workers or soldiers. In many countries, children are not regarded as special or as in need of protection. For example, in Mexico, it is estimated that 1.9 million children live rough on the streets – 240 000 of these have been abandoned by their parents. In Brazil, 1000 homeless children are shot dead every year by people who regard them as vermin.

- Even in a country such as Britain, experience of childhood may differ across ethnic and religious groups. For example, there is evidence that Muslim, Hindu and Sikh children generally feel a stronger sense of obligation and duty to their parents than White children. Generational conflict is therefore less likely or is more likely to be hidden.

- Experiences of childhood in Britain may vary according to social class. Upper-class children may find that they spend most of their formative years in boarding schools. Middle-class children may be encouraged from an early age to aim for university and a professional career, and they are likely to receive considerable economic and cultural support from their parents. Working-class childhood may be made more difficult by the experience of poverty. For example, research by Jefferis et al. (2002) found that children who experienced poverty had significantly fallen behind children from middle-class backgrounds in terms of maths, reading and other ability tests by the age of 7.

- Experiences of childhood may differ according to gender. Boys and girls may be socialized into a set of behaviours based on expectations about masculinity and femininity. For example, there is some evidence that girls are subjected to stricter social controls from parents compared with boys when they reach adolescence.

We also need to acknowledge that some children's experiences of childhood may be damaging. Different types of child abuse have been rediscovered in recent years, such as neglect and physical, sexual and emotional abuse. The NSPCC points out that each week at least one child will die as a result of an adult's cruelty, usually a parent or step-parent, while 30 000 children are on child protection registers because they are at risk of abuse from family members. The negative effects of divorce have been documented in several surveys of teenagers. In conclusion, not all children experience the family or their parents as positive – for many children and teenagers, the family is exploitative and dangerous.

focus on research

Morrow (1998)
Children's views of the family

A qualitative study of 183 children aged between 8 and 14, carried out by Morrow in 1998, found that children's views do not necessarily conform to stereotypical images of the nuclear family. The research asked pupils to draw and write about 'who is important to me?', and to complete a sentence on 'what is a family?' and 'what are families for?'. They were also given a short questionnaire asking whether or not five one-sentence descriptions of family type counted as family. Group discussions also took place which explored their responses to the questionnaire. The children were found to have a pragmatic view of family life – love, care and mutual respect were regarded by them as the essential characteristics of family life. They also had a very inclusive view of who was family – absent relatives and pets were regarded as family members. This research can be downloaded from **www.jrf.org.uk**.

1 In what ways did the children's views about the family not conform to the 'typical' nuclear family?

Check your understanding

1 What do sociologists mean when they describe childhood as a 'social construction'?

2 How does Aries believe children were treated in pre-industrial society?

3 What were the main causes of society becoming more child-centred at the end of the 19th century?

4 How does the conventional approach to childhood view children?

5 What problems are associated with this approach?

KEY TERMS

Child-centred treating the needs of children as a priority.

Economic asset something that brings money in.

Infant mortality rate the number of babies who die in their first year of life, as a proportion of all live births.

Social construction something that is created by society.

research ideas

- In order to document the changing experience of and attitudes towards childhood, design a survey asking three generations about their experience of family.

- Using textbooks, CD-Roms and government websites, such as those of the Home Office and Lord Chancellor's department (accessible via www.open.gov.uk), compile a detailed time-line outlining state intervention in children's lives and the rights children now have.

web.task

Visit the website www.child-abuse.com/childhouse

This contains links to a number of excellent sites that look at childhood and children's rights across the world.

Alternatively, visit the NSPCC website www.nspcc.co.uk to get an idea of the degree of child abuse in UK society.

Item A The social construction of childhood

<< Most of us tend to think of childhood as a clear and distinct stage of life. 'Children', we suppose, are distinct from 'babies' or 'toddlers'. Childhood intervenes between infancy and the onset of adolescence. Yet the concept of childhood, like so many other aspects of our social life today, has only come into being over the past two or three centuries. In traditional and pre-industrial cultures, the young move directly from a lengthy infancy into working roles within the community. Right up to the start of the 20th century, in the UK and most other Western countries, children as young as 7 or 8 years old were put to work at what now seems a very early age. There are many countries in the world today, in fact, in which young children are engaged in full-time work, often in physically demanding circumstances (coalmines, for example). The idea that children have distinctive rights, and the notion that the use of child labour is morally wrong, are quite recent developments.>>

Giddens, A. (1997) *Sociology* (3rd edn),
Cambridge: Polity Press, p. 38

Item B Childhood and the law

The changing nature of legislation concerning children has reflected the changing views towards children over time. In the 19th century, the idea gradually developed that children were not simply little adults, but were vulnerable members of society who needed care and protection. This concept of the child as vulnerable dominates 20th-century thinking. For example, the Children Act of 1908 resulted in the criminal justice system treating and punishing criminal adults and children in different ways for the first time. In 1952, local authorities were given the duty to investigate cases of neglect or cruelty with regard to children, while the 1989 Children Act made it clear that the child's best interests must be central to any decision made about the welfare of the child. The child's views are therefore sought and taken into account. Such legislation reflects the fact that we are now a child-centred society.

Adapted from Moore, S. (1998)
Social Welfare Alive (2nd edn),
Cheltenham: Stanley Thornes, pp. 366–7

Item C Diversity of childhood experiences

Childhood is tremendously varied, from the sheltered preschooler of Western nations to the maimed street beggar or gun-carrying 'freedom fighter' of less industrialized nations. Even in the UK, children may grow up in a wide variety of different and potentially damaging situations. There are occasional alarming reports of child prostitution linked to runaway children and drug use. We know from recent studies that many children of less than 10 years old may be the main carer in family situations where their parent is chronically ill or disabled. For many children, childhood may involve the direct experience of oppression, abuse, exploitation, not to mention parental divorce, poor health and poverty. Childhood experience, then, is extremely diverse by way of region, social class, housing quality, income, culture and ethnicity, prejudice, diet, disease and abuse.

Adapted from Bernardes, J. (1997)
Family Studies: An Introduction,
London: Routledge, p. 115

1 **Explain what is meant by the phrase 'a child-centred society' (Item B).** (2 marks)

2 **Suggest two ways in which the experience of being a child in a less developed nation may differ from the experience of a British child (Item C).** (4 marks)

3 **Identify and briefly explain three ways in which the state protects the rights of children today (Item B).** (9 marks)

4 **Describe two differences between childhood in pre-industrial society and childhood in contemporary industrial society.** (10 marks)

Exam practice

5 a **Identify and explain two reasons why the UK has become a more child-centred society.** (15 marks)

 b **Outline and discuss the view that childhood is socially constructed.** (30 marks)

Power and control in the family

getting you thinking

(a) Making sure that you had sandwiches for lunch or the money to pay for a school dinner.

(b) Making sure that your favourite food was in the fridge.

(c) Arranging with other parents for you to go to a party or around to somebody's house for tea.

(d) Making sure that you had a clean swimming costume and towel on the days of school swims.

(e) Changing the sheets on your bed.

(f) Supervising your bath-time.

(g) Picking you up from school.

(h) Buying a present for you to take to another child's birthday party.

(i) Reassuring you if you had a bad dream in the night.

(j) Anticipating that you needed a new pair of shoes because you were about to grow out of your old pair.

1 Consider the list of tasks above. Which adult in your home was mainly responsible for each when you were aged 5 to 7?

2 What other aspects of power and control in the home are neglected if we only focus on household tasks?

3 Who exercises power in your home and what forms does this take?

In 1973, Young and Willmott claimed that the traditional **segregated division of labour in the home** – men as breadwinners and women as housewives/mothers – was breaking down. The relationship between husband and wife (the **conjugal relationship**) was becoming – at least in middle-class families – more joint or **symmetrical**. This trend towards **egalitarian** marriage was caused by the decline in the extended family, and its replacement in the late 20th century by the **privatized nuclear family**, as well as by the increasing opportunities in paid employment for women. Some media commentators were so convinced by these arguments that in

the 1980s, it was claimed that a 'new man' had appeared, i.e. males who were in touch with their feminine side and who were happy to meet women's emotional and domestic needs.

However, the exercise above should have shown you that much of women's labour in the home is neglected by studies that focus only on obvious and highly visible tasks. A good deal of what women do in the home is mental and emotional as well as physical, involving anticipating and fulfilling the needs of family members. These more subtle responsibilities tend to be missed by researchers, some of whom have concluded that men and women are becoming more equal in the home – on the basis of their sharing some of the more glamorous domestic tasks, such as cooking. These sorts of surveys can also miss other influences that ensure that power and control in the home remain firmly in male hands – violence, the lack of status associated with the mother/housewife role, the belief that working mothers damage children, the fact that being a mother limits job opportunities, and so on.

Studies of housework and childcare

The idea that equality is a central characteristic of marriage is strongly opposed by feminist sociologists. Studies of professional couples indicate that only a minority genuinely share housework and childcare. For example, Dryden's (1999) qualitative study of 17 married couples found that women still had major responsibility for housework and childcare. Similarly, studies of unemployed men indicate that, although they do more around the home, their wives, even when working full time, do the lion's share of housework and childcare. As Young comments on the findings of the British Household Panel Survey:

<< *Women do more when they are working and the man unemployed, when they are working longer hours than the man, when they are both employed full time – whatever the setup.* >>

Some sociologists have suggested that unemployed men resist increased involvement in housework because it threatens their masculinity, especially if their wife is the main income earner.

A survey carried out for the insurance firm Legal & General in April 2000 found that full-time working mothers spent 56 hours per week on housework and childcare, compared with men's 31 hours. This increased to 84 hours if the women had children aged 3 and under. The Future Foundation survey of October 2000 was more positive. It found that women were receiving more help in the home from husbands and boyfriends. Two-thirds of men said they did more around the home than their fathers. However, even at this rate, women will have to wait until at least 2015 before tasks are shared equally!

The quantifiable evidence, therefore, indicates that women are still likely to have a **dual burden** – they are expected to be mainly responsible for the bulk of domestic tasks despite holding down full-time jobs. Dryden found that such inequality was a constant source of friction between couples and a number of studies of marriage, notably by Hart (1976), have argued that this is a major cause of marital breakdown.

Women are also responsible for the emotional well-being of their partners and children. Studies such as that carried out by Duncombe and Marsden (1995) have found that women felt that their male partners were lacking in terms of 'emotional participation', i.e. men found it difficult to express their feelings, to tell their partners how they felt about them and to relate emotionally to their children. Duncombe and Marsden argue that this increases the burden on women because they

feel they should attempt to compensate and please all parties in the home. Women consequently spend a great deal of time soothing the emotions of partners and children. This leads to the neglect of their own psychological well-being, and can have negative consequences for their mental and physical health. For example, Bernard's study of marriage (1982) confirms this – she found that the men in her study were more satisfied with their marriage than their wives, many of whom expressed emotional loneliness. Moreover, these men had no inkling that their wives were unhappy.

Decision-making

Some sociologists have focused on the distribution of power within marriages. Edgell (1980) discovered that middle-class wives generally deferred to their husbands in decision-making. Edgell concluded that the men in his sample were able to demand that the interests of their wives and families be subordinated to the man's career, because he was the main breadwinner. Similarly, surveys of young married couples with children conclude that the decision to have children, although jointly reached, dramatically changes the life of the mother rather than the father. However, Gillian Leighton (1992) discovered that the power to make decisions changed when males became unemployed. In her study of professional couples, working wives often took over responsibility for bills and initiated cutbacks in spending.

Fatherhood

An important part of the New Right critique of one-parent families is the view that most of them lack fathers. Dennis and Erdos (2000), for example, suggest that fatherless children are less likely to be successfully socialized into the culture of discipline and compromise found in nuclear families and so are less likely to be successful parents themselves. It is suggested that such children lack an authority figure to turn to in times of crisis and as a result the peer group and mass media have increased in influence. It is argued that such influence is likely to lead to an increase in social problems, such as delinquency, sexual promiscuity, teenage pregnancy and drug use.

There is no doubt that de-partnering, whether from marriage or cohabitation, leads to some degree of de-parenting, i.e. one or other parent, usually the father in the UK, becomes less involved in the parenting of a child. The law in the UK tends to uphold traditional ideas about gender roles and custody of children is mainly awarded to the mother. Bernardes notes that the Children Act clearly states that the mother should have parental responsibility for a child if the parents are not married. It is estimated that 40 per cent of fathers lose complete touch with their children after two years; others will experience irregular contact or conflict with their ex-partners about access arrangements. The recent publicity campaign by Fathers4Justice has aimed to draw attention to what they see as an unjust mother-centred legal system which denies fathers their right of access to their children.

Other commentators have suggested that we should focus on the quality of fathering. In the early 1990s, many sociologists concluded that the role of fathers was changing. For example, men in the 1990s were more likely to attend the birth of their babies than men in the 1960s, and they were more likely to play a greater role in childcare than their own fathers. Burghes (1997) found that fathers were taking an increasingly active role in the emotional development of their children. Beck (1992) notes that, in the postmodern age, fathers can no longer rely on jobs to provide a sense of identity and fulfilment. Increasingly, they look to their children to give them a sense of identity and purpose.

Warin *et al.* (1999), in their study of 95 families in Rochdale, found that fathers, mothers and teenage children overwhelmingly subscribed to the view that the male should be the breadwinner, despite changes in employment and family life, and that mothers were the experts in parenting. Fathers in this study felt under considerable pressure to provide for their families and this was intensified by demands from teenage children for consumer goods and designer-label fashion items. Men who were in low-paid jobs, sick, disabled or unemployed expressed feelings of frustration and sadness, and were likely to see themselves as failures for being unable to supply their children with what they wanted. The study claims that the contributions of fathers to families often goes unrecognized. Fathers were aware that they were expected to do more than previous generations and they expressed this by acting as a taxi service for their children, sharing in the shopping, carrying out informal sports coaching and going to watch children at sporting events. The researchers imply that fathers today are under considerable pressure, attempting to juggle the role of provider with the emotional support role traditionally provided by mothers. They conclude that the pressures of work and family were turning men into 'all-singing, all-dancing superdads'.

However, despite Warin and colleagues' conclusions, it is important not to exaggerate men's role in childcare. Looking after children is still overwhelmingly the responsibility of mothers, rather than jointly shared with fathers. Recent research has also focused on the pressures of work in the 21st century. It suggests that these may be negatively impacting on the ability of fathers to bond effectively with their children and spend time with them. For example, in 2003, a survey by Dex noted that half her sample of fathers reported that 30 per cent (as well as 6 per cent of mothers) worked more than 48 hours a week on a regular basis. It is unlikely that fathers in this situation will be spending quality time interacting with their families.

Patriarchal ideology

Feminists have highlighted the influence of patriarchal ideology (see Unit 1, Topic 7) on the perceptions of both husbands and wives. Surveys indicate that many women accept primary responsibility for housework and childcare without question, and believe that their career should be secondary to that of their husband. Such ideas are also reflected in state policy, which encourages female economic dependence upon men. Moreover, patriarchal ideology expects women to take on jobs that are compatible with family commitments. Surveys suggest that a large number of mothers feel guilty about working. Some actually give up work altogether because they believe that their absence somehow damages their children.

The housewife experience

The housewife role has low status compared with paid work, and this may lead to feelings of boredom, loneliness and dissatisfaction. As a result, some housewives may see themselves as worthless or as mere extensions of their husbands and children. They may see themselves as redundant when their children grow up and leave home. Such feelings may be responsible for the high levels of depression experienced by women in modern industrial societies. Feminists would argue that these findings are yet further evidence of inequalities within marriage.

The mother/housewife role and work

Some feminist sociologists have concluded that women's participation in the labour market is clearly limited by their domestic responsibilities. Because of these responsibilities, very few women have continuous full-time careers. Mothers, then, tend to have 'jobs', while their husbands have 'careers'. As a result, women don't have the same access to promotion and training opportunities as men. Some employers may believe that women are unreliable because of family commitments and, consequently, discriminate against them.

Modern marriages appear far from equal. On all the criteria examined so far – the distribution of housework and childcare tasks, decision-making, and the impact of being a mother/housewife on employment – we see women at a disadvantage compared with men.

Children, power and control

Some writers have criticized the role of the family in socializing children. David Cooper (1972) was very sceptical about the claim that the family provides emotional support for children. He argued that family socialization was actually bad for children because it destroyed free will, imagination and creativity. Children are turned into unthinking robots who blindly obey their superiors and happily discriminate against others because they have uncritically internalized their parents' prejudices. These controversial ideas have recently been criticized by New Right commentators, such as Melanie Phillips (1997), who argue that teenagers show little sign of conformity or blind acceptance of authority. Rather, she argues, rates of teenage delinquency and antischool cultures indicate that children today are ill-disciplined, aggressive and enthusiastically willing to challenge all forms of traditional authority.

Afshar H. (1994) 'Muslim women in West Yorkshire: growing up with real and imaginary values amidst conflicting views of self and society', in H. Afshar and M. Maynard (eds) *The Dynamics of 'Race' and 'Gender'*, London: Taylor & Francis

Haleh Afshar
Muslim women in West Yorkshire

Haleh Afshar spent nearly a decade researching a group of Muslim women in West Yorkshire. Her sample, which was selected using the snowball method, was made up of women living in three-generational households, consisting of grandmother, bride and granddaughter. Interviews were conducted by a researcher who spoke Urdu and who did not live in the locality where the respondents lived. The intention was to allow the voices of the women themselves to be heard. All the interviews were taped. Those respondents who spoke in English had their words reported verbatim whilst those who did not had their words interpreted as closely as possible to the original. Afshar found that arranged marriage for young Muslim women involved men exchanging the services received from their mother for those received from their wives. Islamic marriage recognizes men and women as partners in life but married women are not expected to assert their rights. They are to be help-mates and obedient partners. They are expected to excel at their new role of wifehood. Within a year or two, they are expected to give birth, preferably to a son, and to transmit positive family values to the next generation.

1 Why do you think Afshar used the snowball sampling technique?

2 Why do you think Afshar chose to do qualitative research?

3 Why might some sociologists suggest that Afshar's methods are unreliable?

Theoretical explanations of inequalities in power and control in families

There are four major theoretical perspectives on the distribution of power and control in the family:

1 *Functionalists* see the sexual division of labour in the home as biologically inevitable. Women are seen as naturally suited to the caring and emotional role, which Parsons terms the 'expressive role'.

2 *Liberal feminists* believe that women have made real progress in terms of equality within the family and particularly in education and the economy. They generally believe that men are adapting to change and, although they culturally lag behind women in terms of attitudes and behaviour, the future is likely to bring further movement towards domestic and economic equality.

3 *Marxist–feminists* have focused on the contribution of domestic labour i.e. housework and childcare, to capitalist economies. They point out that such work is unpaid but has great value for capitalist economies. In other words,

capitalism exploits women. Moreover, men benefit from this exploitation.

For example, the Marxist-feminist Margaret Benston (1972) suggested that the nuclear family is important to capitalism because it rears the future workforce at little cost to the capitalist state. Women's domestic labour and sexual services also help to maintain the present workforce's physical and emotional fitness. Mothers and housewives are also a useful reserve army of labour that can be hired cheaply as part-time workers in time of economic expansion and let go first in times of recession. Finally, it can be argued that the capitalist class directly exploit women's domestic labour by hiring women as cleaners, nannies and cooks. This enables the wealthy of both sexes to pursue careers outside the home.

4 *Radical feminists* such as Delphy (1984) believe that 'the first oppression is the oppression of women by men – women are an exploited class'. The housewife role is, therefore, a role created by patriarchy and geared to the service of men and their interests (see Topic 2, p. 58). Like functionalism, both Marxist and radical forms of feminism see women's exploitation and oppression as rooted in their biological role as mothers.

Criticisms of these theories

- These theories fail to explain why women's roles vary across different cultures. For example, the mother/housewife role does not exist in all societies.
- Feminism may be guilty of devaluing the mother/housewife role as a 'second-class' role. For many women, housework and childcare, like paid work, have real and positive meaning. Such work may be invested with meaning for women because it is 'work done for love' and it demonstrates their commitment to their families. Thus, boring, routine work may be transformed into satisfying, caring work.
- Feminists may underestimate the degree of power that women actually enjoy. Women are concerned about the amount of housework men do, but they are probably more concerned about whether men show enough gratitude or whether men listen to them, etc. The fact that many women divorce their husbands indicates that they have the power to leave a relationship if they are unhappy with it. Catherine Hakim (1996) suggests that feminists underestimate women's ability to make rational choices. It is not patriarchy or men that are responsible for the position of women in families. She argues that women choose to give more commitment to family and children, and consequently they have less commitment to work than men have.

Whatever your favoured perspective, it appears that the view that a 'new man' is emerging – sharing domestic tasks, engaging emotionally with women and showing interest in developing his fathering skills – is an overoptimistic picture of life in many conjugal relationships.

Check your understanding

1. What did Willmott and Young claim about conjugal roles in the 1970s?

2. What have recent surveys concluded about the distribution of domestic tasks between husbands and wives?

3. In what circumstances might wives acquire more power over decision-making in the home?

4. What do studies generally conclude about women's experience of the mother/housewife role?

5. What effect does the mother/housewife role have on women's job opportunities?

KEY TERMS

Conjugal relationship the relationship between married or cohabiting partners.

Dual burden refers to wives taking responsibility for the bulk of domestic tasks as well as holding down full-time jobs.

Egalitarian based on equality.

Privatized nuclear family a home-centred family that has little contact with extended kin or neighbours.

Segregated division of labour in the home a traditional sexual division of labour in which women take responsibility for housework and mothering, and men take responsibility for being the breadwinner and head of the household.

Symmetrical similar or corresponding.

research ideas

- Conduct a survey of parents using the list of tasks in the 'Getting you thinking' exercise on p. 80. An interesting variation is to ask parents separately whether they think they and their partner are doing enough around the home.

- Interview a selection of mothers in different social situations – e.g. full-time mothers, those who have full-time or part-time jobs, those who have children who have left home, etc. Try to construct an interview schedule that measures how they feel about the mother/housewife role.

web.task

Use the search engines of the following news websites which contain some excellent summaries of research conducted between 2002 and 2004 on housework. Often these pages contain good links to other news stories on the same or related subjects.

- www.bbc.co.uk/news
- www.dailymail.co.uk
- www.guardian.co.uk

Item A Working mothers

<< Working mothers spend more hours a week on housework than on their full-time job, a survey revealed yesterday. The survey of 543 parents of children under 18 was carried out for Legal & General. It found that full-time working mothers spend 56 hours a week on housework, part-time working mothers do 68 hours and housewives put in 76 hours, while fathers do only 31. Mothers spend around 14 hours a week cooking, compared with fathers' four hours, and 21 hours washing and ironing, compared with eight-and-a-half hours for men. Mothers clean for 13 hours a week, compared with their husbands' four hours, and women spend about an hour sewing compared with 10 minutes for men. Fathers do four hours a week of gardening, an hour more than mothers.>>

Guardian, 10 March 2000

Item B Why don't men do more housework?

Why does such a pronounced division of domestic labour persist? Women who continue to see housework and childcare as an essential part of being a 'good wife and mother' are more likely to be satisfied with an unequal domestic division of labour than women who reject such roles. Baxter and Western (1998) argue that women may deal with situations over which they have little control by defining them as 'satisfactory'. Men may have inflexible and demanding work schedules that make it difficult for them to meet family obligations. However, in criticism of this, men do tend to have greater control and freedom over how they spend their time outside of work. Women are often unable to 'clock on and off' from their caring responsibilities. The most plausible explanation for the persistence of an unequal domestic division of labour is that it suits men and so they resist change.

Adapted from Leonard, M. (2000) 'Back to the future: the domestic division of labour', *Sociology Review*, 10(2)

Item C Fatherhood

<< The report 'Fathers and Fatherhood in Britain' by Louie Burghes directly challenges the idea that men are abandoning a role in the family. The report found that, increasingly, fathers are taking an active involvement in the emotional side of child-rearing. Despite continuing to be the main earner in the family and working long hours, fathers are tending to spend more time with their children. The amount of time fathers spent with children was found to have increased fourfold over a generation between 1961 and 1995.>>

Denscombe, M. (1998) *Sociology Update*, Leicester: Olympus Books

---

1 Explain what is meant by the phrase 'unequal domestic division of labour' (Item B). (2 marks)

2 Identify two ways in which Item A confirms that a traditional sexual division of labour still exists in the modern family. (4 marks)

3 Identify three ways in which the mother–housewife role may limit women's employment opportunities. (9 marks)

4 Identify and explain two reasons why the sexual division of labour in the family continues to exist (Item B). (10 marks)

Exam practice

5 a Identify and explain two ways in which men are making a greater contribution to the domestic division of labour. (15 marks)

  b Outline and discuss the view that the relationship between men and women in families in the 21st century is characterized by inequality. (30 marks)

The dark side of family life

gettingyouthinking

> 'In 1877, a man could beat his wife with a stick – if it was no thicker than his thumb. *So what's changed?'*

Text used in a Women's Aid poster from the 1990s

Helpful and unhelpful explanations for male violence

- She should stick with it – he'll change
- I bet she drove him to it
- You gotta feel sorry for him
- They should have a cuddle and make up!
- She must have asked for it
- She came from a bad lot
- She's a loony!
- She can't leave him – what about the kids?
- She's a nagger
- At least he doesn't knock her about
- She was too demanding

A MORI poll conducted in 1994 found that 18% of men and 13% of women reported being victims of domestic violence by a partner. The poll estimated 3.5 million men have been or are currently victims of domestic violence.

The 2000 British Crime Survey reported that 10% of violent incidents reported by men were domestic compared with 40% reported by women. It suggests that one in four adult women suffer domestic violence at some stage.

1. With regard to domestic violence, what does the Women's Aid Federation think has changed since 1877?
2. Why do you think the statistics on each side of the photograph tell a different story about domestic violence?
3. Look at the 'Helpful and unhelpful explanations for male violence'. In what ways might society blame a woman for domestic violence perpetrated against her?

The family is traditionally seen as a loving institution in which people can find protection and safety. As we have already seen in Topic 1, p. 52, functionalists see the family as a system of positive relationships which meet the basic human need for love and intimacy. Marriage is seen as particularly important as a source of companionship, emotional gratification and psychological support. Overall, the nuclear family is seen as good for society and positive for the individuals who comprise it. Such thinking is echoed by New Right thinkers – familial ideology (see Topic 2, p. 57) portrays nuclear family life as the ideal to which we should all strive.

However, this rosy picture of nuclear families has come under sustained attack from two broad fronts. First, Marxist and feminist writers have suggested that modern nuclear families do not function for the good of society – rather it is suggested that such families benefit the powerful rather than the powerless, and men rather than women. Second, it is argued that, for some individuals, the family is a very dangerous place. For example, if we examine official criminal statistics, a very **dysfunctional** picture of the family emerges. Most recorded murder, assault and child abuse take place within the family unit.

Marxist views

Marxists generally see the nuclear family as serving the interests of the ruling class by promoting capitalist values. For example, nuclear families encourage their members to pursue the capitalist-friendly goals of materialism, consumerism, **individualism** and 'keeping up with the Joneses'. Marcuse (1964) claimed that working-class families are encouraged to pursue '**false needs**' in the form of the latest consumer goods and to judge themselves and others on the basis of their possessions. He noted that this served the interests of capitalism because it both stimulated the economy and distracted workers from the fact that capitalism exploited them.

Marxists argue that class inequality is also reproduced and maintained through primary socialization, which stresses to children that the main route to happiness and status lies in material possessions. In addition, the way in which nuclear families are traditionally organized (that is, with the male as the head of the household) encourages passive acceptance of authority, obedience, hierarchy and inequality – the very qualities the capitalist class would like the workforce to possess, because it makes them less likely to challenge ruling-class power and wealth.

Marxists argue that the capitalist ruling class has deliberately discouraged the working-class extended family because such families encourage mutual support and community. These qualities are seen as problematical because such shared experience may politicize people and help them become aware of wider economic and social inequalities. This, in turn, might lead to ruling-class power being challenged.

Marxist-feminist views

Marxist-feminists, too, are sceptical about the functionalist claim that the nuclear family meets the needs of society in general. They suggest that the nuclear family benefits the capitalist class at the expense of the working class. However, it also benefits men – even working-class men benefit from the domestic labour of working-class women.

Marxist-feminists agree that a traditional familial ideology exists and this benefits capitalism because the focus on women as mothers puts considerable cultural pressure on women to have children and take time out of the labour market to bring those children up. This not only benefits capitalism by ensuring the creation of a future workforce but also benefits men, because women do not compete on an equal playing field for jobs or promotion opportunities. State policies also support familial ideology and benefit men – for example, the focus on maternity leave and pay, and the lack of similar paternal rights, reinforce the view that children are mainly the responsibility of mothers rather than both parents (see Topic 2).

Radical feminist views

Radical feminists argue that both males and females are socialized into a set of ideas that largely confirm male power and superiority. In other words, familial ideology is patriarchal ideology (see pp. 58 and 82). The family is the main place for transmitting this ideology through the socialization of children into gender roles. Such socialization encourages the notion that the sexual division of labour is 'natural' and unchangeable. It is argued that women are also primarily portrayed by patriarchal familial ideology as either sexual objects, when single, or mothers/housewives, once married.

Radical feminists suggest, therefore, that the emergence of the modern nuclear family meets the needs of men rather than the needs of all members of society. The family is essentially a patriarchal institution which exploits and oppresses women.

The critique of feminism

However, these feminist criticisms of the family have been criticised for three main reasons:

1 Like functionalism, they have dated fairly badly, because they fail to account for recent economic and social changes, such as the feminization of the economy, the educational success of young females, women's use of divorce and many women's rejection of domestic labour as their unique responsibility.
2 They portray women as passively accepting their lot – the reality, however, is that women can adopt a range of active social identities today, many of which do not involve playing a secondary role to men. In other words, many young women are resisting traditional male definitions of what their role should be.
3 There is an implicit assumption that all male–female relationships involve male exploitation of women. However, the bulk of male–female relationships are probably based on mutual love and respect, rather than domination and subordination.

Violence in families

Both Marxist and radical feminists have drawn attention to the problem of domestic violence. This is usually defined as the power of men to control women by physical force, although Davidson (2003) argues that men are also victims of female domestic violence.

Domestic violence is estimated to be the most common type of violence in Britain, although it is notoriously difficult to measure and document, because it takes place behind closed doors, often without witnesses. It is also difficult to define. As Sclater (2001) notes, some behaviour, such as kicking and punching, is easily recognizable as violent, but behaviours such as threats, verbal abuse, psychological manipulation and sexual intimidation are less easy to categorize and may not be recognized by some men and women as domestic violence.

The **official statistics** tell us that violence by men against their female partners accounts for a third of all reported violence. Stanko's (2000) survey found that one incident of domestic violence is reported by women to the police every minute in the UK. Mirrlees-Black (1999), using data from the

British Crime Survey, found that women were more likely to suffer domestic violence than men – 70 per cent of reported domestic violence is violence by men against their female partners. It is estimated that one in four adult women will experience domestic violence at some stage in their lives. These figures are thought to be an underestimate because many women are reluctant to come forward, either because they love their partners and think they can change them or because they blame themselves in some way for the violence. Many women fail to report violence because they feel they may not be taken seriously or because they are afraid of the repercussions.

Some sociologists have reported increases in female violence on men, but it is estimated that this only constitutes at best 5 per cent of all domestic violence. Moreover, as Nazroo's research indicates (1999), wives often live in fear of men's potential domestic violence or threats, while husbands rarely feel frightened or intimidated by their wives' potential for violence. They are also less likely to be subjected to a repeated pattern of abusive behaviour.

Feminist approaches to domestic violence

Feminists suggest that domestic violence is a problem of patriarchy. In particular, research indicates that men's view that women have failed to be 'good' partners or mothers is often used to justify attacks or threats. These gendered expectations may be particularly reinforced if a woman goes out to work and earns more than her partner.

Liberal feminists suggest that domestic violence arises from two sources:

- *Different gender-role socialization* – Boys are socialized into 'masculine' values, which revolve around risk-taking behaviour, toughness, aggression, proving oneself, etc. Many boys and men are still brought up in traditional ways to believe that they should have economic and social power as breadwinners and heads of household. Socialization into femininity, on the other hand, involves learning to be passive and subordinate, which may be a reason why some women tolerate violence.

- *A* **'crisis in masculinity'** – Traditional masculinity is facing a number of significant cultural attacks. First, men's traditional source of identity, i.e. work, is no longer guaranteed. Many of the new jobs becoming available in the labour market are for women. Working women and unemployment have challenged men's status as head of the household and breadwinner. Second, women may be demanding more authority in the home and insisting that unemployed men play a greater domestic role – some men may see this domestic responsibility as threatening their masculinity. Violence may be an aspect of the anxiety men are feeling about their economic and domestic role, an attempt to re-exert and maintain power, status and control in a rapidly changing world.

Feminists also point out that society has, until fairly recently, condoned male violence in the home. Both the state and the criminal justice system have failed to take the problem seriously, although there are positive signs that the Labour government

focus on research

British Crime Survey
Computer-assisted interviewing

Questions on domestic violence are now part of British Crime Surveys which aim to gain an insight into the true amount of crime in society by talking to victims. The designers of this survey realized that face-to-face interviewing was an unreliable method because victims are often too embarrassed to talk about their experiences of violence. The 1996 survey was the first to use the alternative method of computer-assisted interviewing in which a lap-top is passed over to the respondent, who reads the questions on screen and enters their answers directly onto the computer without the interviewer being involved. It is thought that the confidentiality factor associated with this type of interviewing on such a sensitive issue has improved both the reliability of the method (producing on average a 97 per cent response rate) and the validity of the data collected, people are more willing to talk about their feelings and experiences.

1 Why is computer-assisted interviewing likely to produce more valid data than face-to-face interviewing or questionnaires?

2 Why is the subject of domestic violence always going to be problematical for sociologists to investigate?

and police forces are now willing to condemn and punish such violence. Whatever the explanation, some feminists would argue that as long as men have the capacity to commit such violence, there can never be equality within marriage.

Child abuse

A recent national study of parents found little agreement on what constitutes reasonable punishment for children. Ghate *et al.* (2003) found that many parents in their study, for example, agreed with smacking, but there was little consensus on when this form of discipline turned into abuse. For example, 9 per cent of parents reported using 'severe' physical punishment on children aged under 12 – this was defined as 'slapping around the face or head, hitting with a hard object, kicking and punching'. These parents did not see their behaviour as 'excessive'.

However, sociologists working within this field (who are few and far between) have identified four categories of abuse:

1 *Physical abuse* – Over the years, there have been a number of high-profile cases involving the death of children at the hands of their parents, stepparents or relatives, e.g. Maria Colwell, Jasmine Beckford and Victoria Climbie.
2 *Neglect* – As recently as 2004, five children were found in Sheffield in an advanced state of malnutrition. The NSPCC described it as the worst case found outside the developing world.
3 *Emotional abuse* – A number of sociologists and psychologists, such as Edmund Leach (1967), have suggested that intense family relationships can become emotionally abusive as parents use children as weapons against each other, or expect too much of their children and take out their disappointment in the form of verbal abuse ('You're no good to anyone – you're useless').
4 *Sexual abuse* – This type of abuse was generally not discussed until its 'rediscovery' in the mid-1980s after the organization Childline was set up by the television personality, Esther Rantzen.

Steve Taylor (1991) has drawn our attention to the problems in defining and therefore measuring child abuse. He is particularly critical of the research methods used to collect information about child abuse. Taylor points out that they are based either on official statistics collected by the Home Office or organizations such as Childline or from **victim surveys**. However, he argues these are flawed for several reasons:

- There is a disproportionate number of working-class or poor families in the official statistics. This is because these families tend to have regular contact either with social workers or with the police for reasons other than child abuse. Contact with these authorities means that any problems in terms of abuse are likely to be uncovered. However, Taylor suggests that they may not be representative of abusers in general, who may be just as common in well-to-do families, but are less likely to be detected because they have little or no contact with the authorities.
- Moral panics – sensationalist coverage of child abuse by tabloid newspapers – may distort the statistics by oversensitizing society to the 'problem'. For example, staff at photo developers have reported people to the police for being photographed in their baths with their children.
- Victims may not realize they are being abused or they may not be believed. For many years, children were not regarded as reliable witnesses.
- Some forms of abuse, such as those involving physical injury or neglect, may be more likely to arouse suspicion than sexual or emotional abuse, which are extremely difficult to detect from outward signs.

- What counts as child abuse changes over time and varies between cultures and subcultures. Surveys of child abuse only measure how that society or set of researchers define behaviour at that moment in time. For example, child prostitution was an inevitable social evil in Victorian England, whereas today, the smacking of children in Scotland is actually a criminal act.
- Response rates to victim surveys are very poor. There may be problems arising from the respondents' willingness and ability to recall things that happened long ago. Moreover, people generally do not share the same interpretations of what constitutes abuse in all its forms.

Taylor, therefore, suggests that the concept and measurement of child abuse is riddled with problems. However, despite this sociological dithering over definition and measurement, the facts are harsh. In March 2002, 59 700 children were in care in England, the most common reason being abuse or neglect (44 per cent).

Explanations of child abuse

The disease model of child abuse

Early theories of child abuse focused on physical abuse and neglect. Most of these theories can be grouped together to form a 'disease' model of abuse. This assumes that child abuse is the product of illness or abnormality – a defect in the character/personality of particular parents. This approach is paralleled by the media approach to child abuse, which suggests that abusers are 'monsters' or 'perverts'. The disease model, therefore, sees child abuse as the product of unusual family circumstances. Child abusers are viewed as unique individuals who may be 'spotted' before they do much harm by vigilant social workers. If children die, the media often blame social workers for not recognizing the symptoms of the problem.

The functionalist theory of child abuse

Functionalist thinking has touched upon the problem of child abuse through the work of Bell and Vogel (1968), who suggested that the dysfunction of child abuse may be a 'lesser evil' than the breakdown of the family! They seem, however, to be focusing on emotional child abuse, i.e. where the child is used as an emotional weapon by feuding parents. They suggest that such emotional abuse may be preferable to divorce, with all its attendant problems. Although this approach raises a number of ethical problems, there is some evidence that variations on this theme seems to have influenced social policy. Certainly up to the 1980s, many social services departments seem to have operated with the view that it was important to keep the family together, even if physical abuse was suspected. It was believed that constant surveillance of 'problem' or dysfunctional families would minimize the problem of physical child abuse and neglect. However, the well publicised deaths of two children in the 1980s – Maria Colwell and Jasmine Beckford – called into question the morality of this policy.

Structural theories of child abuse

Nigel Parton (1989) is critical of both the above models because they suggest that child abuse is only found in 'extreme' cases. Parton argues that child abuse is more routine than society likes to admit. He argues that both the disease model and the New Right model are problematical because they give the impression that only certain sections of society, such as one-parent families and those in poverty, are likely to commit child abuse. He argues that they fail to take into consideration that affluence may disguise child abuse. In other words, it may just as common in middle-class households.

Moreover, Parton argues that physical child abuse must be located in its social or structural context. He suggests that at the lower end of the socio-economic scale, it may be a reaction to the stress of poverty, unemployment, debts, marital problems, etc. Middle-class physical abuse of children may be due to similar structural problems, such as lack of job satisfaction, financial anxieties, fear of redundancy. It is important to note that Parton is not attempting to justify child abuse. He is simply stating that the structural circumstances in which people live can put great strain on personal relationships.

Feminist theories of child abuse

The feminist perspective focuses mainly on sexual child abuse, which it mainly sees as a symptom of male power in a patriarchal society. Feminists suggest that sexual abuse is the product of a society where males are socialized into seeing themselves as sexually dominant and into sexually objectifying females. It is argued that boys are encouraged by patriarchal ideology in the media 'to view their sexuality as something powerful that can be used to dominate, to compensate for feelings of powerlessness, or to express anger' (Saraga 1993). Feminists argue that these processes may be even more pronounced within the family, which they see as a patriarchal arena in which women are oppressed in a number of ways. The feminist analysis of sexual child abuse states that some men may sexually objectify both wife and daughters and view them as sexual property to be exploited.

Feminists do acknowledge that women, too, can abuse children, but point out that this is very rarely sexual abuse. They suggest that female physical abuse and neglect of children may be the product of their experience of childcare in a patriarchal society. Women's anger and frustration, expressed through physical abuse, may be the product of the fact that childcare in UK society is regarded as low-status work, is often carried out in isolation and may be stressful, boring and unrewarding. Men's physical abuse, on the other hand, is simply an expression of masculinity and of men's need, learnt through the socialization process, to be powerful and dominant.

KEY TERMS

Crisis in masculinity the idea that traditional roles for men are in decline and that men are not coping well with this change.

Dysfunctional not working well.

False needs the idea, promoted by advertising, that particular consumer goods are essential when, in reality, they are not.

Individualism the idea that you should put yourself first, i.e. before your community or society in general.

Official statistics statistics collected by government departments, e.g. on crime.

Victim surveys surveys, such as the British Crime Survey, which collect information about crimes from victims, who may or may not have reported the crime committed against them.

Check your understanding

1. In what ways does the nuclear family serve the interests of capitalism, according to Marxism?

2. How does the Marxist-feminist critique of the nuclear family differ from the Marxist critique?

3. How is patriarchy transmitted from generation to generation according to radical feminists?

4. Identify three criticisms of how feminists see family relationships.

5. What are the two sources of domestic violence, according to liberal feminists?

6. Identify two causes of emotional abuse in families.

7. Why is Melanie Phillips critical of the view that children are not encouraged to think critically in families?

research idea

- Research and prepare a report on the extent of domestic violence and recent policy responses to it, using the following websites:

  www.homeoffice.gov.uk/crime/domesticviolence/

  www.womensaid.org.uk

  www.metpolice.uk/enoughisenough

  www.womenandequalityunit.gov.uk/domestic_violence

web.task

Visit the National Society for the Prevention of Cruelty to Children website at www.nspcc.co.uk for their definition of child abuse and for the latest statistics.

exploring the dark side of family life

Item A Male and female violence

Both the quantitative and qualitative data presented supports the feminist position in two ways. First, they clearly demonstrate that male- and female-perpetrated marital violence are very different in both their meanings and consequences, and there does appear to be a link between much of men's use of violence in marriage and their (successful) attempts to dominate their partners. Second, it appears that almost all of the female violence described does not carry that sense of intrinsic 'wrongness' that Strauss attributes to all violence, because it is clearly not intimidating and nowhere near dangerous. Even if men are abused, they are far more likely to have access to the resources necessary to escape. For example, I am reminded of a man recently interviewed on British television who described how his wife seriously assaulted and injured him with a saucepan. However, despite this assault he was able to pick up his wallet and car keys and leave. How many women in such a situation would have the resources to be able to do the same, even if they did not have children to consider?

Adapted from Nazroo (1999)

Item B Patriarchy and the family

The radical feminist, Christine Delphy argues that the productive and reproductive activities that take place in the family are controlled by husbands, that women's labour in the family is performed free, and that the main beneficiaries of women's labour are husbands. This situation is sustained by marriage, which is for Delphy an arrangement whereby men gain control over women's labour. Moreover, in Delphy's view, women's entry into paid work does not bring women independence, for they continue to provide domestic services free and their wages from paid employment are likely to be controlled by their husbands. Women are thus in a common and oppressed class position, men are their oppressors, and marriage is the main instrument of their oppression. Delphy concludes that women should mobilize to overthrow this patriarchal system of production and reproduction.

Adapted from Robertson Elliot, F. (1986)
The Family: Change or Continuity?,
Basingstoke: MacMillan, p. 108

Item C Family abuse

The 'discovery' of family abuse in the 1970s stimulated a very large literature. Within the term 'family abuse' are included family practices involving emotional, psychological, sexual and physical abuse of family member(s) by other family member(s). A great deal of the literature has adopted simplistic notions of essentially powerful males abusing less powerful females and children. Whilst this was an important step, it was only one step in the right direction. What the largely feminist revelation of family abuse has suggested is that 'ordinary families' may contain abuse. Moreover, we should recognize that victims and perpetrators do not divide neatly into the abused and non-abused. Given the high levels of violence by young people, especially males, it seems likely that 'teenage thugs' are just as violent at home towards siblings and parents.

Adapted from Bernardes, J. (1997)
Family Studies: An Introduction,
London: Routledge, pp. 72–3

1 **Explain what is meant by the phrase 'patriarchal system' (Item B). (2 marks)**

2 **Identify two ways in which men may benefit from the traditional family. (4 marks)**

3 **Identify and explain three reasons why it is difficult to measure the extent of violence within the family. (9 marks)**

4 **Identify and explain two ways in which the 'meanings and consequences' of 'male- and female-perpetrated marital violence' may be different (Item A). (10 marks)**

Exam practice

5 a **Identify and explain two ways in which the family might be a negative experience for its members. (15 marks)**

b **Outline and discuss the view that the family is both exploitative and dangerous. (30 marks)**

Childhood

New Right view
Childhood is biological state ← → Children in need of protection

Childhood as social construction
- Aries
- Influence of class
- influence of gender
- Influence of ethnicity
- Global experience

Family decline

New Right arguments
- Nuclear family dying out
- Marriage in decline
- Cohabitation replacing marriage
- Divorce too easy

Critique of New Right
- Divorce sign of higher expectations
- Marriage still valued goal
- Cohabitation prelude to marriage
- Remarriage very popular

Why more divorce?
- Legal changes
- Less stigma
- Lesser evil than domestic violence
- Changes in women's attitudes
- Rejection of empty-shell marriage

Family diversity

Types of family in modern society
- One-parent
- Reconstituted
- Homosexual
- Lone persons

Ethnic diversity
- African-Caribbean lone parents
- Obligations to parents and extended kin
- Mixed marriages
- Arranged marriages

Government encourages women to go out to work

Benefit culture encourages single mothers and teenage pregnancy

Divorc Reform 1970

Fa Ho

More emphasis c fatherhoo today

Functionalists stress egalitarian marriage

Empirical studies conclude inequality is still the norm

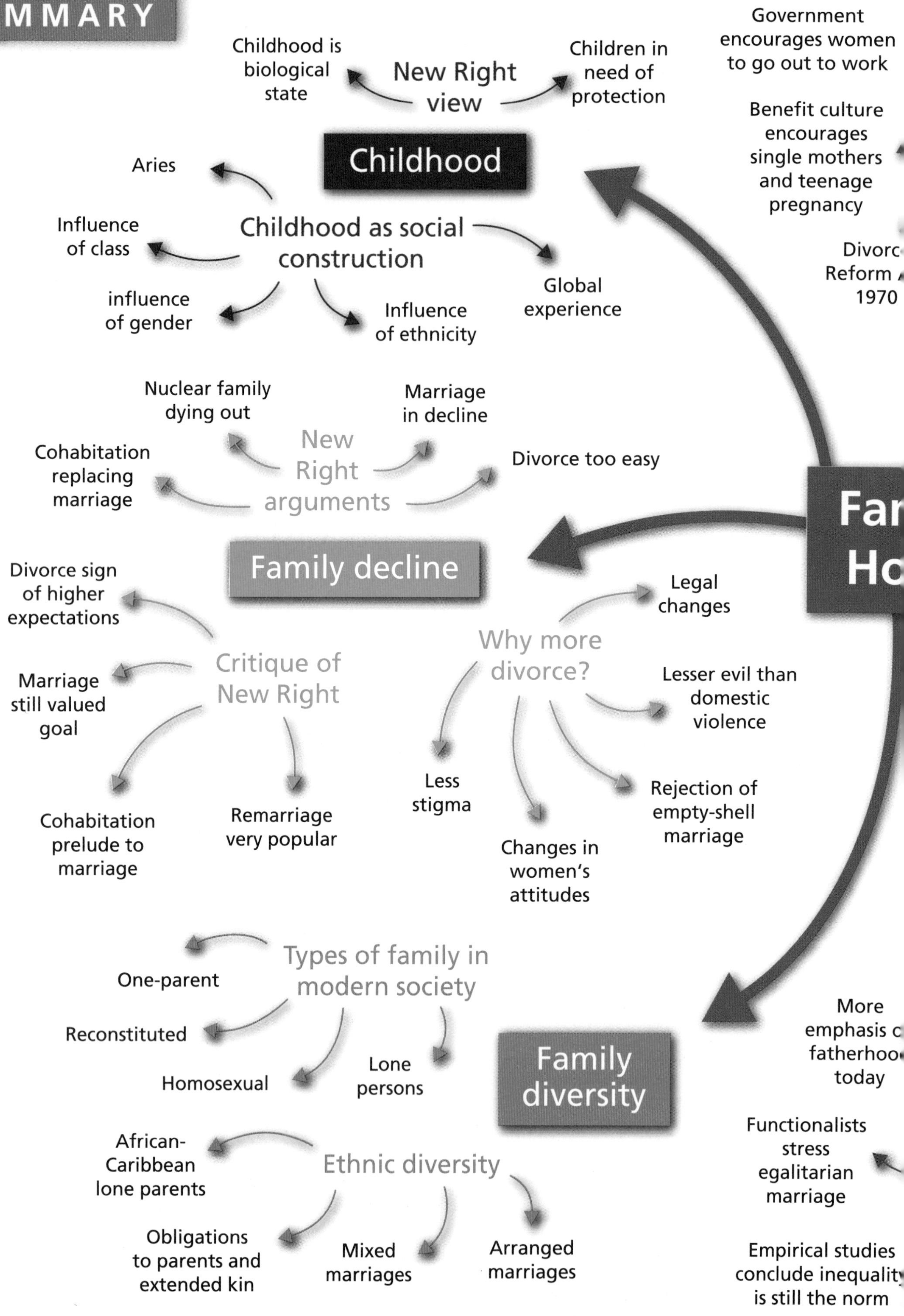

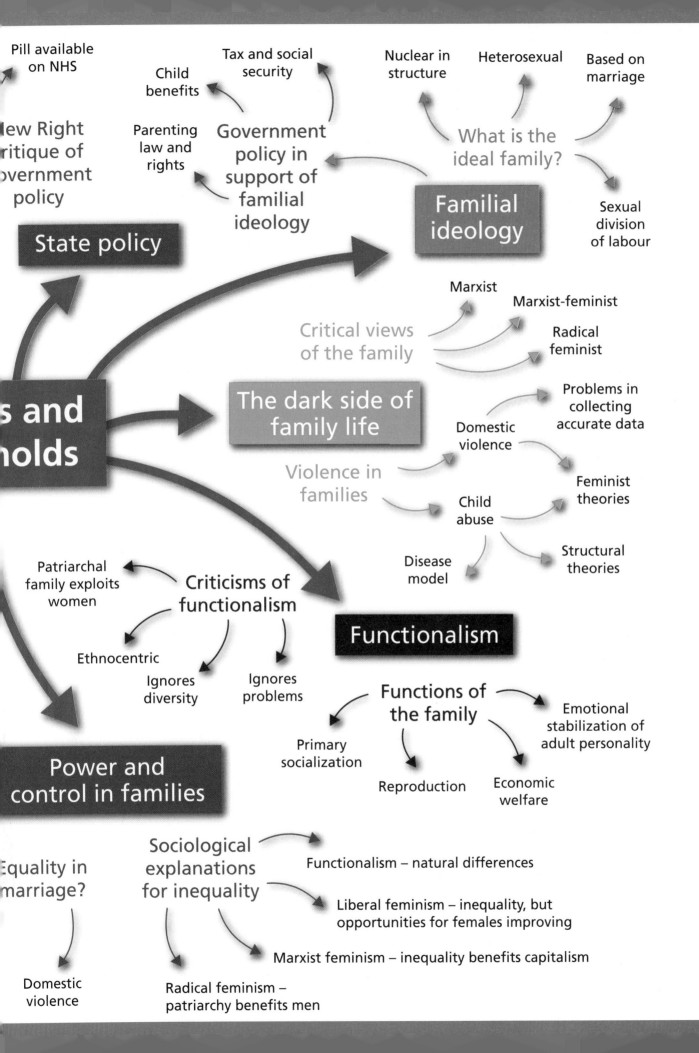

Pill available
on NHS

Child
benefits

Tax and social
security

Nuclear in
structure

Heterosexual

Based on
marriage

New Right
critique of
government
policy

Parenting
law and
rights

Government
policy in
support of
familial
ideology

What is the
ideal family?

Familial
ideology

State policy

Sexual
division
of labour

Critical views
of the family

Marxist

Marxist-feminist

Radical
feminist

s and
holds

The dark side of
family life

Problems in
collecting
accurate data

Violence in
families

Domestic
violence

Feminist
theories

Child
abuse

Patriarchal
family exploits
women

Criticisms of
functionalism

Disease
model

Structural
theories

Functionalism

Ethnocentric

Ignores
diversity

Ignores
problems

Functions of
the family

Emotional
stabilization of
adult personality

Power and
control in families

Primary
socialization

Reproduction

Economic
welfare

Equality in
marriage?

Sociological
explanations
for inequality

Functionalism – natural differences

Liberal feminism – inequality, but
opportunities for females improving

Marxist feminism – inequality benefits capitalism

Domestic
violence

Radical feminism –
patriarchy benefits men

DEFINING AND ILLUSTRATING WHAT WAS MEANT BY THE MASS MEDIA used to be very simple. 'Mass media' simply referred to channels through which messages are conveyed from a single point to a very large number of other points. A newspaper or a radio broadcast clearly fitted this criterion. The term was also used to describe media which the majority of the population consumed. This latter definition may still apply to newer media forms, but the initial definition may not. New terms have been developed to reflect the changing nature of communication:

● **Interpersonal media** involve messages which are conveyed between single points, such as mobile phones and email.
● **Interactive media** allow a limited degree of communication back from the individual points to the point of origin – examples include digital TV and the internet.
● **Network media** permit messages to be passed between individual, small or large numbers of points in any direction – examples include video conferencing and intranets.

The term 'new media' is used to describe media associated with information and communications technology (ICT). New generation mobile phones, PCs and the internet, computer games consoles and MP3 players are examples of **new media**. Because their consumption can be more individual, they tend to involve smaller audiences. The term 'narrowcasting' is sometimes used to distinguish the new media from the 'broadcasting' of more traditional mass media forms.

The relative ease of access and cheapness of the new media in the affluent nations of the world has enabled its use to spread at a truly dramatic rate. In the first quarter of 2004, 49 per cent of households in the UK (12.1 million) could access the internet from home, compared with just 13 per cent (3.2 million) in the same quarter of 1999.

It's not surprising that the study of the mass media has changed to reflect the changes described above. In this unit, we cover the key debates regarding the ownership, content and consumption of the mass media, and consider their changing patterns and influence.

OCR specification	topics	pages
Media institutions		
Trends in ownership and control of the mass media	These trends, as well as explanations of them, are covered in Topic 1.	96–101
The relationship between ownership, control and production: the influence of proprietors and professionals	Topic 1 includes discussion of the influence of proprietors and professionals. The role of media professionals is also considered in Topic 3.	96–101 106–111
Ownership and trends in production and consumption (e.g. internet, cable TV); the implications for state regulation	Topic 2 covers issues surrounding developments in terrestrial and satellite TV. It also focuses on the debate about public service broadcasting and the effects of deregulation.	102–105
Content and representation in the mass media		
The role of media professionals in constructing the news and moral panics	Topic 3 covers the construction of the 'news'. Moral panics are considered in relation to representations in Topic 7.	106–111 128–133
Media stereotypes; gender, ethnicity and class	Representations of gender are the focus of Topic 6, ethnicity and class in Topic 7.	122–127 128–133
Theories of media content, e.g. pluralism, Marxism and postmodernism	Topic 1 covers pluralist and Marxist theories while postmodernism is the focus of Topic 8.	96–101 134–137
The effects of the mass media		
The effects of the mass media on audiences	Media effects theories are covered in Topic 4.	112–115
Media effects and the implications for censorship	The debate about censorship and violence in the media is the focus of Topic 5.	116–121
Mass communication and globalization	Covered in Topic 8.	134–137

Mass media

TOPIC 1   Ownership and control of the mass media **96**

TOPIC 2   Public service broadcasting **102**

TOPIC 3   The content of the mass media: making the news **106**

TOPIC 4   How do the media affect people? **112**

TOPIC 5   Is there too much violence in the media? **116**

TOPIC 6   Gender and the media **122**

TOPIC 7   Media representations **128**

TOPIC 8   Postmodernism and the media **134**

UNIT SUMMARY **138**

Ownership and control of the mass media

gettingyou**thinking**

then ...

... now

1 How do the cartoons illustrate changing patterns of ownership of the mass media?

Sociological debates about media ownership have had to change as the nature of that ownership has itself changed. The press barons, film studio magnates and record company bosses of the past were immensely powerful men (and they were invariably men) in their own fields. Their modern-day equivalents can wield power across far wider aspects of human communication.

The low labour costs (increasingly overseas) and lower skill demands involved in assembling modern media hardware have significantly reduced its cost, making ownership ever more widespread. Virtually every household now has at least one TV, which the average person watches for 25 hours each week. Over 20 million people read a daily newspaper; almost 50 per cent of British households have access to a personal computer and it seems almost everyone has a mobile phone, with the latest models providing multimedia capabilities (BFI 2001).

The owners and controllers of the media have potentially more power than ever. In order to examine the possible extent of this power, we need to know a bit more about trends in ownership and consumption.

Trends in ownership

Technological convergence

The ability of digital technology to combine previously separate forms of communication, such as the internet and mobile phones (WAP), has encouraged media companies to merge. The even bigger companies that are created, such as Viacom/CBS and Time Warner/AOL, have more ability to develop a wider range of products and markets.

In the near future, it will be possible for all those who can afford it, or have access to the technology, to conduct all communications via a unified interactive receiver – capable of use as a telephone, computer, wordprocessor, radio, TV and video, from which many interactive commercial, retail, leisure and learning services will be accessible, including pay-per-view TV, video on demand, internet services and home shopping, banking and market research.

Media commentators now talk of **synergy**. This has two aspects:

1 Media products which were once distinct can now be produced as part of a package. For example, products based on the film *Spiderman 2* include a soundtrack CD, computer game, ring tones, action figures, clothing, and so on.

2 The ownership of these different aspects of production and consumption is increasingly in the hands of one massive organization. This means that a range of media products can be promoted together to a global market in a process known as **intracorporate self-promotion** or **cross promotion**.

Transnational ownership

Media companies are no longer restricted by national boundaries, particularly now that ownership rules have been relaxed in the world's richest nations. Media ownership is becoming a global concern with huge media producers combining forces as new technology breaks down old barriers between them. These giant media corporations buy up smaller companies all over the world. There is some concern that this could undermine smaller and more distinctive national and local production.

Media concentration

Media companies are bought and sold at an alarming rate. Over the last 20 or 30 years, the media have become more and more concentrated into fewer and fewer hands. If the American media were owned by separate individuals, there would be 25,000 owners. Instead, only five huge corporations own everything (Bagdikian 2000).

Vertical integration

This refers to the process whereby all the stages in the production, distribution and consumption of a media product are owned by one company. For example, a newspaper owner might own the sawmills that produce the wood, the paper mills that produce the paper, newspaper offices, printing facilities, lorries and newsagents. This cuts costs and increases profits. Vertical integration has been a common feature of some aspects of the media, such as film and the press, for some time. However, the process is spreading to other areas of the media.

Cross-media ownership

This occurs where more than one form of media – say radio and TV stations – come to be owned by the same company, creating what is known as a **media conglomerate**, such as NewsCorp.

Diversification

Many companies move into areas outside the media so that one part of the business can support another until things improve. Granada, for example, owns TV studios, TV and computer rental outlets and motorway service stations. Sony owns film studios and music recording studios although its main source of income is through electronic consumer goods.

Ownership and control

So do the owners of the media actually control its content? Is our information about the world distorted through the eyes of a few, very wealthy, media barons? The extent to which this occurs is an area of intense debate, which centres around the interconnected roles of media proprietors (owners), media professionals (those who work for them) and us, the consumers.

Sociologists have come up with three basic theories to explain the links between ownership and control.

Traditional Marxism

According to this view, the media help maintain the unfair and exploitative capitalist system by 'brainwashing' the public. Media owners are rich and successful people who benefit considerably from capitalism and therefore have a vested interest in ensuring its survival. Because of this, they directly manipulate media output so that it reflects their interests. The media encourage us to support the system and to hold values that enable capitalism to thrive. Marxists call these values capitalist **ideology**.

There is considerable evidence of direct manipulation. Rupert Murdoch, who owns and controls NewsCorp (a huge media corporation which owns, or has a controlling interest in the *Sun*, *The Times*, the *News of the World*, Sky and Fox, as well as over 1000 other media concerns in five continents), has been accused of manipulative practices on many occasions. He allegedly would not allow legitimate coverage of TV reports regarding the Chinese government's suppression of dissidents to be broadcast on Sky News because it might affect business negotiations between Murdoch's companies and the Chinese authorities.

Some commentators suggest that the political power of those who now own most of the media cannot be underestimated. It has been said that the likes of Murdoch and Bill Gates (head of Microsoft) have more global influence than the President of the USA. In the UK, Murdoch has even been dubbed 'the Phantom Prime Minister'.

Critics of the traditional Marxist view highlight the wide range of views which exist in society, which, they claim, would not exist if media manipulation was as powerful as is suggested. Also, they point out, it is impossible for owners to be directly involved in all aspects of their business to the extent that they have any real influence. Their businesses are too immense and they could not possibly find the time. In addition, media owners are not free to act totally as they wish because they are governed by a number of laws and other regulations – for example, the Official Secrets Act and libel laws. Their activities are also monitored by a number of **watchdogs**, such as the Press Complaints Commission.

Because of these criticisms, many Marxists do not agree with the traditional view. They still believe that the media reflect the views of the powerful, but they have a slightly different explanation.

Hegemonic Marxism

This view is similar to the traditional Marxist view in that it believes that the media provide the public with an ideology – views and information that support the capitalist system. However, this group of Marxists does not believe that the content of the media is under the direct control of the owners. Instead, they believe that this ideology is transmitted constantly via institutions such as schools and churches, as well as the media. Eventually, nobody even notices it – the views of the

focus on research

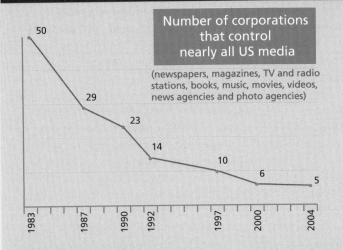

Number of corporations that control nearly all US media

(newspapers, magazines, TV and radio stations, books, music, movies, videos, news agencies and photo agencies)

Ben Bagdikian
The New Media Monopoly (2004)

In 1983, 50 corporations controlled the vast majority of all news media in the USA. At the time, Ben Bagdikian was called 'alarmist' for pointing this out in his book, *The Media Monopoly*. In his 4th edition, published in 1992, he wrote 'in the US, fewer than two dozen of these extraordinary creatures own and operate 90 per cent of the mass media' – controlling almost all of America's newspapers, magazines, TV and radio stations, books, records, movies, videos, news agencies and photo agencies. He predicted then that eventually this number would fall to about half a dozen companies. This was greeted with scepticism at the time. When the 6th edition of *The Media Monopoly* was published in 2000, the number had fallen to six. Since then, there have been more mergers and the scope has expanded to include new media like the internet market. More than 1 in 5 internet users in the USA and 1 in 7 in the UK now log in with AOL Time-Warner, the world's largest media corporation.

In 2004, Bagdikian's revised and expanded book, *The New Media Monopoly*, shows that only five huge corporations – Time Warner, Disney, Murdoch's News Corporation, Bertelsmann of Germany, and Viacom (formerly CBS) – now control most of the media industry in the USA. General Electric's NBC is a close sixth.

Media Reform Information Center 2004 (www.corporations.org/media/)

1 Why were Bagdikian's original claims perceived as 'alarmist'?

2 How do Bagdikian's claims illustrate the process of concentration of media ownership?

ruling class have become 'common sense'. Of course, it's always easier to dominate and control people if they are happy to go along with you, and the media have played a key role in bringing about this situation, which is known as **hegemony**.

But why, ask hegemonic Marxists, do the media present views that support the unfair capitalist system? Because of their background, journalists and broadcasters (who tend to be White, middle-class and male) usually subscribe to a 'middle-of-the-road', unthreatening set of viewpoints, which will, they believe, appeal to the majority of readers. Anyone outside the consensus is seen as an extremist. Alternative views are sometimes represented but usually ridiculed.

Agenda-setting

Meetings usually have an agenda – a list of issues to be discussed. The media provide an agenda for discussion in society. How often do you hear people talking about the latest news stories, scandals or soap operas? Hegemonic Marxists argue that the media present us with a fairly narrow agenda for discussion. We talk about the size and shape of a female singer, but don't often discuss the massive inequalities that exist in society. We are more likely to be outraged by the latest events in Albert Square than by the number of people living in poverty. In this way, the public are distracted from really important issues, and the workings of capitalist society are never questioned because its worst points are rarely presented.

But, you may ask, don't we get different political views presented to us so that we can make real choices about how society should be run? In the run-up to the 1997 General Election, only two national newspapers supported the Labour Party, and six supported the Conservatives (although the *Express* and *Sun* switched their allegiance to Labour in the final weeks). People frequently argue that, since New Labour emerged, there has, in any case, been very little difference between the parties, so the agenda for discussion has narrowed even further.

Both of the positions we have looked at argue that the media support the capitalist system by controlling – consciously (traditional Marxism) or unconsciously (hegemonic Marxism) – media output so that it benefits those in power.

The third and final position (**pluralism**) is the one that, unsurprisingly, the media themselves tend to support.

Pluralism

From a pluralist viewpoint, the media are seen as offering a wide selection of the views of the various groups in society. Modern society is democratic and people have freedom of choice. If they did not like the output of the media, they would not buy it or watch it. The media have to give the public what they want – otherwise they would go out of business.

Pluralists raise a number of points in support of their view:

- The media are not all-powerful – governments have tried at various times to legislate against media owners having too much power. For example, **vertical integration** has been considered unfair for two reasons: first, it doesn't allow competition to survive because smaller companies can't compete with the cheaper costs of the conglomerates; and second, it reduces customer choice, because one person's or group's views or products can become too dominant.

- In the USA, the huge film studios have been prevented from owning film production, film distribution and cinemas at the same time. Many countries have **cross-media ownership** rules preventing companies from owning more than one media form in the same area.

- In the UK, however, since the Broadcasting Act of 1996, the rules have been relaxed regarding media and cross-media ownership and Broadcasters are less constrained by rules regarding content. The Communications Act of 2003 has weakened ownership restrictions further, allowing major TV and radio broadcasters to expand their share of the UK media market and this includes non-EU companies or individuals whose potential share was much more restricted previously. Similar restrictions on ownership have been relaxed in the USA and Europe.

The power of the media owner
Rupert Murdoch and News Corporation

Sometimes it is not necessary for powerful media owners to influence the content of the media directly, in order to put their own views across. In the passage below, Richard Searby, Australian chairman of News Corporation (see p. 118), discusses the influence of its owner, Rupert Murdoch.

<< *The management style of News Corporation is one of extreme devolution punctuated by periods of episodic autocracy. Most company boards meet to take decisions. Ours meets to ratify Rupert's. For much of the time, you don't hear from Rupert. Then, all of a sudden, he descends like a thunderbolt from hell to slash and burn all before him. Since nobody is ever sure when the next autocratic intervention will take place (or on what subject), they live in fear of it and try to second guess what he would want, even in the most unimportant of matters. It is a clever way of keeping his executives off balance: they live in a perpetual state of insecurity. Everybody in the company is obsessed with him, he is the main topic of conversation, even among executives who have not heard from him for months; everybody is desperate for any titbit of information about him, especially if it sheds light on what his latest thoughts and movements are.* >>

Richard Searby quoted in Neill, A. (1996) *Full Disclosure*, Basingstoke: Macmillan

1 How does the quotation above provide an example of self-censorship?

- Pluralists also point out that journalists and editors often refuse to go along with what their owners want of them.
- Finally, the media have a strong tradition of **investigative journalism** which has often targeted those in power. For example, two reporters on the Washington Post forced the then President of the USA – Richard Nixon – to stand down after they exposed him for authorizing the bugging of his opponents' offices at Watergate in 1972.

Whether direct manipulation goes on or not, pluralists claim that there is no proof that audiences passively accept what they are fed. Audiences are selective and, at times, critical. To suggest that they can be manipulated is to fail to recognize the diversity of the audience or the ways in which they use the media. This will be considered more fully in later topics.

Check your understanding

1 How have recent developments in media increased the power of media owners?

2 How does traditional Marxism view the influence of media owners on media output?

3 Give an example of the direct manipulation of media output by a media proprietor.

4 How would hegemonic Marxists challenge the view that the media present us with a wide range of opinion?

5 What are the differences between traditional Marxism and hegemonic Marxism?

6 Give examples of three arguments put forward by pluralists to show that the media do not just represent the views of the powerful but cater for everyone in society. To what extent might these views be seen to be out of date?

research ideas

- Conduct a small-scale social survey to discover to what extent people of different ages and/or ethnic and/or class backgrounds believe that the content of the media reflects the wide variety of views present in British society.

web.task

Use the internet to investigate the extent of product synergy in the marketing of the *Harry Potter* stories.

KEY TERMS

Agenda-setting controlling what issues come to public attention.

Cross-media ownership occurs where different types of media – e.g. radio and TV stations – are owned by the same company.

Cross promotion (or **intra-corporate self-promotion**) an aspect of synergy where different areas of a company's business promote other areas owned by the same company.

Diversification the practice of spreading risk by moving into new, unrelated areas of business.

Hegemony domination by consent (used to describe the way in which the ruling class project their view of the world so that it becomes the consensus view).

Ideology the norms and values adopted by a particular group or society.

Investigative journalism journalism that aims to expose the misdeeds of the powerful.

Media concentration the result of smaller media companies merging, or being bought up by larger companies, to form a small number of very large companies.

Media conglomerate a company that owns various types of media.

New Media digital media offering images, text and sounds plus the capability for the user to interact, such as the internet, 3G mobile phones and digital television.

Pluralism a theory that society is made up of many different groups, all having more or less equal power.

Synergy a mutually advantageous combination of distinct elements, where the working together of two or more things produces an effect greater than the sum of their individual effects.

Technological convergence the tendency for once diverse media forms to combine as a result of digital technology.

Vertical integration owning all the stages in the production, distribution and consumption of a product.

Watchdog an organization created to keep a check on powerful businesses.

Item A Public hygiene and the media

<< These cost accountants or their near clones are employed by new kinds of media owners who try to gobble up everything in their path. We must protect ourselves and our democracy, first by properly exercising the cross-ownership provisions currently in place, and then by erecting further checks and balances against dangerous concentrations of the media power which plays such a large part in our lives. No individual or company should be allowed to own more than one daily, one evening and one weekly newspaper. No newspaper should be allowed to own a television station and vice versa.

A simple act of public hygiene, containing abuse, widening choice and maybe even returning broadcasting to its makers.>>

Dennis Potter: excerpt from the James MacTaggart Memorial Lecture, Edinburgh Film Festival, 1993, reproduced in Potter, D. (1994), *Seeing the Blossom: Two interviews and a lecture*, London: Faber & Faber

Item B All for one

<< When AOL took over Time Warner, it also took over: Warner Brothers Pictures, Morgan Creek, New Regency, Warner Brothers Animation, a partial stake in Savoy Pictures, Little Browne & Co., Bullfinch, Back Bay, Time-Life Books, Oxmoor House, Sunset Books, Warner Books, the Book-of-the-Month Club, Warner/Chappell Music, Atlantic Records, Warner Audio Books, Elektra, Warner Brothers Records, Time-Life Music, Columbia House, a 40-per-cent stake in Seattle's Sub-Pop records, *Time Magazine, Fortune, Life, Sports Illustrated, Vibe, People, Entertainment Weekly, Money, In Style, Martha Stewart Living, Sunset, Asia Week, Parenting,* Weight Watchers, *Cooking Light,* DC Comics, 49 per cent of the Six Flags theme parks, Movie World and Warner Brothers parks, HBO, Cinemax, Warner Brothers Television, partial ownership of Comedy Central, E!, Black Entertainment Television, Court TV, the Sega channel, the Home Shopping Network, Turner Broadcasting, the Atlanta Braves and Atlanta Hawks, World Championship Wrestling, Hanna-Barbera Cartoons, New Line Cinema, Fine Line Cinema, Turner Classic Movies, Turner Pictures, Castle Rock productions, CNN, CNN Headline News, CNN International, CNN/SI, CNN Airport Network, CNNfi, CNN radio, TNT, WTBS, and the Cartoon Network.

The situation is not substantially different at Disney, Viacom, General Electric, or at Murdoch's News Corporation, which is credited with having created the first global media network by investing in both software (movies, TV shows, sports franchises, publishing) and the distribution platforms (the Fox network, cable television and satellite systems) that disseminate the software … >>

Alterman, E. (2002) *What Liberal Media? The truth about bias and the news,* New York: Basic Books

1 Explain what is meant by 'cross ownership' in the context of the mass media (Item A). (2 marks)

2 Identify two ways in which the 'dangerous concentrations of media power' can be checked, according to Potter (Item A). (4 marks)

3 Identify and explain three criticisms of the view that media owners are the main influence upon media output. (9 marks)

4 Identify and explain two ways in which traditional Marxists might criticize cross-media ownership. (10 marks)

Exam practice

5 a Identify and explain two changes in the nature of media ownership over the last 30 years. (15 marks)

b Outline and discuss the view that media owners have little control over media output. (30 marks)

Public service broadcasting

getting you thinking

Annual % share of viewing 1991 to 2003

Year	BBC1	BBC2	ITV (incGMTV)	CH4	CH5	OTHERS (Cable/ Sat/RTE)
1991	34	10	42	10	-	4
1992	34	10	41	10	-	5
1993	33	10	40	11	-	6
1994	32	11	39	11	-	7
1995	32	11	37	11	-	9
1996	33.5	11.5	35.1	10.7	-	10.1
1997	30.8	11.6	32.9	10.6	2.3	11.8
1998	29.5	11.3	31.7	10.3	4.3	12.9
1999	28.4	10.8	31.2	10.3	5.4	14.0
2000	27.2	10.8	29.3	10.5	5.7	16.6
2001	26.9	11.1	26.7	10.0	5.8	19.6
2002	26.2	11.4	24.1	10.0	6.3	22.1
2003	25.6	11.0	23.7	9.6	6.5	23.6

NB: Shares before 1996 have been rounded to nearest whole number

Source: Broadcaster's Audience Research Board, 2003

Qualities of public service broadcasting

- *Quality* – cultural policy (including access to the arts, promotion of domestic and independent film industry) and protection of vulnerable programme types (news, children's programmes, high-cost drama).
- *Accuracy and impartiality* – reliable and credible news, education and information for the public as a contribution to the national political debate.
- *Plurality and diversity* – the allocation of scarce public resources to as wide a range of operators as possible and the promotion of diverse types of content to cater to all segments of society.
- *Access* – universal, affordable access to core services which provide high-quality, accurate news and diverse content.
- *Taste and decency* – consumer protection from an influential medium, including the protection of children from harmful material.

Thomas, A. (1999) *Regulation of Broadcasting in the Digital Age*, Department for Culture, Media and Sport

1 Summarize the trends in the table. What do they tell us about changing patterns in broadcasting?

2 Read the list of qualities of public service broadcasting. To what extent do you think the BBC's current programming meets these requirements. Give examples.

A key strand in the pluralist argument has been that, unlike countries such as the USA, the British media – and broadcasting in particular – are more highly regulated and hence diverse because they are in part publicly owned and controlled.

Public versus private ownership

In the UK, **commercial television** channels, such as ITV1 and Channel 5, are funded mainly through advertising, while **satellite TV** (e.g. Sky/BsB) receives subscriptions from its viewers in addition to advertising revenue. Both types of television, therefore, are concerned with their appeal to advertisers and with profit. However, in the UK, the BBC is a state-owned TV and radio broadcaster. It is controlled by a board of governors appointed by the Home Secretary. The BBC receives its funding from the government via a broadcasting tax known as the **licence fee**. The BBC must, however, satisfy the government that it is providing the service people want in order for this licence fee to be approved. In order to do this, it has to compete with commercial television for viewers/listeners.

All broadcasters have some formal requirements imposed upon them by their **regulators**. There is now a single powerful regulator – the Office for Communications – OFCOM – which has replaced the ITC, Radio Authority, Oftel, Broadcasting Standards Commission and the Radiocommunications Agency.

Public service broadcasting

The BBC and Channel 4 have a much greater obligation to their viewers as particular types of broadcasters. The BBC is expected to provide services of a high standard that inform, educate and entertain. It should offer a wide range of subject matter for local and national audiences, as well as ensuring accuracy and impartiality in its news programming and in coverage of controversial subjects. Channel 4, although funded through advertising, has a remit which centres on complementing ITV through the provision of distinctive output, and is required to show innovation and experiment in the form and content of its programmes.

Some have criticized the values promoted by **public service broadcasting** (PSB) as middle class and patronizing. Many working-class viewers have, until recently, preferred commercial TV since its launch in 1954.

Deregulation

The ITV companies who compete for the right to broadcast in a particular area (Carlton, Granada, Meridian, Grampian, etc.), although regulated and expected to have some PSB remit, have always had greater freedom to pursue profit and mass audiences. However, since the Broadcasting Act was revised in 1990 and 1996, the distinction between state-run PSB and commercial TV has become blurred. Both have had fewer restrictions imposed upon them and, whilst advertising is still not allowed on the BBC, they too have been freer to become more commercial.

The 2003 Communications Act has built upon the **deregulation** introduced by earlier legislation. It has relaxed both ownership and content rules, encouraging greater competition and allowing the free market to play a bigger role in determining content. The 2003 Act, however, was also concerned to preserve PSB in the wake of criticism that it seemed to be under threat.

Many argue that the intentions of the 2003 Act, in part to support all terrestrial broadcasters to deliver PSB, are too little, too late and that public service broadcasting no longer exists. They claim that the public service broadcasters are '**dumbing down**', that BBC1 and C4 increasingly imitate their commercial competitors and are failing in their duty to maintain quality standards for the industry (Liddiment 2001). As the table on the left shows, over the last 15 years an increasingly influential commercial sector has been cable and satellite TV.

Terrestrial TV broadcasters like the BBC and ITV were once the dominant force in Broadcasting. Now they are in direct competition with satellite and cable TV companies, such as

Rupert Murdoch's BSkyB Television, which began to emerge in the late 1980s. Such companies are funded by both advertising and subscriptions, and have the technology to act as global broadcasters. Less bound by regulations over content, they are able to concentrate mainly on popular programming. Therefore, with such large, sometimes **niche audiences** (particular groups of viewers such as 16- to 24-year-old MTV viewers) for certain channels, they can attract massive advertising revenue and so have the capacity to attract viewers away from the terrestrial channels. This increased competition has created a trend towards commercialization for all TV output, giving apparently greater choice, with more and more channels. Terrestrial TV producers have also diversified into cable, satellite and digital TV themselves – for example, with BBC3 and 4, and ITV2. They have also gone into partnership with commercial companies to set up new channels such as UK Gold.

More choice or more of the same?

Since deregulation, there has been the scope for terrestrial TV to bow to pressure to become more commercially successful, in order to compete more effectively with cable and satellite TV. This has meant that quality has been affected as the lowest common denominator among the viewing public has become the main concern.

The aim is to satisfy a mass culture. We don't have more choice, just more of the same thing. There are more repeats and cheap imports, and 50 per cent fewer documentaries, many of which are 'docusoaps' (fly-on-the-wall documentaries such as *Airport* and *Ibiza Uncovered*). There has been a growth of 'infotainment', a mix of news and light entertainment which focuses on personalities and lifestyles of the rich and famous rather than social and political issues. The lifestyles of ordinary people feature more and more with cheap makeover shows of house and garden. Cheap reality TV programmes which make personalities out of unknowns have replaced quality entertainment involving real (and expensive) personalities with genuine talent. Advertising has increased in diversity and influence, with more TV sponsorship and product placement (visible brand identity promoted in mainstream programmes) by advertisers and manufacturers.

On the other hand, popular TV appeals to more people. Who is to say what constitutes good television? The perceived distinction between low culture (or popular culture of the masses) and high culture of the intellectual elite is snobbish and value laden. Popular culture should have equal validity, and may have many equally authentic forms as societies become more fragmented. Besides, PSB is still accessible to everyone, while commercial TV is increasingly becoming a digitized and expensive option for those who can afford it. However, Jackson (2000, 2001) argues that wider social and cultural changes have made the provision of public service broadcasting less necessary, including the view that the concept of minorities is no longer socially meaningful. He concludes that the values of PSB have declining relevance for British society. In any case, as

Cathy Come Home *was an influential TV play about homelessness, first shown in the 1960s.*

Steve Barnett & Emily Weymour
Disneyfication

<<A further critique of television which caught the media's attention in 1999 was the report produced by Steve Barnett and Emily Weymour on behalf of the Campaign for Quality Television. The report entitled 'A Shrinking Iceberg Travelling South: Changing Trends in British Television', compared schedules in 1978, 1988 and 1998, and pointed to a rise in 'quick-fix' TV which is intended to increase ratings. To justify his claim of the 'disneyfication' of British television, Barnett pointed to the fact that the number of single dramas has halved over the last 20 years, while soap operas have increased fivefold, as programmers, pressured to respond to the ratings, are obliged to schedule drama likely to bring the viewers back repeatedly. Barnett quoted from interviews with 30 anonymous programme makers and commissioning editors. These showed, he claimed, increasing disillusionment and a belief that the major ground-breaking dramas tackling social issues, such as *Cathy Come Home,* would not now be funded, as they would be perceived as too risky in the ratings war.

Ultimately, all the problems – centralization, homogeneity, the focus-group mentality – come down to money and ratings in a world of deregulated competition and diminishing budgets. Producers throughout the industry are now expected to perform according to ratings targets and on budgets which are progressively being cut (sometimes even in the middle of filming). In the BBC, the result is a growing culture of self-censorship: 'Every year, they keep cutting. We feel we've become so budget-oriented that we've clipped our own wings – we don't even suggest ideas because we think it will be too expensive'.>>

The Guardian, 25 October 1999

1 Why might ground-breaking dramas which tackle social issues be considered too risky in the ratings war?

2 What sorts of ideas may not be suggested because they may be thought too expensive?

---

the BBC, its main provider, secures a progressively dwindling viewer base, a licence fee for all may become unjustifiable and PSB may cease to have a coherent provider in the future.

One aspect of PSB which has attracted attention in the wake of increasing competition and commercialization is television news, which is discussed in the next topic.

Check your understanding

1 How does the BBC secure its funding? What might happen if programme ratings are poor?

2 How would you define PSB?

3 Why has the BBC and Channel 4 failed to attract working-class viewers?

4 What impact has deregulation allegedly had on terrestrial television?

5 How does the 2003 Communications Act attempt to support PSB?

6 Why is satellite TV so profitable?

7 Give four criticisms levelled against contemporary TV.

8 How might terrestrial TV broadcasters address these criticisms?

KEY TERMS

Commercial television ITV stations that raise revenues from advertising. TV output that has high ratings.

Deregulation the removal of restrictions on the ownership and content of the media.

'Dumbing down' the accusation that TV output is becoming simpler and easier for all to understand in the quest for ratings.

Licence fee a tax on radio and television paid to the government and then passed on to the BBC provided they fulfil their PSB remit.

Niche audiences special cohorts of viewers with a shared interest, e.g. in sport or music, who are willing to pay for specialist channels.

Public service broadcasting output which is accessible to all, serves a diverse audience, contains quality programming and which educates and informs as well as entertains.

Regulators for broadcasting one body – OFCOM – monitors broadcasting to ensure that its regulations are enforced.

Satellite TV similar to other commercial broadcasters, but also able to raise revenue from subscriptions

Terrestrial TV the main channels still broadcasting in analogue that can be received in principle by everyone. These include BBC 1 and 2, ITV1, Channel 4 and Channel 5 as well as S4C in Wales.

Item A Children and television

<< Whilst the annual percentage share of viewing figures shows a decline nationally in terrestrial TV's audience share against a growth in cable/satellite viewing, the figures mask age-related consumption patterns, especially within 'cable-connected' homes, where cable stations accounted for 54 per cent of total viewing by youngsters under 15 and nearly 64 per cent among those aged under 9. This may be due to the fact that distinctive youth genres are available in constant supply through channels such as Nickelodeon and Cartoon Network. Also, the mode of presentation and material outside the regular programmes, e.g. advertising, competitions, graphics and use of comedy, has more appeal. Children's channels are becoming highly lucrative for the broadcasters. As an increasingly affluent consumer group, children are being targeted more and more by advertisers willing to pay the huge rates demanded for advertising time.>>

Adapted from: 'Continental Research for the ITC', *The Guardian*, 23 December 1995

Item B Accessibility

<< The problem for the programme makers, with the ratings-chasers on their backs, is that they dare not risk offering any fare that may be too challenging. That means making programmes that are 'accessible'. What is meant by 'accessible' is anything that we can relate to from experience in our own lives, the patronizing assumption being that anything outside our experience will be a turn-off. So out goes much of the difficult stuff and in comes the story to which we can 'relate'. Or the private lives of the famous. Or crime. Or consumer affairs. Or something funny or whimsical. Anything to do with sex, jealousy, conflict, money, power, suffering, anything from which you can elicit an emotional response, is deemed to be 'accessible'. This is where populist television news takes us. >>

Adapted from J. Humphrys, *The Guardian*, 30 August 1999

1 Explain in your own words what is meant by 'terrestrial TV' (Item A). (2 marks)

2 Suggest two reasons why cable channels may be more popular than terrestrial channels among the young (Item A). (4 marks)

3 Identify and explain three problems terrestrial broadcasters face in attempting to compete with satellite TV. (9 marks)

4 Identify and explain two ways in which programmes are criticized for becoming supposedly more 'accessible', according to Item B. (10 marks)

Exam practice

5 a Identify and explain two ways in which the consumption of the mass media has changed in the last decade. (15 marks)

   b Outline and discuss the view that the relaxation of controls upon broadcasting in the contemporary UK have had a negative impact upon content. (30 marks)

research ideas

● Conduct a survey of TV viewers. Try to find out their favourite programmes. Use a quota sample so that you can see whether there are differences in preferences according to age. Conduct interviews with those choosing PSB-type programmes. Ask whether they feel that TV in general and the BBC in particular has suffered from 'dumbing down'.

web.task

Search the BBCs website (www.bbc.co.uk) for information about its purpose, values, charter and regulation. To what extent do these reflect the values of public service broadcasting?

The content of the mass media: making the news

gettingyouthinking

1 Which aspects of the above screen shots suggest that the news:

- is 'up to the minute'?
- comes from around the world?
- employs the latest technology?

2 Think of the music that introduces news broadcasts. What impression does it give?

News: a 'window on the world'?

For most of us, TV news is the most important source of information about what is going on outside our day-to-day experiences. We rely on TV news to help us make sense of a confusing world. As you probably worked out from the questions above, news broadcasts are carefully managed to give an impression of seriousness and credibility. But do they really represent a 'window on the world'? How do TV journalists and editors decide which of the millions of events that occur in the world on any day will become 'news'?

Critics of the media have pointed out that the news is most certainly not a 'window on the world'. Instead, they argue that it is a manufactured and manipulated product involving a high degree of selectivity and bias. What causes this? Three important elements are:

1 institutional factors both inside and outside the newsrooms (such as issues of time and money)
2 the culture of news production and journalism (how news professionals think and operate)
3 the ideological influences on the media (the cause and nature of bias).

Institutional factors

The 'news diary'

Rather than being a spontaneous response to world events, many news reports are planned well in advance. Many newspapers and TV news producers purchase news items from press agencies (companies who sell brief reports of world or national news 24 hours per day). They also receive press releases from pressure groups, government agencies, private companies and individuals, all of whom wish to publicize their activities.

Schlesinger (1978) highlighted the influence of the **news diary**. This is a record of forthcoming social, political and economic events which enables journalists and broadcasters to plan their coverage, and select and book relevant 'experts'. It also allows them to make practical arrangements – which could include anything from liaising with local authorities and the police over outside broadcasts, or organizing satellite link-ups, to sorting out the catering for location staff. Such events might include the Chancellor of the Exchequer's speech on budget day, royal birthdays, the release of a notorious prisoner or the arrival of a famous entertainment personality.

Financial costs

Financial considerations can also influence the news. Sometimes, so much has been spent on covering a world event (sending camera crews, flights, accommodation for journalists, pre-booked satellite links, etc.) that it will continue to get reported on even though very little that is new has happened.

The point at which the news company's financial year-end falls can also affect how, and even whether, costly news items are covered. This is why the BBC was able to cover the pro-democracy demonstrations in Tiananmen square in China, which provided some of the most memorable footage in recent times, and yet was unable, unlike ITN, to give full coverage of the unification of Germany and the demolition of the Berlin wall which occurred later that same year.

Competition

This highlights another factor: competition. News producers are desperate to be the first to 'break the news'. This can cause them to cut corners – for example, accepting 'evidence' from sources without properly checking it, or relying on official sources because they are more easily accessed. This can lead to a biased view in favour of the official side of the argument (see the work of the Glasgow University Media Group, pp. 109–10).

Time or space available

News items have to be selected from the thousands that flood into the newsroom every day, and they then need to be fashioned into a coherent and recognizable product. The average news bulletin contains 15 items which must take exactly the same amount of time to put across each day. Similarly, a newspaper has a fixed amount of space for each news category. Sometimes stories are included or excluded merely because they fit or don't fit the time or space available.

Audience

The time of a news broadcast (and who is perceived to be watching), or the readership profile of a paper, will also influence the selection of news. A lunchtime broadcast is more likely to be viewed by women, and so an item relating to the supermarket price war might receive more coverage than it would in a late-evening news bulletin.

The culture of news production and journalism

News values

Various studies have attempted to identify what makes an item 'newsworthy' for journalists. Galtung and Ruge (1973) identified several key **news values** that might be used to determine the 'newsworthiness' of events. These included:

- extraordinariness: events that are considered 'out of the ordinary'
- events that concern important or elite persons or countries
- events that can be personalized to point up the essentially human characteristics of sadness, humour, sentimentality and so on
- events that are dramatic, clear and negative in their consequences.

Different media have different ways of prioritizing news values. TV news would see picture values as an important consideration, whilst the tabloid press would tend to prioritize stories based on 'human interest' or famous personalities.

Gatekeeping

Journalists thus make decisions about what is and what is not 'newsworthy'. Their work has been referred to as **gatekeeping**:

Figure 3.1 Gatekeeping and news values

Posh & Becks to split?
Soap star attacked
Share prices crash
Mother of 10 wins lottery
England lose again
New figures show gap between rich aap between rich
9/11 hero in wife swap shock
Tragedy of tsunami orphans
Is it extraordinary? Is it a human interest story? Is it about a celebrity or rich country? Is it dramatic?

they only let a tiny minority of events through the 'gate' to the next stage. Gatekeeping is, however, a very hierarchical process, with increasingly powerful gatekeepers at each stage. Only a small proportion of news items passed upwards at stage one make it into the final news product. Further structuring occurs in the final stages when running order or page positions are decided.

Narrativization

A narrative is a story. We are socialized into a culture in which storytelling has an important role. Stories tend to have a beginning, a middle and an end, and we expect this kind of narrative structure. News broadcasts often follow a format in which normality is disturbed by individuals or groups (often 'baddies') who then cause a problem or create a mystery of some sort. Eventually, the intervention of other causal agents (such as brave or heroic figures) ends the story when normality is restored. However, real events do not necessarily follow this **classic realist narrative** and in making them appear to, journalists inevitably distort the truth.

News programmes themselves also have a narrative structure. They place serious political and economic items at the beginning, and perhaps lighter-hearted stories at the end. News media has to also ensure that the composition of the programme or paper conforms to the brand identity of the medium as well as covering a range of news types, such as domestic news, foreign news, sport and business. All of these factors serve to distort the selection and presentation of news.

Bias against understanding

News production works on a 24-hour cycle. News coverage has to fit into the very short period which has developed over the last short period between bulletins. This means that we rarely get an overall picture of events or are allowed to see them in a historical context. This prevents us from ever truly understanding the cause-and-effect relationships involved.

Ideological influences on the media

As we saw in the previous topic, traditional Marxists argue that all of the news selection described above is deliberate and the result of conscious manipulation. News producers have a vested interest in maintaining the capitalist system, and so they help maintain that system by being directly supportive of the ruling class. The news is biased in favour of the powerful in society, and against those who are a threat to that power. While this view may overstate the case, it is certainly true that the ruling classes are appreciative of the role that the media play.

Table 3.1 Influences on media content	
Owners and controlling companies	Certain owners directly manipulate the media. Owners and controllers have interests that they wish to promote or defend – Rupert Murdoch made sure that his bid for Manchester United was reported in a positive light in his newspapers.
Media institutions	Media institutions have a public image which they need to maintain. This affects their decisions about what to include and how to present it. The *News of the World*, for example, over-reports sex and scandal as this is what its readers want and expect.
The law	The media are subject to legal controls, such as the Official Secrets Act and the Prevention of Terrorism Act, as well as the laws of libel and contempt of court. Contempt of court means that the media cannot report in a way that might affect the verdict in an ongoing court case.
Constitutional constraints	Media organizations are governed by written 'contracts', such as the BBC Charter, which they agree in order to gain the right to publish or broadcast.
Media regulation and self-regulation	The media have their own standards and regulatory bodies which monitor content. Examples are the Press Complaints Commission and the Broadcasting Standards Council. Professional practices are also an influence. Journalists often censor their own work by taking out what they know will not be published.
Economic factors	The amount of money and resources available will inevitably influence the media, as shown by the example of the coverage of the Gulf War and Tiananmen Square.
Advertisers	Most of the media need advertising to survive. This means that the needs of advertisers will be taken very seriously when decisions are made about the content of the media. For example, there were suspicions that the link between smoking and lung cancer was slow to be reported because of the importance of tobacco companies' advertising.
Audiences	It is assumed that different kinds of people watch, listen and read at different times of the day. A lunchtime TV programme is likely to be aimed at women or pensioners, and early evening programming is likely to be aimed at schoolchildren.
Media personnel (class, race, gender, socialization)	The media may reflect a White, male, middle-class viewpoint, as many people in the media are drawn from these social backgrounds.
Sources	With news coverage in particular, certain groups – such as the government – are believed to be more reliable, honest and objective.

Many newspaper proprietors and TV news producers have received recognition through knighthoods or other honours.

For hegemonic Marxists, the way in which journalists learn what makes a good story is governed by their common White, male, middle-class background. Their lifestyle and standard of living are such that they see little wrong with society and rarely adopt a critical stance. This essentially attunes them to taken-for-granted, common-sense assumptions that maintain the system.

In contrast to these views, pluralists would argue that the news reflects the full diversity of viewpoints in society. Certain views will dominate in each situation, but the direction that the bias takes is not consistent, and so there is no overall slant towards a particular viewpoint.

The Glasgow University Media Group (GUMG)

The GUMG have studied news broadcasts for many years. They use a technique called **content analysis** (see Unit 6, p. 261), which involves detailed analysis of the language and visual images used by the media. They have found that the media consistently reflect the common assumptions of the powerful in society, whilst marginalizing the views of others.

In recent studies, the Group have demonstrated the extent to which the need for TV news to entertain creates a bias against understanding. They use both the reporting of the developing world (GUMG 1999) and the Arab/Israeli conflict (Philo 2004) to illustrate how news, because it now exists in a very commercial market, focuses more and more on exciting events, rather than the historical context and explanation of those events.

The reporting of the Colombian earthquake in January 1999 featured scenes of destruction, chaos, collapsed buildings, frantic rescue efforts and appeals for help. But there was nothing said about the impact of the earthquake on Columbia's coffee-growing region or the long-term economic repercussions on unemployment and investment.

They use coverage of the Israeli/Palestinian conflict to highlight how the agenda for discussion in the news is often framed by ideological influences. Israel is closely allied to the United States and there are very strong pro-Israeli lobbies in the USA and to some extent in the UK. The lack of discussion in the news of the origins of the conflict and the controversial aspects of the occupation of former Palestinian territories by Israel operate in Israel's favour. They go further, suggesting that the style and form of language used further highlight this pro-Israeli stance.

Words such as 'murder', 'atrocity', 'lynching' and 'savage cold-blooded killing' were only used to describe Israeli deaths, but never those of Palestinians. Terrible fates befell both Israelis and Palestinians, but there was a clear difference in the language used to describe them. This was so even when the events described had strong similarities. For example, on 10 October 2000, it was reported that Arab residents of Tel Aviv had been 'chased and stabbed'. The

Greg Philo

Bad news from Israel: media coverage of the Israeli/Palestinian conflict

If you don't understand the Middle East crisis, it might be because you are watching it on TV news. This scores high on images of fighting, violence and drama but is low on explanation. The Glasgow University Media Group interviewed 12 small audience groups (a total of 85 people) with a cross section of ages and backgrounds. They were asked a series of questions about the conflict and what they had understood from TV news. The same questions were then put to 300 young people (aged between 17 and 22) who filled in a questionnaire. We asked what came to their mind when they heard the words 'Israeli/Palestinian conflict' and then what was the source of whatever it was. Most (82 per cent) listed TV news as their source and these replies showed that they had absorbed the 'main' message of the news, of conflict, violence and tragedy, but that many people had little understanding of the reasons for the conflict and its origins. Explanations were rarely given on the news and when they were, journalists often spoke in a form of shorthand which assumed quite detailed knowledge of the origins of the conflict. For example, in a news bulletin which featured the progress of peace talks, a journalist made a series of very brief comments on the issues which underpinned the conflict: Journalist: 'The basic raw disagreements remain – the future, for example, of this city Jerusalem, the future of Jewish settlements and the returning refugees.' (ITN 18.30 16.10.2001)

adapted from the Glasgow University Media Unit website at
www.gla.ac.uk/departments/sociology/units/media

1 How did the Glasgow University Media Group try to achieve a representative sample?

2 Why does Greg Philo write that 'if you don't understand the Middle East crisis it might be because you are watching it on TV news'?

reports on television news were extremely brief, but two days later, when two Israeli soldiers were killed by a crowd of Palestinians, there was very extensive coverage and the words 'lynching' and 'lynch mob' were very widely used.

The work of the Glasgow University Media Group shows that the media do not just reflect public opinion, but that they also provide a framework (or agenda) for the public, so that people think about issues in a way that benefits the ruling class. In this respect, the media are a powerful ideological influence. (See also Item A in the 'Exploring' activity on the opposite page.)

Class bias is not the only area of misrepresentation that critics of the pluralist position point to. Women, ethnic minorities, the disabled and the young may also be victims of media bias. The following topics will examine these issues in more detail.

Check your understanding

1 How does the use of a news diary demonstrate that news is not a spontaneous response to world events?

2 Give two examples of the impact of financial factors on news production.

3 Explain in your own words how the format and intended audience for a news programme affect news output.

4 What are 'news values'?

5 Explain in your own words how the process of gatekeeping affects the form that news output eventually takes.

6 Use the work of the Glasgow University Media Group to show how the media influence the way the public thinks about issues.

research ideas

- List the first ten news items from an edition of the BBC evening news. Do the same for ITN news on the same evening. What are the differences? Can they be explained in terms of 'news values'?

- Tape one news programme. Analyse the lead story in terms of the sources that are used, e.g. newscaster's script, live film footage, location report from a reporter at the scene, interview (taped, live or by satellite), archive footage (old film), amateur film, etc.

  Then brainstorm a list of all the people who must have been involved, e.g. reporters, photographers, editors, companies buying and selling satellite time, drivers, outside broadcast crews, film archivists, etc. Discuss how practical problems may have served to structure the story in a particular way.

web.tasks

Look at the web pages of the following daily newspapers on the same day: the *Sun*, the *Daily Telegraph* and the *Guardian*. Compare the presentation of their main stories.

What similarities and differences are there in terms of stories covered and presentation? Why?

Search for the home page of the Glasgow University Mass Media Unit. Find out about their latest research.

KEY TERMS

Classic realist narrative a story which begins with normality being threatened by disruptive forces and is resolved when other forces act to restore normality.

Content analysis a detailed analysis of media content.

Gatekeepers people within the media who have the power to let some news stories through and stop others.

Marginalizing making a group appear to be 'at the edge' of society and not very important.

Narrativization the process of turning into a story.

News diary a record of forthcoming events that will need to be covered.

News values assumptions that guide journalists and editors when selecting news items.

exploring making the news

Item A Ten conclusions from the Glasgow University Media Group

1. News is reported in a simplified and one-sided way.
2. The effects of events tend to be reported rather than their causes. There is no sense of their development.
3. There is biased use of words in TV news – e.g. 'miners' strike' rather than 'coal dispute'.
4. There is biased use of images in TV news. During the Liverpool council workers' strike, the piles of rubbish and unburied bodies reinforced the effects rather than the causes of the dispute, and put the viewer on the side of the management rather than the strikers.
5. Stories are reported selectively – only certain facts are presented and others are left out.
6. Protesters' tactics are more likely to be reported than their views.
7. There is a hierarchy of access to the media – experts and establishment figures are more likely to get their views heard than ordinary people.
8. There is a hierarchy of credibility whereby only certain groups are asked for their opinion, as they are seen to be more reliable and their remarks more valid.
9. The media have an agenda-setting function. Journalists have a 'middle-of-the-road', consensual outlook informed by their common background and experience. They frame events within a very narrow range, limiting the breadth of possible discussion.
10. Personnel in the media act as 'gatekeepers' – they exclude some stories from the news and include others.

Adapted from GUMG's *Bad News* (1976), *More Bad News* (1980), *Really Bad News* (1982), *War and Peace News* (1985), London: Routledge

Item B Tabloid shift in TV news

Broadcasts today – with the exceptions of the BBC's late evening news and Channel 4 news – have shifted away from political stories and foreign affairs towards a tabloid diet dominated by consumer affairs and crime.

The survey of more than 700 evening news programmes between 1975 and 1999 showed that while the 'dire warnings' of dumbing down have not been borne out, the early evening news programmes on BBC and ITV were pursuing a more tabloid agenda.

By contrast, the BBC's late evening news and Channel 4's news programmes have maintained a broadsheet approach. In the BBC's 6 pm news, tabloid content – such as crime, consumer and showbusiness stories – rose from 18 to 30 per cent. Foreign coverage also rose, but numbers of broadsheet stories, such as politics, wars and social affairs, fell.

On ITV, the trend towards tabloid stories in the early evening news was even more marked, more than doubling from 15 per cent in 1975 to 33 per cent in 1999. Content in the relaunched ITV evening news was broadly the same.

Tabloid stories in the BBC's late evening news fell from 16 per cent in 1975 to 13 per cent in 1999. The proportion of foreign stories increased from 24 to 43 per cent.

Adapted from *The Guardian*, 10 July 2000

1. In your own words, explain what is meant by the term 'hierarchy of access' (Item A). (2 marks)
2. Identify two of the groups who 'are asked for their opinion, as they are seen to be more reliable and their remarks more valid' (Item A). (4 marks)
3. Identify and explain three trends in news reporting identified by the research described in Item B. (9 marks)
4. Identify and explain two ways, according to Marxists, in which the content of TV news reflects the interests of the powerful in society. (10 marks)

Exam practice

5. a Identify and explain two ways in which journalists may decide that a story is newsworthy. (15 marks)

   b Outline and discuss the view that the TV news is a 'window on the world'. (30 marks)

Unit 3 Mass media

119

How do the media affect people?

gettingyouthinking

Protesters demonstrate outside the BBC against the showing of the opera Jerry Springer on TV in January 2005

TV and music have a great influence on our students. You only have to hear them sing at a disco to realize they learn lyrics of very sensuous songs off by heart but find it difficult to recite 'Our Father'. It may be useful to discuss, as a class, the frequency of sexual innuendo and references in shows they commonly watch.

What would God say to the following if He appeared before them today?

● Authors of corrupt novels, newspapers, plays, films and indecent styles.
● Those who display eroticism (openly sexual behaviour) in modern music.
● Those who distribute condoms and other contraceptives to the youth of today, knowing full well what behaviour this encourages, and knowing full well that 100 per cent 'safe sex' is a myth.
● Parents who allow their children to watch suggestive and lustful TV shows.

The passage above right is adapted from 'Teachers for Life', an advice leaflet for teachers, produced by a Catholic teachers' group in Western Australia.

1 **What is the writer concerned about?**

2 **What sort of music and TV programmes do you think the writer might object to?**

3 **What do you think is the writer's view of TV audiences and of young people in particular?**

4 **To what extent do you agree with the views expressed in the extract? What arguments could be presented against these views?**

Groups such as the Christian Right in the extract above, fundamentalist clerics and many Conservative politicians, as well as pressure groups such as Mediawatch (formerly the National Viewers' and Listeners' Association), blame the media for corrupting the morals of society – especially the young. According to such groups, the media are responsible for family breakdown, crime, abortion, underage sex and even homosexuality!

But concern about the media is not just limited to these kinds of groups. Many feminists and Marxists also feel that media messages can be corrupting – for example, by encouraging male violence against women, or by brainwashing viewers into being passive consumers.

Most ideas about media effects start by setting out an overall relationship between the media and their audience. For this reason they are often called 'models of media effects'.

'Hypodermic syringe' model

In 1957, Vance Packard wrote a famous book about advertising called *The Hidden Persuaders*. He described how ordinary people were persuaded to consume goods without being aware of the techniques being used. His view was that the mass media were so powerful that they could directly 'inject' messages into the audience, or that, like a 'magic bullet', the message could be precisely targeted at an audience, who would automatically fall down when hit. This view has become known as the **hypodermic syringe model**. According to this model, the audience is:

● passive – weak and inactive
● homogeneous – all the same
● 'blank pages' to be written on – with the media exerting a powerful influence that provokes an immediate response from the audience.

Sociologists are generally very critical of this model. They believe that it fails to recognize the different social characteristics of audience members. They also believe that people are not as vulnerable as the hypodermic syringe model implies. Nevertheless, it has been very influential in **media regulation** in The UK. The 9 p.m. watershed and age restrictions on video hire, along with a range of other controls, have made censorship of the British media among the most restrictive in the free world.

Supporters of the model are particularly frustrated by the difficulties faced in trying to regulate new media.

Regulating internet use

It is not surprising that there is a high level of public concern about the internet. The internet is expanding rapidly as millions go 'on line' each day to access and exchange a vast amount of uncontrolled information. A particular concern is the use of chat rooms by paedophiles – sometimes hiding their identity, contacting children and swapping pornographic images. Recently, police have cooperated across national borders to exchange information about subscribers to child pornography sites and numerous arrests have been made. Some commentators have suggested the public outrage surrounding this issue constitutes a 'moral panic' (see pp. 130–1). There is also more concern about terrorism, especially after '9/11'. For example, the US government has started removing information on nuclear weapons research and nuclear power stations from its own websites some 30 years after a US graduate student published a nuclear bomb design based on publicly available information.

Cultural effects model

The **cultural effects model** also sees the media as a very powerful influence, but it recognizes that the media audience is very diverse. People have different backgrounds and experiences and this means that they interpret what they see, read and hear in different ways. A programme about life in an inner-London borough, for example, may be interpreted as evidence of racial conflict and deprivation, or as evidence of interesting cultural diversity, depending on who is watching.

However, those who produce the media do expect the audience to respond to their work in a particular way. This anticipated response is known as the **preferred (or dominant) reading**. Those who lack direct experience of the issue presented by the media (in many cases the majority of the audience) are likely to accept this preferred reading.

In the Marxist version of this model, the ideas of the dominant groups in society – i.e. ruling-class ideology (see Unit 1, p. 11) – continually bombard audiences from every direction. It becomes difficult for anyone to retain a critical viewpoint. In the end, most people come to believe that ruling-class ideas are right. They consent to the dominance of the powerful without even realizing it. Many elderly people, for example, are so taken in by the media portrayal of social security claimants as 'scroungers' that they don't even claim the benefits that are rightfully theirs.

Rather than having an immediate, direct effect, as the hypodermic syringe model claims, this model suggests that there is a slow, 'drip-drip' process taking place over a long period of time. Eventually, dominant values come to be shared by most people – values such as 'happiness is about possessions and money', 'you must look like the models in magazines', or 'most asylum seekers are just illegal immigrants'.

Active audience approaches

Other theories of media effects see the media as far less influential. They believe that people have considerable choice in the way they use and interpret the media. There are various versions of this view.

Selective filter model

Think of a sieve: some things pass through while others stay in the sieve. The **selective filter model** holds that media messages are similar: some get through, while others are ignored or rejected by the audience.

Klapper (1960) suggests that, for a media message to have any effect, it must pass through the following three filters:

- **Selective exposure** – A message must first be chosen to be viewed, read or listened to. Media messages can have no effect if no one sees or hears them! Choices depend upon people's interests, education, work commitments and so on.
- **Selective perception** – The messages have to be accepted. For example, some people may take notice of certain TV programmes, but reject or ignore others.
- **Selective retention** – The messages have to 'stick'. People have a tendency to remember only the things they broadly agree with.

Uses and gratifications model

Blumler and McQuail (1968) point out that people get what they want from the media. Old people may watch soaps for companionship or to experience family life, whilst young people may watch soaps for advice on relationships or so that they have something to talk about at school the next day. In other words, the media satisfy a range of social needs, and different people get different pleasures – or gratifications – from the media.

Structured interpretation model

This view suggests that the way people interpret **media texts** differs according to their class, age, gender, ethnic group and other sources of identity. Those who hold this view analyse how and why different groups receive media messages. The methods they use are called **reception analysis**.

This is a more optimistic view than the cultural effects model. Media messages may be interpreted in a variety of ways, and even though one interpretation is dominant (the preferred reading), it is not always accepted.

Morley (1980) argues that people choose to make one of three responses:

- **Dominant** – they go along with the views expressed in the media text.
- **Oppositional** – they oppose the views expressed.
- **Negotiated** – they reinterpret the views to fit in with their own opinions and values.

For example, let's say the news contains a report about the Notting Hill Carnival. The report focuses on 12 arrests for drug dealing. A preferred (or dominant) reading might be that Black people can't enjoy themselves without breaking the law. An **oppositional reading** might be that the police or the media are racist, focusing on drug-related crime unnecessarily. After all, 12 arrests are nothing, considering the millions who attend. A **negotiated reading** might be that there is probably a lot of drug use among Afro-Caribbeans, but that it's mostly cannabis use, which should, in the viewer's opinion, be legalized anyway.

How does this illustrate the structured interpretation model?

These **active audience approaches** see the audience as interpreting media messages for themselves, and this makes it difficult to generalize about the effects of the media. Some of the most recent postmodern approaches go even further. Rather than seeing the audience as an undifferentiated mass, or as divided into cultural or other groupings, they argue that generalizations about media effects and audiences are impossible, since the same person may react to the same media message in different ways in different situations. Postmodern thinking on the media will be examined more fully in Topic 8.

Check your understanding

1. **How can the hypodermic syringe model be supported by people of very different views, e.g. Conservative politicians as well as some Marxists and feminists?**

2. **In what way does the cultural effects model suggest a 'drip drip' approach to media effects?**

3. **What is the difference between oppositional and negotiated readings?**

4. **Give two similarities and two differences between the cultural effects model and the hypodermic syringe model.**

5. **'It is no coincidence that Hollywood films were at their height of popularity during the war years.' How does this statement illustrate the uses and gratifications model?**

research ideas

- Complete a media grid for each member of your household, detailing one day's media use. Follow this up by asking each person to state, for each viewing/listening slot, which of the following needs or gratifications it satisfied:
  - diversion (escape from routine)
  - interaction with others (companionship, conversation, etc.)
  - learning (information-seeking, education)
  - advice (personal development, etc.).

  Compare their answers.

KEY TERMS

Active audience approaches theories that stress that the effects of the media are limited because people are not easily influenced.

Cultural effects model the view that the media are powerful in so far as they link up with other agents of socialization to encourage particular ways of making sense of the world.

Hypodermic syringe model the view that the media are very powerful and the audience very weak. The media can 'inject' their messages into the audience, who accept them uncritically.

Media regulation control of what we see, hear and read in the media from outside bodies.

Media text any media output, be it written, aural or visual, e.g. magazine article, photo, CD, film, TV or radio programme.

Negotiated reading an interpretation of a media text that modifies the intended (preferred) reading so that it fits with the audience member's own views.

Oppositional reading an interpretation of a media text that rejects its intended (preferred) reading.

Preferred (or **dominant**) **reading** the intended messages contained within the text.

Reception analysis research that focuses on the way individuals make meanings from media messages.

Selective exposure the idea that people only watch, listen or read what they want to.

Selective filter model the view that audience members allow only certain media messages through.

Selective perception the idea that people take notice only of certain media messages.

Selective retention the idea that people remember only certain media messages.

Structured interpretation model the view that people interpret media texts according to their various identities, e.g. class, gender, ethnic group.

Uses and gratifications model the view that people use the media for their own purposes.

Item A   The War of the Worlds

A classic example of the powerful influence of the media was the radio broadcast in 1938 of H.G. Wells's book *The War of the Worlds*. The dramatized adaptation of an invasion of Martians into a rural area of New Jersey, USA, was so convincing that it generated mass hysteria in many American states. Significantly, though, not all of the six million listeners responded in the same way. «Long before the broadcast had ended, people all over the US were praying, crying, fleeing frantically to escape death from the Martians.»

Research on the audience response was undertaken by Cantril (1940), who found that several factors affected the extent to which people believed the broadcast to be true. For example, listeners who had not heard the beginning of the programme were more likely to be taken in by it, and those who were not able to check out the story with neighbours, to 'reality test' it, were convinced by the broadcast and reacted accordingly. Radio news was at that time the only source of immediate knowledge about the world at large. As the programme was broadcast in the style of a news programme, listeners were more likely to treat it as real.

Adapted from Haralambos, M. (ed.) (1986)
Sociology: New Directions,
Ormskirk: Causeway Press

Item B   Moral issues and bias

The Coal Dispute of 1984 (referred to as the 'miners' strike' by the media) occurred as a result of the decision by the Coal Board to close pits much earlier and in greater number than had been agreed in writing. The police and miners were involved in well-publicized confrontations. The media blamed the miners for both the strike and the resulting violence. They also greatly exaggerated the alleged lack of solidarity among the miners by constantly referring to the 'drift back to work', which, in fact, was the case for only a small minority of miners.

In order to expose the main messages received by the audience, Philo asked audience members, in groups, a year later, to write their own media stories based on photographs. The respondents were shown pictures of violence and asked to put together a news item. Philo found that many of the audience members produced similar stories, focusing on the violence of the picket lines and on the phrase 'drift back to work' (implying that the strike was failing).

Taken at face value this would imply that the audience were all passive victims of the media, as the hypodermic syringe model suggests.

However, in follow-up interviews, Philo discovered that the respondents were perfectly able to create stories 'in the style of a biased media', while not actually believing these stories.

While all believed in the media's view that violence is wrong, there was not common agreement on who should be blamed. Working-class trade unionists blamed the police, whilst middle-class professionals were more likely to blame the pickets for starting the trouble.

Adapted from Philo, G. (ed.) (1990) *Seeing and Believing: The Influence of Television*,
London: Routledge

1 Explain in your own words what is meant by the 'hypodermic syringe' model of media effects (Item B). (2 marks)

2 Identify and briefly explain two cultural factors that may have influenced those who fled the 'Martian attack' (Item A). (4 marks)

3 Identify and explain three ways in which the media manipulated the audience's view of the coal dispute. (9 marks)

4 Identify and explain two reasons why respondents wrote stories which appeared to support the Coal Board's position (Item B). (10 marks)

Exam practice

5 a Identify and explain two ways in which media audiences may use the media. (15 marks)

  b Outline and discuss the view that media content has an immediate and direct effect on audiences. (30 marks)

web.tasks

1 There is a great deal of concern about lack of control of the internet. Search the web using the keyword 'censorship' to find out arguments for and against regulation of the internet.

2 Find the website of the Advertising Standards Authority. Look up some of its adjudications (decisions about complaints) and see to what extent you agree with them.

Is there too much violence in the media?

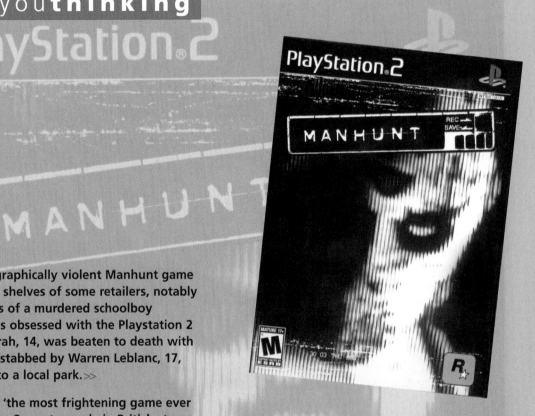

gettingyou**thinking**

« Last month, the graphically violent Manhunt game was pulled from the shelves of some retailers, notably Dixons, after parents of a murdered schoolboy claimed his killer was obsessed with the Playstation 2 game. Stefan Pakeerah, 14, was beaten to death with a claw hammer and stabbed by Warren Leblanc, 17, who had lured him to a local park. »

« It comes billed as 'the most frightening game ever created', but as Doom 3 went on sale in British stores yesterday, its distributors dismissed accusations that the violence on screen can encourage violence off it.

The sci-fi horror game involves the shooter struggling against zombies, lost souls, demons, maggots and various other monsters unleashed from hell. Along the way, graphics depict exploding heads, chainsaws, axes and decapitations.

It has been granted an 18 rating by the British Board of Film Classification.

The original Doom was linked to the Columbine school massacre, when it was claimed that the teenage killers Eric Harris and Dylan Klebold were influenced by the violent nature of the game. »

Adapted from *The Guardian*, 14 August 2004

1 Can you think of other examples of violent video games, films and song lyrics?

2 Do you think retailers were justified in removing Manhunt from their shelves?

3 What sorts of people do you think are most vulnerable to screen violence? Why?

4 What arguments could the distributors of Doom use to dismiss accusations that it would cause violence?

In 2003, about 200 million videos were rented and a further 100 million were purchased in the UK. Probably at least twice this number of people watched these videos. Over 30 million video games were sold. Even today, with television audiences increasingly fragmented across multiple channels, a recent broadcast of the 'violent' movie *Die Hard 2* attracted an audience of over 7 million people on just one night. (Broadcast/BARB 2004). The sheer size of these audiences for popular media have long fuelled speculation that they must have some profound impact on society – that out there, in such vast populations, some – perhaps many – disturbed individuals will act out the violence and horror which they have seen on their screens. And perhaps even worse, there must be a 'drip-drip-drip' effect on everyone. Every year, some event makes such speculation newsworthy or some research is produced where scientists are said to have 'proved the link' between video violence and violence in society.

On 12 February 1993, two 10-year-old boys abducted toddler James Bulger from a shopping mall. They tortured and killed him, according to the tabloid press, by mimicking scenes from a video – *Child's Play 3*. Later that year, the judge, in sentencing the boys, speculated on the significant role that the film had played. An obvious example of the dangerous effects of screen violence, you may think. However, things were not quite that simple. The police stated that there was no evidence at all that either of James's killers had seen the video.

This case illustrates the controversy and confusion that surround the 70 years of debate and research about violence and the media. In the main, researchers have fallen into one of two major camps:

1 *the effects approach* – those who think that everyone is affected in much the same way by screen violence
2 *alternative approaches* – those who think that the media's effect depends on who is viewing and the situation in which that viewing takes place.

The effects approach

The main model underpinning the **effects approach** is the hypodermic syringe model (see Topic 4). The audience is seen as a homogeneous (similar) mass who interpret the media in the same uncritical way and are powerless to resist its influence. A direct **correlation** (connection) is believed to exist between screen violence and violence in society. The following are four examples of the possible effects of media violence.

1 'Copycat' violence

In 1963, Bandura *et al.* showed three groups of children real, film and cartoon examples of a self-righting doll ('bobo doll') being attacked with mallets, whilst a fourth group saw no violent activity. After being introduced to a room full of exciting toys, the children in each group were made to feel frustrated by being told that the toys were not for them. They were then led to another room containing a bobo doll, where they were observed through a one-way mirror. The three groups who had

been shown the violent activity – whether real, film or cartoon – all behaved more aggressively than the fourth group. This is the effect known as **copycat violence**.

2 Desensitization

A more subtle approach was adopted by Hilda Himmelweit (1958). She accepted that viewing one programme was not going to affect behaviour in everyone – only in the most disturbed. She suggested, however, that prolonged exposure to programmes portraying violence may have a 'drip-drip' effect, such that individuals are socialized into accepting violent behaviour as normal.

3 Catharsis

Not all effects research focuses on negative effects. Fesbach and Sanger (1971) found that screen violence can actually provide a safe outlet for people's aggressive tendencies (known as **catharsis**). They looked at the effects of violent TV on teenagers. A large sample of boys from both private schools and residential homes were fed a diet of TV for six weeks. Some groups could only watch aggressive programmes, whilst others were made to watch non-aggressive programmes. The observers noted at the end of the study that the groups who had seen only aggressive programmes were actually less aggressive in their behaviour than the others.

4 Sensitization

Some argue that seeing the effects of violence and the pain and suffering that it causes will sensitize viewers – make them more aware of its consequences and so less inclined to commit violent acts. When filmed in a certain way (i.e. ever more graphically), violent scenes can be so shocking as to put people off violence.

Criticisms of the effects approach

- Most effects studies have been conducted using a scientific approach. Some critics say that this makes their findings questionable, as people do not behave as naturally under laboratory conditions as they would in normal life.
- Effects studies often ignore other factors that may be causing violent or antisocial behaviour, such as peer-group influences.
- Effects theorists do not always distinguish between different kinds of screen violence, such as fictional violence and real-life violence in news and current affairs programmes.
- Recent research (see Morrison's work below) shows that the context in which screen violence occurs affects its impact.
- Effects studies often take a patronizing view of children, seeing them as vulnerable to the damaging effects of the media. Recent work, such as that of Buckingham (see below), shows that children are much more **media literate** than researchers have assumed.

Despite these criticisms, the effects approach remains an influence on government policy. A report by Professor Elizabeth Newsom (1994) presented a strong case for greater controls over the renting of videos and, despite a wave of criticism of its use of the effects approach, led directly to the Video Recordings Act, which gave videos certificates and restricted their availability to children. However, the evidence claimed for television's effects is really quite weak. For example, most of the studies which have looked at how children are affected when television first arrives, have found surprisingly little change. The last study was in St Helena, a British colony in the South Atlantic Ocean, which received television for the first time in 1995. Before and after studies showed no change in children's antisocial or prosocial behaviour (Charlton *et al.* 2000).

Alternative approaches

These approaches focus on the audience as a heterogeneous (diverse) and active group, with different social characteristics and different ways of using and interpreting the media. They draw on 'uses and gratifications', 'cultural effects' and other 'active audience' theories (see Topic 4). The following are four examples of recent research using alternative approaches.

1. Buckingham (1993) looked at how children interpret media violence. He criticizes effects research for failing to recognize that gender, class and ethnic identities are crucially important, as is the changing identity of the child as they grow up. Buckingham does not accept that children are especially vulnerable to TV violence. He argues that children are much more sophisticated in their understanding and more media literate than previous researchers have assumed.

2. Julian Wood (1993) conducted a small-scale study of boys' use of video. He attended an after-school showing of a horror video in the home of one of the boys (the boy's parents were away). Wood describes the boys' comments in detail, and is able to demonstrate that, in this situation, the horror film is used almost as a rite of passage. The boys can prove their heterosexuality to each other, behave in a macho way, swear and, above all, demonstrate their fearlessness. Rather than being a corrupting influence, video violence is merely a part of growing up.

3. Morrison (1999) showed a range of clips – including scenes from *Brookside*, news footage and excerpts from violent films – to groups of women, young men and war veterans. All of the interviewees felt that the most disturbing clip was a man beating his wife in *Ladybird, Ladybird* (see left-hand photograph below), a film by Ken Loach. It caused distress because of the realism of the setting, the strong language and the perceived unfairness, and also because viewers were concerned about the effect on the child actors in the scene. By contrast, the clip from *Pulp Fiction* – in which a man is killed out of the blue during an innocent conversation, spraying blood and chunks of brain around a car – was seen as 'humorous' and 'not violent', even by women over the age of 60, because there was lighthearted dialogue. The right-hand photograph below shows a typically 'messy' scene from the film *Pulp Fiction*.

4. Marsha Kinder's (1999) edited collection of essays, *Kid's Media Culture*, features research conducted within different sociological traditions from both macro- and

Scenes from Ladybird, Ladybird *(left) and* Pulp Fiction *(right) – which film do viewers find the more disturbing?*

microsociology. She asserts that the essays situate children's relationships with media products within broader leisure activities, as well as within complex networks of social relations at home, at school and in the broader public sphere (neighbourhood, region, nation). In all of the essays in this volume, then, the kids are not portrayed as timeless, innocent victims who desperately need to be protected from popular culture. Rather, they are seen as historically situated participants who actively collaborate in the production and negotiation of cultural meanings.

focus on research

A mourner breaks down after the Columbine High School shootings in Denver, USA, in 1999. Thirteen people were killed by two student gunmen Eric Harris and Dylan Klebold

Guy Cumberbatch
The effects of screen violence

Over the years, there have been over 3,500 research studies into the effects of screen violence, encompassing film, TV, video and more recently, computer and video games. This is according to a report commissioned by the Video Standards Council and undertaken by Dr Guy Cumberbatch, Chartered Psychologist and Director of the Communications Research Group, based in Birmingham, who has specialized in the study of media violence for over 25 years.

His Report, published in 2004, concentrated on the more recent epidemic of research, with strong concentration on the most recent, in which computer and video games feature strongly as the subject matter.

Particular reference to computer and video games is made in an oft-quoted USA study by Anderson and Dill (2000), following the Columbine High School massacre. On this infamous study, Dr Cumberbatch concludes:

<< *Anderson and Dill (2000) suggest that violent video games were probably a factor in the massacre at Columbine High School. However, as social scientists,*

they should be ashamed of themselves in offering only second-hand hearsay support for this assertion. Such claims are very common, perhaps often made in good faith, and sound very plausible, but they have never stood up to scrutiny. >>

Dr Cumberbatch states that in 1988, Kate Adie researched for BBC's *Panorama* what seemed to be the best-evidenced cases where a crime had been clearly linked to the mass media. In no case was such a link supported by the evidence to a level that would be acceptable to a serious investigative journalist. Every case turned out to be mere speculation – often by reckless journalists. Cumberbatch concludes that the relationship that audiences enjoy with violence in entertainment is a rich and multilayered one, which studies of video violence effects choose to ignore completely. To suggest that these studies are misleading would be too kind. Many appear simply deceitful. However, the absence of convincing research evidence that media violence causes harm does not mean that we should necessarily celebrate it and encourage more. There may be moral, aesthetic, philosophical, religious or humanistic grounds on which we might consider that excessive representations of violence are a matter of some public interest.

In the Conclusions to his Report, Cumberbatch states:

<< *The real puzzle is that anyone looking for research evidence could draw any conclusions about the pattern, let alone argue with such confidence and even passion that it demonstrates the harm of violence on TV, in film/video and in video games. While tests of statistical significance are a vital tool of the social sciences, they seem to have been more often used in this field as instruments of torture on the data until it confesses something that could justify a publication in a scientific journal. If one conclusion is possible, it is that the jury is still not out. It's never been in. Media violence has been subjected to a lynch mob mentality with almost any evidence used to prove guilt.* >>

Adapted from the Video Standards Council website
(**www.videostandards.org.uk**)

1 What does Cumberbatch say about the validity of recent research findings on media violence?

2 He concludes that there may be reasons other than alleged causal effects for being concerned about screen violence. What do you think he means by this?

Where are we now?

So, thousands of studies later, we have not really made much progress and many questions remain. Are some people less able to distinguish between artificial and real violence? Is some censorship justified in order to protect us? But would more censorship push violence underground, so that even more disturbing material might become available? Does the way in which violence is depicted make a difference to its impact – for example, if there are differences in power between the participants, or if humour is involved?

The more we seek to find the answers to questions about the effects of media violence, the more questions seem to be generated.

web.tasks

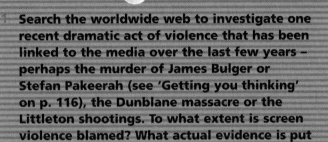

1 Search the worldwide web to investigate one recent dramatic act of violence that has been linked to the media over the last few years – perhaps the murder of James Bulger or Stefan Pakeerah (see 'Getting you thinking' on p. 116), the Dunblane massacre or the Littleton shootings. To what extent is screen violence blamed? What actual evidence is put forward to link media violence to the murders?

2 Go to the page of the American Psychiatric Association's website that covers the effects of media violence at www.psych.org/public_info/media_violence.cfm

What does it suggest about the evidence on this issue?

Compare this page with the view of media sociologist David Gauntlett at www.theory.org.uk/effects.htm

What criticisms does Gauntlett make of the 'effects model'?

Check your understanding

1 Explain in your own words what is meant by the claim that there is a correlation between screen violence and violence in society.

2 How might the media desensitize their audience to violence?

3 Explain in your own words three limitations of the effects approach.

4 What evidence is there that the effects approach still has its supporters today?

5 Identify and explain three insights into the nature of the audience that critics of effects approaches have put forward.

research ideas

● Investigate what types of violence are considered disturbing by people of different ages, genders, classes or ethnic groups. Present your findings quantitatively.

● Conduct a content analysis of part of one evening's TV programmes on any one channel. Add up the number of times acts of violence are depicted. After noting down each act of violence, explain the type of programme (e.g. news, cartoon, drama) and the type of violence (e.g. real, humorous).

What do your results indicate about the amount and type of violence on television?

KEY TERMS

Catharsis the process of relieving tensions – for example, violence on screen providing a safe outlet for people's violent tendencies.

Correlation a relationship between two or more things, where one characteristic is directly affected by another.

'Copycat' violence violence that occurs as a result of copying something that is seen in the media.

Desensitization the process by which, through repeated exposure to media violence, people come to accept violent behaviour as normal.

Effects approach an approach based on the hypodermic syringe model (see Topic 4) which believes that the media have direct effects on their audience.

Media literate an intelligent, critical and informed attitude to the media.

exploring violence and the media

Item A The viewing habits of young offenders

A study by Hagell and Newburn for the Policy Studies Institute compared young offenders' viewing habits with those of non-offending teenagers. They found that there were very few differences between the two groups in terms of what they watched, with hardly any having seen the films that were causing concern at the time. Few members of either group had a particular interest in violent output. The young offenders, in fact, generally had had less access to TVs, video, cable or satellite TV. Other factors beyond the media must be causing the differences in behaviour.

Adapted from A. Hagell and T. Newburn (1994) *Young Offenders and the Media: Viewing Habits*, London: PSI

Item B Crime and media violence

Thirty-seven of the top 40 UK software titles listed for 2004 are games. Twenty-three of those titles contain some sort of violence. Fourteen of those titles include graphic violence throughout the duration of the game. Some of the titles in this category include: *Tom Clancy's Splinter Cell: Pandora Tomorrow, Onimusha: Demon Siege, Full Spectrum Warrior, Medal of Honor: Rising Sun, Grand Theft Auto: Vice City, Red Dead Revolver, Hitman: Contracts* and *Soul Calibur II*.

In contrast, a look at the top 40 grossing films over one weekend (16 to 18 July 2004) only reveals 15 movies with any violence. Among those 15 movies, two were documentaries, and many were comedies or children's movies that contained some cartoon-like violence. A comedy about dodgeball, a Harry Potter movie, and *Shrek 2* were included in the list containing violence.

Despite the exposure of young males to an increasing diet of first-person gaming violence, the British Crime Survey of 2000 showed a 20 per cent fall in victims of violence over the previous four years. In the early 1950s, one quarter of all violent crime recorded was 'serious' violent crime. Today it is less than 10 per cent. This is despite the fact that, with the advent of mobile phones, people are more likely to report crime than in the past. Overall, the idea that we now live in a more violent society is very questionable and, certainly, since computer/video games have become prevalent, crime has gone down.

Source: Sims, L. and Myhill, A. (2001) *Policing and the Public, Findings from the British Crime Survey 2000*, London: Home Office

1 Explain in your own words what is meant by 'desensitization'. (2 marks)

2 Identify and briefly explain two possible reasons why the best-selling computer games are more likely to contain violence than the most popular films (Item B). (4 marks)

3 Identify three reasons why the PSI study concludes that 'other factors beyond the media must be causing the differences in behaviour' between the young offenders and the schoolchildren (Item A). (9 marks)

4 Identify and explain two ways in which the Items challenge the view that media violence is the cause of violence in society. (10 marks)

Exam practice

5 a Identify and explain two ways in which violence on screen may have a positive effect on audiences. (15 marks)

b Outline and discuss the view that violence on screen can cause violence in society. (30 marks)

Gender and the media

getting**you**thinking

Look at these images of women, presented by the media, and then answer the following questions.

1 Which of these women are playing stereotyped female roles? What are these roles?
2 What do these photographs tell us about the way in which women are portrayed in the media?
3 To what extent do you think that images of women in the media are changing?

As women have begun to achieve more visibility outside the home and to compete on a more equal basis with men in the workplace, you might expect this to be reflected in the mass media. Sociological research suggests, however, that, although there is some recent evidence of greater equality, the roles allocated to the sexes across a range of media – such as advertising, television and film – have been restricted in the following ways:

- Women have been allocated a limited range of roles.
- Women are less visible in the media than men.
- Women have been presented as ideals.
- Women have been selected to appeal to men.
- Men have been seen as aggressors, women as victims.

Let's look at these issues in more detail.

A limited range of roles

Women are represented in a narrow range of social roles in the media, whilst men perform the full range of social and occupational roles. Women are especially found in domestic settings – as busy housewives, contented mothers, eager consumers and so on. Tuchman *et al.* (1978) adds sexual and romantic roles to this list.

Women are rarely shown in high-status occupational roles, such as doctors or lawyers. If they are, they are often shown to have problems in dealing with their 'unusual' circumstances. For example, they are portrayed as unfulfilled (motherhood is sometimes offered as the answer to this), as unattractive, as unstable, or as having problems with relationships. If they have children, successful women are sometimes shown as irresponsible, with their children getting into trouble due to their emotional neglect. Men are rarely portrayed in this way.

Whilst these are still the primary representations, there has recently been an increase in the number of 'stronger' roles for women – for example, in TV dramas such as *Sex in the City,* which also have relatively weak 'dorky' men. *Buffy the Vampire Slayer* broke new ground by becoming hugely popular within the typically male-dominated world of science fiction. The lead character is more confident and assertive than many male heroes in contemporary film and TV, such as the Superman character in the *New Adventures of Superman,* who is more caring and sensitive than in earlier versions. Soap operas also tend to promote independent and assertive female characters, whereas male soap characters tend to be weaker. This may be because soaps focus on domestic issues, the only legitimate (accepted) area for female authority.

Visibility

At the beginning of the 1990s, 89 per cent of voice-overs for television commercials were male, probably because the male voice is seen to represent authority. Women were the main stars of only 14 per cent of mid-evening television programmes. Analysis of Hollywood films at that time indicated that few women stars were seen by the major studios as being able to carry a film by themselves, although women were slowly moving into lead roles in traditionally masculine areas, such as science fiction. There are indications that things are improving, with the male-to-female split in speaking parts in prime-time TV now at about 60/40. There are also a growing number of female leads in Hollywood films, such as the *Alien* trilogy and *Tomb Raider*. As Haralambos and Holborn (2004) point out, however, earlier forms of gender representation do not go away. They live on as old programmes recycled on cable and satellite television.

New media also seem to be slow in catching up. A content analysis of 33 popular Nintendo and Sega Genesis video games revealed that there were no female characters in 41 per cent of the games. Females were either absent or cast in the role of victim. In 28 per cent of the games, females were portrayed as sex objects. Almost 80 per cent of the games required violence or aggression as part of the strategy. Almost half of the games included violence directed specifically at other people, with 21 per cent of the games depicting direct violence against women. Most of the game characters were Caucasian (Dietz 1998).

Female issues may still be **marginalized** by the media. Most newspapers have 'women's pages' which focus on women as a special group with special – often emotional – needs. Such pages tend to concentrate on beauty and slimming. Tuchman uses the term '**symbolic annihilation**' to describe the way in which women in the media are absent, condemned or trivialized. Women's sport in particular is underrepresented. Research by Newbold *et al.* (2002) into TV sport presentation shows that what little coverage there is tends to 'sexualize, trivialize and devalue women's sporting accomplishments'. Consider, for example, the way women tennis stars in particular are victims of the male gaze, in a similar way to female characters in many films (see under 'Sex appeal' on p. 124).

Women are also absent from top jobs in the media. An analysis of powerful positions generates the following facts: the majority of media owners are men, as are the higher position holders within media empires. For example, out of 30 top BBC executives in 1996, only four were female. In newspapers, in 1995/96 only 20 per cent of positions of significant decision-making power were held by women. In 2005, fewer than 5 per cent of the chief executives of the largest media companies in Britain and fewer than 10 per cent of editors of national newspapers are female (Equal Opportunities Commission 2005).

Women as ideals

Ferguson (1983) conducted a content analysis of women's magazines between 1949 and 1974, and 1979 and 1980. She notes that such magazines are organized around 'a cult of femininity', which promotes an ideal where excellence is achieved through caring for others, the family, marriage and appearance. Modern female magazines, especially those aimed at teenagers, are moving away from these stereotypes – although Ferguson argues that even these tend to focus on 'him, home and looking good (for him)'. Winship (1987), however, stresses the supportive roles such magazines play in the lives of women, especially as many women are largely excluded from the masculine world of work and leisure. She argues that such magazines present women with a broader range of options than ever before, and that they tackle problems that have been largely ignored by the male-dominated media, such as domestic violence and child abuse. Contemporary women's magazines have moved on a great deal from their historical origins, offering visions of femininity that involve independence and confidence as well as beauty and domestic concerns. However, in magazines like *More*, *Red* and *New Woman* women are still encouraged to look good in order to attract men.

On the other hand, it could be argued that the new crop of men's magazines, such as *Men's Health*, do exactly the same for men. However, the feminist response would be that two wrongs don't make a right; both of these genres are still perpetuating an obsession with appearance that discriminates against women.

It is still the case that most women in films and on television (especially presenters) tend to be under 30. Physical looks, sex appeal and, primarily, youth seem to be necessary attributes for women to be successful in television and in the cinema. The same is not true for men, who are still accepted as sexually appealing until much later in life.

Wolf (1990) points out that the media, especially advertising, present a particular physical image as the 'normal' or 'ideal' body image for women to have, even though this image may be unattainable for the majority of women. Some commentators, such as Orbach (1991), have linked such images to anorexia and bulimia in teenage girls.

Sex appeal

Women are often presented as sexual objects to be enjoyed by men. The most extreme media version of this is pornography and 'Page 3 girls' in newspapers. Mulvey (1975) argues that film-makers employ a 'male gaze', whereby the camera lens essentially 'eyes up' the female characters, providing erotic pleasure for men.

Men's style magazines – such as *FHM*, *Maxim* and *Loaded* – encourage young men to dress, smell and consume in particular ways. There is, however, less of a burden on men to change themselves to conform to this ideal. Whilst women may feel that they need to conform in order to ensure that they are desirable, it is more of an option for men.

Buckingham (1993) argues that many boys and probably most men fear being labelled 'effeminate'. The apparent

feminization of masculinity has therefore to be offset by more conspicuous and 'macho' behaviour. The 'new lad' that has emerged is supposedly counter-balanced by the 'ladette' (e.g. Sara Cox and Denise Van Outen), who leers at males through an alcoholic haze and is also aggressively sexual. In new magazines for young women, such as *More*, girls are encouraged to be sexual aggressors rather than sex objects. Whilst this may appear to be evidence of equality, some feminist critics argue that the outcome is to make women more available to sexual exploitation by men – which is particularly concerning, given that the rise in binge drinking among young women can make them vulnerable to rape and date rape.

Male aggressor, female victim

Many people are concerned about the media's presentation of sexual violence against women. A Channel 4 series, *Hard News*, analysed more than 600 articles in ten national newspapers in early 1990. They found that, despite the fact that such crime only makes up 2 per cent of all recorded crime, almost 70 per cent of crime stories focused on rape. Such stories were often distorted in their reporting. Rape victims were often stereotyped as either 'good' women (e.g. virgins, mothers) who had been violated, or 'bad' women who led men on. Newspapers often **sensationalized** cases and focused on what they saw as the most 'titillating' aspects – usually the details of the defendant's evidence.

Joan Smith (1989) notes how the female fear of violent assault is used as a basis for many films. These films may add to the stock of fear that already exists in society. They contribute to the notion of women as 'vulnerable and potential victims' of the superior strength of men. Yet women are also presented as needing the protection of males. 'Female fear sells films. It's a box office hit. … Terror, torture, rape, mutilation and murder are handed to actresses by respectable directors as routinely as tickets on a bus. No longer the stock in trade only of pornographers and video-nasty producers, they can be purchased any day at a cinema near you' (Smith 1989).

Changing representations of men in film

During the 1980s, action films such as *Commando*, *Die Hard* and *Predator* paraded the bodies of their male heroes in advanced stages of both muscular development and undress. One film in particular, *Rambo: First Blood Part II*, starring Sylvester Stallone, became a particular focus for concern. The figure of Rambo has been taken to represent the re-emergence of a threatening, physical form of masculinity. In an overview of the period, Jonathan Rutherford (1988) put forward the idea that there existed two key images of masculinity in the late 20th century. He termed these images, 'new man' and 'retributive man'. For Rutherford, images of the new man attempt – partly in a response to feminism – to express men's repressed emotions, revealing a more feminized image. Against this, the face of retributive man represents the struggle to reassert a traditional masculinity; a tough authority.

More recently, male violence in cinema has acquired a glamour and stylishness that seems to celebrate the more traditional **representations** of masculinity. Films like *Lock Stock and Two Smoking Barrels* and *Face Off* present men who gain admiration by solving their problems through violence. These kinds of films are currently outnumbering those that represent alternative views of masculinity, such as *The Full Monty*. However, gratuitous violence is no longer the sole province of the sadistic male, with a growing number of violent films with leading female characters, such as *Kill Bill 1* and *2* and *Crouching Tiger, Hidden Dragon*.

Explanations of gender representations

Feminists have been very critical of the representations of men and women in the media. However, they differ in their emphasis. (See Unit 1, Topic 3, pp. 12–13, for explanations of the different types of feminism.)

- *Liberal feminists* believe that media representations are lagging behind women's achievements in society. However, they also believe that the situation is improving as the number of female journalists, editors and broadcasters increases.
- *Socialist- and Marxist-feminists* believe that stereotypical images of men and women are a by-product of the need to make a profit. The male-dominated media aim to attract the largest audience possible, and this leads to an emphasis on the traditional roles of men and women.
- *Radical feminists* feel strongly that the media reproduce patriarchy. Traditional images are deliberately transmitted by male-dominated media to keep women oppressed in a narrow range of roles.

Not everyone accepts these kinds of feminist analysis. Critics argue that they underestimate women's ability to see through stereotyping. Pluralists (see p. 99) believe that the media simply reflect social attitudes and public demand. They argue that the media are meeting both men and women's needs – although the question remains: to what extent are the media actually creating those needs in the first place?

David Gauntlett
Men's magazines

There is a generation of younger men who have adapted to the modern world (in a range of ways), who have grown up with women as their equals, and who do not feel threatened by these social changes. These men and their cultures are largely ignored by the problem-centred discourse of masculinity studies.

Because of this, older self-proclaimed gender-aware men and women would almost certainly fail to understand the playful, humorous discourse about gender that circulates in men's magazines. (These magazines are not wholly antisexist, and there is a legitimate concern that dim readers will take 'joke sexism' literally, of course, but the more significant observation should perhaps be that sexism has shifted from being the expression of a meaningful and serious ideology in former times, to being a resource for use in silly jokes today). The magazines are often centred on helping men to be considerate lovers, useful around the home, healthy, fashionable and funny – in particular, being able to laugh at themselves. To be obsessed about the bits which superficially look like 'a reinscription of masculinity' is to miss the point. Men's magazines are not perfect vehicles for the transformation of gender roles, by any means, but they play a more important, complex and broadly positive role than most critics suggest.

Adapted from Gauntlett, D. (2002) *Media, Gender and Identity: An Introduction*, London: Routledge

1 What does the author mean by the 'playful, humorous discourse about gender that circulates in men's magazines'? Give examples.

2 Do you agree that men's and women's lifestyle magazines 'play a more important, complex and broadly positive role than most critics suggest'?

Check your understanding

1 What might be the reason why women often have independent and assertive roles in soap operas?

2 Describe the differences in gender representation in top positions in the media.

3 How does Winship argue that women's magazines can be supportive?

4 What problems are associated with the 'ideal' body image for women?

5 How does Buckingham explain the emergence of the 'new lad'?

6 According to Joan Smith, what are the effects of media representations of women as victims?

7 How do feminists explain the representations of women in the media?

Sociology AS for OCR

research ideas

- Individually or in groups, conduct a content analysis of a soap opera, a news broadcast, a game show and a TV drama.
    - How many men and women appear?
    - How much time does each gender spend on screen?
    - What roles do they play?
    - How typical is each programme of others of its kind?
    - What conclusions can you draw about men and women in the media?

- Compare the views of young men and young women about the representation of women in the media. You could do this by conducting in-depth interviews or by using a questionnaire. Try showing respondents examples of men's and women's magazines to get them talking.

web.task

David Gauntlett is the author of *Media, Gender and identity: an Introduction.* Go to his book's website at www.theoryhead.com/gender

Click on the discussions between him and other writers regarding issues of gender representations.

Read his article about the sexual assertiveness of young women's magazines. What do you think about Gauntlett's view of these magazines? Write a response either agreeing or disagreeing, explaining your reasons and e-mail it to David Gauntlett using the link provided at the end of the article.

MEDIA, GENDER AND IDENTITY
AN INTRODUCTION · David Gauntlett

STILL NEW! SITE UPDATED WITH NEW MATERIAL, NOVEMBER 2003

Media, Gender and Identity provides a new introduction to the relationship between the media and gender identities today. [More...]

Buy the book online for £14 (UK) or $25 (US). [Click...]

We want to know what you think. If you've read the book, send us comments please. [Reviews...]

This website offers a range of bonus features which complement the material in the book. The website-only extra features include:

- New article on men's magazines in Germany (added September 2003)
- Extended chapter on self-help books and what they tell us about gender and identities today
- New article about the sexual assertiveness of young women's magazines
- Discussion between Amy Jankowicz and David Gauntlett about the impact of men's magazines
- Discussion between Derrick Cameron and David Gauntlett about men's magazines and masculinities

NEW REVIEWS:

"Gauntlett's optimism is infectious, the subject matter engaging, and, as a result, the book is difficult to put aside. It is a thoroughly pleasurable introduction to the ties between self-identities and representations of

Item A Women in the press

Item B Women on television

Level of appearance by gender (terrestrial television)

Level of appearance	Male no.	(%)	Female no.	(%)	Total no.	(%)
Major role	1,482	16	1,080	23	2,562	18
Minor role	1,475	16	693	15	2,168	16
Incidental/interviewer	6,217	68	2,922	62	9,139	66
Total	9,174	100	4,695	100	13,869	100

Source: Broadcasting Standards Commission Report 1999, p. 100

Item C Women in the media

« The presentation of women in the media is biased because it emphasizes women's domestic, sexual, consumer and marital activities to the exclusion of all else. Women are depicted as busy housewives, as contented mothers, as eager consumers and as sex objects. This does indeed indicate bias because, although similar numbers of men are fathers and husbands, the media has much less to say about these male roles; men are seldom presented nude, nor is their marital or family status continually quoted in irrelevant contexts. Just as men's domestic and marital roles are ignored, the media also ignore that well over half of British adult women go out to paid employment, and that many of both their interests and problems are employment related.»

Tunstall, J. (1983) *The Media in Britain*, London: Constable

1 Explain what is meant by the concept of presentation of women in the media being biased (Item C). (2 marks)

2 Identify and briefly explain two assumptions that the covers in Item A make about the interests of young men or young women. (4 marks)

3 Identify and explain three ways in which media representations of males and females are becoming more similar. (9 marks)

4 Identify and explain two ways in which men and women's roles are presented differently in the media. (10 marks)

Exam practice

5 a Identify and explain two ways in which women have been misrepresented by the media. (15 marks)

b Outline and discuss the view that women's representation in the media is distorted and limited. (30 marks)

Media representations

1 How do you think most people would interpret what is
happening in this photograph?

2 Why will they think this?

3 What other possible interpretations can you think of?

In the photograph above, a Black, plain-clothes police officer
leads some of his uniformed colleagues in chasing a suspect.
However, many people are likely to interpret the photograph
differently, believing that the Black man is being chased by the
police. This mistake should come as no surprise, as many people
do associate young Black men with criminality. Why is this?
Perhaps the explanation lies with the **representation** of ethnic
minorities in the media. Ethnic minorities tend to be either
ignored by the media or, when they do actually appear,
portrayed in distorted ways that owe more to **stereotypes** than
to reality. But ethnic minorities are not the only groups who
have reason to be concerned about their portrayal in the media.
This topic will look at media representations of various groups.

Ethnic minorities

Old films, comics and adventure stories that portrayed Black
people as happy, dancing savages with a brutal streak have,

thankfully, largely disappeared from modern television and
films. However, the media still have a tendency to associate
Black people with physical rather than intellectual activities, and
to view them in stereotypical ways. The findings of recent
research generally make for depressing reading:

- underrepresentation and stereotypical characterization in
  entertainment genres
- negative, problem-oriented portrayal in factual and news
  forms
- a tendency to ignore inequality and racism.

Black people are portrayed in the media in the following ways:

- *As criminal* – van Dijk (1991) conducted a content
  analysis of tens of thousands of news items across the
  world over several decades. He found that Black crime
  and violence are one of the most frequent issues in ethnic
  coverage. Black people, particularly African-Caribbeans,
  tend to be portrayed, especially in the tabloid press, as
  criminals – and more recently as members of organized

criminal gangs. The word 'Black' is often used as a prefix if an offender is a member of an ethnic minority, e.g. 'a Black youth'. The word 'White' is rarely used in the same way. In a now famous study by Stuart Hall, *Policing the Crisis* (Hall *et al.* 1978), the alleged crime wave of Black muggers was cited as a moral panic (see pp. 130–1) created by the establishment through the media to justify more repressive social control measures at a time when capitalism was in crisis. The truth is that a Black person is 36 times more likely to be the victim of a violent attack than a White person.

- *As a threat* – Tabloid newspapers are prone to panic about the numbers of ethnic minorities in the UK. It is often suggested that immigrants are a threat in terms of their 'numbers', because of the impact they might have on the supply of jobs, housing and other facilities. The same newspapers are also concerned about refugees and asylum seekers, who are allegedly coming to the UK to abuse the welfare state and take advantage of a more successful economy than their own.

- *As abnormal* – Some sections of the media are guilty of creating false cultural stereotypes around the value systems and norms of other cultures. For example, tabloid newspapers have run stories that suggest that Muslims have negative attitudes towards women. They claim that they 'force' daughters into arranged marriages against their will. The distinction between 'forced' marriage – an extremely rare occurrence, strongly disapproved of by Asian communities – and arranged marriage, which is based on mutual consent, is rarely made. A survey of Asian viewers, by the market research company Ethnic Focus (2003), cited the most common complaint, which was 'that the media divided Asians into two camps; either miserable folk being forced into loveless marriages or billionaires who had come to the UK with nothing and had now made a fortune.'

- *As unimportant* – Some sections of the media imply that the lives of White people are somehow more important than the lives of non-White people. News items about disasters in other countries are often restricted to a few lines or words, especially if the population is non-White. The misfortunes of one British person tend to be prioritized over the sufferings of thousands of foreigners.

- *As dependent* – As the government report *Viewing the World* (2000) points out, stories about less developed countries tend to focus on the 'coup–war–famine–starvation syndrome'. The implication of such stories, both in newspapers and on television, is that the problems of developing countries are the result of stupidity, tribal conflict, too many babies, laziness, corruption and unstable political regimes. It is implied that the governments of these countries are somehow inadequate because they cannot solve these problems. Such countries are portrayed as coming to the West for help time and time again. The idea that the poverty of developing countries may be due to their exploitation by the West is often ignored and neglected.

'One Britain was killed in a plane crash in South Africa today. The Kenyan airlines Airbus was carrying 320 passengers from Nairobi to Johannesburg. No one survived.'

Underrepresentation

Surveys of television, advertising and films indicate that Black people are underrepresented. When they do appear, the range of roles they play is very limited. Black people are rarely shown as ordinary citizens who just happen to be Black. More often they play 'Black' roles, their attitudes and behaviour being heavily determined by their ethnic identity. Some soaps, such as *Eastenders,* have, in fact, included Black and Asian characters as ordinary members of the community. However, its main rival on ITV, *Coronation Street*, has only recently begun to include Black characters despite its 40-year history and despite being set in what would long have been a multicultural area of Manchester.

Ghettoization

Some critics have commented on the recent tendency for ethnic issues and interests to be covered by specialized programming and channels. This, they claim, isolates mainstream audiences from minority cultures and further inhibits their understanding and tolerance. Also, the main channels may decide not to cover minority issues as they consider them to be well catered for elsewhere.

On a more positive note, the media have been very positive in their exposure of problems such as racism. The murder of the Black teenager Stephen Lawrence by White racists in 1993 received high-profile coverage, both on television and in the press. Even the *Daily Mail* presented a front-page story highlighting police racism, and attempted to 'name and shame' the racists who committed the murder.

The cast of BBC TV soap EastEnders at an awards ceremony

BBC research into race
Representation of ethnic minorities on TV

In a recent survey by the BBC in answer to the question 'Are ethnic minorities better represented on TV than they were 10 years ago?', the answers were as follows:

	Total	White	Black	Asian
Yes	78%	80%	73%	67%
No	8%	7%	12%	16%
Don't know	13%	12%	15%	17%

Source: BBC News Online special report: Race UK, 20–31 May 2002, conducted by ICM research for the BBC

1 How might you criticize the phrasing of this question?

An interesting recent development is media recognition of the influence of ethnic cultures on White culture. Comedy shows such as the *Ali G* show and *Goodness Gracious Me* highlight, albeit in a comic way, how Black youth subcultural styles have infiltrated the styles of both White and Asian youth.

Class

The upper classes are often seen in nostalgic representations which paint a rosy picture of a time when Britain was great, and honour, culture and good breeding prevailed. Wealth and social inequality are rarely critically examined. Examples of this type of representation include TV costume dramas such as *Pride and Prejudice*, and films such as *A Room With a View*.

The middle classes are over-represented in the media, possibly because most of the creative personnel in the media are themselves middle class. In news and current affairs, the middle classes dominate in positions of authority – the 'expert' is invariably middle class.

Jhally and Lewis (1992) found that, on American TV between 1971 and 1989, 90 per cent of characters were middle class, whilst the percentage of working-class characters over the period fell from 4 per cent to only 1 per cent. In the UK, members of the working class tend to appear as criminals, single parents, 'welfare scroungers' or delinquent children. Soaps have tended to show working-class life in a more positive, if unrealistic, light – presenting an ideal of a tight-knit community with a shared history and mutual obligations. British cinema has tried to portray working-class life more realistically. In the 1960s, films such as *A Taste of Honey*, and *Saturday Night, Sunday Morning* examined the realities of domestic life. More recently, *Secrets and Lies* and *The Full Monty* have shown working-class problems in a sensitive way, challenging social inequality, racial intolerance and class conflict. Some TV comedy and drama, such as *The Royle Family,* has also begun to adopt a more naturalistic approach to working-class family life.

Gay men and lesbians

Until recently, gay people have generally been either invisible in the media or represented in a negative light – being stereotyped as either 'camp' gay men or 'butch' lesbian women.

Gay men were heavily stigmatized in the wake of the initial Aids reporting, but, since then, sexuality has been more openly discussed. Several celebrities have recently 'come out' (declared their sexual orientation publicly). These include Elton John, George Michael, Stephen Gateley and Will Young. Lesbian sexual orientation has been embraced by mainstream female performers such as Madonna, Britney Spears and Christina Aguilera through stage shows in which the female performers have stunned audiences with open-mouth on-stage kisses.

It appears that homosexuality is now much more acceptable within the popular media. Graham Norton, the openly gay presenter of a popular TV chat show, has a huge following of mainly heterosexual viewers. Two of the last three winners of the *Big Brother* reality game show have been gay. Mainstream television dramas now explore the lives of gay people, while *Coronation Street*, the longest-running soap, has had two main storylines featuring a gay character and a transsexual character, both of whom have been sympathetically portrayed. Such acceptance may be less evident in the news media.

Youth and 'moral panics'

Young people are often presented as a problem by the media. By identifying groups of young people as 'football hooligans' and 'ravers', the media can create a **'moral panic'** – in which the behaviour of such groups is seen as a threat to the moral order and stability of society. The media play a key role in creating moral panics by sensationalizing and grossly exaggerating the threat that these groups pose. They soon become **'folk devils'** – evil people who are threatening our ordinary, everyday lives. Examples of moral panics and associated folk devils are listed in Table 3.2 below.

Ironically, the media's desire to produce sensational stories about youth, sometimes out of nothing, can help create the very behaviour they are attacking. For example, many young people are actually attracted by sensational coverage of youth groups (which they otherwise might not have heard about or recognized). They begin to conform to media stereotypes in order to acquire status and recognition in the eyes of their peers, and some notoriety in the wider society. The prejudiced attitude of the general public and the police drives them further towards deviance (a process known as **deviance amplification**). Thus a real problem is created out of something that would probably have remained fairly small scale had it not been for the media's sensational coverage.

Table 3.2 Moral panics and 'folk devils' – some examples

Dates	Moral panic – the perceived problem	'Folk devil' – the group to blame	Potential victims
Late 1940s–1980s	Violent youth – civil unrest: threat to public order/decency/safety	Most youth subcultures, such as 'mods and rockers'	Ordinary citizens and their property
Every decade	Football hooliganism – street violence; vandalism, damage to life/property	Organized, 'mindless' hooligans who are not 'real' fans	Innocent bystanders; 'real' football fans
Late 1960s	Hippies – a threat due to their alternative lifestyle, drug-taking and sexual freedom	Long-haired, young middle classes	All decent, hardworking people
1960s and 70s	Sex on screen – corruption of children and offence to the unwitting viewer	Irresponsible film and TV producers	The impressionable young; decent folk
1970s	Mugging – threat to peace in the streets and personal security	Black youths	The vulnerable on the street
Mid 1970s	'Scroungers' – social security fraud	Undeserving, fraudulent claimants (often non-White)	Everyone who pays taxes
Early 1980s	Aids – death through 'deviant' sexual practices	Mainly gay men	The sexually active, above all young, single people
1980s, 90s	Glue-sniffing, out-of-control youth; premature death	Youth underclass	All lower working-class youth
Late 1980s–1990s	Club culture – ecstasy – drug deaths; threats to public order	Clubbers; ravers	All young people; the general public
Mid 1990s	Satanic ritual abuse – widespread sexual abuse of children by parents	Mostly incestuous fathers and overzealous social workers	Children and the family unit
Mid 1990s	Children, violence and the family (plus video nasties) – moral decline; family breakdown; corruption of young	Children of 'underclass' families; irresponsible parents	Toddlers; small children
Late 1990s	Paedophilia, child pornography	Middle-aged men, organized through the internet	Every child
2000s	Gun culture	Black drug criminals	All innocent bystanders; corrupted youth
2000s	Overwhelming immigration	Asylum seekers	All decent, tax-paying citizens

KEY TERMS

Deviance amplification the reinforcing of a person's or a group's deviant identity, as a result of condemnation by agencies of social control such as the media.

Folk devils – groups seen by the media as evil and a threat to the moral well-being of society.

Moral panic public concern, created by the media, about the behaviour of certain groups of people who are seen as a threat to the moral order and stability of society.

Representation manner in which the media present an individual, group or event.

Stereotype a typical or 'shorthand' picture of a certain group.

focus on research

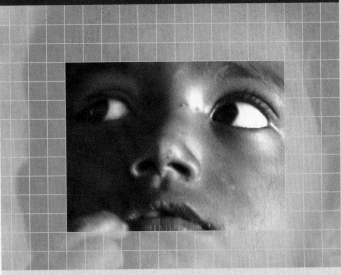

Read the extract on the right and then answer the questions below.

Source: Davies, M.M. and Mosdell, N. (2001) *Consenting Children? The Use of Children in Non-Fiction Television Programmes*, London: Broadcasting Standards Commission

Davies and Mosdell
Children: 'monsters' or 'innocents'?

<< Our *Consenting Children?* analysis indicated a duality in the ways in which children are represented in the media: on the one hand, there was the innocent child who was allowed to play adult-like roles for the sake of entertainment or who was an innocent victim of disasters such as war, famine and disease; on the other hand, there was the controversial child, of interest to the audience because of his/her 'evil' nature, such as children who kill, as in the case of the Bulger killers. Both the 'innocent' and the 'evil' can be found in representations of children at war, often combined in the same children – as has happened with stories covering the child warriors of Liberia. Are they war criminals or victims? News reporters find it difficult to present stories about such children because of the duality of their roles. They are difficult to fit into the standard child-protagonist in media narratives – innocent victim or precociously evil 'monster'. They are clearly both. >>

1 What is meant by the 'duality' in the way children are represented in the media?

2 What happens to this duality in coverage of children at war?

Check your understanding

1 What does van Dijk's study tell us about media representations of ethnic minorities?

2 What do the media suggest is the main motivation for refugees and asylum seekers in coming to the UK?

3 How is the relationship between developing countries and the West portrayed in the media?

4 Compare media representations of the upper, middle and working classes.

5 How is the popular media's attitude to gay people changing?

6 Explain in your own words the terms 'moral panic' and 'folk devils'.

7 How can media coverage of deviant youth groups actually make the 'problem' worse?

web.tasks

1 Find the websites of the Refugee Council at www.refugeecouncil.org.uk and the Campaign against Racism and Fascism at www.carf.demon.co.uk (select 'Features'). What do they have to say about media coverage of minority ethnic groups, refugees and asylum seekers?

2 Find the report, Viewing the World, at the website of the Department for International Development. This can be accessed from the main government website www.open.gov.uk

What methods does the study use and what are its key conclusions about media coverage of development issues?

research idea

● Watch a range of television programmes one evening. Conduct a content analysis by counting the numbers and types of roles taken by older and younger people. What conclusions can you reach about media representations of age?

Item A Press coverage of immigration

In February 2004, there was extensive coverage of the enlargement of the European Union in the national newspapers, centring on the free movement of workers in the new Member States.

Mass-circulation tabloid headlines included the following:

Migrants invasion warning

5 million more migrants by 2031

Blair's bid to save UK jobs from EU gypsies

This culminated in the following:

Britain is warned over the migrants with HIV

(*Daily Mail*, 18 February)

How health tourists will bleed our system dry

(*Daily Express*, 25 February)

In the *Sun*, the 'Sick Britain' front page (24 February) claimed:

Britain will be swamped by sick immigrants from Eastern Europe as the EU expands. People from countries where HIV and TB are rife will be able to come here and use the NHS (health service) despite a new ban on overseas benefit scroungers.

Item B Media turns on gays

<<TV presenter Graham Norton, businessman Ivan Massow, MEP Michael Cashman and activist Peter Tatchell told the *Independent* that they have all been appalled by the way newspaper editors in particular have used gay stereotypes and offensive language in a bid to shift papers. They claim that the media is 'out of touch' with gay culture and riddled with sterotypes.

Stories circulating in the royal gay rape story in particular have been billed to shock. Stories of a gay mafia at work in the palace, servants entertaining rent boys, and the prospect of a member of the Royal family being caught in a compromising situation with a member of staff have been

sensationalized to sell papers.

The newspapers have been having what can only be called as a 'lets take a pot shot at gays' field day. The *Sunday Telegraph*, for example, slammed the government for granting two gay Jamaicans asylum because of homophobia in their country, whilst *The Sun* demanded to know why so many of our MPs are gay.

The battle over gays being allowed to adopt and David Blunkett's announcement that the offence of buggery (anal sex with a male) was to be abolished has given the newspapers even more ammunition.

Labour MEP Michael Cashman said he has seen an increase in

homophobic reporting, but he believes the public have moved on and no longer see homosexuality as the big issue the tabloids like to whip it into.

'Lesbians and gay men are now much more out than ever before. You have openly gay politicians and gay builders,' he told the *Independent*.

With another butler trial looming and further debate over gay couples adopting, the media hasn't finished. Let's just hope the British public see it for what it is – the fish 'n' chip paper of tomorrow.>>

Source: www.uk.gay.com, 25 November 2002

1 Explain what is meant by the term 'underrepresented'. (2 marks)

2 Suggest two possible effects of the headlines described in Item A. (4 marks)

3 Using Item B and your wider knowledge, suggest reasons for the persistence of stereotypical representations of gay people in the media. (9 marks)

4 Identify and explain two ways in which the media could be said to be responsible for creating moral panics. (10 marks)

Exam practice

5 a Identify and explain two ways in which ethnic minorities have been misrepresented by the media. (20 marks)

   b Outline and discuss the view that the representation of ethnic minorities in the media has significantly improved over the last 20 years. (30 marks)

Postmodernism and the media

gettingyouthinking

Family viewing in the 1950s

Media in the home today

Look at the cartoons above.

1 **In what ways do they show that our use of the media is changing?**

2 **How do they show that the media themselves have changed?**

3 **What effect might these changes have on family life?**

4 **To what extent may changes in the media have reduced social interaction?**

5 **To what extent may changes in the media have increased social interaction?**

6 **'Media output was once highly structured for us – now we structure it to suit ourselves.'**
How far do you consider this statement to be true?

People – at least those who can afford the technology – are now exposed to an ever-increasing range of media. Once part of a whole family experience, **media consumption** has become a more individual affair (just look at the cartoons above). But it can also involve a worldwide community, through technology such as the internet. Viewers take in a much wider range of programming and images, often flicking from channel to channel and producing their own viewing schedules through the use of video, DVD and other emerging technologies. They may take digital photos or videos on their phones, e-mail them instantly or edit them before sending them across the world wide web. How has this all come about and what are the implications for societies and their cultures?

Postmodernism and the media

As we saw in Unit 1, Topic 5, it has been suggested that societies have entered a new stage of development known as postmodernism. In economic life, information technology is increasingly becoming more important than manufacturing technology. White-collar workers, who specialize in the production of information and knowledge, now outnumber industrial workers. The globalization of mass media, information technology and electronic communication, such as e-mail and the internet, has led to the decline of national cultures and the growing importance of cultural diversity in our lifestyles.

Dominic Strinati (1995) argues that the mass media are centrally important in the development of postmodern society, for the following reasons:

● The part people played in the manufacture of goods once determined their social, national and local identities. These identities were further structured by factors such as social class, gender and ethnicity. In postmodern society, however, identities are increasingly being structured through consumption patterns. Now, the media provide most of our experience of social reality. What we take as 'real' is to a great extent what the media tell us is real. Our lifestyles and identity are defined for us by the media. For example, TV programmes and lifestyle magazines tell us what our homes and gardens should look like. Advertising tells us what products we need to buy to improve the quality of our lives. Magazines tell us how we can make ourselves attractive to potential partners. The news tells us what issues we should be thinking about. Fly-on-the-wall documentaries reassure us that other people share our anxieties, and so on.

● Image and style have more significance than form or content. In the postmodern world, we learn through the media that the consumption of images and signs for their own sake is more important than the consumption of the goods they represent. We buy the labels and packaging rather than the clothes or goods themselves. People are judged negatively for wearing the wrong trainers, rather than because of some fault in their character or lack of ability.

● In the past, a **cultural hierarchy** existed. Classical music, for example, was considered to be more 'serious' and 'important' than pop music. But in the postmodern world, there are constant crossovers between '**high culture**' and '**popular culture**'. The classical musicians Luciano Pavarotti, Vanessa Mae and Nigel Kennedy have all attempted pop music projects, whilst pop artists such as Paul McCartney have experimented with classical music. Time and place have also become confused and **decontextualized**. For example, Fatboy Slim sampled a few lines from a protest song of the American Civil Rights Movement of the 1960s, 'Praise you', and turned them into a number one record (the result was brilliant dance music devoid of political meaning). Shakespeare's *Romeo and Juliet* was re-presented as a teen movie set in late 20th-century Los Angeles.

The popular media themselves have become the subject of heated intellectual debate. For instance, you can now study towards an honours degree in Star Trek. The 'cultural expert', whose views have more weight than those of ordinary consumers, no longer exists. Now we are all experts.

According to postmodernists, it is the constant bombardment of media imagery in this **media-saturated society** that has caused all of this, transforming not only individual societies but even national identities – to the extent that, as some claim, we now live in a '**global village**'. People all over the world share many of the same consumption patterns and the same image-conscious outlook. Companies such as Disney, Levi Strauss, McDonald's, Sony and Coca-Cola target their products at a global audience. People across the world have real-time access to world news from CNN, while their kids argue about switching over to MTV.

focus on research

Nawal El Saadawi
War, Lies and Videotape

In *War, Lies and Videotape*, media critics and activists examine the newly-emerging global media systems. The following extract is adapted from a contribution by Nawal El Saadawi, a world-renowned Egyptian feminist:

<< Never before in history has there been such domination of people's minds by the mass media ... such a concentration and centralization of media, capital and military power in the hands of so few people. The richest seven countries control almost all the technological, economic, media, information and military power in the world.

To expand the global market, the media plays its role in developing certain values, patterns of behavior and perceptions of beauty, femininity, masculinity, success, love and sex. The media creates a global consumer with an increasing desire to buy what the transnational capitalists (TNCs) produce, thereby maximizing their profits.

In spite of all these obstacles, we have to continue the struggle locally and globally. Globalization from above by the TNCs and their media should be challenged by globalization from below by women and men who are the majority of the world. We have to create our own media and communicate with each other through the internet, e-mail and other electronic devices. With the continuous advance in communication technology, we will be able to reach each other with less money and less time. The decentralization of the media and communication technology is inevitable, and it can be turned to our favor. The unveiling of the mind is our goal, to be accomplished by exercising political power through local and global organizations. >>

Aristide *et al.* (eds) (2000) *War, Lies and Videotape*, New York: International Action Center,

1 **What role has the media played in promoting globalization?**

2 **How and why should globalization be resisted?**

Criticisms of the postmodern view of the media

Postmodernists are criticized for exaggerating the extent to which wider social influences have subsided. Their critics argue that they underplay the continuing importance of class, gender and ethnicity in our lives, and that they exaggerate the changes that the media have brought about. Inequality remains a key issue, as access to the internet, digital television and so on is denied to many millions of poorer people worldwide. How can a 'global village' exist when so many cannot enter it?

Resistance to global media

The growing influence of the global corporations and media giants has not gone unnoticed. They are often accused of eroding national cultures or even undermining them. Islamic countries denounce the Western media for using degrading images of women. Eastern political regimes (e.g. China, Malaysia), fearing undesirable political and moral messages, have boycotted Western-owned satellite broadcasters. Even Rupert Murdoch has realized that, by promoting local culture through the Star satellite that he owns (which broadcasts to Asia), he will gain more government approval – and ultimately bigger audiences – than he would by imposing Western programmes on Eastern audiences.

In parts of Europe, resistance to '**McDonaldization**' (the American take-over of culture) has had a reverse effect. New broadcasting technology is being used for the development of more local and regional programming, aimed at preserving distinctive European cultural traditions and outlooks.

The explosion of satellite, digital and internet technologies has transformed the way in which most of us organize our lives. Families, communities, and national life have all been affected. There is no doubt that – whatever the exact nature of their influence – the media have had an immense impact on modern societies throughout the world, and that, in the process, the world has become a smaller place.

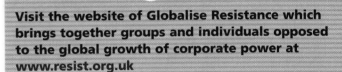

web.task

Visit the website of Globalise Resistance which brings together groups and individuals opposed to the global growth of corporate power at www.resist.org.uk

Check your understanding

1. **Identify three changes associated with the shift towards a postmodern society.**

2. **What is the relationship between consumption and identity? Give an example of your own.**

3. **What is meant by the phrase 'style is more important than substance'?**

4. **Why might postmodernists argue that Fatboy Slim's version of 'Praise you' is just as valid as the original?**

5. **Explain in your own words the term 'globalization'.**

6. **Give examples of two positive and two negative outcomes of globalization.**

research ideas

- Design a questionnaire and conduct a survey within your school or college to assess the differences in access to and consumption of the new media, in relation to class, gender, ethnicity and age. Consider both household ownership and personal consumption of the following media forms: PCs, web TV, cable TV, games consoles, WAP phones, DVD players, videos, MP3 players, digital cameras.

- Draw up a list of the top five terrestrial TV programmes amongst your peer group. What proportion show signs of American influence? How many are reflective of British culture? Do the same for cable/satellite TV.

KEY TERMS

Cultural hierarchy term used to describe how opinions and tastes of particular individuals and groups, who are seen to have more cultural expertise, are valued above the tastes of others.

Decontextualized used to describe something that has been taken out of the situation in which it arose.

'Global village' the idea that the world has become much smaller as the media allow us all to communicate easily with each other and to share ideas and lifestyles.

High culture cultural forms, such as opera, that are associated with high-status or elite sections of society and considered 'superior' to other forms of culture.

McDonaldization the idea that American culture has overwhelmed other national cultures – literally that McDonald's has taken over the world.

Media consumption use of the media.

Media-saturated society a society in which every aspect of social life is influenced by the media.

Popular culture cultural forms, such as soap operas, that are preferred by the majority of the population.

exploring postmodernism and the media

Item A Use of new technology in the UK 1997 to 2004

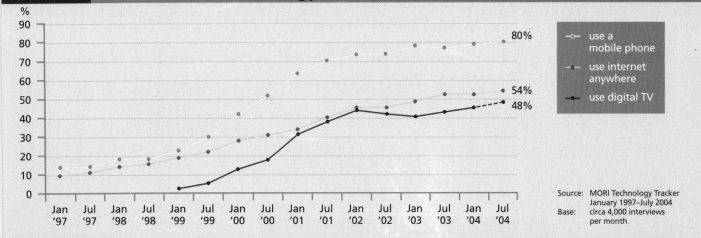

Legend:
— ○ — use a mobile phone
— - — use internet anywhere
— ● — use digital TV

80%
54%
48%

Source: MORI Technology Tracker January 1997–July 2004
Base: circa 4,000 interviews per month

Item B Class differences in the use of new technology

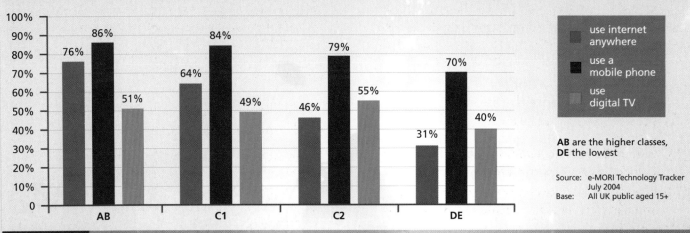

Legend:
use internet anywhere
use a mobile phone
use digital TV

AB: 76%, 86%, 51%
C1: 64%, 84%, 49%
C2: 46%, 79%, 55%
DE: 31%, 70%, 40%

AB are the higher classes, **DE** the lowest

Source: e-MORI Technology Tracker July 2004
Base: All UK public aged 15+

Item C Cultural imperialism

In 1981, American films accounted for 94 per cent of foreign films broadcast on British TV, 80 per cent of those broadcast on French TV and 54 per cent on West German TV. In Western Europe as a whole, American imports represented 75 per cent of all imports. The share represented by US-originated programmes in other parts of the world is even greater. These media products depict Western (often idealized) lifestyles. This cultural imperialism is transnational. More recently, there has been some debate as to whether the US dominance is slipping, with increased competition at regional, national and local levels.

However, what has happened to replace American programming is in many cases a local adaptation of American television formats. Local cultures are re-presented in an Americanized form.

Adapted from Taylor, S. (2001) *Sociology: Issues and Debates*, London: Routledge

---

1 Explain in your own words what is meant by the term 'cultural imperialism' (Item C). (2 marks)

2 Identify and explain two ways in which the use of new technology is increasing (Item A). (4 marks)

3 Identify and explain three possible reasons for differences in the use of new technology according to social class (Item B). (9 marks)

4 Identify and explain two ways in which new technologies have had an impact on social life. (10 marks)

Exam practice

5 a Identify and explain two ways in which use of the media has changed in the last 20 years. (15 marks)

b Outline and discuss the view that we now live in a media-saturated society which defines our lifestyle and consumption patterns. (30 marks)

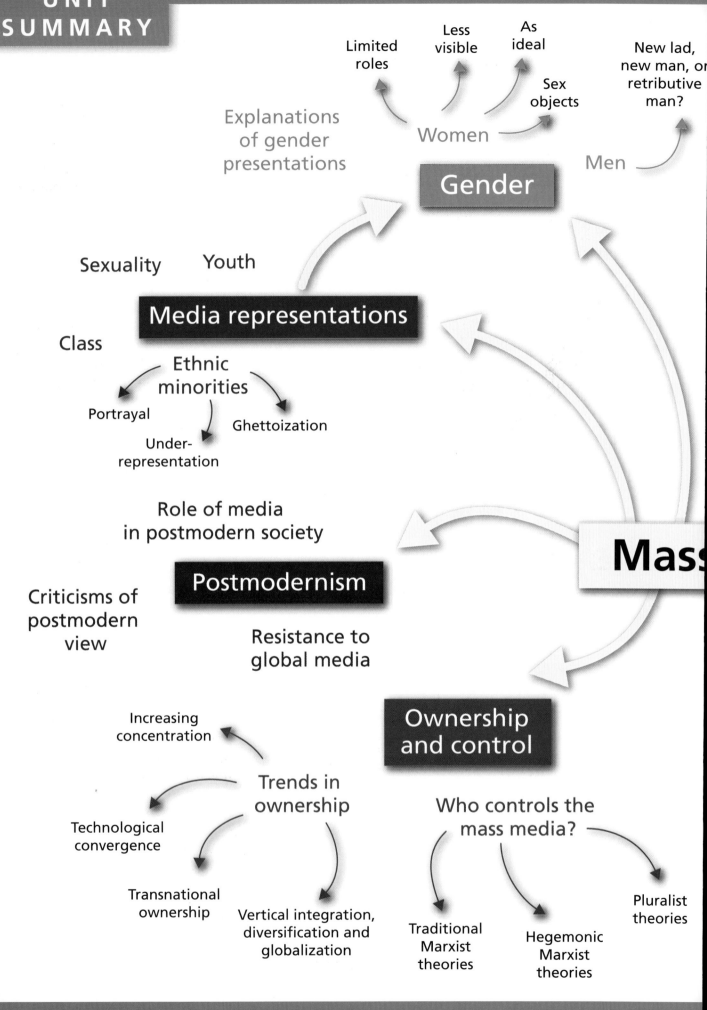

Limited roles

Less visible

As ideal

New lad, new man, or retributive man?

Sex objects

Explanations of gender presentations

Women

Men

Gender

Sexuality

Youth

Media representations

Class

Ethnic minorities

Portrayal

Ghettoization

Under-representation

Role of media in postmodern society

Postmodernism

Criticisms of postmodern view

Resistance to global media

Mass

Ownership and control

Increasing concentration

Trends in ownership

Who controls the mass media?

Technological convergence

Transnational ownership

Vertical integration, diversification and globalization

Traditional Marxist theories

Hegemonic Marxist theories

Pluralist theories

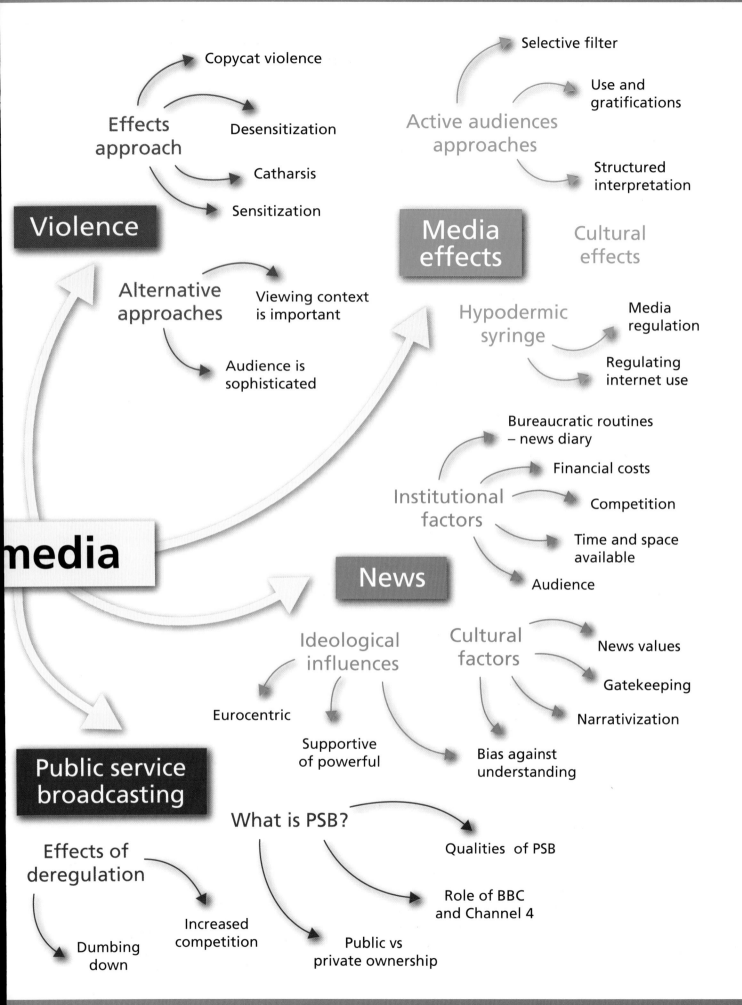

Copycat violence

Effects approach
- Desensitization
- Catharsis
- Sensitization

Violence

Alternative approaches
- Viewing context is important
- Audience is sophisticated

Selective filter

Active audiences approaches
- Use and gratifications
- Structured interpretation

Media effects

Cultural effects

Hypodermic syringe
- Media regulation
- Regulating internet use

media

Institutional factors
- Bureaucratic routines – news diary
- Financial costs
- Competition
- Time and space available
- Audience

News

Ideological influences
- Eurocentric
- Supportive of powerful
- Bias against understanding

Cultural factors
- News values
- Gatekeeping
- Narrativization

Public service broadcasting

Effects of deregulation
- Dumbing down
- Increased competition

What is PSB?
- Public vs private ownership

Qualities of PSB

Role of BBC and Channel 4

BILLIONS OF PEOPLE IN THE WORLD BELIEVE IN SOMETHING that has never been proved to exist. Many of these people base their lifestyles, values and morals on these beliefs. In fact, whole societies are sometimes structured around religious belief.

It's not surprising that sociologists take a strong interest in religion. They wonder about the role of religion in society: why does it exist? What effects does it have? These issues make up the main parts of Topics 1 and 2.

People express their religious beliefs in many different ways. Some are members of huge faiths whose followers are spread across the world, while others express their spiritual beliefs in more personal ways – by consulting tarot cards or crystals for example. Topic 3 focuses on organized religions and Topic 4 on the growth of what have become known as 'new religious movements'.

Religious belief and participation are not free from the divisions that cut across other aspects of social life. Topic 5 looks at gender and religion, including the role of women in religious organizations, feminism and religion, and explanations of women's high rates of religious participation and belief. The focus of Topic 6 is ethnicity and religion – in particular, the importance of religion in the lives of members of minority ethnic groups in Britain.

Finally, Topic 7 asks whether religion is in decline in a world which seems to emphasize scientific explanations and rational ways of thinking. The evidence for and against secularization is considered and the difficulties of generalizing about this complex issue are acknowledged.

OCRspecification	topics	pages
Religious institutions		
Church, denomination, sect and cult. Their relationship to society and to each other	These different religious organizations are covered in Topic 3.	152–157
New Religious Movements. Classifications and explanations of religious innovation and renewal	New religious movements are the subject of Topic 4.	158–163
The appeal of religious institutions to 'spiritual shoppers' and by social profile including class, age, ethnicity and gender	The appeal of different religious organizations is discussed in Topics 3 and 4. Topics 5 and 6 focus on gender and ethnicity specifically.	152–175
The influence of religion on the individual and society		
The secularization debate; definitions and dimensions of secularization	Secularization is covered in Topic 7.	176–181
Religious fundamentalism; crises of meaning and the search for certainty	Explanations of religious fundamentalism can be found in Topic 3.	152–157
Religion and control; ethnicity; gender and sexuality	Gender issues are the focus of Topic 5; ethnicity is covered in Topic 6.	164–175
Religion and classical sociology		
Religion, ideology and conflict – Marxist theory in outline	Marxist theories of religion are covered in Topic 1.	145–146
Religion, stability and consensus – Durkheimian theory in outline	The work of Durkheim – as well as the functionalist perspective in general – is discussed in Topic 1.	143–144
Religion, social action and social change – Weberian theory in outline	Topic 2 concerns the relationship between religion and social change and includes Weberian theory.	148–151

UNIT 4

Religion

TOPIC 1	Religion as a conservative influence on society	**142**
TOPIC 2	Religion as a force for social change	**148**
TOPIC 3	Organized religion and religious institutions	**152**
TOPIC 4	New religious and New Age movements	**158**
TOPIC 5	Gender, feminism and religion	**164**
TOPIC 6	Religion and ethnicity	**170**
TOPIC 7	The secularization debate	**176**
	UNIT SUMMARY	**182**

Religion as a conservative influence on society

gettingyouthinking

Left: A funeral – a rite of passage which enables those left behind to come to terms with the passing of a loved one and to re-establish stability in their lives.

Above: The untouchable caste endure their poverty and perform the worst social duties because they believe that this will assure them of a place in a higher caste in the next life.

Left: Members of a church meet for coffee in the vestry.

1 What purpose does religion serve for the individuals in each picture?

2 What might happen to these individuals if religion suddenly ceased to exist?

3 Suggest some ways in which religion helps people in modern society cope with destabilizing influences in their lives.

Sociologists who have studied the role of religion in society often tend to fall into one of two broad camps:

1 Those who see religion as a **conservative** force – 'Conservative' means keeping things the way they are. These sociologists see religion as a force for stability and order. They may well favour a functionalist (see Unit 1, pp. 6–9) or a Marxist point of view (see Unit 1, pp. 11–12).
2 Those who see religion as a force for social change – Supporters of this position point to the role of religion in encouraging societies to change. They may be influenced by the writings of Max Weber (see Unit 1, p. 12).

The first topic examines the first of these groups of thinkers.

Functionalist approaches to religion

In his famous work, *The Elementary Forms of Religious Life*, Durkheim (1912) relates religion to the overall structure of society. He based his work on a study of **totemism** among Australian aborigines. (A totem is an object, usually an animal or plant which has deep symbolic significance.) He argued that totemism represents the most elementary form of religion.

The totem is believed to have divine properties that separate it from those animals or plants that may be eaten or harvested.

There are a number of ceremonies and rituals involved in worship of the totem which serve to bring the tribe together as a group and consequently reaffirm their group identity.

Durkheim defined religion in terms of a distinction between the **sacred** (holy or spiritual) and the **profane** (unspiritual, non-religious, ordinary). Sacred people, objects and symbols are set apart from ordinary life, and access to them is usually forbidden or restricted in some way.

Why is the totem so sacred?

Durkheim suggests that the totem is sacred because it is symbolically representative of the group itself. It stands for the values of the community and, by worshipping the totem, they are effectively 'worshipping' their society.

Durkheim argues that religion is rarely a matter of individual belief. Most religions involve collective worship, ceremony and rituals, during which group solidarity is affirmed or heightened. An individual is temporarily elevated from their normal profane existence to a higher level, in which they can recognize divine influences or gods. These divine influences are recognized as providing the moral guidance for the particular social group concerned. For Durkheim, however, gods are merely the expression of the influence over the individual of what he calls the '**collective conscience**' – the basic shared beliefs, values, traditions and norms that make the society work. The continual act of group worship and celebration through ritual and ceremony serves to forge group identity, creating cohesion and solidarity. God is actually a recognition that society is more important than the individual.

The functions of religion in modern society

Figure 4.1 on p. 145 summarizes the key functions of religion, outlined in more detail below.

Socialization

In modern societies, the major function of religion is to socialize society's members into a value consensus by investing values with a sacred quality. These values become 'moral codes' – beliefs that society agrees to hold in the highest regard and socialize children into. Consequently, such codes regulate our social behaviour – for example, the Ten Commandments (from the Old Testament) are a good example of a set of moral codes that have influenced both formal controls, such as the law (e.g. 'Thou shalt not kill/steal'), as well as informal controls, such as moral disapproval (e.g. 'Thou shalt not commit adultery').

Social integration

Encouraging collective worship enables individuals to express their shared values and strengthens group unity. It fosters the development of a collective conscience or moral community so that deviant behaviour is restrained and social change restricted.

Civil religion

In modern societies, ritual and ceremony are common aspects of national loyalties. In the UK, street parades, swearing allegiance to Queen and country, and being part of a flag-waving crowd all remind us of our relationship to the nation.

This idea has been developed by some functionalist thinkers into the theory of '**civil religion**'. This refers to a situation where sacred qualities are attached to aspects of the society itself. Hence, religion in one form or another continues to be an essential feature of society. This is very evident in America where the concept of civil religion was first developed by Bellah (1970), himself American. America is effectively a nation of immigrants with a wide range of co-existing cultural and religious traditions. What does unite them, however, is their faith in 'Americanism'. While traditional religion binds individuals to their various communities, civil religion in America unites the nation. Although civil religion need not involve a connection to supernatural beliefs, according to Bellah, God and Americanism appear to go hand in hand. American coins remind their users 'In God we trust', and the phrase 'God bless America' is a common concluding remark to an important speech. Even the phrase 'President of the United States of America' imbues the country's leader with an almost divine quality. The God that Americans are talking about, however, is not allied to a particular faith; he is, in a Durkheimian sense, the God of (or that is) America.

Bellah, however, suggests that even civil religion is in decline, as people now rank personal gratification above obligation to others and there is, in his view, a deepening cynicism about established social institutions. However, the events of 11 September 2001 and their aftermath have undoubtedly led to a reaffirmation of Americanism and its associated symbolism.

1 To what extent can the terms 'sacred' and 'profane' be applied to the situations above?

2 In what ways can the situations in the photos be seen to:

(a) strengthen social solidarity?

(b) act as a conservative influence?

3 To what extent do you agree that the concept of civil religion is helpful in understanding religion today?

4 How might Marxists argue that, like religion, football rivalry diverts the attention of the working class from the real opposition, the ruling class?

Preventing anomie

Durkheim's main fear for modern industrial society was that individuals would become less integrated and their behaviour less regulated. Should this become widespread, **anomie** (a state of normlessness) could occur whereby society could not function because its members would not know how they should behave relative to one another.

Religious and civil ceremony prevents this happening by encouraging an awareness of common membership of an entity greater than, and supportive of, the individual. Some religious movements seem to have grown in times of social upheaval when anomie may have been occurring. For example, the industrial revolution in Britain was marked by a series of revivalist movements such as Methodism and Presbyterianism.

Coming to terms with life-changing events

Functionalist thinkers, such as Malinowski (1954) and Parsons (1965), see religion as functioning to relieve the stress and anxieties created by life crises such as birth, puberty, marriage and death. In other words, such events can undermine people's commitment to the wider society and therefore social order. Religion gives such events meaning, helping people come to terms with change. Most societies have evolved religious 'rites

of passage' ceremonies in order to minimize this social disruption. For example, the death of a loved one can cause the bereaved to feel helpless and alone, unable to cope with life. However, the funeral ceremony allows people to adjust to their new situation. The group mourning also reaffirms the fact that the group outlives the passing of particular individuals and is there to support its members.

Criticisms of functionalism

- It is difficult to see how religion can be functioning to socialize the majority of society's members into morality and social integration if only a minority of people regularly attend church.
- Some have argued that Durkheim's analysis is based on flawed evidence: he misunderstood both totemism and the behaviour of the aboriginal tribes themselves.
- It is difficult to see how Durkheim's analysis can be applied to societies which are culturally diverse.
- Religion often has dysfunctional consequences. Rather than binding people together, many of the world's conflicts have been caused by religion – for example, in Northern Ireland and the Middle East.

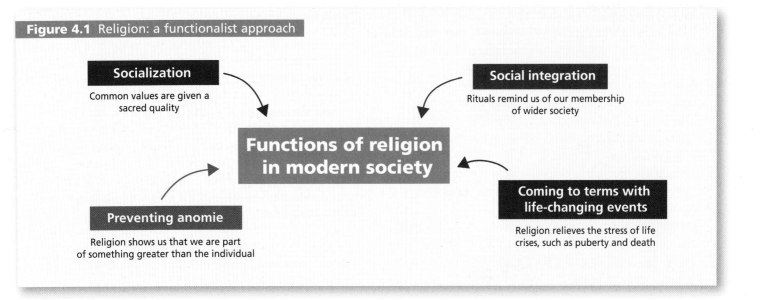

Figure 4.1 Religion: a functionalist approach

Socialization
Common values are given a sacred quality

Social integration
Rituals remind us of our membership of wider society

Functions of religion in modern society

Preventing anomie
Religion shows us that we are part of something greater than the individual

Coming to terms with life-changing events
Religion relieves the stress of life crises, such as puberty and death

Marxism and religion

Like Durkheim, Marx also argued that religion was a conservative force in society. However, he did not agree that this force was essentially positive and beneficial to society. Rather, Marx argues that the primary function of religion is to reproduce, maintain and justify class inequality. In other words, religion is an **ideological apparatus**, which serves to reflect ruling-class ideas and interests. Moreover, Marx describes religion as the 'opium of the people', because in his view it prevents the working classes from becoming aware of the true nature of their exploitation by the ruling class and doing anything about it. Instead, they see it all as 'God's will' and passively accept things as they are, remaining in a state of false consciousness.

Religion is seen by Marx to be ideological in three ways, as summarized in Figure 4.2 on p. 146 and outlined below (Marx and Engels 1957).

1 Legitimating social inequality

Religion serves as a means of controlling the population by promoting the idea that the existing hierarchy is natural, god-given and, therefore, unchangeable. We can particularly see this during the **feudal period**, when it was widely believed that kings had a divine right to rule. During the 18th and 19th centuries, it was generally believed that God had created both rich and poor as reflected in the hymn 'All Things Bright and Beautiful'. This stated (in what is now a little-used verse):

<< *The rich man in his castle,*
The poor man at his gate,
God made them, high or lowly,
And order'd their estate. >>

2 Disguising the true nature of exploitation

Religion explains economic and social inequalities in supernatural terms. In other words, the real causes (exploitation by the ruling class) are obscured and distorted by religion's insistence that inequality is the product of sin or a sign that people have been chosen by God, etc.

3 Keeping the working classes passive and resigned to their fate

Some religions present suffering and poverty as a virtue to be accepted – and even welcomed – as normal. It is suggested that those who do not question their situation will be rewarded by a place in heaven. Such ideas promote the idea that there is no point in changing society now. Instead, people should wait patiently for divine intervention. Religion offers hope and promises happiness. The appeal to a God is part of the illusion that things will change for the better. This prevents the working class from actually doing anything which challenges the ruling class directly.

Evidence to support Marxist views of religion

● Halevy (1927) argued that the Methodist religion played a key role in preventing working-class revolution in 19th-century Britain. Most European nations apart from Britain experienced some type of proletarian attempt to bring about social change in this period. Halevy argued that working-class dissatisfaction with the establishment was, instead, expressed by deserting the Church of England, which was seen as the party of the **landed classes**. Methodism attracted significant numbers of working-class worshippers and Halevy claims Methodism distracted the proletariat from their class grievances by encouraging them to see enlightenment in spirituality rather than revolution. In this sense, religion inhibited major social upheaval and, therefore, social change.

● Leach (1988) is critical of the Church of England because it recruits from what is essentially an upper-class base (80 per cent of bishops were educated at public school and Oxbridge). The Church is also extremely wealthy. Leach argues that as a result, the Church has lost contact with ordinary people. He suggests it should be doing more to tackle inequality, especially that found in the inner cities.

- Religion is used to support dominant groups in America. It has been suggested that modern Protestant **fundamentalist** religions in the USA support right-wing, conservative and anticommunist values. Fundamentalists often suggest that wealth and prosperity are a sign of God's favour, while poverty, illness and homosexuality are indicators of sin.
- Hook (1990) notes that the Pope has a very conservative stance on contraception, abortion, women priests and homosexuality. He points out that the Vatican's stance on contraception is causing problems in less developed areas of the world such as South America. Hook also suggests that the considerable wealth of the Church could be doing more to tackle world poverty.

Criticisms of Marxism

Like functionalism, the Marxist theory of religion fails to consider **secularization**. Surely the ideological power of religion is undermined by the fact that fewer than 10 per cent of people attend church?

There are examples of religious movements that have brought about radical social change and consequently helped remove ruling élites (see Topic 2, p. 149). They demonstrate that religion can legitimate radical revolutionary ideas as well as ideologically conservative ones. Marx failed to recognize this. Neo-Marxists have recognized the way in which religion is sometimes used as the only means to oppose the ruling class. Recently in Britain, for example, churches have often provided safe havens for immigrant groups facing deportation by the government, enabling such groups to publicize their case further and gain time and support.

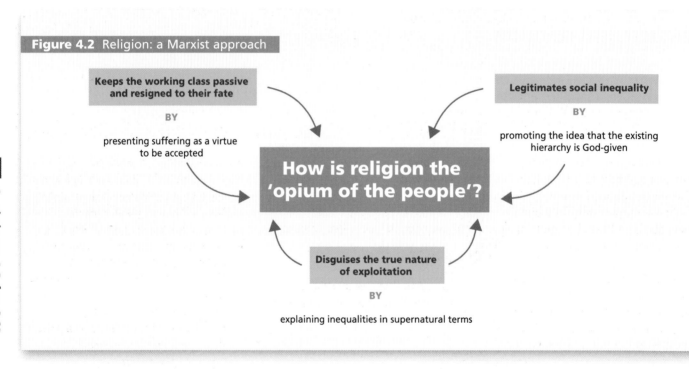

Figure 4.2 Religion: a Marxist approach

Keeps the working class passive and resigned to their fate
BY
presenting suffering as a virtue to be accepted

Legitimates social inequality
BY
promoting the idea that the existing hierarchy is God-given

How is religion the 'opium of the people'?

Disguises the true nature of exploitation
BY
explaining inequalities in supernatural terms

Sociology AS for OCR

KEY TERMS

Anomie a state of confusion and normlessness.

Christian Right fundamentalist and right-wing Christian groups, particularly powerful in the southern states of America.

Civil religion events or activities that involve ritualistic patterns and generate the collective sentiments usually associated with established religions.

Collective conscience beliefs, values and moral attitudes shared by members of a society that are essential to the social order.

Conservative supporting things as they are.

Feudal period medieval period when wealth in society was based on the ownership of land.

Fundamentalist belief in the need to subscribe or return to traditional values and practices, usually involving the literal translation of and belief in a religious text.

Ideological apparatus agencies (such as religion, education and the mass media) that transmit ruling-class ideology to persuade subordinate groups (e.g. the working class) that inequality is natural and normal, thereby ensuring their consent to it.

Landed classes wealthy, land-owning aristocracy.

Profane ordinary, unreligious aspects of life.

Sacred holy or spiritually significant.

Secularization a process whereby religious beliefs and practices lose their social significance.

Totemism primitive religion involving the worship of certain objects seen to have a widespread influence over tribal life.

Check your understanding

1. What is the distinction between the sacred and the profane?

2. What is Durkheim's explanation of the true nature of the 'totem' and 'god'?

3. Identify and explain four functions of religion.

4. Explain, using examples, how civil religion performs similar functions.

5. How have functionalist ideas about religion been criticized?

6. How, according to Marxists, does religion benefit the capitalist class?

7. What evidence is there to support such views?

8. How can Marxist views on religion be criticized?

research ideas

- Interview a sample of people who participate in different religions. Find out their views on the relationship between religion and society. Do they believe that religion should get involved with politics, or is it a purely private matter?

web.task

Go to the archive search at the website of the *Guardian* newspaper (www.guardianunlimited.co.uk) and key in the words 'government' and 'church'. What evidence can you find for the continuing influence of the church on politics in modern society?

exploring religion as a conservative influence

Item A The Christian Right in the USA

‹‹Christian Right groups, as the name implies, consist primarily of Christians, many of them fundamentalists; some have been known to claim that their political positions are, or ought to be, the views of all Christians. In reality, American Christians hold a wide variety of political views. Many elements of the **Christian Right** sympathize with, support and sometimes influence the United States Republican Party. For example, such support is thought to have provided considerable backing for the campaign of US President George W. Bush.

Issues with which the Christian Right is (or is thought to be) primarily concerned with include:

- banning or heavily restricting abortion
- opposition to the gay rights movement and the upholding of what they consider to be 'traditional family values'
- support for the teaching of creationism (the Bible story of creation) in schools
- support for the presence of Christianity in the public sphere, such as the ending of government funding restrictions against religious charities and schools
- opposition to US court decisions widening the separation of church and state beyond historical tradition
- banning of books, music, television programmes, films, etc., that they view as indecent, especially pornography. ››

Source: www.nationmaster.com

1. Explain what is meant by the term 'the Christian Right'. (2 marks)

2. Identify and briefly explain two concerns of the Christian Right in the USA. (4 marks)

3. Take any three items from the bulleted list in Item A and briefly explain why the Christian Right might take those views. (9 marks)

4. Identify and explain two ways in which the Christian Right can be seen as conservative. (10 marks)

Exam practice

5. a Identify and explain two functions of religion in modern society. (15 marks)

   b Outline and discuss the Marxist view that religion is the 'opium of the people'. (30 marks)

Religion as a force for social change

gettingyouthinking

The attacks of September 11th, 2001, and the American response – the so-called 'war on terror' – have often been presented in religious terms, as 'good versus evil', for example. Both sides have used religion to try to change the world.

1 How has religion motivated the individuals in each picture?

2 How might their actions be viewed if religion did not exist?

3 To what extent do you think religion causes or justifies social change?

The problem of theodicy

How do people make sense of a world full of suffering, unfairness, inequality and danger? Why are some people poor, while others are rich? Why are some healthy, while others die of cancer? Why do those we love always die? What will happen to me after I die? Why does God allow such terrible things to happen?

Many sociologists see religion as a means of providing answers to such fundamental questions and these answers are sometimes called '**theodicies**'. Berger (1967) uses the metaphor of a '**sacred canopy**' to refer to the different religious theodicies that enable people to make sense of, and come to terms with, the world. Some of these theodicies justify keeping things as they are – the **status quo** – while others encourage change.

Examples of religious theodicies

- In many Western religions, there is a belief that suffering in this life will bring rewards in the next.
- Hinduism suggests that living the 'right way' in this life will lead to a better future life on earth through **reincarnation**.

- Some theodicies include a belief in fate – that people's lives are predestined and there is nothing they can do to change them. They may, however, devise ways to counter the bleakness of this perception. One way might be to be as successful as possible in order to highlight God's favour and thus reassure themselves of their ultimate place in heaven.

Theodicy and social change

All these theodicies have social consequences. For example, Islamic fundamentalists may gain strength from the **trade sanctions** and other material deprivations they suffer. One Islamic theodicy is the belief that suffering plays a role in gaining entry to heaven. Western sanctions, therefore, are seen as a means to divine salvation and so provide greater resolve.

Max Weber, in his famous work *The Protestant Ethic and the Spirit of Capitalism* (1958, originally 1905), identified one particular theodicy which may have helped to facilitate dramatic social change.

The Protestant ethic and the spirit of capitalism

Calvinists were a Protestant group who emerged in the 17th century and believed in **predestination**. According to them, your destiny or fate was fixed in advance – you were either damned or saved, and there was nothing you or any religious figure could do to improve your chances of going to heaven. There was also no way of knowing your fate. However, it was believed that any form of social activity was of religious significance; material success which arose from hard work and an **ascetic** life would demonstrate God's favour and, therefore, your ultimate destiny – a place in heaven.

Weber argued that these ideas helped initiate Western economic development through the industrial revolution and capitalism. Many of the early **entrepreneurs** were Calvinists. Their obsessive work ethic and self-discipline, inspired by a desire to serve God, meant that they reinvested rather than spent their profits. Such attitudes were ideal for the development of industrial capitalism.

Criticisms of Weber

- Some countries with large Calvinist populations, such as Norway and Sweden, did not industrialize. However, as Marshall (1982) points out, Weber did not claim that Calvinism *caused* capitalism – he only suggested that it was a major contributor to a climate of change. Calvinist beliefs had to be supplemented by a certain level of technology, a skilled and mobile workforce, and rational modes of law and bureaucracy.
- Some commentators have suggested that slavery, colonialism and piracy were more important than Calvinist beliefs in accumulating the capital required for industrialization.
- Marxists are also critical because, as Kautsky (1953) argues, capitalism predates Calvinism. He argues that early capitalists were attracted to Calvinism because it made their interests appear legitimate.

Religion and radical change

Some revolutionary movements have deliberately used religion in an attempt to change society. In some Central and South American countries, such as Guatemala, Chile and El Salvador, where the police and military have been used to crush opposition, religion is the only remaining outlet for dissent. This fusion of Christianity and Marxism is known as '**liberation theology**'. Parkin (1972) argues that political leadership of the Black population in the southern states of the USA was frequently taken on by clergymen and that churches provided an organizational focus for the civil rights movement. He also points out that, in Eastern Europe, the church was the major focus of opposition to communist governments.

Charisma

Another strand of Weberian sociology demonstrates another way in which religion can initiate social change. This is connected to Weber's ideas about authority. Charismatic authority occurs where people are attracted by the ideas of a person who has a powerful personality and they then do what that person wants them to do.

There are many **charismatic leaders** who have caused social change. For example, Adolf Hitler (who was more an advocate of a form of civil religion) changed the world's political landscape. Religion has also had its share of charismatic leaders, such as Jesus Christ and Mohammed. Many religious sects have been founded by charismatic individuals who have had the power of personality to influence others and in so doing cause significant social changes.

Why do some religions encourage social change?

MacGuire (1981) argues that there are a number of factors that determine whether or not religion promotes change.

Beliefs

Religions that emphasize strong moral codes are more likely to produce members who will be critical of and challenge social injustice. The Reverend Martin Luther King and the Southern Baptist Church were at the forefront of the Black civil rights campaign in the 1960s. King's nonviolent demonstrations were important in dismantling segregation and bringing about political and social rights for Black people. Christianity was also a powerful opponent of apartheid in South Africa. Religious beliefs that focus on this world will have more potential to influence it than those that focus on spiritual and otherworldly matters. Christianity and Hinduism thus have more revolutionary potential than Buddhism, for example.

Culture

Where religion is central to the culture of a society, then anyone wishing to change that society is more likely to use religion to help them bring about that change. In India, for example, Gandhi used the Hindu concept of *sarvodaya* (welfare for all) to attack British colonial rule, inspiring rural peasants and the urban poor to turn against the British.

Social location

Where a religious organization plays a major role in political or economic life, there is considerable scope for it to influence social change. Where the clergy come from and remain in close contact with their communities, they are more able to mobilize them against negatively perceived outside influences. An Islamic revolution led by the Ayatollah Khomeini overthrew the Shah of Iran's pro-Western regime in 1979.

Internal organization

Religions with a strong centralized source of authority have more chance of affecting events. The Roman Catholic church was instrumental in bringing about the collapse of communism in Poland through its support of the opposition movement known as 'Solidarity'. This same authority can, however, have the opposite effect by restraining the actions of some parts of its organization. For example, the Pope has expelled some Latin American bishops for supporting liberation theology.

One other aspect of the discussion involves the reactionary nature of some religions – that is, their desire to turn the clock back to a time when society and its moral order were more in line with their religious ideals. Such religions are opposed to what they consider to be the undesirable state of modern society. Christian and Muslim fundamentalists illustrate the position well. This will be further discussed in Topic 3.

KEY TERMS

Ascetic self-denying.

Calvinists a 17th-century Protestant sect based on the thinking of John Calvin.

Charismatic leader leader who has a magnetic and powerful personality.

Entrepreneurs self-made, successful business people.

Liberation theology a fusion of Christianity and Marxism influential in Central and South America.

Predestination belief that an individual's destiny is fixed before their birth.

Reincarnation being reborn after death into another life.

Sacred canopy an overarching set of religious ideas that serves to explain the meaning of life.

Status quo current state of affairs.

Theodicy religious ideas that explain fundamental questions about the nature of existence.

Trade sanctions international boycott of the trade in key goods imposed on a country for its perceived wrongdoing.

Check your understanding

1. What purpose do religious theodicies serve?

2. In your own words, explain one example of a religious theodicy.

3. What does Weber mean by the 'Protestant ethic'?

4. How did Weber suggest that this contributed to the development of capitalism?

5. What criticisms have been made of Weber's work?

6. How can the idea of 'charisma' illustrate how religion can be an initiator of change?

7. What factors may determine whether religion has a radical influence?

8. How is fundamentalism related to both conservatism and change?

web.tasks

1. Search the net for examples of liberation theology. Use a search engine such as Google and type in the following names: Archbishop Oscar Romero, Camilo Torres, Dom Helder Camara.

2. Find the official websites of a range of religious organizations in Britain. Try to find their views on a range of political and moral issues. To what extent are they supporting change?

research idea

- Interview (or conduct a focus group with) a small number of fellow students who attend religious events on a regular basis. Try to cover a range of religions. Ask them about their beliefs and their views about society.

  – Do they argue for social change or are they content with the way things are?

  – If they want change, what sort of changes are they looking for?

  – How do they think these might come about?

Item A September 11th and the mysterious number 11

The incomprehensible events of September 11th have led some to suggest that it was the result of mysterious and influential forces associated with the number 11, which has been linked to mystery and power since ancient times. All forms of number research and study, including Numerology, the ancient science of Gematria, and the secret wisdom of Kabbalah, give significant importance to 11 and its derivatives – 22, 33, 44, etc.

In 1918, World War I ended on the 11th hour, of the 11th day, of the 11th month. To this day, victims and veterans are remembered at that specific time. The USA skipped sequence numbers on the Apollo moon missions to ensure it was Apollo 11 that landed on the moon. In ancient Egypt, King Tutankhamen was buried with combinations of 11 in the jewellery he wore, and he had 11 oars placed on the floor of his tomb. The numbers 11 and 33 have significance to Freemasons, and other secretive groups.

The overwhelming number of 11s related to the 11/9/2001 attacks, is remarkable. It is as if someone or something planned the events to occur around the number 11. If it was not planned, then the coincidence of the numbers, seems even more mysterious and improbable.

- The date of the attack:
  9/11 = 9 + 1 + 1 = 11.
- September 11 has 9 letters and 2 numbers: 9 + 2 = 11.
- The number 911 is the international telephone number for emergencies.
- September 11th is the 254th day of the year: 2 + 5 + 4 = 11.
- After 11 September, there are 111 days left to the end of the year.

- New York City (11 Letters)
- The first plane to hit the towers was American Airlines Flight 11.
- Four of the hijackers on flight AA11 have the initials A.A. for their names: AA=11.
- Flight AA11 had 92 people on board: 9 + 2 = 11.
- Flight AA11 had 11 crew members: 2 pilots and 9 flight attendants.
- The State of New York was the 11th State added to the Union.
- The Twin Towers of the World Trade Center, standing side by side, looked like the number 11.
- The first Fire Unit to arrive at the WTC towers was FDNY Unit 1. Unit 1 lost 11 firemen.
- The WTC towers collapsed to a height of 11 storeys.

Adapted from: www.september11news.com
– a web site dedicated to the events of September 11th, 2001

Item B The Protestant ethic

<< John Wesley, a leader of the great Methodist movement that preceded the expansion of English industry at the close of the 18th century, wrote:

'*For religion must necessarily produce industry and frugality, and these cannot but produce riches. We must exhort all Christians to gain what they can and to save all they can; that is, in effect to grow rich.*'
(Quoted in Weber 1958)

These riches could not be spent on luxuries, fine clothes, lavish houses and frivolous entertainment, but in the glory of God. In effect, this meant being even more successful in terms of one's calling, which in practice meant reinvesting profits in the business.

The Protestants attacked time-wasting, laziness, idle gossip and more sleep than was necessary – six to eight hours a day at the most. They frowned on sexual pleasures; sexual intercourse should remain within marriage and then only for the procreation of children (a vegetable diet and cold baths were sometimes recommended to remove temptation). Sport and recreation were accepted only for improving fitness and health, and condemned if pursued for entertainment. The impulsive fun and enjoyment of the pub, dance hall, theatre and gaming house were prohibited to ascetic Protestants. In fact, anything that might divert or distract people from their calling was condemned. Living life in terms of these guidelines was an indication that the individual had not lost grace and favour in the sight of God. >>

Haralambos, M. and Holborn, M. (2004)
Sociology: Themes and Perspectives,
London: Collins

---

1 Explain what is meant by the term 'ascetic' (Item B). (2 marks)

2 Identify and explain two ways in which the Protestant ethic described in Item B may have aided the growth of capitalism. (4 marks)

3 Identify and explain three reasons why some people might be attracted to the kinds of explanations for the events of 9/11 described in Item A. (9 marks)

4 Identify and briefly explain two ways in which religion can be said to be a conservative force. (10 marks)

Exam practice

5 **a** Identify and explain two ways in which religion may help people to come to terms with life-changing events. (15 marks)

b Outline and discuss the view that religion can be a force for social change. (30 marks)

Organized religion and religious institutions

gettingyouthinking

A Church of England congregation (left), a Jehovah's Witness (centre) and a mass wedding of 'Moonies' (right)

Each of the above pictures shows members of various religious organizations.

1 **How does each organization acquire its members?**

2 **To what extent does each claim to be the only true route to spiritual salvation?**

3 **How much influence does each organization have on its members? What type of influence is it?**

Religious organizations

Religious organizations can be broadly grouped into four main types:

- churches
- sects
- denominations
- cults.

Churches and sects

Weber (1920) and Troeltsch (1931) first distinguished between churches and sects. A church is a large, well-established religious body, such as the mainstream organizations that represent the major world religions – Christian churches (such as the Roman Catholic, Anglican and Eastern Orthodox churches), Judaism, Islam, Hinduism, and so on. However, the term 'church' is particularly associated with the Christian religion and today many prefer to call religions such as Islam and Hinduism 'faiths'. A sect is a smaller, less highly organized grouping of committed believers, usually setting itself up in protest at what a church has become – as Calvinists and Methodists did in preceding centuries (they would now be considered denominations). In terms of membership, churches are far more important than sects. The former tend to have hundreds of thousands or even millions of members, whereas sect members usually number no more than a few hundred. Hence, the often widespread media attention given to sects is somewhat disproportionate.

Denominations

According to Becker (1950) a denomination is a sect that has 'cooled down' to become an institutionalized body rather than an active protest group. Niebuhr (1929) argues that sects that survive over a period of time become denominations because a **bureaucratic**, non-hierarchical structure becomes necessary once the charismatic leader dies. Hence, they rarely survive as sects for more than a generation. While they initially appear deviant, sects gradually evolve into denominations and are accepted as a mere offshoot of an established church. They no longer claim a **monopoly of truth**, and tend to be tolerant and open, requiring a fairly low level of commitment. However, Bryan Wilson (1966) rejects Niebuhr's view and suggests that some sects do survive for a long time without becoming denominations and continue to require a high level of commitment.

Cults

There is some disagreement among sociologists over how to classify a cult, but most agree that it is the least coherent form of religious organization. The focus of cults tends to be on individual experience, bringing like-minded individuals together. People do not formally join cults, rather they subscribe to particular theories or forms of behaviour. Scientology, for example, is claimed to have eight million members worldwide.

The terms 'sect' and 'cult' are often used interchangeably by the media to describe new forms of religious organization and there can be considerable **moral panic** about them, as we shall see in the next topic. Recently, sociologists such as Wallis (1984) have developed the terms 'new religious movement (NRM)' and 'New Age movement (NAM)' to describe these new forms of religion (see Topic 4).

Table 4.1 below summarizes the differences between churches, denominations, sects and cults.

Postmodernity and organized religion

For some sociologists, the advent of postmodern society (see Unit 1, Topic 5) has resulted in:

- previously powerful religious organizations becoming less significant
- an increase in fundamentalist factions within all major world religions
- new types of religious movements and networks, and the development of the so-called 'spiritual shopper'.

Table 4.1 The differences between churches, denominations, sects and cults

This table illustrates key differences between types of religious organization. It is inevitably an over-simplification as religious organizations do not always fit neatly into these categories.

Feature	Churches	Denominations	Sects	Cults
Scope	National (or international); very large membership; inclusive	National (or international); large membership; inclusive	Local or national. Tend to start small but can become extremely large.	Local, national or international; inclusive; varies in size
Internal organization	Hierarchical; bureaucratic	Formal bureaucratic	Voluntary; tight-knit; informal	Voluntary; loose structure
Nature of leadership	Professional clergy with paid officials	Professional clergy; less bureaucratic; uses lay preachers	No professional clergy or bureaucratic structure; often charismatic leader	Individualistic; may be based on a common interest or provision of a service; inspirational leader
Life span	Over centuries	Often more than 100 years	Sometimes more than a generation; may evolve into a denomination	Often short-lived and dies with the leadership
Attitude to wider society	Recognizes the state and accepts society's norms and values. Often seen as the establishment view	Generally accepted but not part of formal structure; seen as a basis of non-conformist views	Critical of mainstream society; often reclusive with own norms and values	May be critical or accepting of society, but has a unique approach which offers more
Claims to truth	Monopoly view of the truth; strong use of ritual with little arousal of strong emotional response	No monopoly on truth; less ritual but clear emphasis on emotional fervour	Monopoly view of truth; aim to re-establish fundamental truths	No monopoly; borrows from a range of sources
Type of membership	Little formal commitment required; often by birth	Stronger commitment and rules, e.g. teetotalism or nongambling	Exceptional commitment	Membership flexible
Examples	Anglicanism, Roman Catholicism, Islam, Judaism, Hinduism, Sikhism	Baptists, Methodists, Pentecostalists	Mormons, Jehovah's Witnesses, Moonies, Branch Davidian, Salvation Army	Scientology, spiritualism, transcendental meditation, New Age ideas

Heelas *et al.* (2004)
The Kendal project

Kendal, a town of 28 000 people in the Lake District, has a church attendance rate slightly above the national average, and is also something of a centre for alternative spirituality, offering the team from Lancaster University an ideal place to explore some of the key questions in current religious studies debates.

The book begins with the claim made by some commentators that traditional forms of religion appear to be declining, while new forms of alternative spirituality are growing.

The focus of the study was, therefore, on the two main types of sacred groupings:

- the 'congregational domain' (the various church congregations)
- the 'holistic milieu' (a range of activities involving the mind, body and spirit – such as yoga, tai chi, healing and self-discovery).

Between 2000 and 2002, questionnaires and interviews were conducted with members of each grouping – 26 congregations and 62 groups with a spiritual dimension, as well as a doorstep survey of over 100 households.

The researchers found that involvement in church and chapel – at 7.9 per cent of the population – still outweighs that in alternative spirituality, with only 1.6 per cent estimated to be committed practitioners. However, alternative spirituality is catching up fast, as church congregations are in general decline (down from 11 per cent of the population in 1980) while the holistic milieu is growing. Furthermore, those churches which emphasized individuals 'in the living of their unique lives' were thriving, compared to those that subordinate all individuality to a higher good, e.g. 'the Almighty', which were contracting.

The writers see this as evidence of a 'spiritual revolution', whereby the forms of religion or spirituality that are doing best are those that help resource individuals in the living of their unique lives. These can be Christian or alternative. What people are seeking are forms of religiosity that make sense to them, rather than those which demand that they subordinate their personal truth to some higher authority. In other words, we are witnessing a '**subjectivization**' of the sacred.

While the study reaffirmed an overall decline in total numbers involved in sacred activities, the growth in the holistic milieu, primarily by women practitioners (80 per cent), seems to reflect the 'subjective turn of modern culture', whereby people see themselves more as unique individuals with hidden depths. This is part of a general process of perceiving individuals as consumers who can express their own individuality through what they buy, or buy into. The findings also suggest that the sociology of spirituality ought to take gender more seriously.

However, the age profile of the holistic milieu was very uneven, with 83 per cent who were over 40 and many who were ex-hippies who had maintained their affiliation with alternative spiritualities since the 1960s. Many in the holistic milieu also worked in people-centred, caring jobs, where personal wellbeing is a major concern. Given the relatively small number in such jobs and the other demographic and cultural factors, this would suggest that the rate of growth of the holistic milieu is likely to slow down. Nonetheless, on the basis of the Kendal research, the writers predict that holistic milieu activity will exceed church attendance within the next 20 to 30 years.

Adapted from Heelas, P., Woodhead, W., Seel, B., Tusting, K. and Szerszynski, B. (2004) *The Spiritual Revolution: Why religion Is giving way to spirituality*, Oxford: Blackwell.

1 What problems might the researchers have encountered when conducting a 'doorstep survey' about religious and spiritual belief and behaviour?

2 What do the researchers mean by:
  (a) 'spiritual revolution'?
  (b) subjectivization?

According to Lyotard (1984), postmodern society is characterized by a loss of confidence in **meta-narratives** – the 'grand' explanations provided by religion, politics, science and even sociology. The 'truths' that these subjects and belief systems claim to be able to reveal have not been forthcoming. This has led to what Bauman (1992) calls a 'crisis of meaning'. Traditional religions, in particular, seem unable to deal with this crisis. Take, for example, the social conflicts caused in the name of religion and its inability to reconcile this with the claim to preach love rather than hate. Consequently, newer expressions of **religiosity** have become more individualistic and less socially divisive. This has enabled individuals to restore meaning to their lives without having to rely on religious institutions imposing their monopoly of truth. This can be seen in the decline of religious monopolies and the rise of NRMs and NAMs. Some established religions that remain have attempted to respond to these changes by watering down their content – according to Herberg (1960), they have undergone a process of internal secularization. Examples of this include the increased acceptance of divorce, homosexuality and the ordination of women in the Christian church, and the increasing popularity of Reform Judaism and Progressive Judaism.

Fundamentalism

Other established religions have encouraged a counterresponse to internal secularization and perceived moral decline by returning to the fundamentals, or basics, of their religious roots. Hence, there has been a rise in what has become termed religious **fundamentalism**. Examples include Zionist groups in Israel, Islamic fundamentalists in Iran, Afghanistan and elsewhere, and the Christian Right in the USA. In the past 30 years, both Islamic and Christian fundamentalism have grown in strength, largely in response to the policies of modernizing governments and the shaping of national and international politics by **globalization**. The increasing influence of Western consumerism, for example, on less developed societies may be perceived as a threat to their faith and identity, thus provoking a defensive fundamentalist response. As Bauman puts it (1992), 'fundamentalist tendencies may articulate the experience of people on the receiving end of globalization'.

According to Holden (2002), fundamentalist movements, such as Jehovah's Witnesses, offer hope, direction and certainty in a world that seems increasingly insecure, confusing and morally lost.

Fundamentalism can sometimes lead to violence, especially where fundamentalists value their beliefs above tolerance of those who do not share them. In some cases, these beliefs can be so strong as to overcome any respect or compassion for others. They can sometimes even overcome the basic human values of preserving one's own life and the lives of others. The bombing of abortion clinics in the USA and the attacks on the Pentagon and World Trade Center Towers on September 11th, 2001, are specific examples.

Table 4.2 Key features of fundamentalist groups

What fundamentalists do	Why they do it
They interpret 'infallible' sacred texts literally	They do this in order to counter what they see as the diluting influence of excessive intellectualism among more **liberal** organizations. They often make use of selective retrieval of evidence from such scriptures.
They reject **religious pluralism**	Tolerance of other religious ideas waters down personal faith and consequently fundamentalists have an 'us' and 'them' mentality.
Followers find a personal experience of God's presence	They define all areas of life as sacred, thus requiring a high level of engagement. For example, fundamentalist Christians are 'born again' to live the rest of their lives in a special relationship with Jesus.
They oppose secularization and modernity and are in favour of tradition	They believe that accommodation to the changing world undermines religious conviction and leads to moral corruption.
They tend to promote conservative beliefs including patriarchal ones	They argue that God intends humans to live in heterosexual societies dominated by men. In particular, they condemn abortion and detest lesbian and gay relationships.
They emerge in response to social inequality or a perceived social crisis	They attract members by offering solutions to desperate, worried or dejected people.
Paradoxically, they tend to make maximum use of modern technology	To compete on equal terms with those who threaten their very existence, the Christian Right, for example, use television (in their view the prime cause of moral decay) to preach the 'word'. Use of the internet is now widespread by all fundamentalist groups.

Features of fundamentalist groups

Sociologists such as Caplan (1987), Hunter (1987), and Davie (1995) provide a useful summary of some of the key features of fundamentalist groups (see Table 4.2 on the previous page).

Individual choice and the postmodern world

The next topic explores the postmodernist view that society has encouraged the development of NRMs, as people assert their identity through individual consumption rather than group membership. The information explosion created by new technologies has provided an opportunity for people to pick and choose from a vast array of alternatives in a virtual 'spiritual supermarket'. Those in developed countries where this choice is greatest, act as **spiritual shoppers**, picking those beliefs and practices which suit their current tastes and identity, but dropping them or substituting them for other products if those identities change.

However, postmodernists have been criticized for overstating the extent of individual choice. Critics, such as Bruce (2002), point to the continuing influence of group membership on identities, as evidenced by the ways in which factors such as class, gender and ethnicity continue to influence the spiritual life course. This is explored further in later topics, especially Topic 5 (gender) and Topic 6 (ethnicity).

Check your understanding

1. Briefly define 'church', 'denomination', 'sect' and 'cult', giving examples of each.

2. What evidence is given for the claim that previously dominant religious organizations have become less significant?

3. What does Herberg mean by the phrase 'internal secularization'?

4. In your own words, outline the key features of fundamentalism.

5. Give two possible reasons for the rising number of fundamentalist groups across the globe.

6. What do you understand by the term 'spiritual shopper'?

7. How does Bruce criticize the postmodern view of religion?

KEY TERMS

Bureaucratic centralized form of organization run by official representatives.

Globalization a process whereby social and economic activity spans many nations with little regard for national borders.

Liberal a concern with individual freedoms.

Meta-narrative (see Unit 1 Topic 6 key terms).

Monopoly of truth a view that only the viewpoint of the holder can be accepted as true.

Moral panic media-induced panic about the behaviour of particular groups.

Religiosity the importance of religion in a person's life.

Religious pluralism where a variety of religions co-exist, all of which are considered to have equal validity.

Spiritual shoppers a postmodern idea that people consume religion in much the same way as any other product.

Subjectivization the increasing relevance of the self and personal experiences as a dominant feature of religion in late-modern society.

research idea

- Identify a small sample of students who participate in organized religious activity. Conduct semi-structured interviews with them, aiming to discover what appeals to them about the particular religious group. Do you find any differences between those who are involved in different kinds of religious organizations?

web.task

There are many sites that represent and discuss churches, sects and cults. Many are the websites of the groups themselves.

Search for the websites of churches, sects and cults. Compare the organizations using some of the criteria in Table 4.1 on p. 153. What other differences and similarities can you identify?

Item A From OM to Amen (via Harvey Nicks)

Geri Halliwell's at it, and even disgraced Tory MP Jonathan Aitken swears it's changed him forever. It's the Alpha course, a free intensive and informal course in Christianity. A poll conducted by MORI in September 2000 revealed that over three and a half million adults in the UK – 6 per cent of the population – have now either done an 'Alpha' course or know someone in their circle who has. The course is now running in over 18 000 churches in 122 countries around the world and the materials have been translated into 33 different languages, including Shona, French, Croatian, Chinese and Russian.

Perhaps it's proof that, despite the popularity of Eastern mysticism, many still crave traditional, structured religion. New recruits attend study meetings and go on retreats in their search for God. Alpha sessions are held at Holy Trinity Brompton in London's Kensington – said to be the Church of England's answer to Harvey Nicks. Apparently, anyone who's anyone goes there darling.

Adapted from Zoe Seymour, *She* magazine, March 2002

Item B What caused the 'Islamic Revolution' in Iran in 1978–9?

In the late 19th century, the inability of the Muslim world to resist the spread of Western culture in any effective way led to reform movements seeking to restore Islam to its original purity and strength. A key idea was that Islam should respond to the Western challenge by affirming the identity of its own beliefs and practices. Such ideas sparked the revolution, which was initially fuelled by internal opposition to the modernizing Shah of Iran, who had tried to promote Western forms of modernization, such as land reform, extension of the vote to women, and the introduction of secular education. The movement that overthrew the Shah (the Mojahadin, some but not all of which was attached to Islamic fundamentalism) possessed a key figure, the Ayatollah Khomeini, who provided a radical reinterpretation of Shi-'ite ideas. Following the revolution, driven by the Islamic socialism of the Mojahadin, he established a government organized according to traditional Islamic law. Religion, as specified in the Qu'ran, became the direct basis of all political and economic life. Men and women are kept rigorously separated, women are obliged to cover their bodies and heads in public, practising homosexuals are sent to the firing squad and adulterers stoned to death.

The aim of the revolution was to Islamicize both the state and society, such that Islamic teachings become dominant in all spheres of life.

There are differing factions within Iran: some wish to push forward to complete this process and export it elsewhere; some feel it has gone far enough, wishing to maintain the status quo; there are also those who wish to open up the economy to foreign investment and trade, and oppose the strict imposition of Islamic codes on women, the family and the legal system. The tensions are evident in Iran today and have gradually surfaced since the death of Khomeini in 1979.

Adapted from *The Guardian*, 10 July 2000

1 Explain what is meant by the term 'traditional structured religion' (Item A). (2 marks)

2 Identify and explain two reasons which may account for the appeal of the Alpha course (Item A). (4 marks)

3 Identify and explain three ways in which those who came to power after the Iranian revolution could be described as fundamentalist (Item B). (9 marks)

4 Identify and explain two reasons for the Iranian revolution suggested in Item B. (10 marks)

Exam practice

5 a Identify and explain two characteristics of religious fundamentalism. (15 marks)

b Outline and discuss the view that religion is becoming more individualized. (30 marks)

New religious and New Age movements

gettingyouthinking

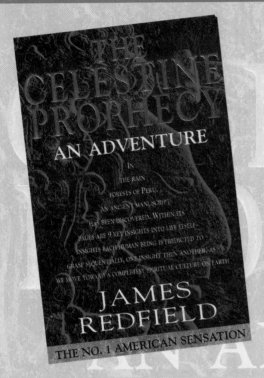

The Celestine Prophecy

The Celestine Prophecy by James Redfield fast became one of the top commercial publishing events of the1990s, hovering at the top of the *New York Times* best-seller list for several months. Originally self-published in 1992, it grew through New Age bookstore popularity to an $850 000 purchase by Time Warner books and sales approaching a million copies. The fictional narrative centres around a search for ancient Mayan manuscripts known as the 'Nine Insights'. These insights purport to contain information and ancient wisdom about ultimate reality and man's place in it. Essentially, according to the book, life's 'chance coincidences', strange occurrences that feel like they were meant to happen, are actually events, indicative of another plane of existence and following them will start you on your path to spiritual truth – a oneness of human spirit with the forces of the universe.

The author and publisher have not made a tremendous effort to explain that the book's story never actually happened. A recent New Age journal points out this oversight: 'A true story? Well, not exactly, though many Celestine devotees have apparently thought so. (Some reportedly walked out on readings after getting the facts.) And booksellers, too: At least one major chain had the novel prominently displayed in the non-fiction section.'

Body, Mind and Spirit,
July/August 1994

1 Have you ever experienced strange coincidences? Do you think that there may be something more to them than mere coincidence?

2 Do you think there is something beyond the physical world that traditional religions are unable to explain?

3 Do you believe that human beings have a spiritual aspect to their nature? Explain the reasoning behind your answer.

4 Which of the following would you be more interested in and why:

(a) an alternative religion or movement that promised you greater spiritual fulfilment?

(b) an alternative movement or religion that offered you the opportunity to be more financially and romantically successful?

If you answered 'yes' to any of questions 1 to 3, you are not alone. As the Kendal project showed (see Topic 3, p. 154), an increasing number of people are rejecting traditional religious explanations of spirituality as well as scientific accounts of the natural world. Some are even prepared to make life-changing commitments to realize their goal of spiritual fulfilment. This process of what some have called '**resacrilization**' has been accelerating since the 1960s.

The emergence of new religious movements (NRMs)

As we saw in the previous topic, membership of established 'mainstream' churches has dropped dramatically. However, affiliation with other religious organizations (including Pentecostal, Seventh-Day Adventists and Christian sects) has

Peter Brierley
Membership of NRMs

Membership of new religious movements, UK 1980 to 2000

	1980	1990	2000
The Aetherius Society	100	500	700
Brahma Kumaris	700	900	1500
Chrisemma	–	5	50
Da free John	35	50	70
Crème	250	375	510
Eckankar	250	350	450
Elan Vital*	1200	1800	2400
Fellowship of Isis	150	250	300
Life training	–	250	350
Mahikari	–	220	280
Barry Long Foundation	–	400	–
Outlook seminar training	–	100	250
Pagan Federation	500	900	5000
The Raelian movement	100	100	100
Shinnyo-en UK	10	30	60
Sahaja Yoga	220	280	365
Solara	–	140	180
3HO	60	60	60
Hare Krishna	300	425	670
Others	50	575	1330
Total	3925	7710	14 625
% of UK population	0.007	0.014	0.028

* previously known as the Divine Light Mission

Compiled from: Brierley, P. (ed.) (2000) *Religious Trends 2000*, London: HarperCollins,

1 Assess the reliability of the figures above.

2 Identify key patterns in the figures and suggest explanations for them.

risen just as noticeably. It is estimated that there may now be as many as 25 000 new religious groups in Europe alone, over 12 000 of whose members reside in the UK (see the Focus on research on the left).

Difficulties in measuring affiliation to NRMs in the UK

There are a number of difficulties in measuring affiliation to NRMs in the UK:

- Many of the organizations above have a large number of followers who are not formally registered in any way. It is estimated that about 30 000 people have attended meditation courses run by Brahma Kumaris, for example.
- Some groups have disbanded their organizations but still have 'devotees' – an example is the Divine Light Mission, whose followers, once initiated with 'the Knowledge', continue to practise the techniques of meditation independently.
- Many organizations are based overseas and their supporters in the UK are not traceable.
- The commitment required varies enormously between organizations. While those who devote themselves full time to their movement are generally quite visible, part-time commitment is more difficult to identify.

Affiliation through practice and belief is much higher than formal membership for both traditional and new religions.

Classifying NRMs

Sociologists have attempted to classify such movements in terms of shared features. One way is to identify their affinities with traditional mainstream religions. For example, some may be linked to Hinduism (e.g. Hare Krishnas) and others to Buddhism (various Zen groups). Some NRMs, such as the Unification Church (Moonies), mix up a number of different theologies, while others have links with the Human Potential Movement, which advocates therapies such as transcendental meditation and Scientology to liberate human potential.

Wallis (1984) identifies three main kinds of NRM:

- world-affirming groups
- world-rejecting groups
- world-accommodating groups.

World-affirming groups

These are usually individualistic and life-positive, and aim to release 'human potentials'. They tend to accept the world as it is, but involve techniques which enable the individual to participate more effectively and gain more from their worldly experience. They do not require a radical break with a conventional lifestyle, nor strongly restrict the behaviour of members. Research suggests that these are more common amongst middle-aged, middle-class groups – often disillusioned and disenchanted with material values and in search of new, more positive meanings. These groups generally lack a church, ritual worship or strong ethical systems. They are often more like 'therapy groups' than traditional religions. Two good examples of world-affirming groups are:

- *The Church of Scientology* founded by L. Ron Hubbard – Hubbard developed the philosophy of 'dianetics', which stresses the importance of 'unblocking the mind' and leading it to becoming 'clear'. His church spread throughout the world (from a base in California). Its business income is estimated at over £200 million per year through the courses members pay for, as well as through the sale of books.
- *Transcendental meditation* (or TM) was brought to the West by the Hindu Mahareshi Mahesh Yogi in the early 1950s and was further popularized through the interest shown in it by the Beatles in the 1960s. Adherents build a personal **mantra**, which they then dwell upon for periods each day. Again, the focus is on a good world – not an evil one – and a way of 'finding oneself' through positive thinking.

World-rejecting groups

These organizations are usually sects, in so far as they are always highly critical of the outside world and demand significant commitment from their members. In some ways, they are quite like conventional religions in that they may require prayer and the study of key religious texts, and have strong ethical codes. They are exclusive, often share possessions and seek to relegate members' identities to that of the greater whole. They are often **millennarian** – expecting divine intervention to change the world. Examples include:

- The Unification Church (popularly known as the Moonies), founded in Korea by the Reverend Sun Myung Moon in 1954. The Unification Church rejects the mundane secular world as evil and has strong moral rules, such as no smoking and drinking.
- Members of Hare Krishna (Children of God, or ISKCON International Society for Krishna Consciousness) are distinguished by their shaved heads, pigtails and flowing gowns. Hare Krishna devotees repeat a mantra 16 times a day.

World-rejecting sects are the movements that have come under most public scrutiny in recent years, largely because of the public horror at the indoctrination that has even led to mass suicide. There is a growing list of extreme examples:

- the mass suicide of Jim Jones's People's Temple in Jonestown, Guyana in 1987
- the Aum Supreme Truth detonating poisonous gas canisters on a Tokyo underground train in 1995, leaving 12 dead and 5000 sick
- the suicidal death in 1997 of the 39 members of the Heaven's Gate cult in California.

The anticult movement

While most of these new religious forms have adopted strategies no different from those of other religions, they are commonly seen by the press and public as deviant – in particular, those that involve open sexuality (thus challenging conventional religious ethics). A small number of sects, for example, have recruited members by sending young female members into the community to promise sexual favours to encourage converts. Others promote very open relationships, where members have many sexual partners within the group. Such sects are particular targets of the 'anticult' movement. (Note that the term 'cult' is misused in this context, 'sect' being more accurate.)

A number of individuals and agencies have attempted to raise public concern about what they feel are serious emotional, spiritual and physical abuses by some NRMs. Some parents of 'cult' members and disillusioned former members have become '**deprogrammers**'. For a fee (which in some cases in the US has exceeded $10 000), deprogrammers hold cult members against their will in order to make them abandon their religious faith. Sometimes, techniques such as physical and mental abuse, and sleep and food deprivation, are used. It is ironic that deprogramming involves the use of the very same practices that the 'cults' are accused of.

Cult apologists

Cult apologists, such as Haddon and Long (1993), while not members themselves, both defend the right of such groups to exist and argue for more religious tolerance. They claim that:

- most cults are simply misunderstood minority 'religions'
- these movements only seem weird because people don't know enough about them and believe sensational media accounts
- anticult organizations and individuals misrepresent the beliefs and practices of such movements
- anticult organizations are intolerant of religious freedom.

World-accommodating groups

This final category of religious movement is more orthodox. They maintain some connections with mainstream religion, but place a high value on inner religious life. The Holy Spirit 'speaks' through the Neo-Pentecostalists for example, giving them the gift of '**speaking in tongues**'. Such religions are usually dismayed at both the state of the world and the state of organized mainstream religions. They seek to establish older certainties and faith, while giving them a new vitality.

New Age movements

The term 'New Age' refers to a large number of religions and therapies that have become increasingly important since the 1970s. Many New Age movements can be classed as 'world affirming' (see above) as they focus on the achievement of individual potential.

Bruce (1996) suggests that these groups tend to take one of two forms:

- *Audience cults* involve little face-to-face interaction. Members of the 'audience' are unlikely to know each other. Contacts are maintained mostly through the mass media and the internet as well as occasional conferences. Both astrology and belief in UFOs would be good examples. Audience cults feed a major market of 'self-help therapy' groups and books which regularly appear in best-seller lists.
- *Client cults* offer particular services to their followers. They have led to a proliferation of new 'therapists' (from astrological to colour therapists), establishing new relationships between a consumer and a seller. Amongst the practices involved are **tarot readings**, **crystals** and **astrology**. Many bookshops devote more to these sorts of books than to books on Christianity.

NAMs seem to appeal to all age groups, but more especially to women (see Topic 5). Bruce (1995) suggests that those affiliated, however, already subscribe to what Heelas calls the '**cultic milieu**' (1996) or '**holistic milieu**' (2004) – a mish-mash of belief in the power of spirituality, ecology and personal growth and a concern that science does not have all the answers. An annual celebration of New Age beliefs – the Festival for the Mind, Body and Spirit – takes place in London and Manchester.

The appeal of NRMs and NAMs

For sociologists, one of the most interesting questions is why people join or support NRMs.

Pragmatic motives

Motivations for affiliation with world-affirming groups can be very practical – financial success and a happier life, for example. These **pragmatic motives** are not the sort that many religious people would recognize and this is probably one of the main reasons why the religious nature of many NRMs is questioned.

Spiritual void

Since the decline in the importance of established religion, people seek alternative belief systems to explain the world and its difficulties. In addition, as postmodernists argue, there is also an increased cynicism about the ability of science to provide solutions to these problems. In the absence of either **grand narrative** (religion or science), people may seek to acquire a personal rationale. This can involve a process of 'spiritual shopping', trying out the various alternatives until they find a belief system that makes sense to them.

Marginality

Weber (1920/1958) pointed out how those marginalized by society may find status and/or a legitimizing explanation for their situation through a theodicy that offers ultimate salvation. This could explain the appeal of world-rejecting sects to some members of ethnic minorities or young social 'drop-outs'.

Tarot readings: an example of a client cult

Relative deprivation

People may be attracted to an NRM because it offers something lacking in the social experience of the seeker – whether spiritual or emotional fulfilment. This could explain the appeal of NRMs to certain members of the middle class, who feel their lives lack spiritual meaning.

The appeal to the young of world-rejecting movements

Many young people are no longer children but lack adult commitments, such as having their own children. Being unattached is an outcome of the increasing gap between childhood and adulthood which, as Wallis (1984) has argued, has been further extended by the gradual lengthening of education and wider accessibility of higher education. It is to these unattached groups that world-rejecting movements appeal. They try to provide some certainty to a community of people who face similar problems and difficulties. What seems to be particularly appealing is the offer of radical and immediate solutions to social and personal problems.

Barker, in her famous study *The Making of a Moonie* (1984), found that most members of the Unification Church (the 'Moonies') came from happy and secure middle-class homes, with parents whose jobs involved some sort of commitment to public service, such as doctors, social workers or teachers. She argued that the sect offered a **surrogate** family in which members could find support and comfort beyond the family, while fulfilling their desire to serve a community, in the same way as their parents did in the wider society. High patterns of drop-out from NRMs suggest that the need they fulfil is temporary.

The appeal of world-affirming movements

World-affirming sects appeal to those who are likely to have finished education, are married, have children and a mortgage. There are two issues in the modern world that add to the appeal of world-affirming movements:

1 As Weber suggested, the modern world is one in which rationality dominates – that is, one in which magical, unpredictable and ecstatic experiences are uncommon.

2 There is tremendous pressure (e.g. through advertising) to become materially, emotionally and sexually successful.

According to Bird (1999), world-affirming sects simultaneously do three things that address these issues:

- They provide a spiritual component in an increasingly rationalized world.
- They provide techniques and knowledge to help people become wealthy, powerful and successful.
- They provide techniques and knowledge which allow people to work on themselves to bring about personal growth.

In some ways, there are common issues which motivate both the young and old. They both live in societies where there is great pressure to succeed and hence great fear of failure. Religious movements can provide both groups with a means to deal with the fear of failure by providing techniques that lead to personal success.

Check your understanding

1. Why are the numbers of those involved with NRMs probably much higher than membership figures suggest?

2. Briefly explain what Wallis means by the term 'world-affirming movements'. Give examples.

3. How does Bruce classify New Age movements?

4. What does Wallis mean by the term 'world-rejecting movements'? Give examples.

5. What is the response of mainstream society to world-rejecting movements?

6. What are world-accommodating movements? Give examples.

7. Identify and explain two examples of beliefs that predict fundamental world change.

8. Give three reasons for the appeal of NRMs/NAMs.

9. What is the relationship between age, social attachment and the appeal of NRMs?

KEY TERMS

Astrology the study of the positions and aspects of celestial bodies (stars, planets, moon) in the belief that they have an influence on the course of natural earthly events and human affairs.

Crystals belief in the healing power of semiprecious stones.

Cult apologists non-cult members who are religiously tolerant and challenge the misinterpretation of cult practice common in the wider society.

Cultic or holistic milieu a range of activities involving the mind, body and spirit, such as yoga, tai chi, healing and self-discovery.

Deprogrammers individuals or groups who remove people from sects and resocialize them back into mainstream society.

Grand narrative belief system, such as religion or science, that claims to explain the world.

Mantra personal word or phrase given by a religious teacher (guru) which is used to free the mind of non-spiritual secular awareness and provide a focus for meditation.

Millennarian belief in a saviour.

Pragmatic motives desire to acquire personally beneficial practical outcomes.

Resacrilization renewed interest and belief in religion and therefore a religious revival.

Speaking in tongues the power to speak in new (but often incomprehensible) languages – believed to be a gift from God.

Surrogate replacement.

Tarot readings an occult practice which claims to predict the future through analysis of specific cards which are alleged to relate to the fate of the client.

web.task

Go to the website of the Cult Information Centre (www.cultinformation.org.uk). Explore some of the organizations and incidents mentioned. Now go to the website of Inform (www.inform.ac/infmain.html). Compare the attitude to NRMs, cults and sects on each site. To what extent do you think their accounts of 'cults' are biased?

research idea

- Conduct a survey or interview a sample of other students to discover the extent of New Age beliefs, such as reincarnation, among your peers. Try to assess their knowledge and experience of New Age phenomena such as tarot cards, crystal healing and astrology.

Item A The Waco siege

The siege of the headquarters of the Branch Davidian sect in Waco, Texas, in 1993 provides an interesting illustration of the relationship between world-rejecting movements and the wider society. The sect predicted the end of the world and separated itself from the wider society. Its leader, David Koresh, was seen to be a charismatic 'God incarnate'. Membership involved whole families, as well as people who had left their families to join. The view of wider society was that Koresh had captured and indoctrinated people and was sexually abusing them. The group had also armed themselves in preparation for the 'end' and this became the excuse for police, military and FBI involvement. A 51-day stalemate between federal agents and members of the cult ended in a fiery tragedy after federal agents botched their assault on the sect's compound. About 80 Branch Davidians, including Koresh himself and at least 17 children, died when the compound burned to the ground in a suspicious blaze in September 1993. The FBI claim that the fire was a mass suicide attempt by members of the sect, while survivors claim that the FBI fired an incendiary device. Jurors in the criminal trial of surviving cult members were unable to determine who fired the first shot. Cult apologists and surviving members, many of whom still believe that Koresh will return, continue to criticize the Federal government, both for its religious intolerance and selective application of gun controls in a state which generally defends the right to possess firearms.

Adapted from: Jorgensen, N., *et al.* (1997) *Sociology: An Interactive Approach*, London: Collins Educational and Britannica.com

Item B The 'New Age' Movement

The NAM 'is a miscellaneous collection of psychological and spiritual techniques that are rooted in Eastern mysticism, lack scientific evaluative data, and are promoted zealously by followers of diverse idealized leaders claiming transformative powers' (Michael D. Langone (1993) *Cult Observer*, 10(1)).

There are four main streams of thought within the NAM:

1 the 'transformational training' stream, represented by groups such as 'est' (Erhard Seminar Training) and Lifespring
2 the intellectual stream, represented by publications such as *The Tao of Physics*
3 the lifestyle stream, represented by publications such as *Whole Life Monthly* and organizations such as the Green Party
4 the occult stream, represented by astrology, tarot, palmistry, crystal power, and the like.

It is important to keep in mind that within this diversity, there is much disagreement. Many intellectual new agers, for example, ridicule believers in the occult stream of the new age.

The NAM is similar to traditional religions in that it subscribes to the existence of a supernatural realm, or at least something beyond 'atoms and the void'. But the NAM believer considers that spiritual knowledge and power can be achieved through the discovery of the proper techniques. These techniques may be silly, as in crystal power. But they may be very sophisticated, as in some forms of yoga. Its concepts have permeated our culture in a quiet, almost invisible way. For example, a Gallup survey of teenagers, several years ago, found that approximately one third of churchgoing Christian teenagers believed in reincarnation, a fundamental new age belief.

Professor Arthur Dole, University of Pennsylvania, *Cultic Studies Journal*, 7(1), 1990

1 **Explain what is meant by the term 'New Age Movement' (Item B).** (2 marks)

2 **Identify and briefly explain two reasons for the Waco siege suggested in Item A.** (4 marks)

3 **Identify and explain three reasons for the growth of the New Age Movement.** (9 marks)

4 **Use Item B and any other information to show how 'New Age concepts have permeated (seeped into) our culture in a quiet, almost invisible way'.** (10 marks)

Exam practice

5 a **Identify and explain two characteristics of new religious movements.** (15 marks)

 b **Outline and discuss the view that the emergence of new religious movements is a response to social disorganization and change.** (30 marks)

Gender, feminism and religion

gettingyouthinking

Gender and church attendance in Britain and Northern Ireland

Attendance (per cent)	Britain		Northern Ireland	
	Men	*Women*	*Men*	*Women*
Frequent	37	63	39	61
Regular	35	65	57	43
Rare	48	52	49	51

Source: *British Social Attitudes Survey* (1991) quoted in S. Bruce (1995) *Religion in Modern Britain*, Oxford: Oxford University Press

1 Summarize the patterns of church attendance given in the table above.

2 Using both the table and the article above, identify reasons that can be given in support of the ordination of women.

3 Suggest reasons why women appear to be more religious than men.

Women as Priests

It is now more than 10 years since the Church of England allowed women priests to be ordained. In fact, in 2004, the number of new female ordinands is, for the first time, equal to the number of male ordinands. The impact of a more feminized job market and positive representations of female priests in the media – in programmes such as *The Vicar of Dibley* (see left) and *A Seaside Parish* (which follows the work of Rev Christine Musser, an Anglican parish priest in Cornwall) – have been cited as contributory factors.

There is a lively debate in the Roman Catholic Church, however, over whether women should be allowed to be ordained as priests. In July 2004, seven women who were ordained by a rebel Austrian Bishop were excommunicated by the Pope (ejected from the Catholic Church). Both sides of the debate are supported by groups of both men and women.

Arguments for women priests include gospel evidence that Jesus was close to women and treated them as equals, and that there is some evidence that the early Church ordained women. For some, the ordination of women priests is about basic equality. Other people point out that many women have a more compassionate nature than men and so would be better suited to the role, especially given the fact that more women attend church than men.

Those opposed to women priests point out that Jesus was a man and that the person who represents him in the Church should therefore also be a man. According to the organisation Women Against the Ordination of Women, the full acceptance of women is a blasphemous deviation from biblical truth. Also, they say that the Apostles were all men and that, while men and women may be equal before God, they are also different. Other opponents to women's ordination also point out that allowing women priests could cause an irreparable split in the Church and so do more harm than good. Many Anglican male priests opposed to the ordination of women have, for example, defected to the Roman Catholic Church.

The decline of the goddess

Women have not always been subordinate to men where religion is concerned. In fact, until about 4000 years ago, the opposite appeared to be so. Large numbers of **effigies** of naked, pregnant mother–goddess figures have been uncovered by archaeologists across Europe and Asia. In those prehistoric days, people worshipped the gods of nature, who were believed to provide sustenance to humans. They relied upon them for good weather, fertile land, abundant food to harvest, healthy offspring and so on. The female sex was seen as closer to nature, representing the mysteries of life and fertility. As Armstrong (1993) put it:

<<*The Earth produced plants and nourished them in rather the same way as a woman gave birth to a child and fed it from her own body. The magical power of the Earth seemed vitally interconnected with the mysterious creativity of the female sex.*>>

Armstrong argues that male aggression exhibited through the invasion of these societies by more male-dominated cultures from the Northern hemisphere and the Middle East, needed a **patriarchal rationale** in order to justify such behaviour. Male gods became increasingly important, introducing a more aggressive spirituality. **Monotheism** – the belief in one God rather than many gods (**polytheism**) – was the final death knell for the goddess, as several major world religions came to adopt a single, male god.

Images of God in different religions

Although there is only one god for most contemporary religions, men and women tend to view that god differently. Davie (1994) showed that:

- women see God more as a god of love, comfort and forgiveness
- men see God more as a god of power and control.

An implicit recognition of the female connection with spirituality can also be seen in the Jewish religion, in which a person can only be Jewish if their mother is. On the other hand, though, some Orthodox Jewish men include the following words in daily prayer:

<< *Blessed art thou O Lord our God that I was not born a slave. Blessed art thou O Lord our God that I was not born a woman.*>>

Christianity is also inherently patriarchal, with men made in 'the image and glory of God' and women made 'for the glory of man', as the following passage from the New Testament shows:

<<*Wives be subject to your husbands, as to the Lord. For the husband is the head of the wife as Christ is the head of the church.*>> (Ephesians 5:22–24)

There are many female characters in the biblical texts, and some are portrayed as acting charitably or bravely, but the primary roles are reserved for males. All the most significant Old Testament prophets, such as Isaiah and Moses, are male, while in the New Testament, all the apostles are men.

The most prominent females in the bible, Eve and Mary mother of Jesus, can be interpreted as reinforcing patriarchal ideas regarding, on the one hand, the dangers of female sexuality and, on the other, the virtues of motherhood. Similarly, the Qur'an, the sacred text of Islam, contends that 'men are in charge of women'. Even Buddhism (in which females appear as important figures in the teachings of some Buddhist orders) is dominated (like Christianity) by a patriarchal power structure, in which the feminine is mainly associated with the secular, powerless, profane and imperfect.

Sexuality and religion

Women's bodies and sexuality are also felt to be dangerous by many religions. Because women menstruate and give birth, they are considered to have a greater capacity to 'pollute' religious rituals. In addition, their presence may distract the men from their more important roles involving worship.

Bird (1999) points out that sexuality is an important issue in many religions. Roman Catholic priests are expected to be **celibate**, while (some interpretations of) Christianity and Islam (amongst others) are opposed to homosexuality.

Turner (1983) suggests that a disciplinary role with respect to sexuality is central to religion. Widespread importance is given to **asceticism**, a self-disciplined existence in which pleasure (especially physical pleasure) is repressed. This means that, in order to carry out priestly duties properly, there needs to be a degree of policing of the body – and the presence of women makes this more difficult.

Women in religious organizations

Patriarchal attitudes have meant that, until recently, women have been barred from serving as priests in many of the world's great religions and the more traditional factions continue to do so. Islamic groups, Orthodox Jews and the Roman Catholic church continue to exclude women from the religious hierarchy.

Although women ministers have long been accepted in some sects and denominations, the Church of England persisted in formally supporting inequalities of gender until 1992, when its General Synod finally voted to allow the ordination of women. However, Anglican churches in other countries (such as Hong Kong, the USA, Canada and New Zealand) had moved to ordain women during the 1970s.

Feminism and religion

Many Christian feminists argue that there will never be gender equality in the church so long as notions of God continue to be associated with masculinity. Mary Daly (1973,1978) goes as far as to suggest that Christianity itself is a patriarchal myth.

Although herself originally a Catholic, she argues that the Christian story eliminated other 'goddess' religions. She argues that Christianity is rooted in male 'sado-rituals' with its 'torture cross symbolism', and that it embodies women-hating.

Simone de Beauvoir in her pioneering feminist book, *The Second Sex* (1953), saw the role of religion in a similar way to Marx. However, she saw it as oppressive to women in particular. Religion is used by the oppressors (men) to control the oppressed group (women). It also serves as a way of compensating women for their second-class status. Like Marx's proletariat, religion gives women the false belief that they will be compensated for their suffering on earth by equality in heaven. She concludes:

<< [Religion] gives her the guide, father, lover, divine guardian she longs for nostalgically; it feeds her daydreams; it fills her empty hours. But, above all, it confirms the social order, it justifies her resignation by giving hope of a better future in a sexless heaven. >>

El Sadaawi (1980), a Muslim feminist, does not blame religion in itself for its oppressive influences on women, but the patriarchal domination of religion that came with the development of monotheistic religions. Such religions, she argues, 'drew inspiration and guidance from the patriarchal and class societies prevalent at the time'. Men wrote their scriptures, and the interpretation of them was almost exclusively male-orientated. This has, on many occasions, enabled men to use religion as an abuse of power. In the 14th century, for example, the Catholic Church declared that women who treated illnesses without special training could be executed as witches. Clearly, the traditional remedies administered by women were seen as as a threat to the authority of the emerging male-dominated medical profession.

Is religion necessarily patriarchal?

It should not be assumed that all religions are equally oppressive to women. In Roman Catholicism, for example, becoming a nun can be viewed as either oppressive or highly liberating. Holm and Bowker (1994) go as far as to suggest that religious organizations developed exclusively for women are the forerunners of the modern women's movement, in that they separate women from men (and therefore oppression) and they enhance women's sense of identity.

There have been some successful challenges to the patriarchal structure of organized religion. Gender-neutral language has been introduced in many hymns and prayers and the requirement in the Christian marriage ceremony for the bride to promise to obey her husband is now also optional.

Judaism has allowed women to become rabbis in its non orthodox denominations since 1972, and even some Christian religions, particularly Quakerism, have never been oppressive to women. According to Kaur-Singh (1994), Sikh gurus pleaded the cause for the emancipation of Indian womanhood, fully supporting them in improving their condition in society.

Some writers highlight how there are signs of hope developing. Gross (1994) detects signs of a post-patriarchal

focus on research

Helen Watson
The meaning of veiling

According to the Qu'ran, women should exercise religious modesty or *hijab* because their seductiveness might lead men astray. Many writers, including some Islamic feminists, have argued that this has been misinterpreted by men to mean that women must cover their bodies and faces in the presence of men who are not relatives, with the patriarchal motive of controlling women. Western commentators also are critical of the practice, seeing it as evidence of repression. As Julie Burchill (2000) writing in the *Guardian* commented, 'such women carry round with them a mobile prison'.

Watson (1994) however, demonstrated that the veil has the potential to liberate. She interviewed three Muslim women who had alternative perspectives on the practice of veiling. Nadia, a second-generation British Asian woman studying medicine at university chose to start wearing a veil at 16. She commented, 'It is liberating to have the freedom of movement to be able to communicate without being on show'. She found that far from being invisible it made her stand out as a Muslim and also helped her to avoid 'lecherous stares or worse' from men. The second woman, Maryam, was a middle-aged Algerian living in France. Upon moving to France she felt it more appropriate to wear a veil. She commented that 'it is difficult enough to live in a big foreign city without having the extra burden of being molested in the street because you are a woman'. The Islamic revolution in Iran had also made her more aware of the importance of Islam and she felt her conduct set a good example for the future generation. The third respondent, Fatima, was an older woman. She was less positive about veiling, seeing it as 'just a trend', but recognized that to turn against some of the less desirable Western values, e.g. the over-emphasis on women as sex objects, was a good thing. In her opinion veiling should be a matter of choice.

Adapted from: Watson (1994)

1 What criticisms could be made of Watson's research?

2 How does Watson's work serve as a caution to sociologists who interpret the practices of unfamiliar religions in simplistic terms?

Buddhism developing in the West which does not differentiate roles for male and female members. Leila Badawi (1994) has noted aspects of Islam that are positive for women, such as being able to keep their own family name when they marry. In fact, most converts to Islam are female. Numerous writers have highlighted how veiling (the covering of the entire face and hair in the company of men outside the family), rather than being a submission to patriarchy, is in fact a means of ethnic and gender assertiveness. Leila Ahmed (1992) suggests that the veil is a means by which Muslim women can become involved in modern society, while maintaining a sense of modesty and correctness. As she puts it: '[Islamic dress] is a uniform of both transition and arrival signalling entrance into and determination to move forward in modern society.'

Why are women more religious than men?

Whatever women's influence and status may have been in religious organizations, studies have consistently shown that women are more religious than men. Miller and Hoffmann (1995) report that women:

- are more likely to express a greater interest in religion
- have a stronger personal religious commitment
- attend church more often.

These patterns appear to hold true throughout life, irrespective of the kind of religious organization (cult, sect or church) or religious belief (astrology, magic, spirits, and so on).

One explanation for the more religious orientation of women is offered by Greeley (1992). He argues that before women acquire a partner and have children, their religiosity is not dissimilar to men's (although slightly more committed). But, 'once you start "taking care" of people, perhaps you begin implicitly to assume greater responsibility for their "ultimate" welfare'. Greeley contends that women are more involved in caring than in practical responsibilities. Caring, it seems, tends to be associated with a more religious outlook.

Miller and Hoffmann (1995) identify two main explanations for such gender differences.

1 Differential socialization

Females are taught to be more submissive, passive, obedient and nurturing than males. These traits are compatible with religiosity, as such characteristics are highly esteemed by most religions. By the same token, men who internalize these norms tend to be more religious than men who do not.

2 Differential roles

Females have lower rates of participation in paid work and this, it is argued, gives women not only more time for church-related activities, but also a greater need for it as a source of personal identity and commitment. They also have higher rates of participation in child-rearing, which also increases religiosity because it coincides with a concern for family wellbeing.

Women and NRMs

Sects

Women tend to participate more in sects than men. Although it is difficult to estimate, Bruce (1995) has suggested that the ratio of female-to-male involvement is similar to that in established religion at about 2:1.

Women are more likely than men to experience poverty, and those who experience economic deprivation are more likely to join sects. As Thompson (1996) notes: 'They may not have the economic and social standing of others in society, but sect members have the promise of salvation and the knowledge that they are enlightened.'

Glock and Stark (1969) identify a number of different types of deprivation in addition to the economic, all of which are more likely to apply to women. They suggest that people who form or join sects may have experienced one or even a number of these.

- *Social deprivation* – This may stem from a lack of power, prestige and status. For example, if people experience a lack of satisfaction or status in employment, they may seek these goals via a religious sect. Those in unsatisfying lower-middle-class jobs (mainly occupied by women) may find satisfaction in the **evangelical goals** set by **conversionist** sects such as Jehovah's Witnesses or Mormons.
- *Organismic deprivation* – This is experienced by those who suffer physical and mental problems (again more likely among women than men). For example, people may turn to sects in the hope of being healed or as an alternative to drugs or alcohol.
- *Ethical deprivation* – People may perceive the world to be in moral decline and so retreat into an **introversionist sect** that separates itself from the world, such as Jim Jones' People's Temple. Again, women tend to be more morally conservative than men.

In the 19th century, many sects were initiated by women: Ellen White set up the Seventh Day Adventists, Mary Baker Eddy founded Christian Science, Ann Lee founded the Shakers, and the Fox sisters began the Spiritualist movement.

Cults

Cults involve a highly individual, privatized version of religious activity. This is mainly (although not exclusively) involved with promoting a notion of personal 'improvement'. Even where wider issues are addressed (such as social problems of crime, unemployment or the destruction of the environment), the solutions offered tend to be couched in personal terms (meditation, greater consciousness, etc.). This 'private sphere' of cult activity relates to traditional gender roles for women, which are based in the 'private' arena of the home. Women are also more inclined to see in themselves a need for self-improvement.

Women and NAMs

Historically, wherever nature is conceptualized, the role of women has been seen in terms of their 'essential femininity', that is, as being naturally different creatures to males – more attuned to the supposed natural rhythms of life. Thus, within the philosophies of New Age cults, women tend to be afforded a much higher status than men. This is one reason that may explain higher female involvement in NAMs, as many of them emphasize the 'natural', such as herbal and homeopathic remedies, aromatherapy and massage.

Women and fundamentalism

The resurgence of religious fundamentalism over the past decade has played a major role in attempting to reverse the trend of women's increasing autonomy and their pursuit of fulfilment beyond motherhood.

- In the USA, opposition to women controlling their fertility through abortion has sometimes ended in violence with right-wing, religious fundamentalist pro-life groups adopting near terrorist tactics to close clinics down.
- Despite India's long history of reform and modernization, the rise of Hindu fundamentalism has made it difficult for governments there to intervene in family life or encourage greater freedom for women, despite their commitment to preventing the oppression of members of certain lower castes.
- Fundamentalist groups in Iran, Israel, Afghanistan and parts of the former Soviet Union similarly insist on ruthlessly conserving or reinstating women's traditional positions.

Cohen and Kennedy (2000) suggest that 'the desire to restore fundamentalist religious values and social practices is associated with the fear that any real increase in women's freedom of choice and action will undermine the foundations of tradition, religion, morality and, it could be argued, male control'.

Women's traditional roles centre around child-rearing and the home. They are thus responsible for transmitting religious values from one generation to the next and upholding all that is most sacred in the lives of family members. Fundamentalism, both in the West, such as the Christian Right or the **Nation of Islam** in the USA, and elsewhere, has often emphasized the significance of protecting and defending women. The spin-off is that this re-empowers men by removing some of the **ambiguities** that have been associated with the modern world. But, as feminists assert, the apparent position of importance such women experience in upholding the faith, brings with it powerlessness and sometimes abuse at the hands of husbands and kinsmen.

However, not all women are unwilling victims of the return to traditional roles – as the work on Muslim women and veiling demonstrates. Research by Woodhead and Heelas (2000) shows how women converting to orthodox Judaism in the US are actually attracted by the status in the home that it provides them with. Such women can also be seen as seeking to remove the ambiguities of modernity, as they perceive them.

Check your understanding

1. What evidence is there to show that women were not always subordinate to men in religion?

2. What caused men to dominate religion and religious practice?

3. What evidence for patriarchy is there in the world's major religions:
   (a) in terms of their scriptures?
   (b) in terms of roles in religious institutions?

4. Why, according to Bird, is sexuality such an important issue for many religions?

5. How do feminists view the role of religion?

6. What evidence is there to show that some religions are not necessarily patriarchal?

7. (a) What evidence is there for women's greater religiosity?
   (b) What explanations have been given for this?

8. Why is it more difficult to measure the extent of women's involvement in sects?

9. What reasons are given for women's greater involvement in NRMs?

10. How has the resurgence of fundamentalism affected the role of women?

KEY TERMS

Ambiguities uncertain issues, having more than one meaning.

Asceticism the practice of severe self-discipline and denial of individual pleasure.

Blasphemous insulting to religious beliefs.

Celibate deliberately refraining from sexual activity.

Conversionist religious groups whose aim is to convert people to their faith

Effigies images or statues.

Evangelical goals the aim of converting others to your faith.

Introversionist sect world-rejecting sect.

Monotheism belief in one god.

Nation of Islam Black, radical, American Islamic organization.

Patriarchal rationale an explanation of events motivated by a desire for male domination.

Polytheism belief in many gods.

Item A Women in religious organizations

Simon and Nadell (1995) conducted research on women in religious organizations, drawing upon evidence from in-depth interviews with 32 female rabbis and 27 female members of the Protestant clergy. They concluded that the women conduct themselves in totally different ways to the male members of their religious organizations.

They asked the female rabbis whether they carried out their duties differently from male rabbis of the same age and training. Almost all of the women replied 'yes'. They described themselves as less formal, more approachable, more egalitarian, and more inclined to touch and hug. Seventeen out of the 27 female members of the Protestant

clergy described themselves as less formal, more people oriented, more into pastoral care and less concerned about power struggles than the male clergy.

Adapted from: Simon, R.J., and Nadell, P.S. (1995) 'In the same voice or is it different? Gender and the clergy', *Sociology of Religion*, 56 (1)

Item B Jewish women seeking traditional gender roles

Despite feminist criticisms of the prescriptive roles ascribed to women by many religions, significant numbers of women continue to be attracted to such religions. Davidman (1991) explored the reasons why culturally advantaged North American women were converting to Orthodox Judaism. Davidman's conclusion is that it is precisely because such religion maintains a clear distinction between the sexes

that it becomes attractive to women who, in an increasingly dislocating world, value domesticity and their future role as wives and mothers. In contrast to the feminist goal of sexual liberation, careers and variation in family patterns, Orthodox Judaism offered clear gender norms, assistance in finding partners and explicit guidelines for family life. It legitimated their desires for the traditional identity of

wives and mothers in nuclear families. Also, women are seen as central in the Jewish religious world and are given special status. In contrast to the liberal feminist goal of equality, such women seek the alternative of equity – the idea of equal but separate roles.

Adapted from: Woodhead, L. and Heelas, P. (2000) *Religion in Modern Times: An Interpretive Anthology*, Oxford: Blackwell

1 Explain the meaning of the term 'prescriptive roles' (Item B). (2 marks)

2 Identify and briefly explain two reasons why the women described in Item B want to convert to Orthodox Judaism. (4 marks)

3 Identify and explain three reasons why the research findings described in Item A might imply that women might make better religious leaders than men. (9 marks)

4 Identify and explain two ways in which representations of 'Gods' are a representation of patriarchy. (10 marks)

Exam practice

5 a Identify and explain two reasons why church attenders are predominately female. (15 marks)

 b Outline and discuss the view that religion, in general, has negative consequences for women. (30 marks)

web.task

Search the web for 'the role of women in religion' using any search engine of your choice. Select an article on women in various religious organizations past and present and summarize it. Compare your reading with others in the class.

research idea

- Using an equal sample of males and females from amongst your peers, try to assess the extent of gender differences in **religiosity**. Focus on formal religious practice (e.g. church attendance), belief/non-belief in God, the nature of God (compassionate or powerful) and alternative beliefs, e.g. spirituality.

Religion and ethnicity

gettingyouthinking

Group	1970	1980	1990	2000	
Christian: Trinitarian* of whom:	9272	7529	6624	5917	*mainly White ethnic majority*
Anglican	2987	2180	1728	1654	
Catholic	2746	2455	2198	1768	
Free Churches	1629	1285	1299	1278	
Presbyterian	1751	1437	1214	989	
Orthodox	159	172	185	235	
Christian: Non-Trinitarian**	276	349	455	533	
Buddhist	10	15	30	50	*mainly ethnic minority*
Hindu	80	120	140	165	
Jewish	375	321	356	383	
Muslim	130	305	495	675	
Sikh	100	150	250	400	
Others	20	40	55	85	

(Membership in the UK (thousands))

*Trinitarian churches are those which accept a view of God as the three eternal persons: God the Father, God the Son and God the Holy Spirit. These are the great majority of Christian churches.

**Non-Trinitarian churches accept a range of different views of God. These include sects such as: Christian Scientists, the Church of Scientology, Jehovah's Witnesses, Mormons (Church of Jesus Christ of Latter Day Saints), Spiritualists and the Unification Church (Moonies).

Adapted from: Brierley, P. (ed.) *Religious Trends 2000*, London: HarperCollins

1 What is the overall trend in the membership of Trinitarian churches?

2 What do the figures tell us about ethnicity and religious practice?

3 In what ways does religion influence the way that you lead your life?

4 How important is it to you that children practise their faith or that they pass on their religious heritage to their children?

5 Does religion give you a personal motivation and strength that helps you to cope with the stresses and difficulties involved in society?

It is likely that most White members of the class would have had little to say with regard to the role of religion in their lives. On the other hand, students from different ethnic backgrounds may have said a great deal more. The statistics above show the continuing importance of religion in the lives of many minority groups in Britain. Why this is the case is much more difficult to explain and this is even harder when you take into account differences between first-generation immigrants and their children who were born in Britain.

The United Kingdom in the 21st century is a multifaith society. Everyone has the right to religious freedom. A wide variety of religious organizations and groups are permitted to conduct their **rites** and ceremonies, to promote their beliefs within the limits of the law, to own property and to run schools and a range of other charitable activities. For the first time in the UK since 1851, the 2001 Census included a question on religion. Although it was a voluntary question, over 92 per cent of people chose to answer it.

Religion and community solidarity

A study by the Policy Studies Institute (1997) found that 74 per cent of Muslim respondents said that religion was 'very important'. This compared with around 45 per cent for Hindus and Sikhs. In contrast, only 11 per cent of White people described themselves as belonging to the Church of England. Amongst Muslim men over the age of 35, four in five reported that they visit a mosque at least once every week.

There are various possible reasons why immigrants to Britain have placed a greater emphasis on religion than the long-established population:

- People had high levels of belief before migration and, as Weber (1920/1958) has suggested, being members of deprived groups, they tended to be more religious. Religion provides an explanation for disadvantage and possibly offers hope of salvation, if not elsewhere on earth then in the afterlife.
- Religion helps bond new communities – particularly when under threat. As Durkheim (1912/1961) has argued, it provides members with a sense of shared norms and values, symbolized through rituals that unite them as a distinctive social group.

However, religion has also become a basis for conflicts between cultures. The dominant culture often sees minority cultures in a negative light, as there is the feeling that newcomers to British society should **assimilate**. Ethnic minority issues, such as arranged marriages, the refusal of Sikhs to wear motorcycle helmets and the growth in the number of religious temples and mosques (while many Christian churches have closed) suggest an unwillingness to assimilate and have created resentment from the host community. However, many second- and third-generation ethnic-minority Britons were born in the UK and their refusal to assimilate fully has led to a re-evaluation of what being British actually means.

In studying religion and ethnicity, it is clear that religions offer much more than spiritual fulfilment. They have the power to reaffirm the ethnic identity of their adherents, albeit in uniquely different ways, as is clear from Table 4.3 below.

Religion and ethnic identity

While there are significant differences in **religiosity** within the Asian and African-Caribbean communities, it is possible to make some initial generalizations about them. African-Caribbeans were mainly Christian on arrival in the UK, but were unable to access the existing religious institutions. However, Hindus, Sikhs and Muslims (for whom religion was part of their 'difference') had virtually no existing religious organizations and places of worship in Britain to join. From this flowed different experiences. On the one hand, the African-Caribbeans tried to join existing religious institutions and often had to come to terms with the racism displayed by the Church and its congregations, a racism pervasive in British society at the time.

On the other hand, Asians had to make a collective effort to establish and practise their faith in a radically new social setting. As Modood et al. (1994) point out, for Asians their religion was intricately connected with their status as an ethnic group, but this was not the case for African-Caribbeans (see Table 4.3 below). Even for those who saw their Christianity as part of family tradition and culture, their religion was not significantly part of their sense of ethnic difference. However, distinctively African-Caribbean forms of Christian spirituality in both the mainstream churches and in the Black-led churches have mushroomed in the last 20 years, as some African-Caribbeans have sought to establish their own churches and styles of worship.

Table 4.3 Differences in the significance of religion for first-generation Asian and African-Caribbean migrants to Britain

	African-Caribbean	Asian
Role of religion	Religion is used as a means of coping with the worries and the pressures of life through the joyful nature of prayer, as much through its immediacy and mood-affecting quality as its long-term contribution to personal development.	Asian groups tend to speak of control over selfish desires and of fulfilling one's responsibilities to others, especially family members. Prayer is seen in terms of duty, routine and the patterning of their lives.
Religion and family life	Used to develop trust, love, mutual responsibilities and the learning of right and wrong within the context of the family. African-Caribbeans express an individualistic or voluntaristic view of religion. Children should decide for themselves whether they maintain religious commitment into adulthood.	Used in a similar way, but Asians tend to adopt a collective or conformist approach. The expectation of parents is that their children will follow in adulthood the religion they have been brought up in; not to do so is to betray one's upbringing or to let one's family down.
Religion and social life	Little importance beyond fostering and maintaining a spiritual, moral and ethical outlook. The church offers opportunities to socialize and to organize social events in an otherwise privatized community of member families.	Muslims tend to see conformity to Islamic law and Islam as a comprehensive way of life, affecting attitudes to alcohol, food, dress and choice of marriage partner. The influence of religion is less extreme for most Sikhs and Hindus, but its importance for the first generation is still great.

Adapted from: Modood, T., Beisham, S. and Virdee, S. (1994) *Changing Ethnic Identities*, London: Policy Studies Institute

The second generation

When examining the position of members of ethnic minorities born in Britain, Modood *et al.* (1994) found that there appears to be an overall decline in the importance of religion for all of the main ethnic groups and fewer said they observed the various rules and requirements. Even those who said that religion was important wished to interpret their religious traditions and scriptures flexibly. Also, fewer second-generation respondents regularly attended a place of religious worship. The least religiously committed were Sikhs. When asked how they saw themselves, virtually none of the second-generation Punjabis spontaneously said 'Sikh'. However, a decade earlier Beatrice Drury studied a much larger sample of 16- to 20-year-old Sikh girls and found that, if prompted, all saw their Sikh identity as fundamental (reported in Drury 1991).

Single-faith schools

Perhaps as a consequence of this decline in religious observance, many parents of ethnic-minority children want the option for their children of attending a faith school. In their view, such schools can be a positive influence on strength of religious commitment as well as in maintaining strong ethnic identities. Though these schools are currently relatively few in number (see Table 4.4), the government proposes to expand this aspect of educational provision. However, the events of September 11th, the continuing problems in Northern Ireland (in particular the events outside Holy Cross School in the Ardoyne) and the racial unrest which fuelled riots in Bradford and other English cities in 2001, all show ethnic fracture lines in our society. Opponents of faith schools see them as socially divisive, inhibiting understanding between communities and providing an easy target for racists.

Refer back to the table in 'Getting you thinking' (p. 170) and compare the proportion of different religious schools in Table 4.4 to the proportion of members of different religions. How fair is the current distribution of religious schools?

However, parents may be being overpessimistic in their perception of a loss of ethnic identity among their children. Johal (1998) has pointed out how in a country such as Britain,

spotlight on

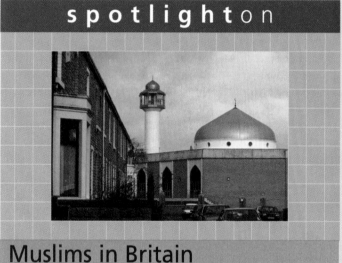

Muslims in Britain

Although early migrants saw themselves as temporary visitors, successive changes to immigration laws encouraged them to settle. The subsequent restructuring of manufacturing industries in the 1970s and the disappearance of many of the jobs in northern Britain for which South Asians had originally been recruited, encouraged a large number of them to become self-employed in the service sector. This was also affected by religious and cultural factors. A survey in the 1990s (Metcalf *et al.* 1996) found that two thirds of self-employed Pakistani people mentioned that being their own boss meant it was easier for them to perform their religious duties. Their strong religious faith gave them confidence to set up on their own despite a lack of formal qualifications and poor access to finance.

By the 1970s, Pakistanis and Bangladeshis no longer had the intention of 'returning home' and, as relatives joined them, they established a wide range of community organizations. They began at the same time to be more self-consciously Muslim and more observant in the practice of their faith. Factors affecting this strengthening of religious belief and practice included:

- the desire to build a sense of group identity and strength in a situation of material disadvantage, and in an alien and largely hostile surrounding culture
- the desire, now that communities contained both children, on the one hand, and elders on the other, to keep the generations together, and to transmit traditional values to children and young people
- the desire for inner spiritual resources to withstand the pressures of racism and **Islamophobia**, and the threat to South-Asian culture and customs posed by Western materialism and permissiveness.

The increased influence of Islam in the politics of Pakistan and Bangladesh in the 1970s, and the increased influence of oil-exporting countries in international affairs, most of which were Muslim, contributed to Muslim self-confidence and assertiveness within Britain. In addition, a sense of community strength grew through the 1980s from successful local campaigns to assert Muslim values and concerns – for example, for **halal food** to be served in schools and hospitals. The Rushdie affair in 1988 prompted demands by British Muslims for prosecution of the author of the book *The Satanic Verses* (Salman Rushdie) under British blasphemy laws. Though their demands were refused, this raised the profile of Muslims in Britain, especially when the Ayatollah Khomeini of Iran imposed a *fatwah* on Rushdie – a death sentence to be carried out by any Muslim, which lasted for 10 years. The Islamophobic aftermath following the bombing of the World Trade Center in 2001 also served to promote even greater assertiveness in defending both their community and Islam.

One key consideration in discussing the experience of Muslims in particular, concerns their younger age profile compared to all other groups. Around 70 per cent of all British Muslims are under the age of 25.

Pentecostalism

[im]migrants from the Caribbean have settled throughout [Bri]tain but are concentrated in inner-city areas. Many have [est]ablished strong, culturally distinctive communities in [ur]ban areas such as Brixton in South London. However, [wh]ile religious institutions are central to Asian [co]mmunities, this is not necessarily the case where African-[Ca]ribbeans are concerned. Committed Christian African-[Ca]ribbeans often have a more individualist relationship to [th]eir religion, which means that the issue of identifying [wi]th a wider culture through religion, common with Asian [re]ligions, is less evident. African-Caribbean culture gives [m]ore choice about whether to be religious or not, and [th]ose that are, see their involvement as one aspect of their [liv]es rather than central to all aspects. Moreover, many [Af]rican-Caribbeans are fully assimilated into British society [an]d do not see the loss of religion as a threat to their [id]entity. Indeed, like many White Britons, many do not [gi]ve any significance to religion in their lives.

Many African-Caribbeans belong to racially mixed [Ch]ristian denominations. However, the largest distinctively [A]frican-Caribbean churches consist of the Pentecostalist [an]d the **charismatic** or **'house church' movements**. These [ch]urches have a distinctive style of worship with its roots [in] the Caribbean, Jamaica in particular. According to Stuart [H]all (1985), when White Anglican missionaries met ex-[sl]aves whose Jamaican folk religion included magical [b]eliefs and behaviours, Christianity was assimilated into [fo]lk beliefs to form an 'Afro-Christianity'. Common [fe]atures were **ecstatic trances**, night gatherings, [pr]ocessions led by a 'captain' to the sound of muffled [d]rums. Afro-Christianity gave key biblical events high [p]rominence and some struck a chord within the African [h]eart. The story of Moses, for example, liberating the [Is]raelites and leading them to the promised land, echoed a [d]esire for many to return to Africa. (**Rastafarians** have also [p]icked up on this biblical theme.) Many African churches [a]re characterized by the literal reading of the bible. They [a]lso maintain distinctively African folk traditions. '**Speaking in tongues'** is believed to involve languages [s]pecifically given by God to improve communication with [G]od, while divine healing is thought to prove God's power [t]o redeem the people from sin.

Table 4.4 Voluntary aided schools 2000

Denomination	Number of Schools	
	Primary	Secondary
Church of England	4523	193
Roman Catholic	1752	356
Other Christian	47	27
Jewish	25	5
Muslim	4	3 (1 boys 2 girls)
Sikh	2	2 (girls)
Hindu	1	–
Total with a religious character	6354 (35%)	586 (13%)

Source DFES (2000)

where **religious pluralism** is still a long way off, many British Asians have chosen to preserve and uphold the religious and cultural doctrines of their parents as a means of asserting a coherent and powerful identity and of resisting racism. As Johal puts it, 'holding on to these doctrines can provide a kind of **empowerment** through difference'. He also notes that many second- and third-generation Asians carefully manage their religious and cultural values. Issues such as choice of marriage partners, intra-ethnic marriage and diet 'often lead to the adoption of a position of selective cultural preference, a kind of juggling act in which young Asians move between one culture and another, depending on context and whether overt "Britishness" or pronounced "Asianness" is most appropriate'.

It certainly appears to be the case that Muslim women, often commented on for their apparent submissiveness and repression, have actually adapted well to the challenge of maintaining their cultural and religious identity, while at the same time becoming effective, well-integrated members of mainstream society. A number of studies such as that of Butler (1995) have explored this **cultural hybridity**. Recent research shows how veiling and the wearing of traditional dress may actually give Muslim girls greater freedom from patriarchal attitudes experienced by many White girls. (This was discussed further in Topic 5.)

Differences in styles of worship

While worship in Anglican churches is dominated by older people and women, and demands limited formal involvement of the congregation, Pentecostal church congregations are comprised of every age group and an equal balance of the sexes. There is a greater emphasis on religious experience than **religious dogma**, and worship is concerned with demonstrating publicly the joyous nature of religious conversion and the power of religion to heal people, both physically and mentally. Considerable involvement is required from worshippers in the form of dancing and 'call and response' between congregation and clergy.

Bird (1999) suggests that Pentecostalism has played a dual role for African-Caribbean people:

1 For some, it has enabled them to cope with and adjust to a racist and unjust society. It serves as an 'opium' for the people, as Marx has suggested.
2 For others, such as Pryce (1979), it encourages hard work, sexual morality, prudent management of finances and strong support of the family and community. In this sense, it reflects the Protestant ethic that Weber saw as essential in the development of capitalism (see Topic 1).

There are many other ethnic-minority religions, all of which can help to define and maintain a cultural identity, traditions and customs. Some provide direction and enable their members to cope in a racist and unjust society (e.g. Rastafarianism). Some religions or religious factions are antagonistic to society and the ambiguities of modernity. They offer solutions that may involve resistance and/or a return to fundamental principles felt to have been eroded through spiritual and moral decline. Such fundamentalism is discussed further in Topic 3.

Check your understanding

1 **Give two reasons why immigrants to the UK have placed a greater emphasis on religion.**

2 **(a) How did the experience of Asian and African-Caribbean groups differ when they originally came to Britain?**

   (b) How did this affect their sense of identity?

3 **According to Modood, what changes have there been for second-generation Asians?**

4 **Identify arguments for and against the existence of religious schools?**

5 **Why have many second-generation Asians chosen to hold on to their religious identity?**

6 **Give examples of how recent world events have served to reaffirm religious commitment for many minority ethnic groups.**

7 **What are the reasons for the growing popularity of Pentecostal churches?**

8 **What role does Pentecostalism play for African-Caribbean believers?**

KEY TERMS

Assimilate blend in and integrate.

Charismatic church a church in which the preacher has a powerful influence through their beauty of speech which can sway the congregation by the power of language.

Cultural hybridity to mix and match different cultural influences.

Ecstatic trances an apparently hypnotic state where worshippers appear overwhelmed by their religious experience and unaware of the immediate physical world around them.

Empowerment to be given greater power and recognition.

Halal food food prepared and blessed according to Islamic law.

House church movement a church body which doesn't assemble in an established church building but in the homes of its members. By their very nature, house churches tend to be smaller in size and counter-cultural in many ways, i.e. have a sect-like, world-rejecting quality. They exist all over the world.

Islamophobia obsessive fear and hatred of Islam and Muslims.

Rastafarianism Rastafarians (Rastas) worship Haile Selassie I (known as Ras [Prince] Tafari), former emperor of Ethiopia, considering him to have been the Messiah and the champion of the Black race. Rastas believe that Black people are the Israelites reincarnated and have been persecuted by the White race in divine punishment for their sins. They will eventually be redeemed by exodus to Africa, their true home and heaven on earth.

Religious dogma rules and regulations, commandments and formal requirements of a particular religion.

Rites customary religious practices, e.g. baptism.

research ideas

● Interview a number of respondents from different religious backgrounds who wear religious artefacts such as Jewish headwear, the hijab or crucifixes.

Try to determine how important they consider this right to display religious commitment to be. Are their motivations mainly cultural or religious?

web.task

Find articles containing evidence of Islamophobia using the website of the *Muslim News* on www.muslimnews.co.uk/news/

Summarize any two articles.

Item A Pressures and influences on young Muslims

1 **The family** – The generation gap may be wider for Muslim children, who may clash with parents over priorities which they feel have not moved on since emigration from the 'mother country'.

2 **The mosque** – Up to the age of 14, most Muslim children attend a local mosque school. There is an increasingly widespread perception in Muslim communities that imams (teachers in the mosque schools), who mainly received their education outside Britain, are not equipped by their own training to help young British Muslims cope with issues such as unemployment, racism and Islamophobia, drugs, the attractions of Western youth culture, and so on.

3 **Extremist Muslim organizations** – Their simplistic messages can be attractive to young people, since they appear at first sight to give a satisfactory picture of the total world situation (the West is the root of all evil) and appear to have a clear practical agenda (resistance and struggle). However, they have far fewer active supporters than the mainstream media claim.

4 **The Islamophobic messages of the mass media** – These can undermine young people's self-confidence and self-esteem, their confidence in their parents and families, and their respect for Islam.

5 The largely **secular culture of mainstream society**, encountered in the education system and the mass media, and in employment and training, which is largely indifferent to all forms of religious commitment, not only to Islam. The Policy Studies Institute's recent research showed a clear decline in religious observance amongst younger Muslims. Vertovec's (1993) sample of young Pakistanis in Keighley were not interested in practising Islam ('I will be a proper Muslim when I'm old' was the prevailing attitude), but were emphatically proud to be Muslims.

6 The **street culture of the young people themselves** – There are trends amongst young British Muslims, particularly those who are unemployed or who expect to be unemployed, towards territoriality and gang formation, and towards antisocial conduct, including criminality. In the prison population of England and Wales, the numbers of Muslims increased by 40 per cent in the period 1991 to 1995.

Adapted from *Islamophobia: A Challenge for Us All*, compiled and published by the Runnymede Trust in 1997

Item B What we stand for: the right to wear the hijab

Note: The French government's position is that a ban 'on the "hijab" (Islamic headdress) in state schools acts as a vital antidote to rising Muslim fundamentalisms, and growing risks to France's secular underpinnings.'
(France is the only country without a reference to God in its constitution, the separation of church and state being central to French political life.)

The ban on religious symbols in France and the hijab in particular, has caused widespread outrage amongst many communities – Christian, Jewish, Sikh and Muslim – as the ruling clearly illustrates the French government's disregard for basic human rights. All citizens of France have the freedom to practise their religion, and this freedom must be applicable to all Muslims within France. An attack on the hijab is an attack on the right to have the freedom to practise one's chosen religion. Placing a ban on the hijab is an act of oppression and this act challenges the identity of a Muslim.

We cannot separate this attack on the Muslim community in France from the wider Islamophobia that has become the discourse of both the Far Right and now, it seems, even mainstream Governments across Europe. The banning of the *hijab* in France is the flip side of the anti-Muslim rhetoric of the British Home Secretary and his draconian anti-terrorism legislation, which imprisons Muslims without charge and trial – in direct contravention of international human rights standards.

Adapted from an article by George Galloway MP writing in the RESPECT e-zine 28 April 2004

1 Explain what is meant by the term 'religious symbols' (Item B). (2 marks)

2 Identify and briefly explain two threats to the continued commitment of young Muslims to Islam (Item A). (4 marks)

3 Identify and explain three pressures which could create more extreme commitment to Islam for young Muslims (Item A). (9 marks)

4 Identify and briefly explain two reasons which the French government may use for justifying a ban on the hijab in schools (Item B). (10 marks)

Exam practice

5 a Identify and explain two reasons why some ethnic minorities in the UK are more committed to religion than the rest of the population. (15 marks)

b Outline and discuss the view that 'Britain is a multifaith society in which members of all religious groups can freely express themselves'. (30 marks)

The secularization debate

gettingyouthinking

'Christianity will go. It will vanish and shrink. I needn't argue with that – I'm right and I will be proved right. We're more popular than Jesus now. I don't know which will go first – rock 'n' roll or Christianity.'

John Lennon (The Beatles), *London Evening Standard*, 4 March 1966

Right: the Swaminarayan Hindu Mandir (Temple), in Neasden, NW London, opened in 1995

1 **How do the photographs above challenge or support the view that religion in the contemporary UK is declining in significance?**

2 **What types of religion in Britain appear to be declining and which thriving?**

3 **Why do you think that John Lennon's comments caused international uproar, especially in the United States?**

Above: a former cinema in Woolwich, South London, now being used as an evangelical church

Left: a former church now housing a carpet warehouse

What is secularization?

The idea of '**secularization**' suggests that religion is becoming less prominent in society and its institutions less important and influential in the lives of individuals. One group of writers believes it is happening, while other writers consider it to be a myth and that religion is merely changing. The problem with the debate is that writers use different definitions of religion. As Hanson (1997) points out, such definitional diversity leads to 'much misunderstanding and talking past one another'. Even before it starts, the debate can never be conclusive.

There are two main ways in which religion is defined:

● Substantive definitions – These define a religious belief system as involving relations between the 'natural' and 'supernatural' spheres. This includes beliefs in God or gods, the afterlife, heaven, spirits, prophecy, and so on. Thus religion is defined in terms of the structure and content of people's beliefs rather than what religion does for them.

- Functional definitions – Functional definitions characterize religion in terms of the functions it performs for individuals and society. These definitions are also called **inclusive** because they include beliefs that have a religion-like influence but which theorists from the substantive camp would not include. For Marx, religion was the 'opium of the masses' and for Durkheim a form of 'social cement'. The same 'religious' functions may be now performed by television, going to a football match or civil ceremonies such as events involving the Royal Family. Using the functional definition, all these could be considered 'religious'.

The relationship between these two senses is clearly a problem. However, as Wilson (1982) has pointed out, those who define religion in substantive terms are more likely to support the secularization thesis because they can show that religious belief has declined as people accept other more **rational** explanations of the world. But those who see religion in functional terms are more likely to reject the secularization thesis. If the functions of religion are essential to the smooth running of society, they argue, even though religion may change, these functions still need to be fulfilled. What we call religion, must simply remain in some form or another to fulfil them.

Practice and belief

It is also important to consider changes in the ways people practise religion. Does declining church attendance necessarily indicate a reduction in religiosity? People may still believe, but are too busy to attend, or see churches as inappropriate these days because they think that religion is a private matter. On the other hand, those who attend church may do so for reasons other than religion, to appear respectable or to make new friends. Making comparisons with the past can be difficult, too, as it is impossible to know exactly what people's motives for religious commitment were in previous generations.

What is the evidence for secularization?

One of the most influential supporters of the secularization thesis, Wilson (1966) defines secularization as 'the process by which religious institutions, actions and ideas lose their social significance'. He suggests that this is mainly reflected statistically in declining church attendance and membership, but he also argues that religion is losing influence over public life and affairs. Wilson mainly focuses on statistical evidence relating to religious institutions and their activity.

Attendance

The strongest evidence for secularization in Britain comes from church-attendance statistics. According to the 1851 Census, approximately 40 per cent of the population attended church. By 1950, this had dropped to 20 per cent, and attendance was less than 7.5 per cent in 2000 (Brierley 1999). Sunday school attendance is also in decline (see Table 4.5).

Table 4.5	Church membership in the UK 1900 to 2000			
Year	Members (000s)	Population (000s)	Members as % of population	% of population attending Sunday School
1900	8664	32 237	27	55
1920	9803	44 027	22	49
1940	10 017	47 769	21	36
1960	9918	52 709	19	24
1980	7529	56 353	13	9
2000	5862	59 122	10	4

Source: Brierley, P. (ed.) (2000)

Membership

Hamilton (2001) also points out that fewer people are church members (see Table 4.5).

Critics of the secularization thesis point to the growth of new churches and the fact that ethnic-minority churches have pretty much held their own. However, it is clear that the big organizations such as the Church of England and the Catholic church have declined badly, whereas those that have stayed stable or grown are the smaller ones (see Topic 6).

Age bias

Brierley also points out that the gross figures of decline hide a trend even more worrying for the future of Christianity in Britain: age bias. For each of his three English surveys (1979, 1989, 1999), he estimates the age profile of the various groups of denominations. With the exception of the Pentecostal churches, he notes that churchgoers are considerably older than non-churchgoers. This is the case even when the general ageing of the population is taken into account – see Table 4.6.

Table 4.6	Percentage of churchgoers aged over 65, 1979–99		
Church	1979	1989	1999
Anglican	19	22	29
Catholic	13	16	22
Methodist	25	30	38

Source: Brierley, P. (ed.) (2000)

It would seem that fewer and fewer younger members are attending church – suggesting that, eventually, many congregations may die out altogether.

Reduced moral influence

Church weddings now only make up approximately 40 per cent marriages compared with about 75 per cent 30 years ago

(Brierley 2001). This fact, together with the rising divorce rate, increase in cohabitation and the proportion of children born outside marriage, is seen as evidence that religion and its moral value system exert little influence today.

Lower status of clergy

As the number of clergy has fallen, their pay and status have declined. As Bruce (2001) states, the size of the clergy is a useful indicator of the social power and popularity of religion. In 1900, there were over 45 000 clerics in Britain; this had declined to just over 34 000 in 2000, despite the fact that the population had almost doubled.

Other aspects of secularization

Bryan Wilson (1966) and others, notably, Bruce (1995) and Wallis (1984), cite evidence for secularization in addition to statistics. They argue that secularization is a development rooted in **modernity** and focus on three key processes: **rationalization**, **disengagement** and **religious pluralism**.

Rationalization

It is suggested that rational thinking in the form of science has replaced religious influence in our lives, because scientific progress has resulted in higher living standards. Moreover, science has produced convincing explanations for phenomena which were once the province of religion, such as how the world was created. Further, drawing on the work of Weber who saw rationalization as being linked to the Christian tradition, Berger (1973) has suggested that Christianity has ultimately been its own gravedigger. Protestantism focused attention on this life, work and the pursuit of prosperity, rather than on the domain of God and the afterlife.

Disengagement

The disengagement, or separation, of the church from the wider society is an important aspect of secularization. The church is no longer involved in important areas of social life, such as politics. Moreover, Wilson argues, religious belief is no longer central to most people's value systems or personal goals. People are now more concerned with their material standard of living, rather than with spiritual welfare, and are more likely to take moral direction from the mass media than the church. Hamilton (2001) has suggested that churches themselves have secularized in an attempt to compromise with those who have rejected more traditional beliefs. For example, he argues the Church of England no longer supports ideas of the virgin birth, hell or even God as a real external force.

Religious pluralism

Bruce (1995) suggests that industrialization has fragmented society into a marketplace of religions. Wilson (1966) argues that, as a result, religion no longer acts as a unifying force in society. He points to the **ecumenical movement** as an attempt

by institutionalized religion to reverse secularization because such unification only occurs when religious influence is weak. In particular, the growth in the number of sects, cults and NRMs has also been seen by Wilson as evidence of secularization. He argues that sects are 'the last outpost of religion in a secular society' and are a symptom of religion's decline. Competition between religions is seen to undermine their credibility as they compete for **'spiritual shoppers'**.

Evidence against secularization

Many interpretivist sociologists (see Unit 6, Topic 2, p. 236) suggest that statistics which appear to indicate religious decline should be treated with caution. Statistics relating to the previous century are unreliable because **reliable** data-collection practices were not in place. Martin (1978) claims that relatively high attendance figures from the Victorian age may be a reflection of non-religious factors, such as the need to be seen by social superiors. As Hamilton (2001) points out, the notion of an 'age of faith' is an illusion partly created as a result of concentrating on the religious behaviour of the elite, about which we have more information than the vast majority of ordinary people. This may mean that the past was no more or less religious than the present.

Contemporary statistics, too, may not be reliable because different religious organizations employ different counting methods. The **validity** of such statistics is also in doubt, because people who attend church are not necessarily practising religious belief, while those who do believe may not see the need to attend. Grace Davie (1995) has characterized the situation in Britain as 'believing without belonging' and there may even be a case for suggesting that church attendance in the UK reflects 'belonging without believing'. Religion is a private experience for many and, consequently, may not be reliably or scientifically measured.

Religious belief

Despite very low levels of church attendance and membership, surveys show that there seems to be a survival of some religious belief. According to the 1998 British Social Attitudes survey, 21 per cent of those surveyed agreed to the statement 'I know God exists and I have no doubt about it', whereas only 10 per cent said that they did not believe in God at all. However, there may be a moral connotation attached to such surveys, such that people feel more inclined to answer 'yes', whether or not they actually believe in God.

Other criticisms of the secularization thesis

There is evidence that people prefer 'religious' explanations for random events such as the early death of loved ones. Many people still subscribe to the concept of 'luck' or 'fate', as evidenced by the growth of gambling opportunities such as the National Lottery and the relaxation of gambling laws.

There can be little doubt that religion plays less of a political role than it did in earlier centuries. However, national debates about issues such as the age of homosexual consent, the family, abortion and so on are given a moral dimension by the contribution of religious leaders. The media still shows a great interest in issues such as women priests, while religious programmes such as *Songs of Praise* still attract large audiences (7 to 8 million viewers). Some sociologists, notably Parsons (1965), have argued that disengagement is probably a good thing because it means that the churches can focus more effectively on their central role of providing moral goals for society to achieve.

According to Hamilton (2001), decline in religious practices may be part of a more general decline in organizational membership and increased privatization. For example, fewer people join trade unions or political parties. It may be that they still 'believe', but are more committed to spending their time with family or on individual priorities.

Thompson (1996) suggests that the influence of the new Christian evangelical churches is underestimated. In the absence of mass political campaigning, church-inspired campaigns have a high media profile, especially in the USA. Many New Right policies on abortion, media violence and single parents are, he argues, influenced by the evangelical churches.

Stark and Bainbridge (1985) argue that religion can never disappear nor seriously decline. They see religion as meeting the fundamental needs of individuals. We all seek compensations for what seems unattainable at any given time. The frustration a Marxist feels in an unjust capitalist society is compensated for by the promise of inevitable revolution; for a stressed Sociology student, the compensation may be the prospect of a university place and well-paid job. Stark and Bainbridge argue that sometimes individuals want rewards which are so great that the possibility of gaining them can only be contemplated alongside a belief in the supernatural – for instance, answers to our most fundamental questions, or a life after death.

Only religion can answer these questions and therefore provides **religious compensators** to meet universal human needs. Furthermore, the more religious organizations move away from the supernatural, the more people will turn to different organizations that continue to emphasize it. This might explain the relative success of traditional Orthodox and 'New' churches at holding on to their congregations, compared to the modernizing established churches, as well as the growth of NRMs. The quest to rediscover more spiritual religion has, they argue, led to greater pluralism.

Religious pluralism as religious revival?

Rather than seeing religious pluralism as a sign of secularization, studies by Greeley (1972) and Nelson (1986) argue that the growth of NRMs indicate that society is undergoing a religious revival. G.K. Nelson (1986) argues that, in the 1980s institutional religion lost contact with the spiritual needs of society because it had become too ritualized and predictable. In this sense, Nelson agrees with Wilson that established religion is undergoing secularization. The young, in particular, are 'turned-off' by such religion. However, Nelson argues that a religious revival is underway, and is being helped by the success of evangelical churches. These churches offer a more spontaneous

religion which is less reliant on ritual and consequently more attractive to the young.

But Bruce (1986) and Wallis (1984) point out that neither NRMs nor those churches that have increased their membership have recruited anywhere near the numbers of those lost from the established churches. Brierley (1999) estimates that the growth of non-Trinitarian churches of half a million members, amounts to about only one-sixth of those lost to the main churches.

The secularization myth? A global perspective

Many writers have pointed out that secularization has tended to be seen in terms of the decline of organized established churches in Western industrialized countries. However, if one looks at the world globally, then religion is as overwhelming and dominant a force as ever. As Berger (1997) comments, 'the world today with some exceptions is as furiously religious as it ever was and in some places more so than ever'. Religious revival among Christians in the USA, Jews in Israel and Muslims throughout the world has gone unexplained by proponents of the secularization thesis. Hervieu Leger (1993) suggests that what secularizationists see as religious decline is merely the reorganization of religion so that it better suits the needs of modern societies. He suggests that religion now serves to support emotional communities in increasingly impersonal societies by providing a focus for cultural identity. While established religion may appear to be in decline in Western countries such as Britain, the growth of their immigrant

---

KEY TERMS

Disengagement the increasing separation of the institutions of the church from the state and government and their reduced influence in wider aspects of social life.

Ecumenical movement where churches come together in joint worship, each seeing the other as having something to offer.

Inclusive all encompassing.

Modernity the modern age, based on science and reason.

Rational based on reason, logic and science.

Rationalization the use of reason and science to replace spiritual and religious thinking.

Reliability the need for research to be strictly comparable.

Religio-political events instances of religion coming into conflict with governments which have national and sometimes international consequences.

Religious compensators aspects of religion that provide temporary answers to fundamental queries about the nature of existence and satisfy universal needs.

Secularization thesis belief in the declining influence of religion in society.

Spiritual shoppers a postmodern idea that people consume religion in much the same way as any other product.

Validity quality achieved when research provides an accurate measurement of the concept being investigated.

populations is causing an increase in religiosity. Islam is the fastest-growing religion in Britain and non-Trinitarian church membership has mushroomed.

The postmodernist view

Postmodernists, too, see the development of New Age beliefs, what Heelas (2004) calls a '**holistic milieu**', as a rejection of science and modernity in the postmodern age. The true extent of New Age beliefs cannot be known, but the number of internet sites feeding such interests indicates that they are widespread. This new explosion of spirituality doesn't at first seem to detract from the secularization thesis because these private beliefs don't impact upon the way society runs. But, as postmodernists argue, consumption is the way society runs now, or is at least a very significant factor. So this is precisely where we should look to find openings for religious activity.

Secularization: an over-generalization?

The general picture painted by supporters of the idea of secularization disguises some important variations. Even institutionalized religion is not necessarily dying in some modern societies:

- The USA has a much more committed religious population than any other Western country, with 40 per cent of the adult population regularly attending church. About 5 per cent of the US television audience regularly tune in to religious TV and 20 million watch some religious programming every week.
- Religious participation also varies between social groups, with some who have continued to be extremely religiously committed – and in many cases have become more so. As we saw in Topic 6, this is true of many minority ethnic groups in Britain and elsewhere.
- If we accept the view of Bellah (1970) that civil religion has increased in influence (see Topic 1, p. 143), then this too constitutes a new form of religiosity.

As far as the UK is concerned, it is fairly obvious that profound changes are occurring in institutional religion. However, whether these changes can be described as secularization is difficult to ascertain. Religious participation through organized religion has declined, but the extent and nature of continuing belief still proves difficult to determine. Further, increased globalization has meant that **religio-political events** elsewhere have global significance and this is bound to have an impact upon religious influence in Britain. Bauman (1997) and Giddens (2001) for example, argue that religion is becoming more important in the late modern/postmodern world. According to Giddens:

<<*Religious symbols and practices are not only residues from the past: a revival of religious or more broadly spiritual concerns seems fairly widespread … not only has religion failed to disappear; we see all around us the creation of new forms of religious sensibility and spiritual endeavour.*>>

Check your understanding

1. What does Hanson mean when he says that definitional diversity leads to 'much misunderstanding and talking past one another'?
2. Why are those who support substantive definitions likely to support the idea of secularization, while those who adopt functionalist definitions reject it?
3. What evidence on religious participation does Wilson give to support the secularization thesis?
4. How do interactionist sociologists refute this?
5. What, according to Wilson, is the significance of rationalization and disengagement for the secularization thesis?
6. Identify four arguments that refute this.
7. What, according to Stark and Bainbridge, is the reason why religion can never disappear?
8. In what ways does a more global perspective demonstrate that secularization is a myth?
9. How do postmodernists view the secularization thesis?

research idea

- Interview parents/grandparents and other older relatives to ascertain the level of belief and participation in religion, both past and present, in your family. Design a questionnaire measuring religious belief and practice to compare with your own age group. Collate the results for the whole class, and compare them.

web.task

Using a search engine of your choice, type in 'Keep Sunday Special Campaign'. Summarize the main objections Christian groups have to the secularization of Sunday.

Evaluate their arguments.

Item A | Women and secularization

Brown (2001) suggests that participation has declined in the established churches mainly because of the changing role of women. When female church-attendance and participation were high, the same was true for both children and men. Women, with their domestic and maternal roles heavily emphasized in both secular and religious literature right down to c. 1960, were the primary churchgoers, with children in tow and husbands – sometimes reluctantly – following suit.

Brown further suggests that from the 1960s, feminism and the media presented women with other ways of understanding their identities, their sexuality and their lives generally than traditional Christian notions. 'British women secularized the construction of their identity, and the churches started to lose them (and their husbands and children).'

Adapted from: Brown, C.G. (2001) *The Death of Christian Britain: Understanding Secularization 1800–2000*, London: Routledge

Item B | Predicting religion globally

1 Across the globe, religions which can accommodate democracy, greater personal freedom and empowerment will do well.

2 Religions that place a particular emphasis on human rights will fare well in developing countries (as in Bangladesh and Indonesia).

3 Religions which serve to support emerging endangered local, ethnic or national identities will do well, often (in the West) as pockets of protest.

4 Particularly outside the West, modernizing religions will do well, i.e. religions which encourage the development of modernity and adaptation to a global capitalist economy without following a Western secularizing model and so losing their distinctive traditions, identities and faiths.

5 Spiritualities of life, such as the so-called New Age movement, will not fare as well as many have predicted, because they fail to provide a clear framework for living, by focusing solely on the Self, which may not be strong enough to sustain belief.

6 In contrast, experiential religions (where there is active participation in the spiritual quest rather than passive acceptance of the word of those in authority) will do better because they cater for the Self and the relational, as well as the different and the universal.

7 Religions that do best will be those which are able to mobilize the most resources, both financial and human. The accumulation of wealth over a long period of time may sustain older faiths that might otherwise have disappeared.

Adapted from: Woodhead, L. and Heelas, P. (2000) *Religion in Modern Times: An Interpretive Anthology*, London: Blackwell

---

1 Explain what is meant by the term the 'established churches' (Item A). (2 marks)

2 Identify and explain two reasons why religion became less popular for women (Item A). (4 marks)

3 Identify and explain three types of religion that the author of Item B predicts will be successful. (9 marks)

4 Examine the reasons why 'experiential religions (where there is active participation in the spiritual quest)' may be successful (Item B). (10 marks)

Exam practice

5 a Identify and explain two ways in which religion continues to be a significant influence on society. (15 marks)

  b Outline and discuss the view that the influence of religion on UK society is declining. (30 marks)

Evidence against

Problems of:
- Reliability and validity of statistics
- Survival of religious belief
- Continuing moral influence
- Thompson: influence of Christian evangelism
- Stark & Bainbridge: need for 'religious compensators'
- Nelson: growth of NRMs indicate religious revival

BUT
- Bruce: numbers in NRMs much less than those lost from established churches

Evidence for

- Attendance
- Membership
- Age bias
- Reduced moral influence
- Lower status of clergy
- Disengagement
- Religious pluralism

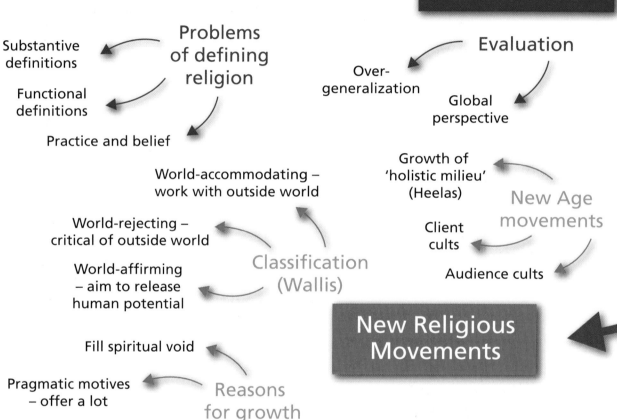

Secularization

Problems of defining religion

Substantive definitions

Functional definitions

Practice and belief

Evaluation

Over-generalization

Global perspective

Growth of 'holistic milieu' (Heelas)

Client cults

Audience cults

New Age movements

World-accommodating – work with outside world

World-rejecting – critical of outside world

World-affirming – aim to release human potential

Classification (Wallis)

New Religious Movements

Fill spiritual void

Pragmatic motives – offer a lot

Marginalization

Deprivation

Reasons for growth

Effect on Society

Force for social change

Reasons include:
- Leader's charisma
- Beliefs
- Culture
- Social location
- Internal organization

Spirit of capitalism

Protestant ethic (Weber)

Conservative force

Functionalist approaches (Durkheim):
- Collective conscience
- Agent of socialization and social integration
- Role of civil religion
- Preventing anomie
- Coping with life changes

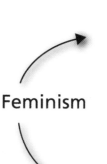
Women and NRMs

Experience of deprivation attracts women to NRMs

Higher status in NRMs

Greater participation in sects and cults

Differential socialization

Differential roles

Women more religious than men

Feminism

Religion as patriarchal:
- Decline of goddess figures
- Development of monotheism
- Women's bodies 'dangerous'
- Women barred from priesthood
- Fundamentalism stresses traditional roles

BUT signs of change:
- Christianity: changes in rituals/hymns, etc.
- Increasing acceptance of women priests
- Postpatriarchal Buddhism
- Feminist interpretations of veiling in Islam

Gender

Ethnicity

Importance of religion to minority ethnic groups in UK

Butler: development of cultural hybridity

Bonds new communities

Reaffirms ethnic identity

High levels of belief before migration

Counter to racism and hostility

Religion

Religious Organization

Postmodernity and individualization

Notion of 'spiritual shopper'

Growth of individualist expressions of religiosity

Bauman: 'crisis of meaning'

Growth of fundamentalism

Traditional and conservative

Literal interpretation of texts

Response to social crisis

Rejection of pluralism

Personal experience of God

Offers direction and certainty in confused world

Church
Denomination
Sect
Cult

Differences in:
- Size
- Structure
- Permanence
- Claim to monopoly of truth
- Level of commitment demanded

FOR THE MAJORITY OF PEOPLE, youth is the period in life when they begin the move away from the family and towards adulthood. Attitudes and interests diverge from those of childhood and often from those of one's parents. For many, it is a period for experimentation in fashion, music and sex. For a considerable number of young people, particularly males, it is also a time when they engage in minor acts of lawbreaking.

It seems something 'natural' which is part of life and, we think, has always been part of life. Yet sociologists argue that this understanding of youth is, in fact, fairly recent. Youth and youth culture developed during the 20th century, and have both fuelled and reflected huge social changes. It is this social construction of youth and the linked social changes which are the focus of this unit.

This unit begins, in Topic 1, by examining the development of youth culture and the modern understanding of youth. We then move on to look at the theoretical explanations for the existence and forms of youth subcultures. These are complex, so we explore them over two linked topics: Topic 2 looks at functionalist and conflict theories of youth culture, while Topic 3 examines late-modern and postmodern theories.

Topic 4 focuses on sociological explanations of youth crime. It shows how the concept of subculture has been used in a variety of ways to explain delinquency.

Topic 5 moves on to look at an emerging phenomenon associated with a small number of young people – the gang. Although relatively unimportant at present in Britain, gangs are very significant in American cities and there is considerable evidence to show that they are becoming more prominent in the UK too.

Finally, in Topic 6, we explore the much more commonplace experiences of young people in schools today.

OCR specification	topics	pages
Youth culture and subcultures		
The distinction between youth culture and youth subcultures; middle-class and working-class subcultures	Topic 1 contains a discussion of the idea of youth culture. Topics 2 focuses on a range of youth subcultures.	186–191 192–197
The significance of class, ethnicity and gender for contemporary youth	These issues are covered in Topics 2 and 3.	192–203
Theories of youth subcultures, e.g. Marxism, feminism, postmodernism	The full range of theories is covered over Topics 2 and 3.	192–203
Youth and deviance		
Delinquency; the patterns and trends of delinquency according to social profile, for example class, gender and ethnicity	Delinquency – youth deviance – is the subject of Topic 4.	204–209
Gangs: territory, values, rituals and sanctions	Topic 5 focuses on gangs.	210–215
Theories of delinquent subcultures, e.g. functionalist, Marxist and feminist accounts	These are all covered in Topic 4.	204–209
Youth and schooling		
Experiences of schooling: class, gender and ethnicity	All these issues concerning youth and schooling are covered in Topic 6.	216–223
Proschool and antischool cultures		
Femininity, masculinity and subject choice		

TOPIC 1   Youth culture **186**

TOPIC 2   Functionalist and conflict theories of youth culture **192**

TOPIC 3   Late-modern and postmodern theories of youth culture **198**

TOPIC 4   Subcultural theories of youth offending **204**

TOPIC 5   Gangs **210**

TOPIC 6   Youth and schooling **216**

UNIT SUMMARY **224**

Youth culture

gettingyouthinking

Clockwise from top left: Beyonce, Duran Duran (in the 1980s), Eminem and the Beatles (in the 1960s)

1 Who is your current favourite singer or band? Why do you like them?

2 Do you think that they influence the way you dress, speak or behave?

3 Which singer/band do you most dislike? Why?

4 Who was the singer/band you most liked when you were 14? Do you still like them? Explain the reasons.

5 Do your parents have the same musical tastes as you? What are your views on your parents' musical and clothing tastes?

Youth culture: a natural or social creation?

Ageing is a physical and natural process which happens to everyone and has always happened. However, childhood, youth, adulthood and old age are associated with different behaviour, tastes and lifestyles. Different societies – and even the same societies over different historical periods – have divided ageing into different stages. These stages have then had different meanings attached to them. For example:

- Nowadays, childhood is seen as a period of innocence, although it was once seen as a period of potential evil.
- Old age, now seen as a period of dependence, was once viewed as a time of wisdom.
- The typical image of youth is characterized by two overlapping images of enjoyment and bad behaviour.

These age categories are not 'natural', but created by society – that is, they are **social constructions**.

Around 50 to 60 years ago, for the first time, a **youth culture** appeared to be emerging – young people appeared to be developing their own values, customs, tastes, clothes, music and language.

The origins of youth culture

The modern concept of youth culture developed in the early 1950s, although, as we shall see later, the idea of youth as a phase in life has a longer history. There is no single reason for the development of youth culture in Britain; rather, it came about as a result of a number of different social changes occurring at the same time. These developments included:

- the increasing economic power of young people
- the increasing diversity of society
- the impact of American culture
- the development and specialization of the media
- the emergence of 'rock and roll' music
- the lengthening of the period of transition between childhood and adulthood
- an increase in the birth rate.

Increasing economic power of young people

The 1950s were a period of rapid economic growth in Britain. With much of the housing and industry destroyed during the Second World War (1939–45), a huge amount of reconstruction occurred. This, in turn, led to a high demand for workers and, as employers competed for their services, wages rose. The first person to realize the impact this was having on young people was Abrams (1959), who analysed the increased economic power of the 'teenage consumer'. He demonstrated that real earnings of young people increased by over 50 per cent between 1938 and 1958, double the increase of adult earnings over the same period. Abrams also researched spending patterns and concluded that, by the late 1950s,

young people were the age group spending the highest proportion of their income on leisure activities and music, clothes and cosmetics. This increase in economic power created the conditions for the emerging youth culture to develop. For the first time, young people had significant amounts of money to spend.

Social change

The Second World War marked the beginning of a powerful change in British society. In sociological terms, it was the beginning of the decline in modernity and the move towards late modernity (see pp. 20–1 and 199–200 for discussions of modernity and late modernity). Before 1939, Britain was characterized by a rigid class structure and, although this continued into the 1950s, cracks were beginning to show. Changes in the economy and an opening-up of the educational system coincided with new ideas about equal opportunities and individual expression. These ideas did not fully flower until the 1960s and 1970s, but the 1950s saw them emerging. The result was that rigid ideas of superior and inferior social classes and of hierarchy began to be challenged. It was in this 'social space' of challenge and change that new forms of cultural expression emerged. Cinema, art, literature and theatre began to explore new ideas. Amongst the many new ideas was that young people were a distinctive group with new values and ideas about their place in society.

The impact of American culture

Today, the dominance of American culture is simply taken for granted in Britain. **Globalization** has made brands such as Coca-Cola and Nike internationally known. It is difficult for people living in the 21st century to imagine a world which is not dominated by US products. Yet it was not until the Second World War that American products and culture came to Britain (at least, on such a large scale). With the changing culture and the growth in affluence of the 1950s, there was a ready market for American goods and culture, which included rock and roll music and other products aimed at the new 'teenage market'.

Growth and specialization of the media

The next element in the mixture of factors which led to the development of youth culture in Britain was the growth and specialization of the media. Compared to today, the media of the 1950s were tiny in number and variety. However, the 1950s saw an explosion of different sorts of media. These included:

- the emergence of television to rival the cinema as the most common form of leisure activity
- the diversification and specialization of magazines, as they sought new audiences – for example, The New Musical Express (NME) was started in this period.

This media explosion was only possible because of the growth in social diversity and an increase in spending power that persuaded companies (very often American) to spend large amounts of money advertising in the new media. As a high-spending and newly discovered group, young people became the target for advertisers and hence the commercial media competed to attract this market.

The emergence of new musical forms

The early 1950s saw the arrival in Britain of a new harder-edged style of singing and guitar playing, which had developed in the USA out of blues and country music. The new style of music challenged accepted 'crooning' styles and carried with it a barely disguised sexual orientation. Its development from Black blues music also added the issue of race. For many younger people looking for a distinctive cultural identity and a break from their parental culture, rock and roll provided the answer. For the American companies and the new media, rock and roll provided a useful commercial opportunity.

Longer transition from childhood to adulthood

Transition refers to the movement from being economically and socially dependent on parents towards independence. The length of transition increased over the 20th century as the average period spent in education increased. During the 20th century, the typical age of leaving education (and hence dependency) increased from 12 years of age to 18 or even 21. This means that typical adult responsibilities were taken on increasingly later in life, leaving young people with a number of years where they were physically mature but without the responsibilities of adulthood.

Increase in the birth rate

The final factor that combined to generate youth culture was the dramatic increase in the birth rate soon after the end of the 1939–45 War. The armed forces had conscripted millions of young British men (and women), and hundreds of thousands had been sent abroad. Many couples were separated for a period of up to six years. For others, their first sexual experiences might have been delayed for some years. The result was that when the men were released from the armed forces in 1945/46, there was a huge increase in the birth rate. Although many of the children born at this time were not 'teenagers' until the end of the 1950s, they did ensure that youth culture continued and grew as a cultural form.

The key characteristics of youth culture

So far we have described the emergence of youth culture without actually saying what marks it off as a separate culture. Abercrombie *et al.* (2000) have suggested that it has three distinguishing features: leisure, style and peer group. It is useful to add a fourth feature: **consumption**.

Leisure

Until relatively recently, most adult cultures – or at least adult male cultures – were based on work. Studies by sociologists of male life from the 1950s to the 1970s constantly return to the importance of work in social life. Income, political attitudes, awareness of social position and general social identity were all tied up with occupation. This did not weaken until the 1980s, when leisure and consumption patterns began to rival work as important elements of male adult lives. But the move towards leisure as a defining characteristic of young people's culture began much earlier in the 1950s and has subsequently continued.

To some extent, this has been linked to the increased length of time that young people spend in education, which we discussed earlier. Young people are unlikely to experience work until a later age, so that it is not atypical for people to delay entry into the workforce until 21. As a consequence, young people have fewer financial responsibilities and are less likely to be 'tied in' to the discipline of employment, with its requirements to attend work for a set number of hours each day, to have limited holiday opportunities and to dress in the way required by the employer.

The importance of style

The importance of image is a key element of youth culture, with style being perhaps the core component. Style is composed of two main elements:

- how one appears to others
- how one sounds to others.

What clues does the style of the people in the photograph give to their interests, musical taste and use of language?

Appearance is related to clothes, hairstyle and make-up. These give clues as to the interests and musical likings of the person. How one sounds is equally important and this is demonstrated by use of **argot** (special language). The combination of these elements will give strong clues as to musical allegiance, leisure choices and even social class. Once again, youth culture predated the changes in the wider culture, where style has become more important to a range of age groups.

The importance of the peer group

The term **peer group** refers to a group of people of a particular age who share similar interests and attitudes. Young people have strong affiliation to peer groups, which partially replace or complement the relationships provided by the family. Functionalist sociologists (see Topic 2) argue that the peer group provides a bridge between childhood and adulthood.

Consumption

Youth culture is based upon consumption. As we have already seen, this is a period in life where money can be spent on nonessential items. Youth culture is closely linked with specific styles of clothing, cosmetics, recorded music and a range of other items which serve to demonstrate membership of a particular form of youth culture.

Images of youth

Earlier we said that youth culture emerged in the early 1950s; however, ideas of youth or 'adolescence' as a distinct phase in people's lives (as opposed to a distinct youth culture) has a much longer history. Certainly, ideas about youth (although very different from today's concept) existed when Shakespeare was writing in the early 17th century. This history also illustrates the double-edged image of youth that persists today. According to

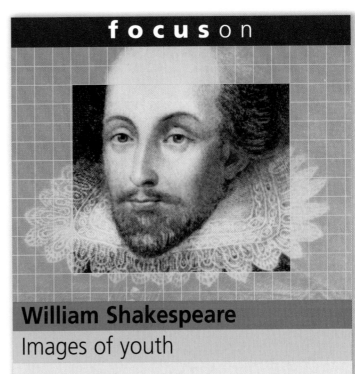

focus on

William Shakespeare
Images of youth

<< *I would that there were no age between sixteen and three and twenty, or that youth would sleep out the rest; for there is nothing in the between but getting wenches with child, wrong the ancientry, stealing, fighting.* >>

William Shakespeare (1611) *The Winter's Tale*

1 How does Shakespeare's age of 'youth' differ from today's?

2 How is Shakespeare's account of youth similar to the way some people view young people today?

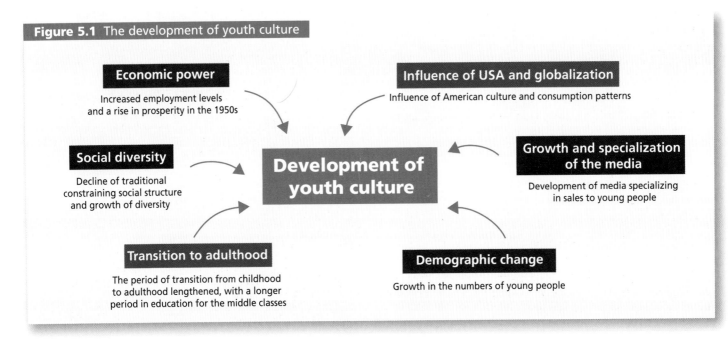

Figure 5.1 The development of youth culture

Economic power
Increased employment levels and a rise in prosperity in the 1950s

Influence of USA and globalization
Influence of American culture and consumption patterns

Social diversity
Decline of traditional constraining social structure and growth of diversity

Development of youth culture

Growth and specialization of the media
Development of media specializing in sales to young people

Transition to adulthood
The period of transition from childhood to adulthood lengthened, with a longer period in education for the middle classes

Demographic change
Growth in the numbers of young people

Aries (1962), modern ideas of youth began to emerge in the 19th century. At this point, the more affluent middle classes began to expand the length of their children's education with the hope that they would emerge with a more mature view of the world and ready to take on adult responsibilities. As the 19th century progressed, the length of this maturation period lengthened and these affluent young people became more separated from the adult world.

According to Pearson (1983), by the late 19th century, middle-class youth were joined by working-class young people who were reluctant to enter regular employment, preferring to 'get by' in rather different ways including petty theft. Two different **discourses** (way of thinking and acting) towards young people began to emerge, seeing youth as either 'trouble' or a time of fun and enjoyment, or indeed both. These two discourses have run along together for the last 150 years. As Hebdige puts it:

<< *The two image clusters, the bleak portrayal of juvenile offenders and the exuberant cameos of teenage life, reverberate, alternate and sometimes they get crossed.*>>
(Hebdige 1988)

When youth culture emerged in the 1950s, it fitted into these existing attitudes towards young people and so is viewed suspiciously by adults as both a time of crime and of fun and enjoyment.

Check your understanding

1 Explain how the age group 'youth' is socially constructed.

2 Give two examples of how the same 'age' has changed its meaning over time.

3 What is the relationship between the increase in young people's income and the development of youth culture?

4 Explain the social changes identified in the text. How did they impact on youth culture?

5 How did the development of rock and roll music influence youth culture?

6 Explain why leisure has become more important to young people since the 1950s.

7 In what ways are the following important to youth culture:
(a) style?
(b) consumption?

8 Identify the two dominant images of youth.

Two images of 1960s youth: mods and rockers fighting on the beach (right) and a poster for the hit film Summer Holiday (below). How do these photographs illustrate the two discourses about youth?

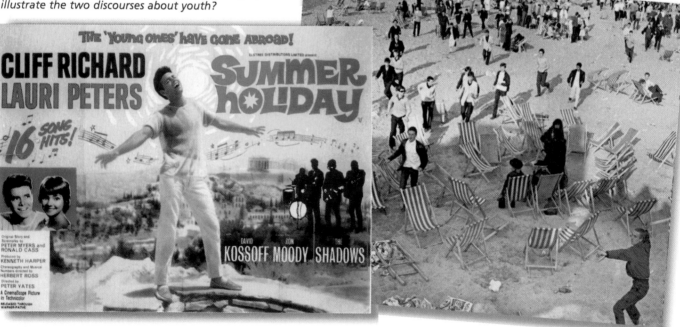

KEY TERMS

Argot the use of special terms for everyday items, only understood by the members of that culture.

Consumption a term used to describe the process of buying goods, usually for status and pleasure reasons.

Discourse way of thinking about a particular group or issue.

Globalization describes the fact that political, economic and social forces now operate across the world rather than in national boundaries.

Peer group a group of people of similar age and interests.

Social construction something that is created by society.

Transition the process of moving from childhood to adulthood.

Youth culture a set of values and behaviour shared by young people that is distinctive from the culture held by the older generations.

exploring youth and culture

Item A The extension of youth

<< 'Growing up', in many Western countries, has been significantly extended due to dissatisfaction or exclusion from the Labour market, increased participation rates in further and higher education, lower marriage rates and greater dependency on the family household. As a result, there is evidence of a period of 'extended' or 'post' adolescence in which an array of youthful lifestyles and identities are visible much longer. Importantly, as the population continues to age, post adolescents – those in their late twenties and into their thirties – will increasingly become targets for future nightlife provision. Further, for many young adults, traditional social relations and places of identity formation (such as the workplace) are weakening, with consumption, leisure and popular culture becoming more influential elements in the formation of youth identity. >>

Chatterton, P. and Hollands, R. (2001) *Changing our 'Toon'*, Newcastle: University of Newcastle

Item B Teenage culture

<< Young people were distinguished from other age groups not by their 'bad' behaviour, but simply in terms of their market choices, and it was these choices that revealed a new 'teenage culture'. This culture was defined in terms of leisure and leisure goods – coffee and milk bars, fashion clothes and hair styles, cosmetics, rock'n'roll records, films and magazines, scooters and motorbikes, dancing and dance halls. >>

Frith, S. (1984) The *Sociology of Youth*, Ormskirk: Causeway

---

1 Explain what is meant by the phrase 'youthful lifestyles and identities' (Item A). (2 marks)

2 Identify two ways in which the new 'teenage culture' was defined (Item B). (4 marks)

3 Identify and explain three ways in which the media contributed to the growth in youth culture. (9 marks)

4 Identify and explain two ways in which youth can be described as a social construction. (10 marks)

Exam practice

5 a Identify and explain two ways in which youth culture can be seen as a distinctive culture from that of adults. (15 marks)

   b Outline and discuss the view that youth culture developed as a result of increases in the income of young people. (30 marks)

---

web.task

Summaries of sociological research projects on the changing nature of youth culture in Newcastle, Bristol and Leeds can be found at: www.ncl.ac.uk/youthnightlife/home.htm

Browse the reports and find out the methods used and the key findings.

research idea

● Interview two adults, such as your parents, and, if possible, older adults such as grandparents, about the music and stars of their youth. What clothes did they wear? Were there any ways of expressing themselves (argot) they can recall? How did their parents react to their behaviour? What are their views on current youth culture?

Functionalist and conflict theories of youth culture

gettingyouthinking

1. **What names would you give to the youth cultural styles pictured here? When were they most popular? Are they still popular?**
2. **Identify as many youth cultures as you can.**
3. **Take one of these and try to work out what attracts young people to this particular style.**
4. **How many of your friends would identify with a particular youth cultural style?**
5. **To what extent do you think youth cultural styles are important to young people?**

In Topic 1, we saw how youth culture developed in the 1950s as a result of a number of different social changes occurring together. However, sociologists are interested in looking beyond this to see if there are any general theoretical explanations for the development of youth culture.

Four major theoretical schools have provided competing overall explanations for the nature and existence of youth culture. These are:

- functionalist
- conflict
- late modern
- postmodern.

Because these approaches cover such wide ground, we have divided them into two topics. In this topic, we are going to explore functionalist and conflict (or Marxist-derived) approaches. In Topic 3, we move on to look at countercultures, late-modern and postmodern theories. In both topics, we will

choose various youth subcultural styles that sociologists have studied and use them as examples of the theories. We will also include discussion on 'race' and gender issues where they are relevant. However, you must remember that both topics are closely related and, in order to gain a full understanding, you need to combine the insights of both topics.

The functionalist approach: youth as transition

Functionalist theories are based on the idea that if something exists in society, then it must be there for a purpose. Their argument is simple: youth culture undoubtedly exists and it must, therefore, serve some purpose. This approach to understanding social phenomena has a long history in sociology. It can be traced back as early as the end of the 19th century in the work of Emile Durkheim and then, in a more sophisticated form, in the writings of Talcott Parsons in the middle of the 20th century.

Parsons argued that in most traditional societies, young people go through a 'rite of passage', a ceremony marking the move from childhood into adulthood. In contemporary societies, these ceremonies have largely fallen into disuse, though a few remnants remain, such as the Jewish bar mitzvah and 18th-birthday celebrations. According to Parsons, youth culture has taken over this 'rite of passage' role, extending it over a number of years, but still essentially acting as form of transition from childhood to adulthood. Young people, he suggests, have to find a way of moving from the secure, cosy world of the family into the competitive adult world of work, where individual talent and sharp competition with others bring the financial rewards. The role of youth culture smooths this path by providing a link between the conflicting values of the home (childhood) and work (adulthood).

Eisenstadt (1956) took Parson's general ideas a little further. According to him, most young people need to find a way to distinguish themselves from their parents. They need to move from the **ascribed** position of being the child of a particular adult, to the **achieved** position of being an adult person in one's own right. However, breaking away from the home and family is difficult and emotionally stressful. Youth culture provides a mechanism for coping with this period of stress by providing a peer group of like-minded people of a similar age who adopt the same styles of dress and attitudes.

This serves the twin purposes of setting young people apart from their parents and providing them with a model of how to behave during this potentially stressful period. According to Eisenstadt, therefore, youth culture is a method of helping young people make the transition from childhood to adulthood. As this is the sole purpose of youth culture, the actual style and the content of the youth culture is of absolutely no importance. Eisenstadt further argues that any differences in the backgrounds of young people and between the various forms of youth cultures are unimportant. The important point to him is that all youth need some kind of transition mechanism, and it is unimportant what cultural form it takes.

Age: the new social division

A development of functionalist youth culture was the argument put forward by Roszak (1970) amongst others that a new division in society was emerging between young people and the older generations – a 'generation gap'. The values, interests and behaviour of youth was the replacement for divisions based on class, gender and race. Roszak argued that age cut across all these, making them outdated and irrelevant. This approach became extremely influential, Murdoch and McCron (1976), for example, argued that youth culture was 'a generation in itself', the advanced guard of a whole new culture which would radically change society, eliminating the out-dated divisions of social class. (These sorts of analyses have also been used to explore the nature of countercultures – see Topic 3, p. 199.)

Youth culture or youth subcultures?

Those who subscribed to the functionalist school and those that argued that youth formed the most significant division in society all used the term 'youth culture' in their analyses. A **culture** refers to a set of values and beliefs that provide clear guidelines on how to act in different situations. Cultures are complete in themselves, providing a 'world view'. Most tribal societies have only one culture shared by all their members. However, in modern, complex societies, although there is one main culture which most people share, within that there are numerous variations that tend to be known as **subcultures**.

If we apply this distinction to youth, we come to the heart of a major debate between sociologists. Can we say there is one youth culture, shared by all young people and highly distinctive from the adult culture, or are there, rather, a series of different youth subcultures reflecting social divisions of class, ethnicity and gender? Functionalist writers argue that there is essentially only one youth culture – or at least any variations are of little or no importance. Other writers, however, argue that the variations in youth that functionalists ignore are actually very important indeed. For example, according to the subcultural conflict models, there is no one, single youth culture, but instead, a variety of youth subcultures. So, while functionalists see no importance in analysing the content of youth culture, the conflict approach (along with the postmodern approach, discussed in Topic 3) argues that understanding the content and style of youth subcultures is crucial for an understanding of modern youth. They suggest that the idea of a division of age replacing class is simply not true.

The conflict approach: subculture as solution

In Britain in the 1970s, conflict theories based on Marxism were very influential. Conflict theories are derived from the Marxist theory that modern, capitalist societies are based on the exploitation of the population, but especially the working class, by a small ruling class. Because of this exploitation, the working class and the ruling class are routinely in conflict. The ruling class, according to conflict theorists, use a variety of mechanisms to control the working class. The obvious form of control is the criminal justice system and the police. However, a much more important method is by controlling the very values of society, so that capitalism and inequality seem 'natural'. This concept of controlling values is known as **hegemony** and is achieved through control of the mass media and of the values taught in schools.

It was within this academic tradition that a group of sociologists from what was Birmingham University's School of Contemporary Cultural Studies, began to study youth subcultures. Writers such as Hall and Jefferson (1976), argued that working-class young people (particularly those who had done poorly at school) formed the weakest point in the ruling class's control of society, as unlike adults they were not tied into capitalist society through jobs and family commitments. This partly explains the reason why there is so much control of young people by the police and the other control agencies. This set of views became known as the 'critical cultural studies approach'.

We saw earlier that, for functionalist writers, youth culture is a means of helping young people in the transition from childhood to adulthood, and that they viewed it as essentially positive. However, for conflict theorists, youth culture is a form of **resistance** against capitalism and, as such, is hostile to the dominant culture. Young people cause 'trouble' because they are engaging in class conflict, whether or not they are aware of this. Youth culture is an **inarticulate** means of resolving the problems faced by each generation of working-class youth. These problems consist of being offered a life of routine and low-paid employment, or perhaps no employment at all, just like their parents before them. Working-class youth cultures are a response to this bleak future – a way of expressing their anger and resistance.

However, if working-class youth face the same futures over generations, why do the forms or 'style' of youth culture alter over time? After all, expressing their opposition to their futures could be achieved in the same way by each generation. The answer to this, according to the Centre for Contemporary Cultural Studies, was that each generation of young people encounter the same problems, but in very different circumstances. For example, the 16-year-old growing up in the 1950s will have had a different experience of life compared to a 16-year-old today, with different cultural expectations, media output, leisure possibilities, drug availability and so on. Yet underneath these cultural differences, similar inequalities in jobs and life in general remain.

The outcome of all this is that youth subcultures alter over time and place in response to these wider changes.

Resistance through style

The problem for the critical cultural studies writers was how to prove their ideas were true. Their answer was to analyse the style and content of youth subcultures in the belief that these would demonstrate that they contained 'symbols of resistance' to capitalism. They therefore undertook what is known as **semiotic analysis**. Semiotics refers to the study of signs – symbols that communicate something – to find out what they mean. The cultural studies analysts therefore began to **decode** the meaning of the choice of clothes, haircut, hair colour, music, argot and ritual forms of behaviour of a range of youth subcultures in order to demonstrate how they were really expressions of opposition to capitalism.

The outcome was a series of studies of working-class youth subcultures, each of which explored in great detail the clothes worn, the music listened to, and the general form of slang language used. The aim of this research was to uncover the real, underlying meaning of the content of the subcultures.

Examples of working-class subculture

Teddy boys

Hall and Jefferson (1976) researched Teddy Boys, a 1950s working-class youth subculture. The rise of Teddy Boys in the early 1950s coincided with the expansion of employment and the general rise in affluence as a result of the major resurgence of industry after the Second World War. However, according to Fyvel (1961), the Teddy Boys were drawn from those youths who had been excluded from this – they had lost out in the education system and missed out on the affluence. Like generations of young people after them, they had nowhere to go and in their case, took over local cafes which they used as bases for hanging around. The Teddy Boys' trademarks were their Edwardian style jackets, suede shoes and bootlace ties. Hall and Jefferson then analysed the symbolic meaning of each of these articles of clothing. He suggested that the bootlace ties were from characters in Western films who had to live off their wits – the sort of characters whom working-class lads could aspire towards. Furthermore, the jackets and shoes were a subversion of the Edwardian Dandy style which had become popular with the upper middle class. Their use by the working-class Teddy Boys showed contempt for the class system by usurping the clothing style of their supposed 'social superiors'.

Skinheads

Phil Cohen (1972) conducted a similar semiotic study of skinheads. Skinheads (both male and female) wore an exaggerated version of traditional working-class male clothes, comprising cropped hair, braces, half-mast jeans and Doc. Marten boots. Their drug of preference was alcohol. Their clothes represented both a 'caricature and reassertion of solid, male, working-class toughness'. This reassertion of values was a response to a number of factors linked to the decline in working-class inner-city communities, which were threatened by the decline in the large-scale manufacturing and dock work that had traditionally provided the economic basis for the inner-city communities. They were also an attempt to deal with the large-scale immigration into these areas by poorer Asians (particularly from Pakistan), whom the White working class perceived as destroying their communities and taking their jobs. Skinhead subculture was therefore wrapped in racism. Much of the activity of the skinheads was involved in reclaiming territory, and this was often played out through football violence, which allowed groups to claim ownership of a club and the area around it.

Punk

Dick Hebdige (1979) studied Punk subculture. He suggests that a process of 'bricolage' (the reuse of ordinary objects in a different way to create challenging new meanings) occurred in Punk subculture. Punk emerged in the 1970s as a response to the dominance of the media, fashion and music industries. It had various routes: on the one hand, working-class young people disenchanted with their economic and social situation, and on the other side, art college students attracted by its creativity and energy. Punk attempted to undermine and disrupt existing styles, with the Punks seeing themselves outside existing cultures and class structures. Hebdige (1979) coined the term the 'blank generation' to describe this, saying that the only thing that Punks had in common was their rejection of anything orderly, restrained and sacred. Punk was one of the

Iain Borden
Skateboarding subculture

Iain Borden claims a certain 'outlaw' status for skateboarders as figures standing apart from and against the 'rule of the commodity' (the reduction of everything to profit-making). In particular, skateboarders reject the control of urban streets by profit-making leisure industries and the repressive legislation which supports this, such as laws of trespass and antisocial behaviour. He argues that skateboarders are a 'countercultural'/'subcultural' group, primarily consisting of 'youth', who seek to reclaim the city space. Skateboarding is a collective act of resistance:

≪ *Skateboarding, like other subcultures, attempts to separate itself from groups such as the family, to be oppositional, appropriative of the city, irrational in organization, ambiguous in constitution, independently creative of its marginal or 'sub' status'.* ≫

Adapted from: Borden, I. (2001) *Skateboarding, Space and the City: Architecture and the Body*, Oxford: Berg

1 What is the nature of skateboarding subculture?

2 In what ways can skateboarding be a form of 'resistance'?

was based on subverting the normal use and meanings of items. Clothes were ripped and drawn from a variety of sources, hair shaped in unusual ways and bodies pierced. Safety pins changed from household objects to body-piercing ornaments; bin liners became clothes; bondage gear was removed from the bedroom to everyday use. Hebdige's point was that, unlike the analyses of Jefferson and Cohen, youth subculture did not have to look to the past to be **oppositional**, but could be innovative too.

Race, conflict and subcultural style

By the 1960s, there were significant enough numbers of young people of African-Caribbean origin in Britain to forge their own distinctive youth subcultures. Hebdige (1979) suggests that the first subcultural style was that of Rude Boys. In Jamaica, 'Rudies' formed a subculture based on looking cool, dealing in cannabis and pimping. The image of coolness was transferred to the UK along with ska music and, like any other youth subculture, a degree of minor offending. Overlapping with the Rude Boys' subculture was the Rastafarian Movement. The Rastafarian Movement developed in Jamaica, but sees Ethiopia as the Holy Land and the last Ethiopian Emperor, Haile Selassie (or Ras Tafari) as their leader. Rastafarianism sees Babylon (or White colonial capitalism) as evil, and salvation coming from an eventual move back to Ethiopia. Marijuana plays a key role in the religion, as it allows the user to enter into an altered, apparently higher, state of consciousness.

Rastafarianism and the Rude Boy culture of Jamaica provided a cultural context for a generation of Black youths that was distinctive from White culture, according to Sivanandan (1981). He argues that the distinctive Black youth cultures emerged in Britain as a result of the experiences of a second generation of Black young people, who were born and raised in Britain, and yet were socially and economically marginalized by the wider White society on the basis of 'race'. Sivanandan suggests that the Black subcultures were a continuation of a colonial struggle transposed to Britain. Whilst working-class White youths expressed their opposition through forming subcultures such as the skinheads, Sivanandan argued that the 'Black' youth subcultures were different styles, but driven by the same sense of opposition to capitalist and racist society.

The response of the media to these Black subcultural forms was different from their treatment of White subcultures. There were some attempts to exploit them by the music and leisure industries, but the media generally opted to represent Black youth subcultures as threatening and criminal. In particular, as Hall *et al.* (1978) pointed out, young Black men were closely linked in the media with street crime.

Magic!

A related, though distinctive version of a critical sociological approach to youth cultures is provided by Brake (1984).

Brake is sympathetic to the idea that youth subcultures are a form of resistance to capitalism, but he also notes that they do nothing to alter the power and economic differences in society that create the problems for working-class youth in the first

few 'resistance' subcultures that did have political elements to it. The lyrics of bands such as The Clash were about experiences of life on estates, unemployment benefit and 'White riots'. In many ways, Punk was the complete opposite of skinhead subculture and yet, at the same time, significant elements of it dealt with problems of unemployment and the drabness of working-class life. Punk style was a deliberate attempt at a do-it-yourself culture, which cost very little and place. In terms of actually challenging capitalism, they are therefore pointless. Nevertheless, according to Brake, they do provide a 'magical' solution for working-class youth's plight.

By using the term 'magical', Brake means that whilst they appear to provide a way out for each generation through new forms of subculture, in fact this is merely an illusion (as most magic tricks are). Each generation uses this trick to convince themselves they are different and are not going to become like their parents. However, in reality, the same economic and social structures that have constrained their parents' behaviour eventually constrains them too. They form relationships, get jobs, have kids and so on. But the magic trick keeps each working-class generation believing they are different.

Brake also explored middle-class youth subcultures and suggested that these are significantly different from those of working-class youth. Brake argues that middle-class youth subcultures are more all-encompassing than working-class ones and are more likely to be 'countercultural'. By this he means that they can provide complete cultural alternatives (for example political or religious) to the existing mainstream culture.

Criticisms of the critical cultural studies approach

The cultural studies analyses of working-class youth subcultures were immensely influential, but have been strongly criticized:

- Stan Cohen (1972) argued that these writers wanted to find forms of resistance in the style and argot of the working-class subcultures and were biased in their analyses. They therefore interpreted argot and style in a way that supported their political beliefs. Cohen pointed out that there were various different ways of interpreting the symbols, most of which were not supportive of the critical cultural studies approach.
- This approach completely ignored middle-class youth subcultures. This could be because, according to this approach, there really should not be any, as middle-class youth do not face the same problems.
- Critical cultural writers credit working-class youth with an amazing ability to create complete, highly sophisticated subcultures based on a complex set of symbols. Cohen suggests this is very naive, ignoring as it does the role of the media and other commercial interests in developing and exploiting young people.
- A final criticism came from McRobbie (1991), who argues that critical youth cultural writers have largely ignored girls' subcultures. She argues that these are very different in content and style, and do not fit the theoretical framework of the conflict approach.

Female youth culture

What sociologists most commonly state when exploring youth subcultures is that females are largely missing. Indeed, the term '**invisible girl**' is often used. McRobbie and Garber (1976) comment that the place of young women in youth culture

reflects their general position in society. Although they are present in all youth subcultures, they are pushed to the margins of this largely male social activity. McRobbie argues that the range of possibilities open to females in subcultures is much more limited than that of the males. According to her, youth cultures let males have 'temporary flights' away from the responsibilities and constraints imposed upon male adults in society, but females are denied this possibility because of greater parental control and the constraints imposed by other females concerning appropriate sexual conduct. This is linked to ideas about the 'natural' place of women being in the home rather than hanging around in the streets.

According to McRobbie, this results in girls engaging in 'bedroom culture', where they meet their friends and chat. This is a place, in the home, which is regarded as safe and appropriate for females.

KEY TERMS

Ascribed social position fixed at birth, such as son or daughter.

Achieved social position chosen or earned, such as A-level student.

Culture a complete-in-itself set of values and guide to behaviour.

Decode the process of uncovering hidden meanings.

Hegemony a complete set of ideas and values which provide an explanation for the social world; the term is usually associated with Marxist or conflict theorists, who argue that the ruling class 'imposes' hegemony on society to explain why they should be in control.

Inarticulate unable to express clearly.

Invisible girl a phrase often used to emphasize the way that youth cultures appear to be dominated by males.

Oppositional subcultural values opposed to the dominant hegemony of the ruling class.

Resistance a term used by conflict theorists to refer to a subculture being critical of capitalism and protective of working-class interests.

Semiotic (semiotic analysis) the analysis of signs and symbols in order to uncover the hidden meanings.

Subculture a set of distinctive values existing within a broader culture.

Check your understanding

1. Explain what is meant by a 'rite of passage'.

2. What is the purpose of youth culture according to functionalists?

3. According to Roszak what has the division of age replaced?

4. What is meant by the terms 'oppositional' and 'semiotic'?

5. Why is the term 'invisible girls' used?

6. Identify and explain any one criticism made by Cohen of the critical cultural studies approach.

exploring functionalist and conflict theories

Item A Evaluating critical cultural studies approaches

«Both these themes of resistance and symbols are rich and suggestive. I have only the space to mention a few of the problems they raise. The first arises from the constant impulse to decode the style in terms only of opposition and resistance. This means that instances are sometimes missed when the style is conservative or supportive: in other words, not reworked or reassembled but taken over intact from dominant commercial culture. ...

There is also a tendency in some of this work to see the historical development of a style as being wholly internal to the group – with commercialization and co-option as something which just happens afterwards. In the understandable zeal to depict the kids as creative agents rather than manipulated dummies, this often plays down the extent to which changes in youth culture are manufactured changes, dictated by consumer society.»

Cohen, S. (1980) *Folk Devils and Moral Panics* (2nd edn), Martin Robertson

Item B Symbolic challenges

«For most young people, subcultures are probably, at best, nothing more than a means to create and establish an identity in a society where they can find it difficult to locate a sense of self. At worst, subcultures prove to be 'symbolic challenges to a symbolic order', because by the style that subcultures adopt, they represent that not all young people are willing to be moulded into what adult society considers the norm. They are symbolic because these 'challenges' offer no real danger to a social 'order' that is based purely on aesthetics and fashion.»

Garratt, D. in Roche, J., Tucker, S., Thomson, R. and Flynn, R. (2004) *Youth in Society* (2nd edn), London: Open University Press.

1. Explain what is meant by 'the constant impulse to decode the style in terms only of opposition and resistance' (Item A). (2 marks)

2. Identify the two alternative explanations for youth subculture offered in Item B? (4 marks)

3. Identify and briefly explain three ways in which youth subcultures show that young people are not 'willing to be moulded into what adult society considers the norm' (Item B). (9 marks)

4. Identify and explain two differences between functionalist and conflict approaches to youth. (10 marks)

Exam practice

5. a Identify and explain two ways in which working-class and middle-class youth subcultures have differed. (15 marks)

   b Outline and discuss the view that youth subcultures are a reaction to economic and social conditions. (30 marks)

research idea

- Interview a small sample of young people who dress and behave in ways appropriate to a youth subculture. Find out what attracts them to the particular subculture and what meaning they give to the clothes, music and lifestyle of that group.

web.task

Go to the archives of the web discussion pages of 'Subcultural-Styles' at www.jiscmail.ac.uk/archives/subcultural-styles.html

Here, academics and other interested people ask and answer questions on youth culture. Browse the archives for some fascinating stuff!

Late-modern and postmodern theories of youth culture

gettingyouthinking

1 What do you think attracts young people to become part of the groups pictured in the first two photos above?

2 Look at the young people in the third photograph (below). What attracts them to a night out in the town centre?

In Topic 2, we examined functionalist-based explanations for youth culture, which stressed that:

- youth culture existed to provide a means of transition from childhood to adulthood
- the content or style of youth culture was of no academic importance
- a new 'generation gap' was replacing class as the most significant social division.

Arguing against this were the conflict theorists who claimed that:

- subcultures were an attempt at resistance by working-class youth
- class divisions were still very important
- there were a number of youth subcultures rather than one undifferentiated youth culture.

They claimed that this could be revealed by decoding the style of the subculture.

These debates were illustrated by a range of studies on the working class and on 'race'. In this topic, we will continue our exploration of youth subcultures by discussing two other theoretical approaches: late-modern and postmodern. These two approaches share the belief that the importance of social class and employment has declined as an influence on youth culture. Instead, youth subcultures stretch across class lines and are more concerned with individuals expressing themselves in various ways. The idea of resistance is completely dropped.

Late modernity: consumerism and countercultures

In recent years, sociologists have argued that the traditional social structure associated with capitalism and industrial societies has been swept away. Social class, for example, which was an extremely important determinant of life in the 1950s, has declined considerably. Certainly inequalities still exist, but they are experienced and perceived in different ways by people now. The decline in the importance of social class is just one of many social and economic changes taking place (see Unit 1, Topic 5, pp. 20–1). In order to help us understand these changes, sociologists have suggested using the term **modernity** for the more traditional industrial social and economic arrangements which began to decline in the second part of the 20th century and **late modernity** for society since then. Late modernity is characterized by choice and a stress on the individual. Work as a central focus of most people's lives and identity has increasingly been replaced by leisure and consumption (what you buy).

This shift from modernity to late modernity has very important implications for youth. In particular, it points the direction of youth subcultural studies away from resistance in two very different directions:

1 towards the exploration of self and new social arrangements, which has led to countercultures or new social movements

2 towards the development of youth lifestyles based on consumerism and leisure.

Countercultures

The term 'counterculture' is used to describe subcultures that present proposals as to how society ought to be organized that contrast with – or run counter to – the current arrangements. The term was developed by writers such as Marcuse (1964) and Roszak (1970). The rise of youth countercultures was possibly one of the first indications of the arrival of late modernity.

The first large-scale counterculture in Britain was that of the hippies who sought to withdraw from the organized, technological and bureaucratic lifestyle predominating by the 1960s. Their general beliefs were that love should replace violence and that people should be free to express themselves artistically, musically and socially. Most political movements demand a change in society, but hippies argued first for a change in the way people thought. Changes in society would then follow. The counterculture emerged in the 1960s in San Francisco, where ideas had developed on the use of drugs to liberate the mind.

The 1970s saw the decline of hippies, and counterculture appeared to shrink to its base of the student population, which, at that time, was undergoing a massive expansion. However, the 1980s saw the emergence of new concerns centred less on personal development and more on concerns about the way society was developing and the effects of technological change on society, the physical environment and the animal world (McKay 1996). A wide range of very different groups began to emerge that had few specific interests in common, but that shared a broad philosophy opposed to materialism, urbanism, consumerism and capitalism. McKay describes the New Age counterculture as a 'loose network of loose networks'. It was composed of New Age travellers, eco-warriors and animal liberation activists, amongst others.

The key point about all these countercultures was that, although they were critical of existing social arrangements, their supporters were drawn from a wide range of society and the central themes were the exploration of new directions and new ideas of self. The notion of working-class resistance did not come into it.

Consumerism and leisure

So far, the youth subcultures we have explored have been portrayed as being in some ways critical of existing social arrangements. This is true whether they are setting out specifically to criticize society, such as the hippies or the eco-warriors, or whether they are 'inarticulate' in their opposition, such as punks and skinheads. Coleman (1980), however, has argued that this approach relies too heavily on exploring the relatively few 'spectacular' youth cultures that have hit the headlines and have been used by the leisure and fashion industries as images. Other sociologists, such as Muncie (1984), have argued that young people on the whole are actually very conformist. Though they may follow the fashion, it does not mean that they 'buy into' the meanings that sociologists suggest underpin the subcultures. You can, for example, have 'locks' but not be a Rastafarian. The major interests of young people reflect and correspond to those of the dominant value system, they do not oppose it. In fact, in a national study of young people's attitudes (Roberts 1997), the overwhelming majority were conformist in attitude. What young people want, according to these analyses, is to enjoy the new leisure industries that have emerged in the last 30 years. City centres have become places where young people go out at weekends, engage in drinking, meeting others and generally seeking to enjoy what the leisure industry has to offer. Chatterton and Hollands' (2001) study of nightlife in Newcastle also finds that there is a considerable amount of conservatism in what appears to be irresponsible, drunken nights out at the weekend. They argue that the idea of 'going out' was not to get drunk, to find a sexual partner or to fight, but simply reflected the more obvious desire to go out with friends and enjoy oneself. There is no intention of confronting society – instead, going out provided social space away from education or work, where young people could 'construct their identities'.

According to Roberts (1997) the gender patterns, too, have remained conservative, with male and female youth exhibiting the broader society's attitudes towards expectations of appropriate behaviour for the different sexes.

The shift from modernity to late modernity has, therefore, opened up 'spaces' where very different forms of youth subcultures can exist.

Postmodern youth subcultures

During the 1990s postmodernist approaches began to emerge as a useful way of analysing a range of social issues. **Postmodernism** challenged sociology in a profound way by arguing that most of the social phenomena that sociologists seek to understand are actually impossible to understand through rational analysis. According to postmodernists such as Bauman (1993) there is no coherent, structured social world that can be understood by rational inquiry. They suggest instead that the world is totally complex and confusing. At first, this might seem to herald the end of sociology, but modified forms of postmodernism were successfully adopted by sociologists, and one of the areas most intensively studied was that of youth subculture.

This new postmodernist approach introduced new questions and innovative research methods to the study of youth subculture. In terms of research, for example, Widdicombe and Wooffitt (1995) encouraged young people to talk about their experiences and views of the world. The researchers refused to impose a framework on the conversations they held with the young people (unlike the approach of the Centre for Contemporary Cultural Studies – see p. 193) and argued that youth subcultures did not have fixed meanings or any real independent existence. They suggested instead that young people used the notion of a youth subculture in many different ways. There was, therefore, no one meaning of youth culture or subculture. The anarchy of punk, the oppositional attitudes

of working-class youth or the countercultural ideas of the middle-class youth were, in fact, merely meanings 'imposed' upon young people's activities by sociologists.

The analysis of youth subculture moved away from notions of opposition or counterculture and started to stress the way that subculture was as much about style as anything else. Roberts (1997) argued that young people pick up styles and fashions from those available in the media and others around them and there is no underlying opposition or real meaning.

Other writers such as Maffesoli (1998) suggested that youth subcultures as such had ceased to exist for young people, and instead were being replaced by fluid and open movements or **neo-tribes**'. He uses this term to describe a wide range of groupings, all of which share a commitment to 'the communal ethic', which 'has the simplest of foundations: warmth, companionship – physical contact with one another' (Maffesoli 1998). These neo-tribes, he argues, tend to be based on networks that have developed through the choice to be together for 'elective sociality' (based simply on the desire to be together), rather than for any particular collective purpose.

These sorts of approaches offered explanations for the emergence of a wide range of rapidly changing 'subcultures', such as those associated with raves and clubbing. However, as well as being highly critical of sociologists, postmodern approaches also raised a question that had not previously been discussed adequately by sociologists: whether youth culture emanated from young people themselves or was the creation of the mass media and commercial interests.

Postmodern perspectives on youth culture and the media industry

Functionalist writers had no interest in the basis of youth culture, seeing it as merely a form of transition into adulthood. Critical sociologists, however, were convinced that youth subcultures were generated by young people themselves in their attempts to resist capitalism. Others, such as Coté and Allahar (1996), oppose this view, seeing youth subcultures as products of media manipulation. According to this view, young people are the 'dupes' of commercial interests, and youth subcultures are essentially the products of an industry which wishes to make profit.

>> *What lies at the heart of all this activity, however, is the fact that these media can sell young people some element of an identity they have been taught to crave ... leisure industries such as music, fashion and cosmetics have a largely uncritical army of consumers awaiting the next craze or fad.*>>(Coté and Allahar 1996, p. 149)

In a similar vein, Giroux (1998) argues that the large multinational media and fashion companies are exploiting the multiplicity of social divisions in contemporary society and seeking to make profit out of them. Giroux argues that differences of religion, 'race', locality and gender are simply marketing categories that are being encouraged as new and growing markets to sell music and clothes to.

Postmodern approaches throw a different light on this debate. Kahane (1997) suggests that contemporary youth subcultures are a genuine attempt to construct new and original subcultures from the enormous choice of music, style and language available to young people, based on 'symbols of freedom, spontaneity, adventurism and **eclecticism**'. Thornton (1995) suggests that youth culture is actually a complex mixture of both. On the one hand, youth cultures can be manufactured by commercial interests and then taken up by young people and refashioned in a way never imagined by the music/fashion industry; on the other hand, 'genuine' youth cultures can be generated by young people and then taken over by commercial interests.

Globalization and hybridized youth subcultures

An important element of postmodernist thinking about youth subcultures is that of **globalization**. Writers such as Luke and Luke (2000) argue that in the modern cultural world, influences derive from films, music and other media that are global in nature, not just national or local. They suggest the idea of a '**hybridized**' youth culture, whereby young people take elements from the global youth cultures featured in the media, and then adapt these according to local values and ideas. So, young people in Japan place a Japanese perspective on international music and styles, and young people in Britain place a British cultural perspective on the same music. Even more specific, Muslim young people in Britain will place a different perspective on this than African-Caribbean youth.

Postmodernity and 'race'

This takes us into postmodern debates on 'race' and youth subcultures. The Rude Boy and Rastafarianism subcultures which we discussed in Topic 2 were regarded by Sivanandan as 'oppositional'. He claimed to have found a meaning underpinning ethnic minority youth subcultures. Postmodern analyses present a rather different image.

The first step towards a postmodern approach can be found in the work of Gilroy (1987), who argued that we can understand all ethnic-minority youth subcultures through diasporas (patterns of dispersal) created by the postcolonial migrations. People who have left their place of origin have links there, but also must adapt to their new environment. For Gilroy, all ethnic-minority youth subcultures are, therefore, a mix of their cultural origins and of their present circumstances. Although, at first, this seems the same argument as we saw earlier, what Gilroy is arguing is that the ethnic minority subcultures are very flexible and open, taking elements from a range of influences and constantly changing. This moved sociologists into applying the notions of hybridity to ethnic-minority youth subcultures.

Cashmore (1997) gives a good example of hybridity in his analysis of 'gangsta' rap. This began in the 1960s in Jamaica and then, in the 1970s, became popular in the Black neighbourhoods of New York. By the mid 1980s, it had been

Andy Bennett
Subcultures or neo-tribes?

Bennett set out to see if the claims of the postmodernist sociologist Michel Maffesoli that youth subcultures had been replaced by 'neo-tribes' were true. Bennett researched clubs in Newcastle and found no evidence for youth subcultures. Instead, loose, fluid and relatively short-term youth groupings occurred, which were drawn from a range of social backgrounds. Unlike traditional working-class subcultures which were clearly definable, these new neo-tribes are based around fashion and lifestyle, but without the shared values. Individuals mixed and matched fashion influences and didn't feel they belonged to any definable group. Bennett suggests that youth identity is now very fluid and doesn't involve fixed commitments or norms and values, as claimed by traditional youth subcultural theorists.

Bennett, A. (1999) 'Subcultures or neo-tribes: rethinking the relationship between youth, style and musical taste', *Sociology*, 33(3), pp. 599–617

1 What are the differences between a 'neo-tribe' and a subculture?

2 Explain Bennett's conclusions about youth identity in your own words.

taken up in Los Angeles and from there was promoted world wide. But there are numerous variations of the original rap, which has constantly changed in response to genuinely creative ideas, as well as to the demands of the international music industry. Rap has also crossed the barriers of race and has been taken up enthusiastically by White youth. Youth subcultures therefore draw upon different global elements and then adapt them to local or relevant ethnic circumstances.

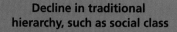

Figure 5.2 Summary of late-modern and postmodern approaches to youth culture

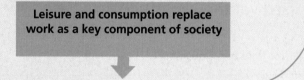

Late modernity and postmodernity

AGREE on the following changes to society:

Late modernity

A range of fast-changing youth styles occur, but also some more long-lasting subcultures and countercultures. The media are extremely influential, as are large commercial leisure organizations.

- Decline in traditional hierarchy, such as social class
- Growth of individualism
- Importance of the media and its presentation of 'reality'
- Leisure and consumption replace work as a key component of society

Postmodernity

No subcultures, but instead a rapidly changing and ever-increasing range of fashions, styles and 'looks'. These are partly genuine innovation by young people, partly manipulation. The individual and the expression of individuality are core experiences.

but they INTERPRET these changes differently:

KEY TERMS

Hybridization the linking of local and global cultures to form youth subcultures.

Modernity the traditional set of social and economic relationships dominated by industry and social class.

Late modernity the period since the 1970s where the structures of modernity have been replaced by individual values and a stress on leisure.

Postmodernism an alternative to late modernity; describes the rejection of rational ways

of explaining action and a stress on emotions.

Globalization refers to international nature of trade and the media.

Neo-tribes temporary groups coming together when they

wish and then parting. An alternative to the idea of more static and long-lasting subcultures.

Eclectic drawn from a wide variety of sources.

Check your understanding

1 What ideas are shared by both late-modern and postmodern sociologists?

2 How did the concerns of countercultural movements change during the 1980s?

3 According to Chatterton and Hollands, what do young people seek when they go out?

4 How do sociologists such as Coleman and Muncie criticize the view that youth subcultures are a way of resisting society?

5 Explain Maffesoli's view of 'neo-tribes'.

6 How do postmodern sociologists attack the view that youth culture is simply the result of manipulation by the media, fashion and music industries?

7 How can the idea of 'hybridity' help us to understand the link between race and youth culture?

---

research idea

- Observe groups of students around your school, college or local town. Observe clothes, hair styles, use of language and behaviour. Is it possible to categorize people into clear styles? If not, why not?

---

web.task

Go to
www.britishbornchinese.org.uk/pages/art6.html

This is a site for British Born Chinese (BBC). Can you find similar information from the internet on other ethnic groups? Are any of the theories you have read in Topics 2 and 3 useful in understanding these groups?

Item A Style

«Style is manifested through dress, look, sound, performance and so on. It is a powerful means of giving a group validation and coherence. It functions rather like the 'totem' according to Emile Durkheim, as something which gives visible expression to an individual's sense of belonging to a group. It allows a group to recognize itself and be recognized (although not necessarily 'understood') by others; it makes a statement which can be sent across the group as well as directed beyond it.»

Gelder, K. and Thornton, S. (1997) *The Subcultures Reader*, London: Routledge, p. 373

Item B Free festivals

The New Age traveller lifestyle has its origins within the hippie counterculture of the 1970s, notably the free festival scene that emerged at that time. Free festivals grew up alongside large commercial festivals and were conceived as utopian models for an alternative society, often referring to an imagined ethos of freedom from the constraints of conventional life.

Adapted from Hetherington, K. (1998) 'Vanloads of uproarious humanity', in T. Skelton and G. Valentine (eds) *Cool Places: Geographies of youth cultures*, London: Routledge p. 330.

Item C Young Asian women: dress and hybrid styles

«For the young women interviewed, dress and style were important topics for discussion. They were well aware of not only how different meanings were attached to individuals depending on what they were wearing, but also how these meanings shifted in different spaces. The participants illustrated how they seek to define their own identities by subverting or redefining the codes associated with different styles of dress. On the one hand they seek to challenge the 'traditional'/'Western' dichotomy. And at the same time they also negotiate the expectations of the local Asian community. The simple opposition between 'Asian' and 'Western' was also undermined when respondents considered the ways in which hybrid styles were being created where fashions were being blended together.»

Dwyer, C. (1998) 'Contested identities. Challenging dominant representations of young British Muslim women', in T. Skelton and G. Valentine (eds) *Cool Places: Geographies of youth cultures*. London: Routledge

1 Explain what is meant by the phrase 'hybrid styles were being created' (Item C). (2 marks)

2 Using Item A, identify two functions of 'style'. (4 marks)

3 Explain the meaning of the term 'counterculture'. In what ways are New Age travellers an example of a counterculture (Item B)? (9 marks)

4 Identify and explain two examples of youth subcultures. (10 marks)

Exam practice

5 a Identify and explain two ways in which postmodern approaches contribute to our understanding of youth subcultures. (15 marks)

  b Outline and discuss the view that distinctive youth subcultures are not significant for young people today. (30 marks)

Subcultural theories of youth offending

gettingyouthinking

Figure 5.3

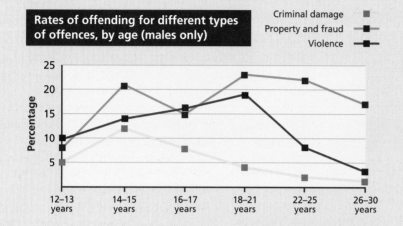

Rates of offending for different types of offences, by age (males only)

Criminal damage
Property and fraud
Violence

Source: Flood-Page, C., Campbell, S., Harrington, V. and Miller, J. (2000) Home Office Research Study 209

Figure 5.4

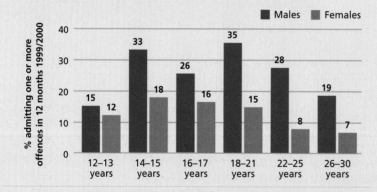

Prevalence of offending in 1999/2000 by age and sex

■ Males ■ Females

Source: Flood-Page, C., Campbell, S., Harrington, V. and Miller, J. (2000) Home Office Research Study 209

Nearly half of all young people in England and Wales have committed a criminal offence, a government survey suggests. The Home Office study says that 57 per cent of young males, aged between 12 and 30, who were questioned admitted committing at least one offence. The figure for young women in the same age group was 37 per cent. For the survey, a sample of nearly 5,000 young people were questioned. The survey found that 10 per cent of juvenile offenders were responsible for nearly half of the crimes committed by those in the 12 to 30 age group.

It also found marked differences in the nature of the crimes committed by the different sexes at different ages. Girls under 16 were most likely to be involved in criminal damage, shoplifting, buying stolen goods and fighting, while over the age of 16 they turned to crimes of fraud and buying stolen goods. Comparatively high rates of offending by 14- and 15-year-old boys reflected their involvement in fights, criminal damage and buying stolen goods. More than a third of offences committed by 16- and 17-year-old boys involved fighting. The highest levels of offending were among 18- to 21-year-old men, with fraud and workplace theft beginning in this age group.

Amended from BBC News Online, Monday 9 October, 2000
http://news.bbc.co.uk/1/hi/uk/963871.stm

1 What percentage of young people admitted to ever having committed an offence?

2 At what age were (a) females and (b) males most likely to commit an offence?

3 In your own words, explain the overall relationship between offending and age for (a) females and (b) males.

4 Which sex is more likely to commit an offence?

5 Look at Figure 5.3. There is information on three different offences here. What are they? In your own words, explain how they change by age.

The statistics above illustrate clearly that there is a strong relationship between young people (or more accurately, young males) and offending – both as victims and as offenders. We can also see that as young men move into their twenties, they are much less likely to offend. In this topic, we explore some of the explanations that sociologists have put forward of the high levels of young men committing offences. These explanations focus on one key concept, that of **subculture**.

The origins of subculture

Subcultural approaches to explaining youth offending are drawn from two traditions. Initially, these two traditions were quite separate, but over time they have become increasingly intertwined, as we shall see. The first of these two traditions is the environmental school, which emerged from studies by sociologists at the University of Chicago in the early to mid 20th century. The second tradition derives from strain theory, first devised by Robert Merton in the 1930s.

Subculture and the University of Chicago

This approach developed as a result of massive social change in American cities in the early 20th century. Sociologists went out into the streets and observed or hung around with gangs in the streets or just observed what was happening amongst deviant groups. A huge number of books were published including Thrasher's *The Gang* (1927) and Whyte's *Street Corner Society* (1955). What emerged from these studies was that these deviant groups had clear norms and values of their own (or subcultures) which they used to justify their deviant behaviour.

Subculture and strain theory

First writing in the 1930s, Merton argued that the offending committed by young people was the result of a poor fit or a **strain** between the socially accepted goals of society and the socially approved means of obtaining those desired goals. This resulting strain led to deviance.

Merton argued that all societies set their members certain socially approved goals and approved ways of achieving these goals. For example, a socially approved goal is have a job and the means to achieving the job is to work hard at school and college, do well in exams, and be awarded the position on merit.

However, if the majority of the population are unable to achieve the socially set goals, because the approved means simply are not available to them (for example, if education is so expensive that only a few affluent people can attend school), then a significant proportion of the population will become disenchanted with the society and seek out alternative (often deviant) ways of behaving. Merton used the term **anomie** to describe the situation where it is difficult for people to achieve the approved goals. In a situation of anomie, people get frustrated and develop a number of responses to deal with the situation:

- carrying on conforming regardless
- seeking new ways of achieving the goals, including crime (innovation)
- simply 'going through the motions', knowing it is pointless (ritualism)
- turning to drugs or alcohol in despair (retreatism)
- rejecting the traditional means and goals, and turning to political, religious or social rebellion.

Merton has been criticized for his belief that there are common goals that people share; critics argue that there are numerous goals in society and equally numerous means of achieving them.

Status frustration

Writing in the mid 1950s, Albert Cohen (1955) drew from both Merton and the Chicago School. He was particularly interested in the fact that a very high proportion of offending by young people does not benefit them financially, but consists of vandalism or violence. The first thing that Cohen noted was that the overwhelming majority of young people committing offences or engaging in antisocial behaviour, were from working-class backgrounds. Cohen suggested the answer lies in **status frustration**, that is, a sense of personal failure and inadequacy. According to Cohen, this comes from the experience of school. Working-class boys are more likely to fail at school and consequently feel humiliated. In an attempt to gain status, they develop subcultures which 'invert' traditional middle-class values such as obedience, politeness and obeying the law. Instead, they behave badly and engage in a variety of antisocial behaviour. Within the values of their subculture, this behaviour provides them with status.

Cohen has been criticized quite heavily for constructing a theory of subculture that is much more applicable to males than to females.

Illegitimate opportunity structure: illegitimate subcultures

Merton's ideas also influence the work of Cloward and Ohlin (1960), who agreed that a mismatch between socially approved goals and means could lead to offending. However, they suggested that Merton had failed to appreciate that there was a parallel illegal set of goals and means to the legal one, which they called the '**illegitimate opportunity structure**'. By this they meant that, for some groups in society, an illegal career was possible. A recent example of this is described in Dick Hobbs' book *Bad Business* (1998). Hobbs interviewed successful professional criminals and demonstrated how it is possible to have a career in crime, given the right connections and 'qualities'.

According to Cloward and Ohlin, the illegal opportunity structure had three possible subcultures:

- Criminal – In this adaptation, there is a thriving local criminal subculture, with successful role models. Young offenders can 'work their way up the ladder' in the criminal hierarchy.

- Conflict – Here, there is no local criminal subculture to provide a career opportunity. Groups brought up in this sort of environment are likely to turn to violence, usually against other similar groups. Cloward and Ohlin give the example of violent gang 'warfare'.
- Retreatist – This occurs where the individual has no opportunity or ability to engage in either of the other two subcultures. The result is a retreat into the subculture of alcohol or drugs.

This explanation is useful and, as Hobbs' work shows, for some people there really is a criminal opportunity structure. But the approach shares some of the weaknesses of Merton's original theory. First, it is difficult to accept that such a neat distinction into three clear categories occurs in real life. Second, there is no discussion whatsoever about female deviance. The explanation is implicitly about males.

Focal concerns: subculture as normal working-class values

Walter Miller (1962) developed a rather different approach to explaining subculture and offending. He suggested that antisocial behaviour was simply an extreme development of normal working-class male values.

Miller suggested that working-class males have six 'focal concerns' which are likely to lead to delinquency:

- trouble – 'I don't go looking for trouble, but ...'
- toughness – a belief that being physically stronger than others (and being able to show it) is good
- smartness – that a person both looks good, but is also witty and has a 'sharp repartee'
- excitement – that it is important to search out thrills
- fate – that the individual has little chance to overcome the wider fate that awaits them
- autonomy – that it is important not to be pushed around by others.

According to Miller, then, young lower-class males are pushed towards crime by the implicit values of working-class male culture. However, Box (1981) has argued that these values could equally apply to males right across the class structure.

Subterranean values: subculture as normal

Matza (1964) has suggested that, in explaining youth offending, we should think less about the notion of subculture and more about subterranean values. According to him, everyone has some deviant values, but they are kept in check most of the time.

All young people crave thrills and excitement and all break rules if it is to their advantage, but most of the time they control these desires and conform. For the majority of young people (and older ones too), these subterranean values only emerge on holiday or a drunken night out. On occasions such as these, most behave badly. But when they do emerge, people will then use excuses to explain why the excesses were justified. Matza

focus on research

Carl Nightingale
On the Edge

Although Merton and Cloward and Ohlin's writings are quite dated, it would be wrong to think that they are irrelevant. In America, there is still a strong tradition which uses their original ideas.

In *On the Edge* (1993), Carl Nightingale studied young Black youth in an inner-city area of Philadelphia. Nightingale noted the way that the youths in his study were avid television devotees, spending many hours watching television and eagerly identifying with the successful characters, both real and fictional. They desperately wanted to be successful like the media celebrities, yet as Black inner-city youths, they were excluded economically, racially and politically from participating in the mainstream US culture. Rather than reacting to this by turning against the dominant culture, they desperately wanted to be successful. For them, this meant having the 'right' clothes, music, cars, etc. – in particular by possessing articles with high-status trade names or logos. The only way to afford this was breaking the law. For Nightingale, the only way to understand the subculture is also to understand that it emerges from a real desire to be part of the mainstream US culture.

1 How does Nightingale argue that youth crime can result from a 'real desire to be part of the mainstream US culture'?

called these excuses techniques of neutralization. The difference between a persistent offender and a law-abiding young person may simply be how often and in what circumstances the subterranean values emerge and are then justified by the techniques of neutralization. Matza is not denying that some groups, or subcultures, are more likely to express subterranean values, but these groups are not completely different from other young people (see Fig. 5. 5)

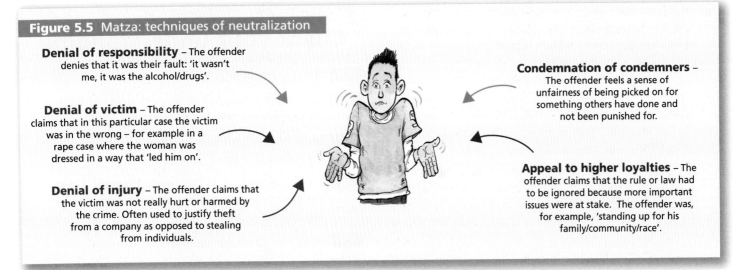

Figure 5.5 Matza: techniques of neutralization

Denial of responsibility – The offender denies that it was their fault: 'it wasn't me, it was the alcohol/drugs'.

Denial of victim – The offender claims that in this particular case the victim was in the wrong – for example in a rape case where the woman was dressed in a way that 'led him on'.

Denial of injury – The offender claims that the victim was not really hurt or harmed by the crime. Often used to justify theft from a company as opposed to stealing from individuals.

Condemnation of condemners – The offender feels a sense of unfairness of being picked on for something others have done and not been punished for.

Appeal to higher loyalties – The offender claims that the rule or law had to be ignored because more important issues were at stake. The offender was, for example, 'standing up for his family/community/race'.

Marxist subcultural theories

In Topic 2, we explored the contribution of Marxist or conflict approaches to youth subcultures. The same approaches are used by Marxist writers to explain youth crime. Young working-class males commit crime as a form of resistance to capitalism (for a full discussion, see p. 193–4).

Left realism and youth subculture

Left-realist approaches to crime emerged from Marxist approaches. Marxist analyses of youth offending saw it as an act of resistance against capitalism. Left realists, such as Lea and Young (1984), however, argue that youth crime harms the working-class people in the neighbourhood in which it takes place.

Lea and Young suggest that youth offending is the result of two linked factors:

1 Young inner-city males (and in particular, ethnic-minority males) feel relatively deprived, as they see affluence all around them, but are unable to gain access to the wealth.
2 They feel socially and politically marginalized, in the sense that they have little status in society and few ways to change the society around them, which they believe causes their poor social and economic situation. The result is that a subculture develops which provides them with status and justifies criminal acts.

Contemporary approaches to subculture

Postmodernity: subculture and emotion

Postmodern ideas relating to youth culture were discussed in Topic 3 (see pp. 200–2), so you may wish to turn there for a more detailed examination of their ideas. Here, we will simply explore their relationship to youth offending subcultures.

The approaches we have looked at so far seek to explain youth offending by looking for some rational reason why the subculture might have developed. Recent postmodern approaches reject this form of explanation.

Instead, they argue that emotions are an important and ignored drive for behaviour that includes youth offending. Two forms of emotion-based explanation are suggested for behaviour which transgresses the accepted boundaries.

● Katz, (1988) argues that crime is **seductive** – young males get drawn into it, not because of any process of rejection, but because quite simply it is thrilling. That is why so much of youth offending is not for financial gain. There is simple pleasure in spraying a 'tag' on a wall or vandalizing a public building. Once a young person has tried this activity, they are drawn (or 'seduced') into repeating the process.
● Lyng (1990) argues that young males like to engage in **edgework**, which he defines as placing oneself in situations of potential harm by flirting with danger. There is no rational explanation for this desire to take risks – attempts to do so fail because they impose a rational explanation on a non-rational emotion. Like Katz, Lyng suggests simply that the rush or pleasure of experiencing danger is something that young males seek. An example of this is the practice of stealing cars and driving them dangerously.

Subculture and gender

Masculinity

Subcultural theories are overwhelmingly about male offending. If you read back through the various explanations in this topic, they are clearly about the behaviour of males.

Collison (1996) points out that if instead of seeing all these explanations as alternatives and instead look at what they all share, we can see that it is the idea of 'being a male'. Amongst a host of other aspects, **masculinity** includes:

● physical toughness
● the ability to take risks and court danger
● looking smart
● maintaining 'face' in the presence of others
● owning status objects.

Collison suggests that exploring the nature of masculinity is the key to understanding youth subcultures. This would involve a broad exploration of how boys are socialized by parents, the education system and the media.

Feminist subcultural explanations

Females are much less likely to engage in **antisocial behaviour** than males as we have seen in Figure 5.4 on p. 204. This has been reflected in the lack of research into female subcultures linked to offending. The majority of studies have actually indicated that female subcultures are far more likely to be restraining girls from offending. McRobbie and Garber (1976) argue that some females are involved in antisocial behaviour, but that within subcultures they tend to be marginalized through the dominance of males. However, McRobbie (1991) has also pointed out that it is actually more difficult for girls to enter youth subcultures, as there is more parental control on their behaviour. They are less likely to be allowed out in the evening and are usually required to explain where they have been. Frith (1983) has argued that **girls' culture** is more likely to be that of the bedroom, where girls can meet, listen to music, chat, compare sexual notes and practise dancing skills.

However, these sociological views are somewhat dated according to Chatterton and Hollands (2001), who studied young people's experience of 'nights out' in Newcastle. Their research suggests that for females aged over 16, the growth of city nightlife, changing attitudes to women's behaviour and increased self-confidence have all combined to change female social behaviour. They are now more likely have a public social life, using clubs, bars and pubs almost as much as young males.

research idea

Devise a questionnaire for a sample of young people to test out some of the theories covered here. Avoid asking whether or not anyone has actually committed a crime. Questions might cover:

- **strain theory** – to what extent the sample share the ambitions of material success and the extent to which they accept the formal means to achieve these goals
- **focal concerns** – whether working-class members of the sample share similar 'focal concerns' to those identified by Miller
- **techniques of neutralization** – whether the sample have ever used any of the techniques identified by Matza
- **seduction** – whether those in the sample believe that deviance can be thrilling and exciting
- **gender** – whether male members of the sample are more tolerant of deviance than female.

Check your understanding

1. What is 'anomie'?
2. Give three examples of normal working-class behaviour that can lead to crime.
3. How does school failure lead to subculture, according to Albert Cohen?
4. What are 'techniques of neutralization' and how do they undermine some subcultural arguments?
5. How can crime be 'seductive'?
6. Why is the idea of 'masculinity' relevant to understanding offending behaviour?

KEY TERMS

Anomie a society overstresses achieving socially approved goals, but does not provide the means for the bulk of the population to achieve these goals.

Antisocial behaviour a wide range of more minor crimes.

Edgework doing dangerous or socially disapproved acts for the thrill of it.

Girls' culture socializing with female friends at home, usually in the bedroom.

Illegal opportunity structure an alternative, illegal way of life to which certain groups in society have access.

Masculinity values traditionally associated with males.

Seductive the pleasure of committing antisocial acts.

Status frustration according to Cohen, when young people feel that they are looked down upon by society.

Strain when the values of a society are difficult to achieve.

Subculture a distinctive set of values which provides an alternative to those of the mainstream culture.

web.task

Go to www.homeoffice.gov.uk/rds/pdfs/hors209.pdf. You will find the Research Study 209 on Findings from the 1998/99 Youth Lifestyles and Leisure Survey. Look at Appendix B, which is the questionnaire from which the statistics in the Getting you thinking section were drawn.

Complete the questionnaire yourself. Do you have any criticisms of these questions as a method of providing accurate information on youth crime?

exploring subcultural theories of youth offending

Item A   Charvers and slappers

Chatterton and Hollands studied nightlife and clubbing in Newcastle. They found clear differences between the various groups in the city. One of the major identifying divisions mentioned in Newcastle's nightlife was through reference to the 'charvers' – this connotes an underlying assumption that the recipient is either welfare dependent, involved in some form of criminal behaviour or resides at the less stable end of the labour market.

Many people we spoke to had a clear understanding of this group:

- Simon: *'They wear Ben Sherman shirts, go out and get pissed.'*
- Jane: *'They go out, have a shag and have a fight.'*
- Clare: *'They do not really go for the music, so much for the chance just to get pissed and maybe have a fight, and they have a good night, then look for a lass.'*

The term 'charvers' is very masculine and refers primarily to rough, local, working-class men. The female equivalent – 'slappers' – connotes a loud, vulgar and promiscuous outlook:

- Sarah: *'Big boobs, boobs are always out. The bigger the better; they are always out.'*
- Susanne: *'Tiny little skirts. Half of cider.'*

Adapted from Chatterton, P. and Hollands, R. (2001) *Changing our 'Toon'*, Newcastle: University of Newcastle, pp. 128–9

Item B   Delinquency and drift

Matza's research found that individual members of a gang were only partially committed to subcultural norms. Rather than forming a subculture which stands against the dominant values, he suggests the delinquent 'drifts' in and out of deviant activity. This is made possible because there is no consensus in society – no set of basic and core values – but a plurality (of values) in which the conventional and the delinquent values continually overlap and interrelate.

Adapted from Muncie, J. (2004) *Youth and Crime*, London: Sage, p. 107

Item C   View from the Boys

Howard Parker's classic study of juvenile thieves in inner-city Liverpool involved him spending three years 'hanging out' with them. Parker found that delinquency was neither a central part of the Boys' activities, nor the main aspect of their behaviour which held them together. Rather, they were a loose-knit peer group which had few educational achievements and lived in a high unemployment area. Theft was important mainly because it provided the resources to allow the Boys to participate in and enjoy leisure. Their criminality was a rational response to their situation.

Adapted from Parker, H. (1974) *View from the Boys*, Newton Abbot: David and Charles

Item D   Masculinities

In *Masculinities and Crime*, Messerschmidt applies an analysis of masculinities to an understanding of youth crime. There are different masculinities depending upon class, location and ethnic background. So, White middle-class youth may construct masculinity in terms of a future of office work, career, economic and status success. Working-class White youths may construct masculinity in terms of physical aggression and hostility to other groups considered 'inferior' to them. Masculinity for certain ethnic-minority males may find expression in the street gang and crime in order to achieve the status they feel is lacking. Therefore, crime or violence provides a way of 'doing masculinity' when other resources are not available.

Adapted from Muncie, J. (2004) *Youth and Crime*, London: Sage, p. 130

1 **Explain what is meant by the phrase, 'drifts' in and out of delinquency (Item B).** (2 marks)

2 **Suggest two ways in which 'the conventional and the delinquent values continually overlap and interrelate' (Item B).** (4 marks)

3 **Identify and explain three ways in which masculinity can be expressed (Item D).** (9 marks)

4 **Suggest two reasons why 'charvers' and 'slappers' (Item A) might behave in the way they do.** (10 marks)

Exam practice

5 a **Identify and explain two reasons why illegitimate opportunity structures may exist.** (15 marks)

b **Outline and discuss the view that youth crime is the result of delinquent subcultures.** (30 marks)

Gangs

East London's Bangladeshi street gangs agree to truce

LEADERS of Bangladeshi youth gangs in the East End of London have put aside their violent vendettas and have formed a committee, to resolve conflicts. It also addresses the desperate problems triggered by the hard drugs that have flooded into the borough of Tower Hamlets in recent years.

Street gangs, such as the Whitechapel-based BLM (the Brick Lane Massif), the Stepney Posse, the East Boys from Bethnal Green and the Cannon Street gang, now work together to keep the peace. Teenage street gangs have been a part of East End culture for generations, but in recent years the old-fashioned punch-up has mutated into lethal violence.

Abul Khayar Ali, 25, a youth worker, estimates that in Tower Hamlets there are 2500 youths affiliated to one of the myriad local gangs. 'The fights used to be with fists and maybe sticks but the new generation of gang members are using machetes, knives, meat-cleavers and baseball bats.'

He said the gang violence, fuelled by machismo, drugs and unemployment, was beginning to replicate that found in American inner cities.

Adapted from Julian Kossof in The Independent on Sunday 30 August 1998, p. 4

1 **Are there any 'gangs' in your neighbourhood? What do you understand by the term 'gang'?**

2 **How do you distinguish (if at all) between a group of friends and a gang?**

3 **Are there any clear characteristics of the gang, for example age, gender, ethnicity or social class?**

4 **Do gangs you know have any 'territory'?**

5 **Do you think the police 'pick on' young people unfairly – assuming that they must be gang members?**

What is a gang?

The first problem in any discussion of 'gangs', is to decide exactly what we are talking about when using the term. Even within sociology, there is some disagreement over the term and certainly the media use of the word 'gang' has been stretched to include virtually any group of friends who hang around together and engage in antisocial behaviour. At one extreme, sociologists such as Miller (1975) have suggested that gangs consist of groups of people with an identifiable leadership and a clear organizational structure, who claim control over a particular territory and who engage in 'violence or other forms of illegal behaviour'. This image of a gang is one of a violent,

criminal organization. At the other extreme, Decker (2001) has suggested that gangs are 'typically disorganized and do not have leaders'.

Finally, Sanders (1994) argues that there are some characteristics that all gangs, as opposed to groups of young people, possess. These are:

● the willingness to use deadly violence
● the importance of defended territory
● the nontransitory nature of the members (this means that the membership remains pretty much the same over a period of time).

Klein (2001) has classified several different types of gang, based on their varying characteristics (see Table 5.1, p. 212).

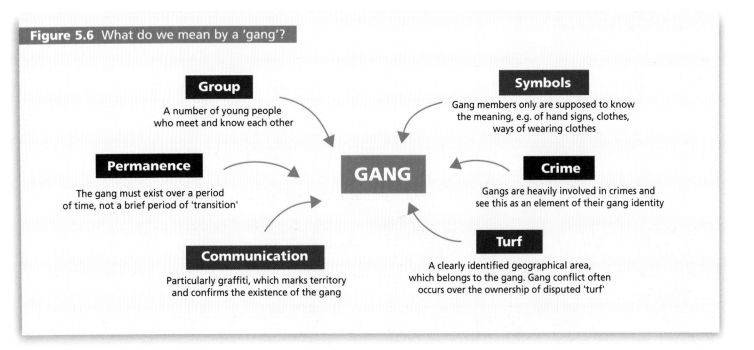

Figure 5.6 What do we mean by a 'gang'?

Group
A number of young people who meet and know each other

Symbols
Gang members only are supposed to know the meaning, e.g. of hand signs, clothes, ways of wearing clothes

Permanence
The gang must exist over a period of time, not a brief period of 'transition'

GANG

Crime
Gangs are heavily involved in crimes and see this as an element of their gang identity

Communication
Particularly graffiti, which marks territory and confirms the existence of the gang

Turf
A clearly identified geographical area, which belongs to the gang. Gang conflict often occurs over the ownership of disputed 'turf'

Gangs in Britain and the USA

If we use Sanders' definition, then gangs can be traced back to the USA in the 1850s, according to Campbell and Muncer (1989). This was a period of massive migration to America from all over Europe. The various national groups settled into distinct neighbourhoods in the large northern cities, such as New York and Chicago. Each group maintained its own languages, traditions and values. The various groups were in competition with each other, trying to improve their economic positions in US society, and this competition heightened the tensions between the various groups. The result was the formation of gangs based on ethnic and cultural divisions.

The first large-scale study of gangs was by Thrasher (1927) in the 1920s, who claimed to have identified over 1000 gangs in Chicago alone. Since then, there have been numerous studies of gangs in the USA, where the phenomenon is common and where the number of gangs appears to have doubled in the last 20 years. It is now estimated that there are about 5000 gangs in the USA. American gangs still tend to be ethnically based and often obtain their income through drug-related activities.

In the UK, there is some dispute about the existence of youth gangs. Pearson (1983) argues that gangs were in existence in the second half of the 19th century. He points out that the term 'hooligan' was first used in 1898 and has stayed in the language ever since. According to his research, gangs fought for territory with each other and engaged in both property crime and violent crime.

However, Humphries (1981) argues that there is little evidence for formal youth gangs as such. He suggested that what existed in England and Wales was more likely to be 'loosely and informally structured', and to consist mainly of groups of friends who 'had no clearly defined hierarchy'. Certainly, there are no studies to show youth gangs existing in Britain from the 1920s until recently. In fact, gangs and gang research has largely been American. The only exception is one study by James Patrick in the 1970s, which claimed to have uncovered the existence of violent gangs in Glasgow.

However, during the 1990s the situation in Britain began to change. Shropshire and McFarquhar (2002) pointed to evidence from the police of a growth of street gangs who were prepared to use extreme violence, including shooting. Their findings coincided with a number of other British studies which suggested that there really was the beginning of a form of gang culture in Britain.

Bullock and Tilley (2002) used the database of Manchester police to obtain information on 23 young males who were reputed to be gang members and then interviewed them. They found that there were four major South Manchester gangs, with memberships ranging from 26 to 67. Gang members were heavily involved in crime, committing a wide variety of offences including property crime and serious violence. Each gang had a core group and a number of additional members. According to Bullock and Tilley, carrying weapons was common among gang members.

Further information was obtained through an observational study by Mares (2001) of two of the four South Manchester gangs. Mares describes the heavy involvement of the two gangs in drug trading. The large majority of the two gangs were African-Caribbean in origin. They were only loosely organized and there were no formal leaders. However, through his links with these gangs, he found out about other gangs in the Manchester area with different structures and different ethnic bases. For example, gangs in Salford (a town near Manchester) were all White and had existed for at least 10 years before the study. Gangs in Wythenshawe (an area of Manchester) were much smaller and consisted of different ethnic groups, with about a quarter of members being female.

The only national study in Britain (or more accurately, in England and Wales), was conducted by Bennett and Holloway (2004). They carried out interviews in 16 towns and cities, over a period of three years with people who had been arrested by the police and were being held in police cells. There are some

Table 5.1 Types of gang

Klein argues that the confusion over what constitutes a 'gang' is simply because there is no single type of organization as a gang. Instead, he suggests that there are different types of gang with varying characteristics.

Type of gang	Length of time in existence	Age of members	Size of gang	Territorial?	Comment
Traditional	Long time (20+ years)	Wide range (10 to 30+)	Large (100+)	Yes, lays claim to territory	
Neotraditional	Fairly long (10+ years)	Limited age range	Medium (50+)	Yes, highly so	Best understood as developing into a 'traditional' gang
Compressed	New	Narrow, similar ages	Small	Not necessarily	Newly formed; future uncertain; could become traditional
Collective	Fairly long (10 to 15 years)	Wide age range, but young	Large	May not be territorial	Although large with fairly long existence and wide age range, has never developed clear-cut structure: 'a shapeless mass'
Speciality	Fairly new (<10 years)	Variable	Small	Commits crime within a particular territory – usually where gang members live	Crime-focused: 'Its principal purpose is more criminal than social, and its territoriality may be a reflection of this.'

Source: Klein, M.W. *et al.* (2001) *The Eurogang Paradox*, London: Kluwer Academic

problems with this research in that interviews were only held with people who were arrested and therefore nothing is known about gang members who were not arrested. Also, for legal reasons, only people aged over 17 were interviewed. This means that the sample may not truly be representative of gang members.

Bennett and Holloway conclude that there are differences between gangs in Britain and the USA, but that identifiable gangs do now exist in Britain that are criminally active and likely to carry weapons including guns. However, the English and Welsh gangs were not ethnically based and the majority of gang members were White. The two biggest ethnic-minority groups involved in gangs were those from African-Caribbean and Asian backgrounds. In terms of gender, only 4 per cent of gang members were female.

Explaining gangs

Traditional subcultural explanations

Thrasher (1927), referred to earlier, suggested that gangs developed to provide young people with the stability and sense of belonging that was not available in inner-city neighbourhoods, which he characterized as being 'socially disorganized'. Whyte (1943) who conducted a famous **ethnographic** study of a gang in Boston, largely agreed with Thrasher, pointing out how mutually supportive members of the gang were. However, in contrast to Thrasher, he suggested that, rather than being in conflict with the community, the gang was an integral part of it.

Albert Cohen (1955), too, studied a youth gang in the mid-1950s and his theory (examined in Topic 4, see p. 205) was based on the idea that the gang was formed by young males who, because of school failure, felt they lacked any status in

society. He coined the term '**status frustration**' to describe this situation. Their antisocial activities were a means of getting back at the society that had denied them status. Cohen's approach is unusual in that he stresses the 'non-utilitarian' nature of the offending behaviour – most of their activities did not get them any financial benefit, whereas most other gang studies demonstrate that financial gain is important.

Amongst the various explanations we examined in Topic 4 was 'strain theory' and it is this particular approach which has been most used to explain gangs. (Reread the description of strain theory on p. 205.) We also saw a development of strain theory called 'illegitimate opportunity structure', which suggested that running parallel to the legitimate ways of achieving the cultural goals, are illegitimate ones.

It is within this broad tradition that theoretical debates about gangs have developed. Davis (1990), in a famous study of Los Angeles, argues that for a large number of poor young people, who are drawn mainly from Black and 'Latino' ethnic-minority groups, there is no possibility of success in US society. Los Angeles has high unemployment levels and is a divided society, with great extremes of wealth and poverty. The young poor people can see the wealth and are bitter about it. Within this context, gangs have developed, but what has caused a massive increase in their numbers and in the levels of violence used, has been the opportunity to escape from poverty by using and dealing in drugs. Davis argues that the formation of gangs is a rational and sensible choice for these young, excluded people.

Davis suggests that in local neighbourhoods, the gangs provide jobs and security from the violence that has engulfed the poorer parts of Los Angeles. Even if they are convicted and sent to prison, there are gang members there who will look after them.

It does seem that drugs and their potential as an alternative means of providing an income have increased the numbers of gangs in Britain. Bennett and Holloway's study of gang activity in England and Wales, Bullock and Tilley's study of Manchester gangs and Mares' ethnographic study of two of these Manchester gangs all come to similar conclusions: selling drugs has become a central element of gangs' activities. Because of the competition between gangs, the use of violence has escalated such that guns are now routinely carried by some gang members. In recent years in Britain, there appears to have been an increase in gangs, so that the situation is moving more towards a US model of drug-trading groups of young men. However, according to Bennett and Holloway, a major difference is that the majority of gang members in Britain are from the White, ethnic majority, unlike the USA, where the majority of gangs are drawn from ethnic minorities.

Postmodernity, gangs and the media

A range of writers have suggested that in order to understand gangs, we need to look at the wider society, the culture and the media.

In the USA, for example, Katz (2000) argues that the fear over ethnic minority gangs reflects concern over levels of immigration. He points out that the current preoccupation with gangs reflects deep concern in Southern California over the levels of illegal immigration through Mexico. Media coverage and political debates on how best to crack down on gangs was occurring at the same time as intense pressure on access to social and health services, caused by increases in the numbers of poorer immigrants (mainly from South and Central America) coupled with financial cutback in the services. He suggests therefore that the gang provides a convenient symbol for issues of migration. Muncie (2004) has suggested that possibly the same thing is happening in Britain, with the 'discovery' of gangs by the media. Although the national research by Bennett and Holloway suggests that gangs are dominated by White youth, the media image is that gangs are drawn largely from ethnic-minority backgrounds.

A more complex theoretical approach to explain gangs has been suggested by Hayward (2004). Looking at the cultural context of crime, he claims that it has been seized upon by some sections of the youth media and turned into something that is 'exciting, cool and a fashionable cultural symbol'. Crime, he argues is being 'rebranded' – for example 'gangster rap' combines images of crime, ways of acting, street life styles and linguistic expression. These all form images that are attractive to youth audiences and are also exploitable by the music and fashion industries. Hayward suggests that there may be relatively few gangs, but the media-created life style is attractive to young people, so gang formation becomes an attractive possibility for groups of young people in certain situations (such as those suggested by strain theory).

Girls in the gang

As with the vast majority of research on youth and offending, female gang members have been the subject of far less study than the males – indeed, in one of the best-known recent studies of gangs in Britain by Bullock and Tilley, girls are not

Laidler and Hunt (2001)
Accomplishing femininity among the girls in the gang

Laidler and Hunt, two American sociologists, wanted to explore how females coped with being gang members and how this influenced their views of themselves as young women. They undertook a comparative, qualitative, longitudinal survey, which began in 1991 and still continued in 2001, the year their research was published. In the first two years of the research, they arranged interviews with 65 active female gang members, from seven different gangs. They used the snowball technique (one gang member passing them on to another member they knew) to find the gang members. All the gangs were based in the San Francisco Bay Area. In the second two years of the study, they arranged interviews with a further 19 female gang members of Southeast Asian origin. The third stage of the study after 2000 was to return to interview the same women plus some new gang members. In order to make sure that the gang members felt relaxed in the interviews, Laidler and Hunt used young, female researchers who had a background in the gang cultures themselves. The outcome of the research is a detailed and complex account of how these women 'accomplish femininity' in the context of violence, poverty and a male-dominated culture.

Laidler, K. and Hunt, G. (2001) 'Accomplishing femininity among the girls in the gang', *British Journal of Criminology*, 41, pp. 656–78

1 What is meant by a 'comparative, qualitative, longitudinal survey'?

2 What are the disadvantages of snowball sampling?

3 What are the disadvantages of using 'female researchers who had a background in the gang cultures themselves' as interviewers?

even mentioned. In terms of membership, estimates vary widely. In Bennett and Holloway's study of people arrested by the police who claimed to be gang members, females formed only five per cent of the membership, but other studies have shown figures as high as 30 per cent (Laidler and Hunt 2001). Thrasher (see p. 211) conducted the first large-scale study and found six 'all-female' gangs out of a total of 13 313 gangs. Girl members of the male-dominated gangs were marginal in all but sexual activities.

The specific reasons why young females would wish to join gangs have not been explored by sociologists, beyond applying the same concepts of subculture, strain and postmodernity used to explain male behaviour. However, the position within the gang for female members has been studied.

The best-known studies on female gang members were by Campbell, who studied Hispanic gangs in New York (1984). The girl members had a difficult task in balancing a number of competing demands and cultural desires. Campbell suggests that they were torn between attempting to have a 'cool' streetwise image and retaining their traditional Puerto Rican values. They were also concerned that they should not get a reputation for sexual 'looseness', whilst still being attractive to male gang members. They also had to balance being seen as aggressive and tough, but also as 'feminine'. However, one value they did demonstrate was the belief that they should not be subordinate to the males. Despite this, their role was largely one of subservience to male gang members.

More recently, Laidler and Hunt (2001) conducted in-depth interviews with 141 gang members. Their research suggests that Campbell's argument that gang members are seeking to reconcile conflicting demands is essentially correct. Female gang members make choices about how they wish to be perceived by other people. The key to this is finding the best way to win 'respect' from others. They may adopt different strategies to gain this, for example by the use of violence, through sexual power over 'homeboys', or by asserting their independence. They may even mix these strategies. Laidler and Hunt use the term 'accomplishing femininity' to describe this process of taking strategies to gain respect.

research ideas

- **Find music videos which use the background and imagery of US gangs. Show it to a group of students – ask them to discuss it. Is Hayward right in his argument that the gang image is attractive to young people?**

- **Conduct an archive search of your local newspaper(s) and national papers to gather information on gangs. What images do the local media portray about gangs?**

Check your understanding

1. **Give one definition of a 'gang'.**

2. **To what extent are gangs a new phenomenon in Britain and the USA?**

3. **What evidence is there to suggest that gangs are increasing?**

4. **What characteristics do the South Manchester gangs have, according to Bullock and Tilley?**

5. **What difference did Bennett and Holloway find between the ethnic background of US and British gangs?**

6. **What did Cohen suggest was the cause of gangs?**

7. **How can strain theory be applied to gangs?**

8. **What role do the media play in the formation of gangs?**

9. **What is the relationship between gender and gang membership?**

KEY TERMS

Ethnography a research method which involves either participant or non-participant observation.

Status frustration Albert Cohen suggested that those who do poorly at school may feel humiliated and consequently are likely to offend.

web.task

Select one of these American gang sites:

- www.iir.com/nygc/ – go to 'Frequently asked questions'

- www.ngcrc.com/profile/profile.html – go to 'Gang profiles'

Do you think the material you are reading here is significantly different from the situation in the UK? In this topic, it states that most of the research into gangs is American. Do you think that this might have any influence on the amount and type of research undertaken? See what information you can find on the web about gangs in the UK.

Item A The effects of youth unemployment

In particular, the deafening public silence about youth unemployment and the growth of poverty amongst young people has left many thousands of them with little alternative but to enlist in the youth unemployment programme operated by the cocaine cartels. Endemic unemployment is at the core of the community's despair.

Adapted from Davis, M. (1990) *City of Quartz: Excavating the future in Los Angeles*, London: Verso

Item B Masculinity and gangs

<< Young men in gangs embody all the problems of power in contemporary society: violence, guns, drugs, poverty, unemployment, decay of community life and educational malaise. Young minority male gang members living in marginalized communities have little access to masculine status in the economy and education. This collectively experienced denial of access to 'legitimate' masculine status creates an arena for exaggerated public and private forms of aggressive masculinity. Street elite posturing among male gang members with dramatized displays of toughness accounts for one cultural form of public aggressiveness. Male gang members' constant and aggressive pursuit of respect represents another way to construct and affirm manliness in an alienated environment. Gang intimidation and violence are more than simply an expression of competitive struggle in communities with little to offer, but rather a vehicle for a meaningful identity and status.>>

Laidler, K. and Hunt, G. (2001) 'Accomplishing femininity among the girls in the gang', *British Journal of Criminology*, 41, p. 658

Item C Gangster rap

<< In recent years, it has become very difficult to tell whether 'gangster rap' imagery and styling is shaping street gang culture in the US or vice versa. Since the 1980s, many cultural symbols of rap music, such as branded sports apparel and designer clothing have been used by street gangs as a means of flagging gang affiliations. Add to this the fact that several major rap artists like Tupac (Shakur) and the Notorious BIG have been murdered in a long-running feud between East and West Coast rap artists, and it immediately becomes apparent that, at least in the field of gangster rap, art and real life are becoming ever more intertwined.>>

Hayward, K.J. (2004) *City Limits: Crime, consumer culture and the urban experience*, London: Glasshouse Press, p. 170

1 Explain what is meant by the phrase 'endemic unemployment is at the core of the community's despair' (Item A). (2 marks)

2 Identify two ways in which members of gangs signal their 'gang affiliations' (Item C). (4 marks)

3 Identify and explain three ways by which gang members construct their masculine identity (Item B). (9 marks)

4 Identify and explain two ways in which the position of females in gang culture has been explained. (10 marks)

Exam practice

5 a Identify and explain two reasons why the media may have influenced attitudes towards gangs. (15 marks)

  b Outline and discuss the view that young people join gangs because they are poor. (30 marks)

Youth and schooling

gettingyouthinking

Separate classes for Black pupils?

Cassandra Jardine and Chloe Rhodes ask several Black teachers how they would solve the problem of Black pupils' underachievement.

BLACK PUPILS start primary school with some of the best scores in baseline assessments, yet within two years they have begun to slip behind and never recover.

At secondary school, the story is gloomier still, with just 43.3 per cent of Black African pupils achieving five good GCSE passes, nine per cent fewer than White children, and only 35.7 per cent of Black Caribbean pupils getting their five A to Cs. Black boys are twice as likely as their White peers to be expelled, and by A-levels, the gap yawns still wider.

So what is the problem, and how can it be addressed? Is materialistic street culture to blame or is it the lack of Black role models for boys? There are few Black teachers in Britain and many pupils have no father at home.

Trevor Phillips, chairman of the Commission for Racial Equality, caused controversy this week by proposing separate classes for Black pupils, following a similar (and successful) experiment in America. But what do Britain's Black teachers think of his ideas?

O'Neill Hemmings, head of St Saviour's, a primary school in Lambeth, says: 'The answer is not separate classes. That will lead to a two-tier system with special schools for Black boys, and if you want integration and mutual respect, that isn't the way forward. There may be influences outside school, but if you want to raise attainment, the place to do that is in school, and the most effective way to do that is for teachers to have the same expectations of all children.'

(School students tell him) they are treated differently because of their culture, dress sense and attitude. 'Some have a chip on their shoulder and don't show respect,' he says. 'Often, they feel that teachers don't expect them to want to become teachers or lawyers, but assume they will become plumbers or electricians.'

'In a secondary school, it is easier to sink, become part of a gang or become resistant to learning. Some teachers accept too readily that a pupil will produce a certain amount of work, rather than encourage him to aim higher.

'If students aren't turned on by the curriculum, then it is not meeting their needs and should be changed. Black students often tell me that all they ever hear about Black history is slavery. A more positive emphasis would make them feel more valued members of society.'

Lesley Morrison, head at St Martin's in the Fields in Lambeth, says that it is vital to create a culture in which it's 'cool' to achieve academically. 'Very often, boys seem to think that being good at sport is how to get street cred,' she says. 'But there are ways of motivating them through sport, such as having a rule that they can only make the football team if their grades are good.'

In her view, segregated classes should be used only as a last resort. 'We've had 40 years of under-achievement among Caribbean pupils. I would hate to see Black boys taken out of the main classroom, but we do often separate boys and girls in subjects where boys under-achieve. It would only ever be part of the solution, though. There are bigger issues involved and we need to address all of them.'

Additional reporting: Liz Lightfoot

Daily Telegraph, 9 March 2005 p. 20

1 Do you think that teaching Black school students separately is a good idea? Give the reasons for your answers.

2 What do you think influences school student's attitudes to studying?

3 What suggestions could you make to improve school students' experience of secondary education?

You probably don't need to be told that students respond to their schooling in different ways. In secondary schools in particular, usually by year 9, different groups emerge with very different attitudes. At one extreme, there are those groups of students who accept the rules and the authority of teachers without question, while at the other extreme, there are those who appear to devote all their attention to rule-breaking and avoiding work. You are probably familiar with this behaviour from your own experiences in education. Sociologists are particularly interested in these groups – or subcultures. Why do they form, and what effect do they have on their members, other pupils, teachers and schools?

The significance of educational experiences for youth

There are four major influences on the attitudes and behaviour of young people – the home, the school, the peer group and the media. These cannot really be separated from each other, as we see throughout this unit. Each has an impact on the other – we have seen examples of this in all the topics so far. In this topic, we will focus on the links between peer groups and the school. In particular, we will examine the way in which issues of social class, gender and ethnicity are played out in the formation of peer groups in the school setting. As you will see, these three forms of social division impact heavily on the development of peer groups and their members' attitudes to school, as well as to life in general.

Social class and the experience of schooling

Early studies of peer groups

The first studies of peer groups in schools took place during the 1960s and concentrated mainly on White, working-class youths. Hargreaves (1967) and Lacey (1970) studied single-sex boys' schools. Both found that working-class boys developed antischool subcultures, partly a result of being labelled by teachers as potential or actual troublemakers and partly because working-class boys were more likely to be consigned to lower streams in these schools. Unable to achieve status in terms of the mainstream values of the school, these pupils substitute their own set of delinquent values by which they can achieve success in the eyes of their peers. They do this by, for example, not respecting teachers, messing about, arriving late, having fights, building up a reputation with the opposite sex, and so on.

Perhaps the best known study into White youths at school during this period was by Willis (1977), who identified two school subcultures. The first, composed of working-class, school 'failures' – the 'lads' – aimed to 'have a laff' by rejecting the values of the school. The second group was more conformist,

accepting the values and aims of the school. This group was referred to by the 'lads' as 'ear'oles'.

Willis' analysis showed that these 'lads' shared a subculture which contained elements of traditional working-class values of 'masculinity'. These were: physicality, toughness, collectivism, territoriality, hedonism/having fun and opposition to authority.

Willis' central argument is that working-class youths at school adopt these values because they can see that they are likely to be school failures. By adopting these, they reject the school and its values, but of course, they also guarantee their own failure.

Writers such as Hargreaves, Lacey and Willis refer to the pro- and antischool cultures as coherent groups, sharing their own uniform set of values. But for a number of writers following them, this was too simplistic.

Later studies of peer groups

Ball (1981) conducted a similar study on a mixed-sex comprehensive school and, whilst generally agreeing with the earlier studies, found there were more complex attitudes to school. Working-class boys did not necessarily reject school – they could also be indifferent to it. So, social class did not necessarily determine attitudes, but was one factor amongst others.

Phil Brown (1987) also criticizes the polarized image of working-class youth that Willis, Hargreaves and Lacey all put forward. Based on his survey of students in a South Wales comprehensive school, Brown argues that the majority of working-class males and females simply want to 'get by'. Brown suggests three different ways working-class students approach 'being in school and becoming adult':

1 The 'getting in' approach – Members of this group were usually low academic achievers (the 'rems'). They wanted to get into working-class culture and a working-class job. They also wanted to leave school at the earliest opportunity.
2 The 'getting out' approach or the 'swots' – Members of this group wanted middle-class jobs and the associated comfortable lifestyle.
3 The third approach – 'getting on' – was taken by the majority of the working-class students who 'neither simply accept nor reject school, but comply with it'.

Brown's view is that the differences between the 'rems' (equivalent to Willis' 'lads') and the ordinary students are quite subtle. The ordinary kids are just as likely to be influenced by outside conflicts, social activities and youth subcultural interests as the rems. It is simply that the ordinary students (the vast majority at the school) never let these develop into full-blown opposition to the school.

Economic influences and opposition to school

In our exploration of working-class experiences of school, we saw that sociological studies found that divisions emerged between the students in terms of their attitudes and behaviour in the classroom, leading to the conclusion that social class does interact with the experience of school to produce different subcultures. The studies differ, however, in the extent to which opposition to school was demonstrated. The explanation for these differences might possibly lie in the wider economy. Riseborough (1993) has suggested that the lads in Willis' study were only able to 'have a laff' because at the time of the study, it was easy to find unskilled work. By the time of Brown's study, these jobs were difficult to find and so the same attitude to school was not really possible. Riseborough found the young people in his study had an awareness of the economic situation which did influence their behaviour. Knowing that there were not many jobs available for unskilled workers made them concentrate more on learning work-related skills.

Schooling and masculinity

The relationship between social class and school subcultures is only one of a number of relationships which sociologists have explored. A second area of research is the way that school interacts with notions of **masculinity**. By masculinity, we mean the use of appropriate attitudes and behaviour that males use to demonstrate to both themselves and to others that they are 'male'. One of the most influential writers on the concept of masculinity is Connell (1995), who argues that the view of what constitutes masculinity changes over time. The dominant view of masculinity at any one time is known as **hegemonic masculinity**. For Connell, there are always competing versions of masculinity striving to become the dominant or hegemonic one. There is always tremendous pressure on males to conform to this hegemonic masculinity. An example of this comes from Haywood (2003), who studied how pupils use language to 'regulate masculinity'. His middle-class sample of hard-working A-level students were referred to as 'wankers', 'bum bandits', 'gays' and 'poofs' – even to their faces. Their 'crime' was not to engage in more 'typical' male behaviour of taking their studies lightly and enjoying an active social life.

But it is not just males who engage in the process of defining and shaping masculinity; women too have an important role in deciding which form of masculinity is dominant. The refusal of women over the last 40 years to accept patriarchy unquestioningly has had an impact on what is currently viewed as hegemonic masculinity. Though it is true too that females play an ambiguous role in 'liberating' males, as Mac an Ghaill's study shows, they also like 'masculine' males. Mac an Ghaill's study (1994) illustrates the complexity of subcultural responses by examining the relationship between schooling, work, masculinity and sexuality. Like the other writers in this tradition, he identifies a range of school subcultures. However, unlike the earlier studies, he also includes middle-class (male) students and also looked at a separate small group of homosexual students.

Working-class youths and masculinity

The 'macho lads'

This group was hostile to school authority and learning, not unlike the lads in Willis' study. However, the economic context which helped to create the 'lads' of Willis' study had changed by the time of this study and the attitudes they had seemed to come from an earlier time. Mac an Ghaill suggested that these youths were facing some degree of crisis, as their masculinity had traditionally been demonstrated in their manual labour. Yet it is precisely this area of employment which was contracting rapidly at the time of the study (and has continued to do so). Nevertheless, few expressed total contempt for school as Willis' 'lads' had done.

The academic achievers

This group were from mostly skilled manual working-class backgrounds and adopted a more traditional upwardly mobile route via academic success. However, they had to develop ways of coping with the stereotyping and accusations of effeminacy from the 'macho lads'. They would do this either by confusing those who bullied them, by deliberately behaving in an effeminate way, or simply by having the confidence to cope with the jibes.

The 'new enterprisers'

Mac an Ghaill suggested that this was a new form of proschool subculture, embracing the 'new **vocationalism**' of the 1980s and 1990s. They rejected the traditional academic curriculum, which they saw as a waste of time, but accepted the new vocational ethos, with the help and support of the new breed of teachers and their industrial contacts. In studying subjects such as business studies and computing, they were able to achieve **upward mobility** and employment by exploiting school–industry links to their advantage.

Middle-class youths and masculinity

'Real Englishmen'

These were a small group of middle-class pupils, usually from a liberal professional background (their parents were typically university lecturers, or writers, or they had jobs in the media). They rejected what teachers had to offer, seeing their own culture and knowledge as superior. They also saw the motivations of the 'achievers' and 'enterprisers' as shallow. Whilst their own values did not fit with doing well at school, they did, however, aspire to university and a professional career. They resolved this dilemma by achieving academic success in a way that appeared effortless (whether it was or not).

Gay students

Mac an Ghaill also studied a number of individual gay students from different educational institutions in the same area. These students did not have a subculture as such, because of their small numbers in each institution. However, they were fully aware of assumptions regarding sexual normality in schools, which took for granted the naturalness of heterosexual relationships and the two-parent nuclear family.

Mac an Ghaill's work can be criticized, however, because it was based on only 11 heterosexual students from one Midland school and a similar small number of homosexual students from other local educational institutions.

'Real men don't work hard'

Sociologists such as Mac an Ghaill (1994) and Haywood (1993) describe the dominant hegemonic masculinity that, in an educational context, is characterized by rejecting academic work as '**feminine**'. The dominance of hegemonic masculinity is achieved through a process of peer pressure to conform to what is perceived to be normal for a boy. For example, if boys want to avoid the verbal and physical abuse attached to being labelled as 'feminine' or 'gay', then they must avoid academic work, or at least appear to avoid academic work.

The result of all this is that working hard at school (or most importantly, appearing to work hard) and achieving educational success actually runs counter to an important form of masculinity.

Female subcultures

In Mac an Ghaill's study, although girls disliked the masculinity of the '**macho** males', many still sought boyfriends with this attitude (see the comments on p. 218 about the female role in enforcing masculinity). Some working-class girls, in particular, even saw work as a potential marriage market. More upwardly mobile girls saw careers more in terms of independence and achievement.

Griffin (1985) studied young, White working-class women during their first two years in employment. Rather than forming a large anti-authority grouping, they created small friendship groups. Their deviance was defined by their sexual behaviour rather than 'trouble-making'. Most importantly, there was not the same continuity between the school's culture and that of their future workplace as there had been for the lads in Willis' study. Instead, there were three possible routes for the girls, which they could follow all at the same time:

1 the labour market – securing a job
2 the marriage market – acquiring a permanent male partner
3 the sexual market – having sexual relationships, whilst at the same time maintaining their reputation, so as to not damage marriage prospects.

Ethnic subcultures

The third element which impacts on the experience of education is ethnicity. This is a complex subject, as various ethnic groupings are responded to differently by teachers and the different groupings may also have very different experiences of racism, economic opportunity and cultural values in the wider society.

The experience of Black males

According to Sewell (2000), the culture of the streets is anti-educational. It is a culture that puts style and instant gratification ahead of the values of school and college. According to Sewell, males of African-Caribbean origin see educational success as 'feminine'. The way for them to get respect is through the credibility of the street, or as Sewell puts it, to be a 'street hood'. Success in the schoolroom marks the Black youth out from his peers or classmates and is likely to make him the target of ridicule or bullying (as we saw earlier). Sewell argues that educational failure becomes a badge to wear with pride.

Mac an Ghaill (1988) also studied the specific effects of ethnicity in an earlier study to the one mentioned above. He found that young male students of African-Caribbean origin responded very strongly to the way they were labelled by teachers, by developing subcultures based strongly on masculine images. The names they gave themselves indicate the nature of their groups – 'The Warriors' and 'The Rasta-Heads'.

O'Donnell and Sharpe's (2000) study of the impact of race and masculinity on schooling, supports the findings of Sewell and those of Mac an Ghaill (in both his studies). They found that the dominant form of masculinity amongst male students from an African-Caribbean background was of being 'macho'. O'Donnell and Sharpe suggest that the only way to understand this construction of masculinity is to see it as a reaction to a range of influences including racism and poor economic prospects. There are many parallels with their attitudes to school and those of the White youths studied by Willis 20 years earlier. However, the economic situation had improved for the White youths, so that their form of masculinity and opposition to school was no longer common, but in the case of the Black youths, the economic prospects remained poor and so opposition to school was still a relevant response.

The experience of Black females

In an investigation of three classes of 5- to 6-year-olds in a multi-ethnic, inner-city primary school, Connolly (1998) found that negative stereotypes are not just confined to boys. Like Black boys, girls were perceived by teachers as potentially disruptive but likely to be good at sports. The teachers in one school tended to 'underplay the Black girls' educational achievements and focus on their social behaviour'. Like their Black male counterparts, they were quite likely to be disciplined and punished, even though their behaviour did not always seem to justify it.

Other studies, such as that by Mirza (1992), point out that females from African-Caribbean backgrounds resent negative labelling and racism in schools – and, in particular, the fact that many teachers expect them to fail. Like males, they develop resistance to schooling. However, they do not form totally antischool subcultures – they realize that these lead to educational failure. Instead, they adopt strategies that enable

focus on research

Source: *Ethnicity and Education: The evidence on minority ethnic pupils research topic paper: RTP01-05,* January 2005, DfES
www.dfes.gov.uk/research/data/uploadfiles/RTP01-05.pdf

Figure 5.7 Proportion of pupils by ethnic group and gender achieving 5 or more A* to C GCSE/GNVQs (2003)

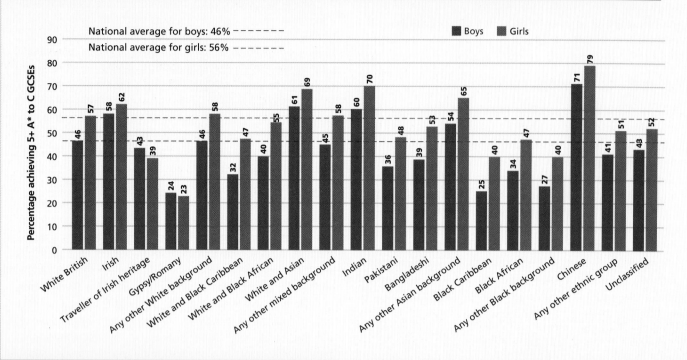

DfES
Ethnicity and education

1 Which group had the highest level of achievement overall?

2 Which group had the lowest?

3 Is there any consistent gender difference?

4 Make a table with the headings of male and female at the top and then complete the information on the percentage gaining 5+ GCSEs grade A* to C from the following ethnic groups.

| Irish | White British | Indian | Pakistani |
| Bangladeshi | Black Caribbean | Chinese | |

5 Are there any explanations in the text which might help explain the differences between the different ethnic groups?

them to get what they need from the system, that allow them to maintain a **positive self-image**, obtain the qualifications they desire and, above all, prove their teachers wrong.

Mirza found that the Black girls in her study, whilst rarely encountering open racism, were held back by the well-meaning but misguided behaviour of most of the teachers. The teachers' 'help' was often patronizing and counterproductive, curtailing both career and educational opportunities that should have been available to the Black girls. For example, the girls were entered for fewer subjects to 'take the pressure off', or they were given ill-informed, often stereotypical, careers advice. The girls, therefore, had to look for alternative strategies to get by, some of which hindered their progress, such as not asking for

help. Alternatively, they helped each other out with academic work, but were seen to resist the school's values by refusing to conform through their dress, appearance and behaviour.

The experience of Asian youths

Connolly (1998) also examined the treatment of South Asian male and female school students. He found that teachers tended to see South Asian boys as immature rather than as troublemakers. Their behaviour was **feminized** and as such was seen as unthreatening. Consequently, much of their bad behaviour went unnoticed by teachers and was not punished to the same extent as that of Black youths. At the same time, the

South Asian boys had difficulty in gaining status as males, which made it more difficult for them to enjoy school and feel confident. However, teachers did have high expectations of their academic potential and they were often praised and encouraged. South Asian girls were seen as even more obedient than the South Asian boys, even though their behaviour, in reality, showed a similar mix of work, avoidance of work and disruptiveness, and was largely indistinguishable from their female peers. Expectations regarding their academic potential were high and it was felt that they needed little help when compared with other groups. These judgements were more likely to be related to the perception that they were largely quiet, passive, obedient and helpful, rather than being related to academic outcomes.

O'Donnell and Sharpe came to very similar conclusions regarding the problems faced by Asian youths. Whereas Black youths were admired by many White youths for their 'macho' behaviour, Asian youths were viewed as falling into one of three categories, which O'Donnell and Sharpe call the 'weakling', the 'warrior' and the 'patriarch':

- Weakling refers to the traditional view of Asian youths as conformist and trouble avoiders.

- Warriors refers to the growing numbers of Asian youths who have taken this image and have set out to cultivate a tougher new edge.
- Patriarch refers to the **cultural tendency** to accept the power of the family, particularly the family males in determining behaviour.

O'Donnell and Sharpe say this crude categorizing of Asian youths fails to appreciate the way that they have successfully 'negotiated' new masculine identities, taking elements from the various cultures surrounding them. They also point out that Asian males and females have been particularly successful in education. Interestingly, the only Asian group which has performed poorly, those from Bangladeshi backgrounds, were those most likely to have been involved in violence and had developed a clear 'macho' image.

Subject choice

Girls are now achieving better academic results than boys at school, yet relatively few choose science or science-related subjects. Males dominate in maths, science and technology,

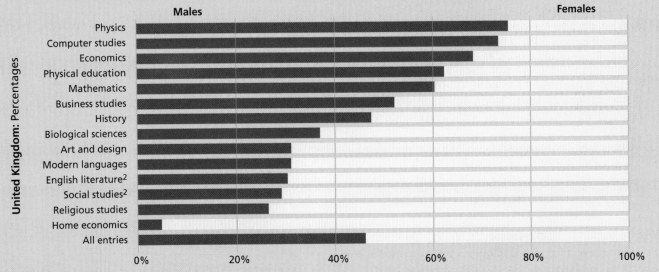

focuson**research**

Social trends
Gender and subject choice

The chart below shows A-level subject entries by gender.

Figure 5.8 A-level or equivalent subject entries for young people[1] by gender, 2001/02

United Kingdom: Percentages

Males — Females

Physics, Computer studies, Economics, Physical education, Mathematics, Business studies, History, Biological sciences, Art and design, Modern languages, English literature[2], Social studies[2], Religious studies, Home economics, All entries

0% 20% 40% 60% 80% 100%

Source: Department for Education and Skills; National Assembly for Wales; Scottish Executive; Northern Ireland Department of Education.

1 Pupils in schools and students in further education institutions aged 16 to 18 at the start of the academic year in England and in Northern Ireland, and aged 17 in Wales. Pupils in Scotland generally sit Highers one year earlier and the figures relate to the result of pupils in Year S5/S6.
2 England and Wales only.

Source: *Social Trends 34* (2004)

1 List the subjects predominantly taken by females.
2 List the subjects predominantly taken by males.
3 Is there any pattern in the type of subjects taken by the different genders?
4 Can you relate this pattern to discussions of masculinity and gender identity discussed in the text?

with consequent implications for future career choices. For example, 60 per cent of working women are clustered in only 10 per cent of occupations. The same is true in vocational subjects, with male students comprising 95 per cent of students studying engineering-based subjects and female students forming 90 per cent of those studying health and care. Mac an Ghaill refers to the '**remasculinization**' of the vocational curriculum.

Our discussions on the role of gender and masculinity are relevant here. Sociologists such as Skelton (2001) show that a **hidden curriculum** exists that helps to perpetuate gender difference by influencing subject choices. This refers to the belief amongst teachers and students about the appropriate behaviour for the various sexes. Included is the belief that certain subjects are regarded as more appropriate for the different sexes. Teachers may make assumptions about the abilities and interests of students and encourage them accordingly.

Peer groups are important too. If a pupil's same-sex friends all choose or reject a subject, the individual may find it hard to be different and so subjects can become stereotyped as 'feminine' or 'masculine'.

However, things have changed since the original sociological studies in these areas in the 1970s and 1980s. Spender (1982), for example, found that female students expected to cease paid work in order to become housewives and mothers and then to work part time. Today, aspirations are higher and women do look for future careers, according to Arnot *et al.* (1999). Riddell (1992), however, argues that girls still carry competing ideas for their futures, influenced partly by choosing subjects useful for future employment, and partly by future ideas of motherhood and domesticity, which remain important parts of their identity as women.

Check your understanding

1 How, according to Hargreaves, did 'low-stream failures' respond to their label?

2 What subcultures did Mac an Ghaill suggest existed?

3 What sorts of subjects do female school students tend to choose?

4 Give three examples of the ways in which the experience of female subcultures is said to be different from that of male subcultures.

5 Explain in your own words the relationship between GCSE achievement and ethnicity.

6 Why, despite their generally positive identification with school, do Black girls remain disadvantaged in the education system?

7 How, according to Connolly, do teachers' perceptions of South Asian pupil subcultures affect their experience of schooling?

KEY TERMS

Cultural tendency process whereby the values of a society stress the normality of a particular form of behaviour.

Feminine stereotypical ideas about women being soft and caring.

Feminized suitable for women.

Hegemonic masculinity the socially accepted idea of what a male should be.

Hidden curriculum ideas and values passed on at school that are not formally taught.

Macho/masculine common ideas about men being tough and strong.

Positive self-image feeling good about yourself.

Remasculinization making something male-orientated again.

Upwardly mobile moving up in the social classes.

Vocationalism skills-based subjects.

research ideas

● Conduct a participant observational survey of your school or college to identify pro- and antischool subcultures. (Use Mac an Ghaill's categories as well as some of your own.)

● Select a sample of male and female A-level students in your school or college. Design a questionnaire to find out what have been the key influences on their A-level subject choice. Analyse the results – do they tell you anything about the relationship between gender and subject choice?

web.task

Go to the government's own site about gender and subject choice at www.standards.dfes.gov.uk/genderandachievement/understanding/subjects What explanations can you find here for the relationship between gender and subject choice?

Follow the link to Women into Science and Engineering (WISE). What is this organization doing to encourage girls into these traditionally male-dominated areas?

Item A   Young money – the three marketeers

<< Despite being fresh out of Torquay Boys' Grammar, Adrian Bougourd, 18, Will Rushmer, 19, and Ryan Hayward, 18, beat the other five teams on the Channel 4 fantasy share game show, Show Me The Money, at the end of the 10-week series. The youngest contestants have made a profit of over £55 000 on an imaginary £100 000 lump sum in only eight weeks.

The teenagers, who have all recently started university, with 11 A-level A grades between them, are not new to stocks and shares. They started taking an interest in the stock market last year when their school entered the ProShare national investment programme. That competition for school pupils ended in May, and was won by a group of girls from Haberdashers' Aske's School, who were still doing GCSEs at the time.

Both Will, who is studying economics at Warwick, and Ryan are hoping for a career in the City, in either fund management or investment banking, once they have finished their degrees. Adrian, who is studying finance, accounting and management at Nottingham University, is toying with the idea of financial journalism. The Three Freshers, as they called themselves for the show, are just one of thousands of investment clubs in the UK. The number of investment groups increased by 3800 last year, pushing the total to more than 9000, according to ProShare, which promotes share ownership. >>

The Times, 11 November 2000

Item B   Do teenagers deliberately fail exams to stay cool?

A poll of 4000 Tyneside teenagers says peer pressure stops many pupils from studying or taking part in lessons.
Researchers say that members of an antischool subculture known as 'charvers' reject school as uncool and refuse to do GCSE course work, meaning they fail their exams. They say the situation could be the same across other UK cities, although the groups might have different names. The charvers typically wear fake designer and sports gear and are usually from poor backgrounds.

Researchers questioned teenagers aged between 15 and 17. They found the charvers' attitude was that school was uncool but college was OK, and that most expected to resit their GCSEs at further education colleges.

The research was by Lynne Howe, director of the South Tyneside Excellence in Cities programme. She said: 'For some youngsters – those known as charvers – being cool and well-thought of among their peers is the most important thing.

'These youngsters were largely from a deprived population but they didn't lack confidence or self-esteem. They deliberately fail their GCSEs because their social standing outside school is more important than any qualification.

'They were scared of being called names, physical threats and damage to the family home and property if they were seen doing homework or answering questions in class, but they consider college cool.'

The former teacher said the teenagers identified five different groups in school, including charvers, radgys (more aggressive than charvers), divvies (impressionable hangers-on to the charvers), goths (wear dark clothes but often work hard) and freaks, who work hard and are considered 'normal' by teachers.

Nearly a third of the 15-year-olds said they had been picked on for doing well at school, while the same proportion admitted teasing others who participated in lessons. More than 90 per cent of bright pupils said they wanted to go to university, but only one in four said they were doing their best at school.

Some said they would rather fail their GCSEs and take resits at college, hoping to get into higher education later, than risk being targeted by bullies while still at school.

Adapted from Leonard, M. (2000) 'Back to the future: the domestic division of labour', *Sociology Review*, 10(2)

1 Explain what is meant by 'antischool subcultures' (Item B). (2 marks)

2 Suggest two ways in which the writer considers educational achievement is affected by peer group membership (Item B). (4 marks)

3 Identify three reasons 'charvers' give for deliberately underperforming at school (Item B). (9 marks)

4 Identify and explain two ways in which the proschool subculture described in Item A differs from the antischool subcultures referred to in Item B. (10 marks)

Exam practice

5 a Identify and explain two explanations for the high proportion of males that choose maths, technology and science A-levels. (15 marks)

b Outline and discuss the view that ethnic subcultures in schools cause underachievement. (30 marks)

Origins of youth culture

Demographic change

Increased economic power

Increasing diversity of society

Impact of globalization

Developed in 1950s

Growth and specialization of the media

Lengthened period of transition from childhood

Theories of youth subcultures

One youth culture

Eases transition from childhood to adulthood

Functionalist

Many youth subcultures

Representing working-class resistance

Conflict

Late modern

Postmodern

Subcultures across social-class lines

Decline of 'spectacular' subcultures

Importance of media

Subcultures no longer exist – replaced by fast-changing styles

Term 'neo-tribes' becomes popular

Subcultural theories of offending

Young people blocked from success turn to non-legal means

Some young people have access to illegitimate ways of achieving material success

Strain theory

Illegitimate opportunity structure

Postmodernists – offending = search for kicks or pleasure

Emotions

Gender

Normality

Status

Females socialized into lower levels of deviance

Males socialized into 'masculinity', leading to offending

Matza and Miller – deviance arises from normal values

School failure leads youths to feel failures

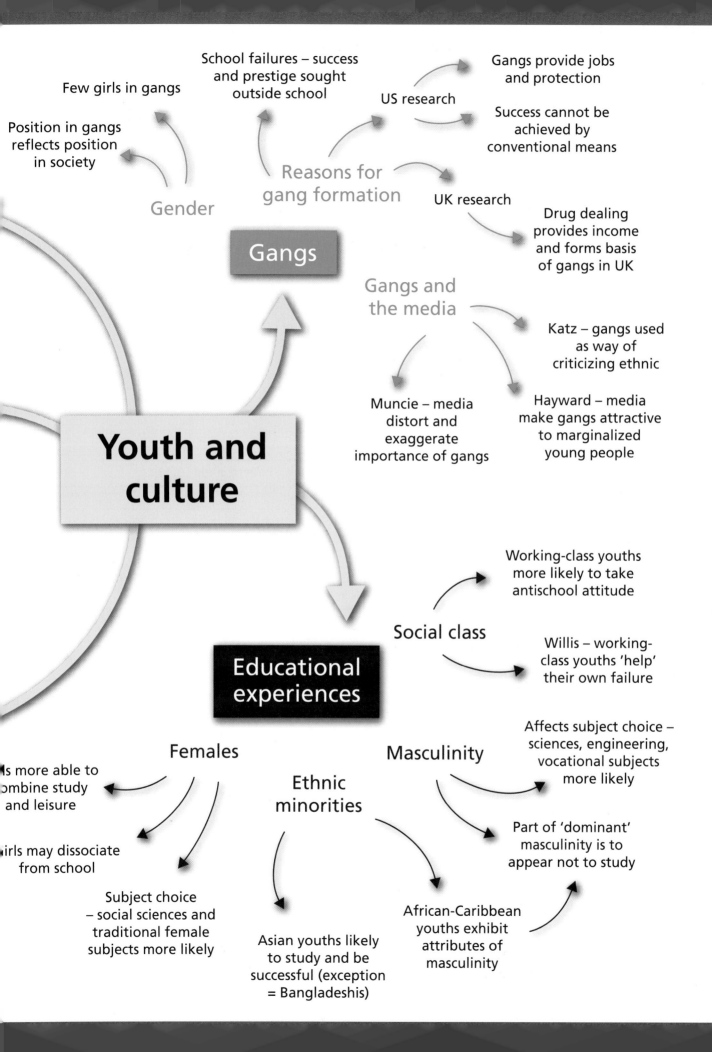

Few girls in gangs

Position in gangs reflects position in society

Gender

School failures – success and prestige sought outside school

Reasons for gang formation

US research

Gangs provide jobs and protection

Success cannot be achieved by conventional means

UK research

Drug dealing provides income and forms basis of gangs in UK

Gangs

Gangs and the media

Muncie – media distort and exaggerate importance of gangs

Katz – gangs used as way of criticizing ethnic

Hayward – media make gangs attractive to marginalized young people

Youth and culture

Educational experiences

Social class

Working-class youths more likely to take antischool attitude

Willis – working-class youths 'help' their own failure

Females

Is more able to combine study and leisure

Girls may dissociate from school

Subject choice – social sciences and traditional female subjects more likely

Ethnic minorities

Asian youths likely to study and be successful (exception = Bangladeshis)

Masculinity

Affects subject choice – sciences, engineering, vocational subjects more likely

Part of 'dominant' masculinity is to appear not to study

African-Caribbean youths exhibit attributes of masculinity

TURN TO ANY PAGE IN THIS BOOK and you'll find claims and debates about the nature of society. There are arguments about the rights and wrongs of family life, the fairness of the education system and the influence of the media to name just three. But how do we know that the contents of the book are accurate? What distinguishes the statements that sociologists make from those of your friends, parents, journalists or people on radio phone-ins?

The answer is that sociology is based on research. And without research, sociologists cannot make any greater claim to explaining the world than anyone else. That means it is vital that all research is of the highest standard – if not, then we cannot rely on it.

Anyone studying sociology must also study the methods sociologists use. Armed with this knowledge, they will be able to carry out their own research and critically examine existing sociological studies. If the research methods in a study are found to be flawed, then the claims made by that sociologist cannot be completely accepted.

In this unit we cover the main methods used by sociologists, and give a wide range of examples of research studies using each method.

OCRspecification	topics	pages
Basic concepts in research design		
Reliability, validity, representativeness and generalization	These key concepts are covered in Topic 1.	228–233
Identifying causes and effects	Also covered in Topic 1.	228–233
Ethics in the research process	Discussion of ethical issues in Topic 2.	234–239
Aspects of data collection		
Sampling; populations and response rates	Sampling is covered in the context of quantitative methods in Topic 3.	240–245
Collecting primary data. Quantitative and qualitative approaches. Piloting, surveys, questionnaires, interviews and observation	The main methods of primary data collection are the subjects of Topics 3, 4 and 5.	240–257
Sources of secondary data. Documents; libraries, official sources and the internet	Secondary data is the focus of Topic 6	258–263
Interpreting and evaluating data		
Interpreting and evaluating quantitative data. Tables and graphs	Interpreting data is discussed in the context of the role of theory in Topic 2. Opportunities to interpret and evaluate quantitative data can be found in Topics 3 and 5.	236 240–245 252–257
Interpreting and evaluating qualitative data	Interpreting data is discussed in the context of the role of theory in Topic 2. Opportunities to interpret and evaluate qualitative data are provided in Topic 4.	236 246–251
Interpreting and evaluating documents, official statistics and other secondary sources	Covered in Topic 6.	258–263
Reporting research results	The effects of reporting research results are discussed in Topic 2.	234–239

Sociological research skills

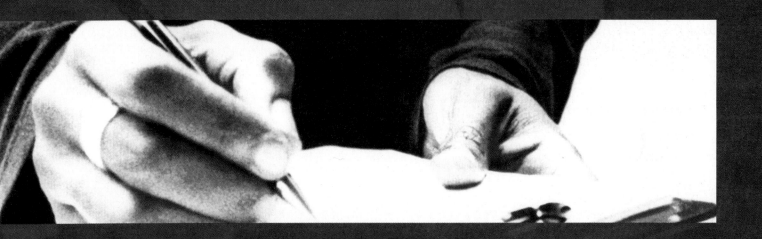

TOPIC 1	Researching social life **228**
TOPIC 2	Methods, theories and ethics **234**
TOPIC 3	Quantitative research: getting 'the truth'? **240**
TOPIC 4	Understanding people: observation **246**
TOPIC 5	Asking questions: questionnaires and interviews **252**
TOPIC 6	Secondary sources of data **258**

UNIT SUMMARY **264**

Researching social life

gettingyouthinking

Big Brother is a television series in which a group of people are required to live together in a house for a period of several months. During that time all their activities and conversations are monitored. Edited versions are shown to a television audience, which then votes one person out each week, until the last remaining 'survivor' is declared the winner.

Marco waves goodbye to the other housemates after being voted off during Big Brother *2004*

1 Do you think that people who live in the *Big Brother* household are representative of the country as a whole?

2 Do you think the people in the household act naturally? If not, why do they behave the way they do?

3 Does *Big Brother* therefore give a 'true' picture of what life would be like if a group of young people lived together? Explain your answer.

4 Do you think that a lot of what goes on is 'edited out' by the producers? What kinds of things are left out? Why?

Sociologists generally try to take a 'sideways' look at social life – seeking to provide insights into the social world that the ordinary person would not normally have. In some ways, this interest in society is shared by journalists and other 'interested observers' of the world, but whereas these people tend to rely heavily on their *common sense* or *personal experience* in exploring society, sociologists reject these as adequate ways of explaining society. Common sense and personal experience, they argue, are usually based on our own very limited and **biased** views of the world. Instead, they claim that the best way to study society is to conduct research which uncovers patterns that would normally remain hidden. This

research is ideally founded on facts rather than opinions. However, the activities of sociologists do not stop at undertaking research – once they have uncovered these patterns, they then seek explanations for the relationships between them. This process of constructing explanations for the social patterns is known as 'theorizing'.

So, research leads – eventually – to theories.

Even that is not the end of it. For once theories exist, other sociologists are influenced by them and will use them as the starting point for their research.

So, research leads to theories, which lead to more research and – yes, you've guessed it – more theories!

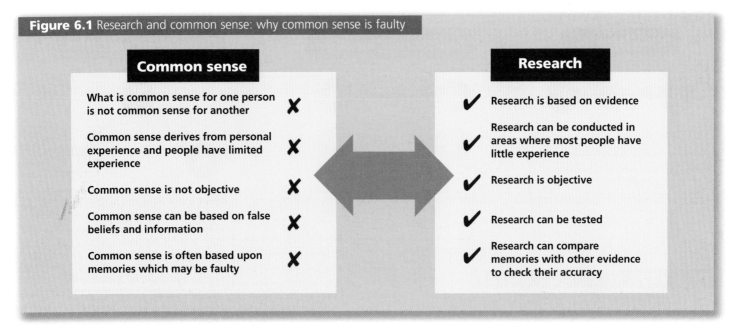

Figure 6.1 Research and common sense: why common sense is faulty

Common sense

- What is common sense for one person is not common sense for another ✗
- Common sense derives from personal experience and people have limited experience ✗
- Common sense is not objective ✗
- Common sense can be based on false beliefs and information ✗
- Common sense is often based upon memories which may be faulty ✗

Research

- ✔ Research is based on evidence
- ✔ Research can be conducted in areas where most people have little experience
- ✔ Research is objective
- ✔ Research can be tested
- ✔ Research can compare memories with other evidence to check their accuracy

What does sociological research set out to do?

Sociological research does three main things: gathers data, makes correlations and suggests or confirms theories.

Gathering data

The first task of research is simply to gather information about the social world. This very basic function is the starting point for any kind of sociological understanding. Knowledge can take the form of statistical information, such as the numbers of marriages and divorces, and sociological 'facts', such as the attitudes of people in society towards marriage as an institution. (This sort of research is conducted by the Office for National Statistics – a government organization which collects data about the UK.) It can also include observations of people in social situations – such as Philippe Bourgois' study of crime and drugs in a New York 'ghetto' (2003) – or people talking about their own lives – Ken Plummer has used this form of biographical research with gay men (1995).

However, we need to be wary about accepting these data at face value. As we shall see later, what is a 'fact' for someone may not be for others, as they may use different theories and methods to interpret the facts. A famous example of this is research on suicide by Durkheim (1897/1952). He collected a large number of statistics and then based his theory of the causes of suicide on these statistics. However, much later, other sociologists looked at exactly the same statistics and produced very different interpretations of these same 'facts'. They argued that the statistics on which Durkheim had based his research were fundamentally flawed. These sociologists said that in only a few cases can we know for certain whether the death was suicide or not, as there are rarely suicide notes. The real research, they argued, was in studying how coroners go about making their decision as to whether or not to classify a death as suicide.

Much effort is made in sociological research to make sure that the data gathered is as clear and accurate as possible, but sociologists always approach any data – whether in the form of statistics, observation or narrative – in a very cautious way.

Establishing correlations

Research can go further than just gathering information. It can help us explore relationships between different elements of society. At its most basic it can be in the form of simple **correlations**. Sociologists describe a correlation as the situation where when one social event occurs, another one tends to do so as well. This is clearer if we use an illustration. Holloway *et al.* (2003) conducted a national research project over a number of years which involved testing the urine of people immediately after they were arrested by the police and being held in police cells. The results of the urine tests demonstrated that the offenders had a very high chance indeed of showing evidence of illegal drug use (as well as alcohol). The statistical results therefore show that there is a correlation between drug use and crime, as when one social event (committing crime) occurs, then another (taking drugs) tends to do so as well.

Cause and effect

The immediate conclusion that most people would draw from this correlation is that drug use causes crime. But this may not be true. It could be argued that people who commit crime are more likely to take drugs – and indeed there is considerable evidence to support this argument (Pudney 2002).

We could also argue that people who like to do drugs also like to commit crime. Therefore a completely different social event causes people both to commit crime and do drugs. There is considerable evidence for this explanation too (Roberts 2004).

Just because statistics demonstrate that two social events tend to occur together – *a correlation* – it does not mean there is actually a **causal relationship**. Identifying and agreeing a causal relationship between social events is often complicated and linked with developing a sociological theory.

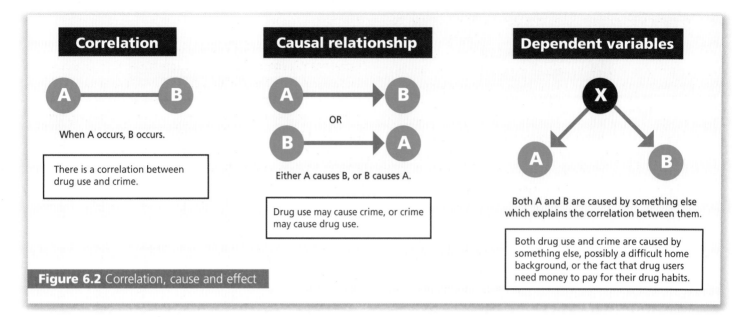

Figure 6.2 Correlation, cause and effect

Developing theories

The final role of research is to support or disprove a **sociological theory**. (A theory is simply a general explanation of social events.) Researchers gather information and statistics which help sociologists to explain why certain social events occur. Often this involves providing an explanation for correlations. So, if a correlation exists between drug use and crime, various theories can be developed. One theoretical explanation for heroin users having high rates of burglary is that they need money to pay for their drug habit. An alternative is that burglars have a high income and so are more likely to have a pleasurable lifestyle that involves using drugs. A third theoretical explanation could be that people with unhappy home backgrounds turn to crime and drugs. It was just this sort of problem that Pudney (2002) tackled in a research project on whether young offenders started taking drugs before they committed crimes or after.

Sources and types of data

Data can come from either primary or secondary sources:

- **Primary data** are those collected directly by the researchers themselves. The most common methods of providing primary data are surveys, observational studies, questionnaire s, interviews and experiments.
- **Secondary data** are those which are used by sociologists but have been collected by other people. These include official and commercial statistics; radio, internet and TV; historical and official documents; personal letters and diaries.

There are two types of data:

- **Quantitative data** is the term used for statistical charts and tables.
- **Qualitative data** is the term used to describe data in the form of observation or other published or broadcast sources.

Table 6.1 Types and sources of data

Types of data	Sources of data	
	Primary data	**Secondary data**
Qualitative data	Interviews, observations	Historical documents, TV programmes
Quantitative data	Statistical surveys	Official statistics

Evaluating data

When conducting research or reading sociological research reports written by others, sociologists are always very critical of the methods employed and the data used. They know that if the methodology is weak, then the research may well be inaccurate. All sociologists are committed to making sure that their research is of the highest quality and achieves what it sets out to do.

When sociologists evaluate research, they need to look at its reliability, validity, representativeness, generalizability and objectivity. Let's look at each of these in more detail.

Reliability

The very nature of sociology means that it has to use a variety of very different methods in a range of circumstances to study people. In these circumstances, it can often be quite difficult to compare one piece of research with another and sociologists accept this. However, what is always expected is that if the same piece of research were repeated by different sociologists, then it should produce the same results. If this is not the case, then we could not rely upon the evidence produced.

Sociologists, therefore, always ask questions about whether or not the research, if repeated, would be likely to produce the same results – the issue of **reliability**. Some methods of research are much more likely to produce results which can be repeated than others. Well-designed questionnaires are probably the method most likely to produce similar research results each time and are therefore regarded as highly reliable. At the other extreme, when a lone sociologist engages in participant observation (that is, joins a group of people and observes their behaviour), the research is likely to be far less reliable, as the research is affected by the specific circumstances surrounding the group and the relationship of the observer to the group. Overall, quantitative methods tend to be more reliable, qualititative methods less reliable.

Validity

The second crucial factor in evaluating research is the extent to which it is **valid**, i.e. how far it gives a true picture of the subject being studied. In evaluating a piece of research, sociologists will ask whether the methods used were those most likely to get to the truth of the matter. Interestingly, validity and reliability do not always go hand in hand. We saw before that questionnaires are likely to be highly reliable, but this does not necessarily mean that they are valid. For example, when asked about embarrassing subjects, such as sex or criminal activity, people often lie. Therefore, if the study were repeated, the results would be exactly the same, yet they would never be true! Observational studies are usually difficult to repeat and so are fairly unreliable. However, if the observation has been done well, then it may actually be very valid.

Representativeness

The third crucial element in any evaluation is that of **representativeness**. Does the sample of people chosen for the research reflect a typical cross section of the group or society the researcher is interested in gaining information about? If the respondents in the study are not representative, then it is simply not possible to generalize to the whole group or society (see the following point). For example, if sociologists wish to talk about the population as a whole, then the chosen group must be representative of society as a whole. Similarly, if they wish to comment on people who are terminally ill, then the study must be of a representative group from this section of society.

Generalizability

The aim of most (though not all) sociological research is to produce knowledge which can aid us in understanding the behaviour of people in general – not just the specific group being studied. If the knowledge gained from studying the group cannot be **generalized** to all society, then it has limited use. This is why many sociologists are concerned that the people they study are typical or representative of a cross section of the society which they wish to generalize about. Overall, the larger the numbers of people in the study and the more sophisticated the methods used to select these people, the greater the chance of the study being representative.

evaluating research

Research into 'cybersex'

The comments on the left were made by a researcher interested in cybersex and describe how he carried out his research.

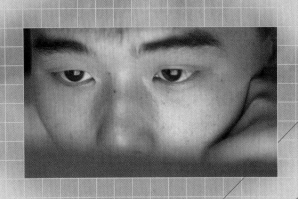

<< In fact, most of my respondents admit that they would not talk with me about cybersex (and other issues it brings up such as solitary masturbation) if I were to interview them face to face. In contrast to this, in the online interviews that I completed, I found that nearly all respondents were almost immediately willing to speak about very intimate details of their sex lives. >>

Source: Hamman, R. (1997) 'The Application of ethnographic methodology in the study of cybersex', *Cybersociology*, 1, October www.socio.demon.co.uk/magazine/plummer.html

1 **Representativeness** – the researcher just posted a message on the website saying that he was researching cybersex and wanted to interview people. He does not know if the people who responded were representative of those who engage in cybersex.

2 **Validity** – what does the researcher mean by 'cybersex' (it isn't defined in the original article), and does it have the same meaning for the respondents as it does to him? **Reliability** – if interviewees use different definitions of 'cybersex', how can their answers be compared?

3 **Validity** – the researcher interviewed people 'on line'. It is generally accepted that it is much easier to lie in this situation than in a face-to-face interview.

4 **Generalizability** – the researcher refers to 'nearly all' and earlier said 'most'; he does not include any statistics. This suggests small numbers. Because of this, it would be very difficult to generalize from these results.

Objectivity

The final key element in ensuring that research is of high standard is the extent to which the researchers have ensured that their own values and beliefs have not had any influence on the design or the carrying out of the research. This is known as **objectivity**. If sociologists allow their own values to intrude into the research process, then this will seriously weaken the research and certainly impact upon the validity of the research. However, we cannot say that all values should be kept out of research, as this is simply impossible, just that there should never be intentional bias.

web.task

Find some of the statistics on drugs and crime. These are available through the Home Office website (www.homeoffice.gov.uk). You will need to select or search for the section on 'Drugs' or 'Drugs and crime'. Give examples of the sort of figures and information provided. Comment on their validity, reliability and representativeness.

Check your understanding

1 Explain the three main aims of sociological research in your own words.

2 Give two reasons why sociological research is more trustworthy than 'common sense'.

3 Explain the difference between a 'correlation' and a 'causal relationship'.

4 What term is used by sociologists for statistical data?

5 Give two examples of:
   (a) primary data
   (b) secondary data.

6 Why is it important for a sociological study to be 'valid'?

research ideas

- Divide into small groups. Each group should write a short questionnaire consisting of three questions. The questions should aim to collect opinions on:
  (a) whether cannabis should be legalized
  (b) whether the use of drugs causes crime
  (c) whether smoking ought to be banned in public places.

- Decide on the wording of your questions and then put them to a sample of six people.

- Compare the answers of the different groups. Are they all similar? If they are different, can you think of reasons why?

- What might this tell us about validity, bias and representativeness?

KEY TERMS

Bias where the views of the researchers affect the research.

Causal relationship where there is a relationship between two social events with one causing the other.

Correlation a statistical relationship between two things. It does not necessarily mean that one causes the other. For example, over 70 per cent of burglars drink coffee, but this does not mean that drinking coffee causes someone to commit burglary.

Data the information uncovered by research.

Generalization if the group sociologists choose to study are representative of the population as a whole, then they will be able to make generalizations about the whole society. If the group is not representative, they will only be able to speak about the particular group studied.

Objectivity quality achieved when a researcher's values do not affect their work.

Primary data information obtained directly by the sociologist.

Qualitative data information from a range of sources which are not statistical, such as observation.

Quantitative data statistical information.

Reliability quality of repeatability: if the same piece of research were repeated by different sociologists, then it should produce the same results.

Representativeness situation where the people sociologists

study are a cross section of the group they wish to generalize about.

Secondary data information obtained from sources originally collected by someone other than the sociologist conducting the research.

Sociological theory (or **theorizing**) an explanation of how different parts of society or different events relate to one another.

Validity the extent to which data give a true picture of the subject being studied.

Item A Dissatisfaction with the NHS

Dissatisfaction with the NHS by age, income and experience of the NHS

	% Dissatisfied		
	1987	1999	2001
Age			
18–36	42	36	44
54+	30	28	35
Household Income			
High	46	41	48
Low	35	28	34
Health Service Experience			
NHS inpatient in previous 12 months	40	40	33
Has private medical insurance	42	41	45

Source: Adatped from Park, A. *et al.* (2002) *British Social Attitudes*, London: Sage (Table 4.6, p. 81)

Item B Assessing a research design

You have been asked to assess a research design in terms of its reliabilty, validity, representativeness and generalizability. The research is about the relationship between drugs and crime.

The research design consists of the following steps:

- selecting a large sample of convicted offenders in prison
- giving each of them a list of reasons why they felt they had committed their crime and asking them to rate these in order of importance
- collecting all the results and making one list using all their replies.

a Briefly explain the concept of 'causal relationship'. (6 marks)

b Using Item A, identify the two main trends of people who were most dissatisfied with the NHS in 2001. (8 marks)

c Using Item B, identify and explain two weaknesses of the research design. (16 marks)

d Outline and assess one sociological research method of collecting information about the link between a person's social class and their dissatisfaction with the health service. (30 marks)

Methods, theories and ethics

getting you thinking

Karen Sharpe studied the lives of prostitutes by acting as a 'secretary' for them. Read the passage (right) about the aims of her research and then answer the questions that follow.

≪ The central objective of my research was to understand why and how women entered the world of prostitution: to discover the motivating factors, the dynamics of the introductory process, and how they learnt the skills, values and codes of conduct of the business. I wanted to explore the importance and impact of prostitution on their lifestyles and to put the 'deviance' of prostitution into context with other aspects of their criminality. I also wanted to discover how the women themselves and their families and friends, subjectively defined, perceived and rationalized their activities. ≫

1 What methods would it have been possible to use in this research? What are their advantages and disadvantages?

2 This research was conducted by a woman. What problems would have been faced by a male researcher?

3 Do you think that this research is justifiable? Explain your answer.

Sharpe, K. (2000) 'Sad, bad and (sometimes) dangerous to know: street corner research with prostitutes, punters and the police' in R.D. King and E. Wincup (eds), *Doing Research on Crime and Justice*, Oxford: Oxford University Press, p. 364

The relationship between research and ethics

Research can have a powerful impact on people's lives. It can do so in both harmful and beneficial ways. Therefore, researchers must always think very carefully about the impact of the research and how they ought to behave, so that no harm comes to the subjects of the research or to society in general. These sorts of concerns are generally discussed under the umbrella term **ethical issues**.

Most sociological researchers would agree that there are five areas of ethical concern:

- choice of topic
- choice of group to be studied
- effects on the people being studied
- effects on the wider society
- issues of legality and immorality.

Choice of topic

The first ethical issue relates to the decision about what to study. Merely by choosing an area, the researcher might be confirming some people's prejudices about a particular issue. For example, many sociologists are concerned about the extent of research into the 'negative' side of African–Caribbean life, with studies on school failure, lower levels of job success and even the claimed higher rate of criminality. Critics argue that merely by studying this, a continued association is made between race and criminality or race and failure.

Choice of group to be studied

One of the trickiest problems that sociologists face is gaining access to study particular groups. The more powerful the group, the less likely it is that the sociologist will manage to obtain agreement to study its members. The result, as you will see, is

1 Kibbutzim can be very small and close, so Lieblich should have realized that details of the research could easily have leaked out into the wider community. She should have thought about the possible consequences.

Lieblich (1996) researched family lives in an Israeli kibbutz (a form of socialist community), reflecting on the way the book had an impact on those involved.

≪An older woman, Genia, who also read the first draft was the person I respected more than any other member of the kibbutz. After the joint meeting with all the 'readers', Genia asked to see me in private. 'I am shocked' she said, 'I cried so much' ... she explained what caused her all the pain were the stories of her two daughters, which were included in the book. I realized that both of them said in so many words that Genia had been a 'bad mother'. During their childhood she dedicated all her time to the affairs of the kibbutz whilst they felt neglected and rejected.≫

Lieblich, A. (1996) 'Some unforeseen outcomes of conducting narrative research with people of one's own culture', in R. Josselson (ed.) *Ethics and Process in the Narrative Study of Lives*, London: Sage (cited in K. Plummer *Documents of Life* (2001) London: Sage, p. 225).

Amia Lieblich
Effects on people being studied

2 Lieblich should have thought about how she could have 'managed the impact' of the book on people's lives as part of the research design.

3 This is a very powerful example of how research can hurt people.

4 Is it morally acceptable to leave a participant in the research project feeling so badly about herself? Or does the knowledge gained outweigh the pain of individuals?

---

that the groups most commonly studied by sociologists are the least powerful – so students, petty criminals and less-skilled workers are the staple diet of sociological research. The really powerful evade study. Does sociology have a duty to explore the lives of the powerful?

Effects on the people being studied

Research can often have an effect on the people being studied. So, before setting out to do research, sociologists must think carefully about what these effects will be, although it is not always possible to anticipate them – see *Focus on research* on the previous page.

One of the reasons why sociologists rarely use experiments, for example, is that these may lead to the subjects being harmed by the experiment. In participant observational studies, where the researcher actually joins in with the group being studied (see Topic 3), the researcher can often become an important member of the group and may influence other members to behave in ways they would not normally.

Effects on the wider society

It is not only the people being studied who are potentially affected by the research. The families of those being researched may have information given about them that they wish to keep secret. Also, victims of crime may be upset by the information that researchers obtain about the perpetrators, as they may prefer to forget the incident.

Issues of legality and immorality

Finally, sociologists may be drawn into situations where they may commit crimes or possibly help in or witness deviant acts. While undertaking research on a prisoner in the USA, Kenneth Tunnell (1998) discovered that the prisoner had actually taken on the identity of someone else (who was dead), in order to avoid a much longer prison sentence. The prison authorities became suspicious and investigated the prisoner's background. Though Tunnell knew the truth, he felt that he owed the prisoner confidentiality and deliberately lied, stating that he knew nothing about the identity 'theft'. As a result, the prisoner was released many years early.

The relationship between theories and methods

Earlier we saw that research findings could be used either to generate new sociological theories, or to confirm or challenge existing theories. However, the relationship between research and theory is even more complicated than this. If a sociologist has a particular interest in a theoretical approach, then this may well influence their research methodology. There are areas in which theory has a strong influence on research – for example, the theoretical approach may:

1 direct people to explore certain areas of research
2 influence the actual techniques chosen
3 influence how researchers interpret the research findings.

Theory and choice of an area of research

One of the great joys of studying sociology is that the variety of different views and theories generates so many different opinions about society. However, when reading sociological research, you must always be aware that sociologists who hold strong theoretical beliefs about society are bound to study the topics that, in their eyes, are the most important, and to be less interested in other areas.

- **Feminist sociologists** see it as their role to examine the position of women in society, and to uncover the ways in which **patriarchy**, or the power of men, has been used to control and oppress women. Consequently, their choice of research projects will be influenced by this.
- **Marxist or critical sociologists** argue that the most important area of study is the question of how a relatively small group of people exploits the vast majority of the population. They will study issues such as the concentration of power and wealth, and the importance of social class divisions.
- **Functionalist-oriented sociologists** think that society is based on a general consensus of values. They are interested in looking at the ways in which society maintains agreement on values and solves social problems. Therefore, they will look at the role of religion or schools in passing on values.

Theory and techniques of study

Various theories may point to different areas of interest, but theories also nudge sociologists into different ways of studying society. Theories in sociology usually fall into two camps – **top-down** and **bottom-up** theories.

Top-down approaches

Top-down approaches, such as functionalism and Marxism, say that the best way to understand society is to view it as a real 'thing' which exists above and beyond us all as individuals. It shapes our lives and provides us with the social world in which we live. Our role is generally to conform.

These sorts of theoretical approaches emphasize that any research ought to bear this in mind and that the researcher should be looking for general patterns of behaviour – which individuals may not even be aware of.

The favoured research methods used by these sociologists tend to be those that generate sets of statistics (such as questionnaires), known as **quantitative methods** (see Topic 2). Sociologists sympathetic to the use of these more 'scientific' methods are sometimes known as **positivists**.

Bottom-up approaches

Bottom-up approaches, such as interactionism, stress that the only way to understand society is to look at the world through the eyes of individuals, as it is their activities and beliefs that make up the social world. Research must start at 'the bottom' and work upwards. The sorts of research methods favoured by those who advocate this approach (known as **interpretive sociologists**) tend to be those that allow the researcher to see the world from the same perspective as those being studied (known as **qualitative methods**). An example is participant observation (see p. 236).

The interpretation of research findings

The final impact of theory on research comes when interpreting the research findings. The research is completed and the results are all there in the computer. How does the researcher make sense of the results? This will depend, of course, on what they are looking for, and that, in turn, depends upon what theoretical approach the researcher sympathizes with. This is very different from bias or personal values – rather, it is a matter of choosing which results are most important, and this will always depend upon what best fits the theoretical framework of the researcher. A feminist researcher will be keen to understand the position of women; the Marxist will be looking for signs of class struggle; the functionalist will be looking at the key indicators to prove that a set of common beliefs exists.

The relationship between practical issues and research

So far we have looked at the ethical and theoretical issues which have an important influence on the research process. As you can see, these are quite difficult 'abstract' issues, which sometimes seem far removed from the reality of everyday life. However, just as important are a range of very down-to-earth influences on the research process.

Funding

All research has to be paid for by someone and those who pay for research have a reason for doing so. These funding organizations may vary from those who wish to extend knowledge about society and to improve the quality of life (such as the Joseph Rowntree Foundation), to private companies wanting to sell more products or services (such as market research organizations). Despite the differences between the funding organizations, each has an aim that constrains the research choices and activities of sociologists.

Probably the largest funder of sociological research in Britain is the government, which pays for a wide range of research into areas such as transport, health, crime and housing. However, anyone conducting research for the government signs a contract that restricts what they can say and publish about their findings.

Academic specialism

Sociologists at university specialize in particular areas within sociology – for example, some will only study the family and others only health issues. Clearly, the research they will wish to undertake will be within their specialism.

Personal reasons

Sociologists, like everyone else, want to have successful careers, be promoted and become respected. Research choices are often influenced by these desires. If there are various areas of research to choose from, the ambitious sociologist chooses that one that may lead to promotion.

Appropriate methods

The research method is often dictated by the situation and the sociologist has no choice, even if they have misgivings. Generally, if a large number of people need to be studied, then the sociologist will use questionnaires or possibly interviews. If a few people need to be studied in depth, then some form of observation will be employed.

focus on research

The British Sociological Association

The British Sociological Association is the official organization for academic sociologists engaged in research. It provides a set of ethical guidelines for its members. Below are some of the key points about the relationships between those who pay for the research (funders) and sociologists (members). You can find the full statement of ethics on the BSA website **www.britsoc.co.uk**

- Members should have a written contract with the funders.
- Members must be totally honest with the funders about their own qualifications and about the advantages/disadvantages of the chosen research methods.
- Members should not agree to research where the funding is dependent upon certain research results.
- Members need to know, before they start the research, that they have the right to publish their research and to let others know who funded it.

1 Take each of the points above and explain why it is important.

KEY TERMS

Bottom-up theories (generally called **micro** or **interpretive** approaches) sociological theories that analyse society by studying the ways in which individuals interpret the world.

Ethical issues refers to moral concerns about the benefits and potential harm of research – to the people being researched, to the researcher her/himself and to society.

Feminist sociology an approach within sociology that concerns itself with studying the way in which women are oppressed by men.

Functionalism an approach within sociology that stresses that society is based on a general agreement of values.

Interpretive sociology an approach which favours the use of qualitative methods such as participant observation which allow the researcher to see the world from the same perspective as those being studied.

Marxist or critical sociology an approach within sociology that stresses the exploitation of the majority of the population by a small and powerful 'ruling class'.

Patriarchy the oppression of women by men.

Positivism the view that sociology should attempt to use more 'scientific' approaches and methods such as questionnaires and official statistics.

Top-down theories (often called **macro** or **structural** approaches) sociological theories that believe it is important to look at society as a whole when studying it.

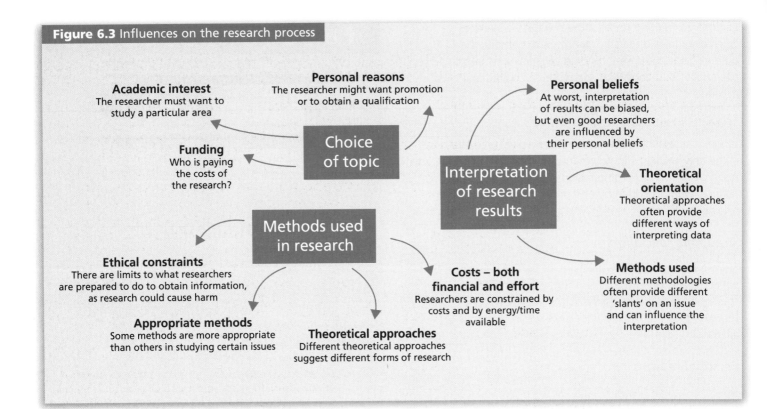

Figure 6.3 Influences on the research process

Academic interest
The researcher must want to study a particular area

Personal reasons
The researcher might want promotion or to obtain a qualification

Personal beliefs
At worst, interpretation of results can be biased, but even good researchers are influenced by their personal beliefs

Funding
Who is paying the costs of the research?

Choice of topic

Interpretation of research results

Theoretical orientation
Theoretical approaches often provide different ways of interpreting data

Methods used in research

Ethical constraints
There are limits to what researchers are prepared to do to obtain information, as research could cause harm

Costs – both financial and effort
Researchers are constrained by costs and by energy/time available

Methods used
Different methodologies often provide different 'slants' on an issue and can influence the interpretation

Appropriate methods
Some methods are more appropriate than others in studying certain issues

Theoretical approaches
Different theoretical approaches suggest different forms of research

Check your understanding

1 Name the three main aims that sociological researchers set out to achieve.

2 Explain in your own words what is meant by the term 'ethical issues'.

3 Illustrate how ethical issues may emerge in:

  (a) the choice of topic to be studied

  (b) the effects on the people being studied.

4 How can a theoretical approach influence:

  (a) the area of study?

  (b) the methodological techniques chosen?

5 Give two examples that show the influence of practical issues on the nature of research.

research ideas

- Look in your school or college library for resources about drugs and alcohol. Who published the material? Can you suggest reasons why they published the material? Could this affect the content of the material in any way?

- Using any textbook of sociology, find one example of feminist research (use the index) and explain how the researcher's feminist approach might have affected the research in any way.

web.task

Go to the website of the British Sociological Association and find the section on 'The Statement of Ethical Practice'. Make a brief list of the key elements. Do you think they are all necessary?

How could 'informed consent' cause problems for studying young people or deviant groups?

Item A Ethical dilemmas

Carolyn Hoyle conducted research into domestic violence against women.

<< ... victims were told who I was, what the research was about, how it was funded and how I would use the data ... However ... this rigorous approach to consent and honesty was not extended to those husbands committing violence against their wives. >>

Hoyle goes on to describe how the violent husband and the victims were interviewed in separate rooms of their homes. The husbands were told that they were being asked the same questions as their wives. This was not true – they were misled as to the true nature of the questions asked of the wives – but Hoyle argued that it allowed the victims to speak freely and be assured that the husband/perpetrator would not know what they were really asked.

She justifies this by arguing:

<< I believe that minimizing the risk of further violence to the victim and having the opportunity to talk openly and honestly to a victim ... justified deliberately misleading the violent husbands.

Although social scientists 'have a responsibility to ensure that the physical, social and psychological wellbeing of research participants is not adversely affected by the research', I believe that these ethical principles are important but have to be weighed against other things ... This weighting should not be based on a researcher's desire to progress her own career, but could be based, for example, on the social desirability of obtaining reliable evidence on a controversial topic, which could help to bring about changes which could improve the lot of the research subjects – in this case the wives. The greater the social problem, the more it may be justified to attach less weight to methodological principles. >>

Adapted from Hoyle, C. (2000) 'Being "a nosy bloody cow": ethical and methodological issues in researching domestic violence', in R.D. King and E. Wincup (eds), *Doing Research on Crime and Justice*, Oxford: OUP, pp. 401–2

Item B Assessing a research design

You have been asked to assess a research design in terms of its reliabilty, validity, representativeness and generalizability. The research is about the relationship between suicide and family relationships.

The research design consists of:

- checking official records of cause of death in selected areas of the country to identify suicides
- writing to the nearest relatives of the deceased asking for an interview and explaining the importance of the research
- carrying out unstructured interviews – interviewing the closest relatives of 10 of the people who committed suicide found from the official records and collecting information on their social-class backgrounds, size of family, relationships between family members and a range of other social factors
- analysing the data to see what social factors are linked to suicide.

---

a Briefly explain the concept of 'ethical issues'. (6 marks)

b Using Item A, identify two ethical issues raised by the research methods. (8 marks)

c Using Item B, identify and explain two weaknesses of the research design. (16 marks)

d Outline and assess one sociological research method of collecting information about the views of victims of sexual crimes about new 'restorative justice' programmes in which the offender and victim can meet and the offender can explain and apologize for the offence. (30 marks)

Quantitative research: getting 'the truth'?

gettingyouthinking

Every year a survey called the Health Related Behaviour Questionnaire takes place. Young people are asked about their experiences of a range of health issues. According to the latest, conducted in 2002:

- **Up to 21 per cent of 10 to 11 year olds had consumed an alcoholic drink during the previous week.**
- **19 per cent of 15 year old males drank more than 11 units of alcohol in the previous week.**
- **Up to 65 per cent of young people will have smoked by year 10.**
- **About one in four pupils in year 10 have tried at least one illegal drug.**
- **Up to 8 per cent of 12 to 13 year olds have taken cannabis.**

Schools Health Education Unit (2003), *Young people in 2002*, Exeter: SHEU

1 How can anyone make these claims? Did they ask every school student in Britain? If they didn't, how is it possible to arrive at these figures?

2 How honestly do you think pupils will answer these questions?

Sociologists choose different methods of research depending upon what method seems most appropriate in the circumstances, and the resources available to them. The approach covered in this topic is quantitative research. This stresses the importance of gathering statistical information that can be checked and tested. Quantitative research usually involves one or more of the following:

- **social surveys (cross-sectional research)**
- **experiments**
- **comparative research**
- **case studies**.

Surveys

A social survey involves obtaining information in a standardized manner from a large group of people. Surveys usually obtain this information through questionnaires or, less often, through interviews. The information is then analysed using statistical techniques. There are three possible aims of social surveys. They can be used:

- to find out 'facts' about the population – for example, how many people have access to the internet
- to uncover differences in beliefs, values and behaviour – for example, whether young people have a more positive view of the internet than older people
- to test 'a hypothesis' – for example, that women are less confident in using the internet than men.

A good example of a survey is the British Crime Survey, which takes place every two years and asks people about their experience of crime. This survey has helped sociologists gain a fuller understanding of patterns of crime. We now know a lot more about issues such as people's fear of crime, the factors affecting the reporting of crime and the likelihood of different social groups becoming victims of crime.

Before a full social survey is carried out, it is usual for a researcher to carry out a **pilot survey**. This is a small-scale version of the full survey, which is intended to:

- help evaluate the usefulness of the larger survey
- test the quality and the accuracy of the questions
- test the accuracy of the sample
- find out if there are any unforeseen problems.

Longitudinal surveys

Social surveys are sometimes criticized for providing only a 'snapshot' of social life at any one time. Sociologists often want to understand how people change over time and in these circumstances the typical **cross-sectional survey** (as these 'snapshot surveys' are sometimes called) is not appropriate. **Longitudinal surveys**, however, get around this problem by studying the same people over a long period of time (as the name suggests) – sometimes over as long as 20 years. Such surveys provide us with a clear, moving image of changes in attitudes and actions over time. The British Household Panel Survey is a longitudinal study that has studied over 10 000 British people of all ages, living in 5500 households. The interviewing started in 1991 and has continued every year since then. The information obtained covers a vast area including family change, household finances and patterns of health and caring. It is used by the government to help inform social policies.

Longitudinal surveys suffer from a number of problems, but the main one is that respondents drop out of the survey because they get bored with answering the questions, or they move and the researchers lose track of them. If too many people drop out, this may make the survey unreliable, as the views of those who remain may well be significantly different from the views of those who drop out.

Sampling

It is usually impossible for sociologists to study the entire population on the grounds of cost and practicality. Instead, they have to find a way of studying a smaller proportion of the population whose views will exactly mirror the views of the whole population. There are two main ways of ensuring that the smaller group studied (the sample) is typical – or **representative** – of the entire population:

1 some form of **random sampling**
2 **quota sampling**.

There are also other forms of sampling which are not representative but are sometimes used. These include:

3 **snowball sampling**
4 **theoretical sampling**.

Random sampling

This is based on the idea that, by choosing randomly, each person has an equal chance of being selected and so those chosen are likely to be a cross-section of the population. A simple random sample involves selecting names randomly from a list, known as a **sampling frame**. If the sampling frame is inaccurate, this can lead to great errors in the final findings. It therefore needs to be a true reflection of the sort of people whom the researcher wishes to study. Examples of commonly used sampling frames are electoral registers (lists of people entitled to vote, which are publicly available) or the Postcode Address File (see *Focus on research* on the right).

The British Social Attitudes Survey: a cross-sectional survey

The British Social Attitudes Survey is a regular survey of the British population which aims to find out attitudes to a wide range of contemporary issues. The 2002 report covered areas as diverse as attitudes to public transport, saving and borrowing, drug use, education, and the importance of family and friends.

Some of the conclusions of the survey in 2002 were as follows:

1 Regular car users were not particularly enthusiastic about moving to public transport and it would be very difficult to change their behaviour without large increases in the costs of motoring.
2 There is growing support for allowing people to smoke cannabis – but not most other drugs.
3 People who have high levels of contact with other family members are less likely to seek friends or join clubs.

The sample consisted of 3287 respondents. The sample was chosen using the Postcode Address File which lists all the addresses held by the Post Office.

Selection was by stratified random sampling across Britain.

Each selected household was sent a letter asking for their help and explaining the purpose of the research.

Interviewers called at the selected addresses (they were not allowed to use other ones) and asked the chosen respondent to complete a questionnaire, which was then taken away by the interviewer.

Park, A., Curtice, J., Thompson, K., Lindsey, J. and Bromley, C. (2002) *British Social Attitudes* (The 19th Report), London: Sage

1 What sampling frame was used in this research?

2 How can 3287 people represent the views of the British population?

3 What problems for the survey may occur when researchers call at selected homes?

Some of the problems faced by interviewers...

However, a simple random sample does not guarantee a representative sample – you may, for instance, select too many young people, too many males or too many from some other group. For this reason, many sociologists break down their list of names into separate categories (for example, males and females) and then select from those lists.

Types of random sampling

There are a number of commonly used types of random sampling which aim to guarantee a representative sample. These include:

- **Systematic sampling** – where every *n*th name (for example, every tenth name) on a list is chosen. It is not truly random – but it is close enough.
- **Stratified sampling** – where the population under study is divided according to known criteria (for example, it could be divided into 52 per cent women and 48 per cent men, to reflect the sex composition of the UK). Within these broad strata, people are then chosen at random. The strata can become quite detailed – for example, with further divisions into age, social class, geographical location.
- **Cluster sampling** – where the researcher selects a series of different places and then chooses a sample at random within the cluster of people within these areas. This method is sometimes used where the population under study is spread over a wide area and it is impossible for the researcher to cover the whole area.

Quota sampling

This form of sampling is often used by market research companies and is used purely as the basis for interviews. Since the main social characteristics of the UK population (age, income, occupation, location, ethnicity, etc.) are known, researchers can give interviewers a particular quota of individuals whom they must find and question – for example, a certain proportion of women of different ages and occupations, and a certain proportion of men of different ages and occupations. The results, when pieced together, should be an accurate reflection of the population as a whole. This form of sampling can only be used where accurate information about the major characteristics of the population is available.

The major advantage of quota sampling over random sampling is the very small number of people needed to build up an accurate picture of the whole. For example, the typical surveys of voting preferences in journals and newspapers use a quota sample of approximately 1,200 to represent the entire British electorate.

Non-representative sampling

Sometimes researchers either do not want a cross-section of the population, or are unable to obtain one.

Snowball sampling

This method is used when it is difficult to gain access to a particular group of people who are the subjects of study, or where there is simply no sampling frame available. It involves making contact with one member of the population to be studied and then asking them to name one or more possible contacts. An example of this is McNamara's study of male prostitutes in New York (1994) where he simply asked prostitutes to identify others, gradually building up enough contacts for the research.

Theoretical sampling

Glaser and Strauss (1967) argue that sometimes it is more helpful to study non-typical people, because they may help generate theoretical insights. Feminist sociologists have deliberately studied very untypical societies where women occupy non-traditional roles in order to show that gender roles are socially constructed – if they were based on biology, we would expect to see the same roles in every society.

Experiments

Experiments are very commonly used in the natural sciences (e.g. physics and chemistry). An experiment is basically research in which all the variables are closely controlled, so that the effect of changing one or more of the variables can be understood. Experiments are widely used in psychology, but much less so in sociology.

This is because:

- it is impossible to recreate normal life in the artificial environment of an experiment
- there are many ethical problems in performing experiments on people
- there is the possibility of the experimenter effect, where the awareness of being in an experiment affects the behaviour of the participants.

Occasionally, sociologists use **field experiments**, where a form of experiment is undertaken in the community. Rosenhan (1973) sent 'normal' people to psychiatric institutions in the USA in the late 1960s to see how they were treated by the staff. (Rather worryingly, the staff treated ordinary behaviour in institutions as evidence of insanity!)

Comparative method

The sociological version of an experiment is the **comparative method**. When a sociologist is interested in explaining a particular issue, one way of doing so is by comparing differences across groups or societies, or across one society over time. By comparing the different social variables in the different societies and their effects upon the issue being studied, it is sometimes possible to identify a particular social practice or value which is the key factor in determining that issue. Emile Durkheim (1897/1952) used the comparative method in his classic study of the different levels of suicide in societies – concluding that specific cultural differences motivated people to commit suicide. In order to arrive at this conclusion, Durkheim collected official statistics from a number of different countries and then compared the different levels of suicide, linking them to cultural differences, including religion and family relationships, which varied across the different countries.

Case studies

A case study is a detailed study of one particular group or organization. Instead of searching out a wide range of people via sampling, the researcher focuses on one group. The resulting studies are usually extremely detailed and provide a depth of information not normally available. However, there is always the problem that this intense scrutiny may miss wider issues by its very concentration. An example of a case study is Grieshaber's work (1997), where she conducted case studies of how families ate their meals, and the rules that the parents and their children negotiated.

Check your understanding

1. What do we mean by quantitative research?
2. Explain in your own words the importance of sampling.
3. Why are random samples not always representative?
4. What is 'quota' sampling? What is the main drawback of this method?
5. Identify and explain, in your own words, three types of random sampling.
6. In what situations might a sociologist use:
   (a) snowball sampling?
   (b) theoretical sampling?
7. Why don't sociologists use experiments?
8. What is a case study?
9. Give one example of a research project that has used the comparative method.

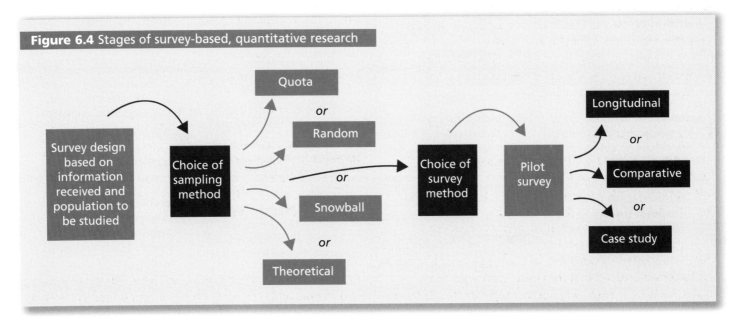

Figure 6.4 Stages of survey-based, quantitative research

Survey design based on information received and population to be studied → Choice of sampling method → Quota *or* Random *or* Snowball *or* Theoretical → Choice of survey method → Pilot survey → Longitudinal *or* Comparative *or* Case study

The table below comes from a recent national research study by the government on school meals in English schools. Although the source is authoritative and the authors are well aware of any problems, it is still a useful habit to look critically at any statistical table.

1 MDS stands for 'multiple deprivation score' – this tells you just how poor the area is in which the school is located. The higher the MDS, the poorer the area.

2 Note that more affluent schools were likely to have participated – might this affect representativeness and generalizability?

3 Look at the relatively high rates of refusal – might this also affect representativeness and generalizability?

Multiple deprivation score (MDS) for participating, non-participating and the issued sample schools

MDS	Participated (n = 79)		Refused (n = 56)		Issued sample (n = 135)	
	n	%	n	%	n	%
0–<10	18	23	7	13	25	19
10–<20	17	21	16	29	33	24
20–<30	17	21	11	20	28	21
30–<40	13	17	8	14	21	16
40–<50	8	10	7	13	15	11
50–<60	2	3	1	2	3	2
60–<70	3	4	5	9	8	6
70–<80	1	1	1	2	2	1

Source: Nelson, M. *et al.* (2004) *School Meals in Secondary Schools in England*, Research Report 557, London: Kings College, National Centre for Social Research, p. 10

KEY TERMS

Case study a highly detailed study of one or two social situations or groups.

Cluster sampling the researcher selects a series of different places and then chooses a sample at random within the cluster of people within these areas.

Comparative method a comparison across countries or cultures; sociology's version of an experiment.

Cross-sectional survey (also known as **social survey** or **snapshot survey**) a survey conducted at one time with no attempt to follow up the people surveyed over a longer time.

Experiment a highly controlled situation where the researchers try to isolate the influence of each variable. Rarely used in sociology.

Field experiment an experiment undertaken in the community rather than in a controlled environment.

Longitudinal survey a survey carried out over a considerable number of years on the same group of people.

Pilot survey a small-scale survey carried out before the main one, to iron out any problems.

Quota sampling where a representative sample of the population is chosen using

known characteristics of the population.

Random sampling where a representative sample of the population is chosen by entirely random methods.

Representative a sample is representative if it is an accurate cross-section of the whole population being studied.

Sampling frame a list used as the source for a random sample.

Snowball sampling where a sample is obtained using a series of personal contacts. Usually used for the study of deviant behaviour.

Stratified sampling where the population under study is divided according to known criteria, such as sex and age, in order to make the sample more representative.

Survey a large-scale piece of quantitative research aiming to make general statements about a particular population.

Systematic sampling where every *n*th name (for example, every tenth name) on a list is chosen.

Theoretical sampling where an untypical sample of the population is chosen to illustrate a particular theory.

Item A   A longitudinal study

The North-West Longitudinal Study involved following several hundred young people for five years between the ages of 14 and 18. The overall aim of this study was to assess how 'ordinary' young people, growing up in England in the 1990s, developed attitudes and behaviour in relation to the availability of illegal drugs, alongside other options such as alcohol and tobacco.

The main technique was a self-report questionnaire initially administered personally by the researchers (and then by post) to several hundred young people within eight state secondary schools in two non-inner-city boroughs of metropolitan north-west England.

At the start of the research the sample was representative of those areas in terms of gender, class and ethnicity. However, attrition (losing participants) partly reduced this over time with the disproportionate loss of some 'working-class' participants and some from Asian and Muslim backgrounds.

A longitudinal study is able to address issues of validity and reliability far more extensively than one-off snapshot surveys, but in turn must also explain inconsistent reporting that occurs over the years.

In general, the research provides a detailed account of how young people develop attitudes and behaviours through time.

Adapted from Parker, H., Aldrige, J. and Measham, F. (1998) *Illegal Leisure*, London: Routledge, pp. 48–9

Item B   Assessing a research design

You have been asked to assess a research design in term its reliabilty, validity, representativeness and generalizability. The research is about how local people can limit crime where there is little trust in the police. The research explores how local people can control crime levels, given that the police were not welcome in many areas.

The research design consists of:

- An urban area in the UK was selected where the police are not welcome – in this particular case, the researchers chose hardline areas of Belfast.
- The sample was obtained by contacting local loyalist and republican organizations and asking them to suggest some names. From that point, a snowball sampling technique was used.
- People were interviewed in their own homes by English researchers, using open questions.

a Briefly explain the concept of a 'longitudinal study'. (6 marks)

b Identify two problems the North-West Longitudinal Study (Item A) would be likely to face. (8 marks)

c Using Item B, identify and explain two weaknesses of the research design. (16 marks)

d Outline and assess one sociological research method of collecting information about the attitudes of British people towards the NHS. (30 marks) .

research ideas

- Work out the proportions needed in your sample if you were to do a quota sample of your school or college.

- Conduct a small survey to discover the extent of alcohol use among students (by age) at your school or college. Compare their use of alcohol with the use of illegal drugs identified in the 'Getting you thinking' exercise at the beginning of this topic (see p. 240).

web.tasks

1 Go to the website 'School Surveys' at www.schoolsurveys.co.uk, where you can organize your own online survey. You will need to get your teacher to register first.

2 Go to the 'Living in Britain' website (part of the government's National Statistics site) at www.statistics.gov.uk/lib2002 What is the General Household Survey and what methods does it use to collect information?

Understanding people: observation

gettingyouthinking

The extract on the right is from a research project which studies the lives and attitudes of door staff ('bouncers') working in night clubs. The researcher narrating the story is a student who has got a job as a bouncer as part of the research project.

1 What is your immediate reaction to the story?

2 Why do you think the girl was attacked by her friend?

3 Have you ever seen a fight outside a club at night? What happened? What did the doorstaff do?

4 Why do you think the researcher chose to get a job as a bouncer in order to study their lives? Could you think of a better way?

‹‹ It's Friday evening outside a club in a city centre … one young woman has shouted an insult at another, the recipient of which has turned on her heel and begun to walk away. The first young woman continues to throw insults until the retreating young woman seemingly has a change of heart, turns, picks up an empty lager bottle from the street and hits the first young woman in the face with it.

A hush descends on the busy street. It isn't funny any more. Nobody is laughing; in fact there was a palpable 'Oh!' sound emitted from the spectators, mixed with the sound of thick glass crashing into tender flesh and bone. The injured young woman has her hand pressed to her mouth – she isn't screaming or crying, but instantly it is possible to tell that she is badly injured.

I snap out of my shocked state when I see Paul (bouncer and colleague) putting his arm around her back to support her unsteady steps … After some gentle coaxing, the woman releases her grip on the wound … blood spurts all over Paul's shirt. Her upper lip is split entirely, right up to her right nostril. It's a wide gash and through the resulting hole it becomes apparent that the woman has also lost at least three teeth. Blood is everywhere. Paul's shirt now appears tie-dyed red with blood.

Later when a policeman calls to take a statement, he informs me that I may be called as a witness in any resulting court case. When I ask how the young woman is, he informs me that 'She lost four teeth, 28 stitches to the upper lip, the usual bruising and swelling … Shame really. Pretty girl.' Turns out she's only 15. ››

Winlow, S., Hobbs, D., Lister, S. and Hadfield, P. (2001) 'Get ready to duck: bouncers and the realities of ethnographic research on violent groups', *British Journal of Criminology*, 41, pp. 536–48

Have you ever watched a sporting event on television and heard the commentator saying what a fantastic atmosphere there is? Yet, at home, you remain outside it. You know there is a fantastic atmosphere, you hear the roar of the crowd, yet you are not part of it. For the people actually in the stadium, the experience of the occasion is quite different. The heat, the closeness of thousands of others, the noise and the emotional highs and lows of the actual event, all combine to give a totally different sense of what is happening.

Some sociologists 'stay at home' to do their research. They may use questionnaires, interviews and surveys to obtain a clear, overall view. On the other hand, there are sociologists who are more interested in experiencing the emotions and sense of actually being there. These sociologists set out to immerse themselves in the lifestyle of the group they wish to study.

Because this form of research is less interested in statistics to prove its point (that is, quantitative research), and more interested in the qualities of social life, it is sometimes known as **qualitative research**. Qualitative approaches are based on the belief that it is not appropriate or possible to measure and categorize the social world accurately – all that is possible is to observe and describe what is happening and offer possible explanations.

The most common form of qualitative research consists of observational studies in which a particular group of people is closely observed and their activities noted. The belief is that, by exploring the lives of people in detail, insights may be gained that can be applied to the understanding of society in general. Observational studies derive from **ethnography**, which is the term used to describe the work of anthropologists who study simple, small-scale societies by living with the (usually tribal) people and observing their daily lives. However, strictly speaking, qualitative research can include a wide variety of other approaches, such as video and audio recording, in-depth interviews, analysis of the internet, or even qualitative analysis of books, magazines and journals.

Types of observation

Observational research is a general term that covers a range of different research techniques. Observational studies vary in two main ways:

1 the extent to which the researcher joins in the activities of the group – the researcher may decide to be a participant or not. The choice is between **non-participant observation** and **participant observation**
2 whether the researcher is honest and tells the group about the research, or prefers to pretend to be one of the group. The choice is between **overt** and **covert** research.

Participant observation

The most common form of observational study is participant observation, where the researcher joins the group being studied.

The advantages of participant observation

- *Experience* – Participant observation allows the researcher to join the group fully and see things through the eyes (and actions) of the people in the group. The researcher is placed in exactly the same situation as the group under study, fully experiencing what is happening. This results in the researcher seeing social life from the same perspective as the group.
- *Generating new ideas* – Often this can lead to completely new insights and generate new theoretical ideas, unlike traditional research, which undertakes the study in order to explore an existing theory or hypothesis.
- *Getting the truth* – One of the problems with questionnaires, and to a lesser extent with interviews, is that the respondent can lie. Participant observation prevents this because the researcher can see the person in action – it may also help them understand why the person would lie in a questionnaire or interview.
- *Digging deep* – Participant observation can create a close bond between the researcher and the group under study, and individuals in the group may be prepared to confide in the researcher on issues and views that would normally remain hidden.

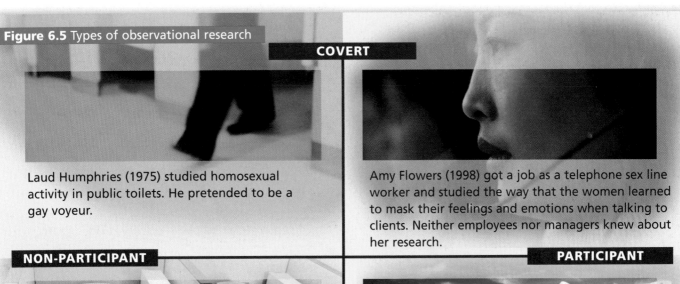

Figure 6.5 Types of observational research

COVERT

Laud Humphries (1975) studied homosexual activity in public toilets. He pretended to be a gay voyeur.

Amy Flowers (1998) got a job as a telephone sex line worker and studied the way that the women learned to mask their feelings and emotions when talking to clients. Neither employees nor managers knew about her research.

NON-PARTICIPANT

Peter Bain and Phil Taylor (2000) studied call centres to research how call centre staff found ways to relieve their frustration at the working conditions through making fun of both clients and managers. They socialized and sat next to workers.

PARTICIPANT

Stephen Lyng (1998) studied 'high risk' groups (sky divers and motorcyclists) to find out why they did it. Lyng never hid the fact he was an academic but joined in all the dangerous activities.

OVERT

- *Dynamic* – Questionnaires and interviews are 'static' – they are only able to gain an understanding of a person's behaviour or attitudes at the precise moment of the interview. Participant observation takes place over a period of time and allows an understanding of how changes in attitudes and behaviour take place.
- *Reaching into difficult areas* – Participant observation is normally used to obtain research information on hard-to-reach groups, such as religious sects and young offenders.

The disadvantages of participant observation

- *Bias* – The main problem lies with bias, as the observer can be drawn into the group and start to see things through their eyes. This may blind the observer to the insights that would otherwise be available.
- *Influence of the researcher* – The presence of the researcher may make the group act less naturally as they are aware of being studied. Of course, this is less likely to happen if the researcher is operating covertly.
- *Ethics* – If the researcher is studying a group engaged in deviant behaviour, then there is a moral issue of how far the researcher should be drawn into the activities of the group – particularly if these activities are immoral or illegal.
- *Proof* – Critics have pointed out that there is no way of knowing objectively whether the findings of participant observation are actually true or not, since there is no possibility of replicating the research. In other words, the results may lack **reliability**.
- *Too specific* – Participant observation is usually used to study small groups of people who are not typical of the wider population. It is therefore difficult to claim that the findings can be **generalized** across the population as a whole.
- *Studying the powerless* – Finally, almost all participant observational studies are concerned with the least powerful groups in society – typically groups of young males or females who engage in deviant activities. Some critics argue that the information obtained does not help us to understand the more important issues in society.

Non-participant observation

Some researchers prefer to withdraw from participation and merely observe.

Advantages of non-participant observation

- *Bias* – As the researcher is less likely to be drawn into the group, they will also be less likely to be biased in their views.
- *Influencing the group* – As the researcher is not making any decisions or joining in activities, the group may be less influenced than in participant observation.

Disadvantages of non-participant observation

- *Superficial* – The whole point of participant observation is to be a member of the group and experience life as the group

experiences it. Merely observing leaves the researcher on the outside and may limit understanding.
- *Altering behaviour* – People may well act differently if they know they are being watched.

Covert and overt methods

Observational research is usually carried out amongst deviant groups or other groups who are unusual in some way, such as religious cults. Usually, these groups will not be very welcoming to a researcher. Before researchers begin their work, therefore, they must decide whether they wish to conduct the research in a covert or overt way.

The advantages of covert research

- *Forbidden fruit* – Researchers can enter forbidden areas, be fully accepted and trusted, and immerse themselves totally in the group to be studied. This can generate a real sense of understanding of the views of the group.
- *Normal behaviour* – The group will continue to act naturally, unaware that they are being studied.

The disadvantages of covert research

- *Danger* – If the researcher's true role is uncovered, they may place themselves in danger.
- *Ethical dilemmas* – First, there is the issue that it is wrong to study a group without telling them. Second, if the group engages in illegal or immoral activities, then the researcher may have to engage in these activities as well. They may then find themselves in possession of knowledge that it may be immoral to withhold from the authorities.

The advantages of overt observation

- *The confidante* – As someone who has no role within the group, the researcher may be in the position of the trusted outsider and receive confidences from group members.
- *Honest* – The researcher is also able to play an open, clear and honest role, which will help minimize ethical dilemmas.
- *Other methods* – Researchers can supplement their observation with other methods, such as interviews and questionnaires.

The disadvantage of overt observation

- *Outsider* – There will be many situations where only a trusted insider will be let into the secrets. Anyone else, even a sympathetic observer, will be excluded.

Doing ethnographic research

The process of doing ethnographic research involves solving some key problems.

Joining the group

Observational studies usually involve groups of people on the margins of society, and the first problem is actually to contact and join the group. The sociologist has to find a place where the group goes and a situation in which they would accept the researcher. Shane Blackman (1997) (see the *Exploring observation* activity on p. 251) studied a group of young homeless people, whom he met at an advice centre for young people. Sometimes sociologists make use of **gatekeepers** – members of the group who help the sociologist become accepted and introduce them to new people and situations. Andy Bennett describes how he gained entry to the local 'hip hop scene' in Newcastle (Bennett 1999):

>> *My route 'into' the local hip hop scene in Newcastle was largely facilitated by a local breakdancer who also worked as an instructor at a community dance project. Through this contact, who essentially acted as a gatekeeper, I gained access to or learned of key figures in the local hip hop scene … and accompanied the gatekeeper and a number of his dance students and other friends to around a dozen weekly hip hop nights held in a bar.*>>

Acceptance by the group

There are often barriers of age, ethnicity and gender to overcome if the group are to accept the researcher. Moore (2004) researched young people 'hanging around'. He was initially unable to gain full acceptance because of his age. He overcame this by using young, female researchers.

Recording information

When researchers are actually hanging around with a group, it is difficult to make notes – particularly if engaged in covert research. Even if the group members are aware of the research, someone constantly making notes would disrupt normal activity and, of course, the researcher would also be unable to pay full attention to what was going on. In participant observational studies, therefore, researchers generally use a **field diary**. This is simply a detailed record of what happened, which the researcher writes up as often as possible. However, the research diary can also be a real weakness of the research.

Research diaries

Ethnographic researchers do not keep regular hours. Their observation may well go on into the night. It can be difficult to write up a diary each evening. Therefore, there is plenty of time to forget things and to distort them. Most observational studies include quotes, yet as it is impossible to remember the exact words, the quotes reflect what the researcher thinks the people said. This may be inaccurate.

Maintaining objectivity

In observational research, it is hard to remain objective. Close contact with the group under study means that feelings almost always emerge. In the introduction to Bourgois' (2003) study of crack cocaine dealers, he comments on how these dealers are his friends and how much he owes to the 'comments, corrections and discussions' provided by one particular dealer.

focus on research

Philippe Bourgois
In Search of Respect: Selling Crack in El Barrio

The biggest-selling research study in the USA in the last 20 years is Philippe Bourgois' study of the life of crack dealers in an impoverished and violent part of New York (East Harlem), known as El Barrio.

Bourgois moved into the area with his wife and young daughter, despite the strongly expressed concerns of their wider family and friends, and continued to live and research there for five years.

Bourgois had close contact with a number of crack dealers and spent a large part of his life in their company during this time – sometimes in very dangerous situations. Bourgois' main problem was that as the only white person in the area, he was often believed to be a policeman and so was at risk of attack.

Bourgois' study revealed that there was a thriving, dangerous, but functioning culture within El Barrio. He argued that street life, drug-dealing and violence in El Barrio were simply responses to the desperate poverty and inequality that these people faced in US society. They were trying to cope as best they could in an unequal society, and actually wanted to belong to mainstream US society, but quite simply had no chance of success in that legitimate world.

Their response was to create a culture of violence and drugs in which the sale and use of drugs, along with prostitution, became the central basis of their economy. The process of buying and selling drugs allowed dealers to make a living and they, in turn, spent the money on a range of goods and services in El Barrio. However, this illegal sale and widespread use of the drugs led to chaotic, violent lifestyles that, ironically, guaranteed their exclusion from the wider society.

1 Is it justifiable for the observer to get involved in dangerous and illegal activities?

2 Is it reasonable for Bourgois to make generalizations about wider society from the one case he has studied?

Influencing the situation

The more involved the researcher is with the people being studied, the greater the chance of influencing what happens. Stephen Lyng (1993) joined a group of males who engaged in 'edgework' – that is, putting their lives at risk through skydiving and (illegal) road motorcycle racing. Lyng became so entangled in this style of life that he actually helped encourage others into life-risking behaviour.

Check your understanding

1 What forms of observational studies are there?

2 What advantages does observational research have over quantitative methods?

3 Identify three problems associated with participant observation.

4 Suggest two examples of research where it would be possible to justify covert observation.

5 Suggest two examples of research situations where observational methods would be appropriate.

6 Suggest two examples of research situations where it might be more appropriate to undertake a survey.

research ideas

- Compare these two pieces of observation:
  - Go to your local library. Spend one hour watching how people behave. Write down as accurate a description as you can.
  - Then spend an evening at home 'observing' your family. Write down as accurate a description of home behaviour that evening as you can.

- Which study is likely to be more biased? Why? Does this make it any less accurate? Are you able to get greater depth studying your family? Why? Do you think it would make a difference if you operated in a covert rather than an overt way with your family?

web.task

Is it possible to do observational studies on the internet? Try observing a chat room or MSN Messenger. What behaviour occurs? Why?

evaluating research Moral issues and bias

In the late 1990's Fleisher spent a year with violent gangs in Kansas City.

Adapted from Fleisher, M.S. (1998) 'Ethnographers, Pimps and the Company Store', in J. Ferrell and M.S. Hamm, *Ethnography at the Edge*, Boston: Northeastern University Press

<< Genuine ethnography, spending six months to a year with informants in natural settings, (creates a sort of 'marriage' between researcher and the researched.) When I commit myself to a neighbourhood and its people, that commitment obtains the right to see things (other researchers never see, ask questions others never ask, get answers others never get.) But that privilege has a dark side. That dark side is the personal damage that seeing kids in pain who inflict pain on others has caused me. I see child abuse and teenage prostitution, drug addiction and drug dealing and (have even heard murder contracts and street-to-prison drug smuggling being arranged over the phone.) For this privilege (I pay a heavy price.)

(My research and my bad dreams are worth it, only if my writing results in a better life for these people. But that's not up to me. >>)

1 Might this close relationship cause problems of bias?

2 This is the big advantage of participant observation – to get detailed information other methods simply couldn't obtain.

3 There are moral problems with this. Should the researcher intervene and tell the police?

4 Ethnographic research can be difficult because of the moral dilemmas and also the exhaustion of living a different type of life.

5 Isn't there a bit of moral 'hand-washing' here? Is it right for sociologists to say the consequences of their research are not their concern?

Covert observation where the sociologist does not admit to being a researcher.

Ethnography describes the work of anthropologists who study simple, small-scale societies by living with the people and observing their daily lives. The term has been used by sociologists to describe modern-day observational studies.

Field diary a detailed record of events, conversations and thoughts kept by participant observers, written up as often as possible.

Generalizability the ability to apply accurately the findings of research into one group to other groups.

Gatekeeper person who can allow a researcher access to an individual, group or event.

Non-participant observation where the sociologist simply observes the group but does not seek to join in their activities.

Participant observational studies where the sociologist joins a group of people and studies their behaviour.

Qualitative research a general term for approaches to research that are less interested in collecting statistical data, and more interested in observing and interpreting the ways in which people behave.

Overt observation where the sociologist is open about the research role.

Reliability refers to the need for research to be strictly comparable (not a great problem with questionnaires and structured/closed-question interviews). This can pose a real problem in observational research, because of the very specific nature of the groups under study and therefore the difficulty of replicating the research.

exploring observation

Item A Youth homelessness in Brighton

In 1992 Shane Blackman spent several months with a group of young homeless people in Brighton.

<< As the study proceeded my research role expanded to also include that of action researcher, drinking partner, friend, colleague and football player. In terms of techniques, I found that the conventional social research interview was an impossibility with the individuals in the study, due to their suspicion of such forms of enquiry. The main research instrument was the field diary.

Where social research focuses on individuals and groups who are on the margins of society, the method through which data is collected is often of a highly intimate nature. The researcher is drawn into the lives of the researched and the fieldworker feels emotions while listening to respondents' accounts of their own lives ...

Ethnographic descriptions are able to convey experience from the perspective of the subject of the research and to develop theories based on feeling. >>

Adapted from Blackman, S. (1997) 'An ethnographic study of youth underclass' in R. McDonald (ed.), *Youth, the Underclass and Social Exclusion*, London: Routledge

Item B Assessing a research design

You have been asked to assess a research design in terms of its reliability, validity, representativeness and generalizability. The research concerns the experiences and activities of young people hanging around a shopping centre in a run-down housing estate.

The research design consists of:

- selecting a city using a quota sampling technique
- analysing the youth and community facilities in the neighbourhood
- appointing two young researchers
- approaching a group of young people who hang around the shops
- hanging around with them for a period of three months through using a covert participant observation technique
- producing a report for the local authority on what needs to be done for local youth.

a Briefly explain the concept of 'covert observation'. (6 marks)

b Using Item A, identify two insights that participant observational research gives compared to other methods. (8 marks)

c Using Item B, identify and explain two strengths of the research design. (16 marks)

d Outline and assess one sociological research method of collecting information about the informal work practices of the people employed by a fast-food chain. (30 marks)

Asking questions: questionnaires and interviews

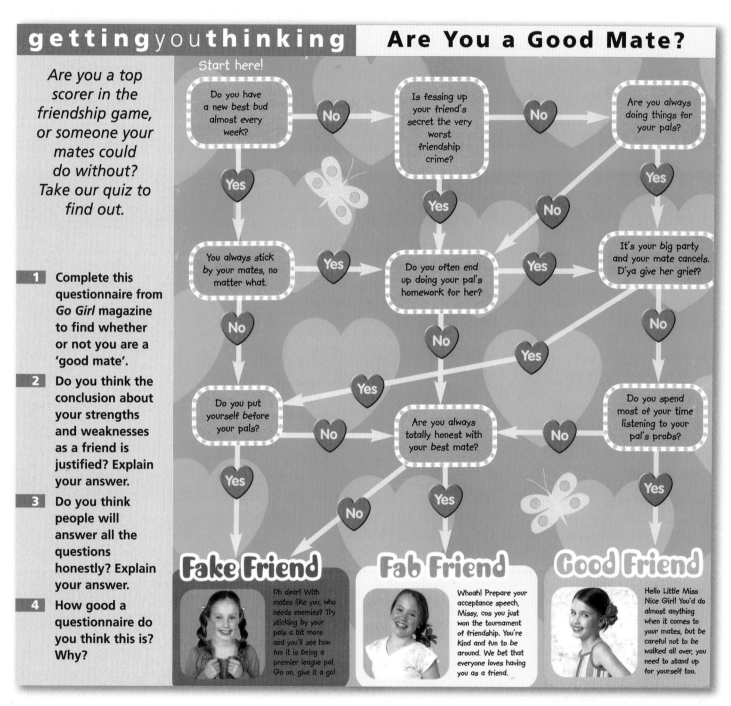

gettingyou**thinking** — **Are You a Good Mate?**

Are you a top scorer in the friendship game, or someone your mates could do without? Take our quiz to find out.

1 Complete this questionnaire from *Go Girl* magazine to find whether or not you are a 'good mate'.

2 Do you think the conclusion about your strengths and weaknesses as a friend is justified? Explain your answer.

3 Do you think people will answer all the questions honestly? Explain your answer.

4 How good a questionnaire do you think this is? Why?

Start here!

Do you have a new best bud almost every week? — No → Is fessing up your friend's secret the very worst friendship crime? — No → Are you always doing things for your pals?

You always stick by your mates, no matter what. — Yes → Do you often end up doing your pal's homework for her? — Yes → It's your big party and your mate cancels. D'ya give her grief?

Do you put yourself before your pals? — No → Are you always totally honest with your best mate? — No → Do you spend most of your time listening to your pal's probs?

Fake Friend

Oh dear! With mates like you, who needs enemies? Try sticking by your pals a bit more and you'll see how fun it is being a premier league pal. Go on, give it a go!

Fab Friend

Whoah! Prepare your acceptance speech, Missy, cos you just won the tournament of friendship. You're kind and fun to be around. We bet that everyone loves having you as a friend.

Good Friend

Hello Little Miss Nice Girl! You'd do almost anything when it comes to your mates, but be careful not to be walked all over, you need to stand up for yourself too.

The most obvious way of finding out something is to ask questions. It is not surprising, then, to find that one of the most common methods of research used by sociologists is just to ask people questions about their attitudes and actions.

Sociologists ask questions in two main ways:

1 asking the questions face to face – the interview
2 writing the questions down and handing them to someone to complete – the questionnaire.

Which of the two methods is chosen depends upon which way of asking questions seems to fit the circumstances best – and has the best chance of gaining the information required.

Questionnaires

The essence of a good questionnaire

When constructing a questionnaire, the sociologist has to ensure that:

- it asks the right questions to unearth exactly the information wanted
- the questions are asked in a clear and simple manner that can be understood by the people completing the questionnaire
- it is as short as possible, since people usually cannot be bothered to spend a long time completing questionnaires.

When to use questionnaires

Questionnaires are used for reaching:

- a large number of people, since the forms can just be handed out
- a widely dispersed group of people, as they can simply be mailed out.

Self-completion questionnaires are also less time-consuming for researchers than interviewing, as they do not require the researcher to go and talk to people face to face.

Anonymous questionnaires are also very useful if the researcher wishes to ask embarrassing questions about such things as sexual activities or illegal acts. People are more likely to tell the truth if they can do so anonymously than if they have to face an interviewer.

Types of questionnaires

There are many different types of questionnaire. They vary in the way in which they expect the person to answer the questions set. At one extreme are '**closed**' questionnaires, which have a series of questions with a choice of answers – all the respondent has to do is tick the box next to the most appropriate answer. At the other extreme are '**open**' questionnaires that seek the respondent's opinion by leaving space for their response. Some questionnaires contain a mixture of both open and closed questions.

Issues in undertaking questionnaires

- Unfortunately, many people cannot be bothered to reply to questionnaires – that is, unless there is some benefit to them, such as the chance to win a prize. This is a serious drawback of questionnaires in research.
- A low **response rate** (the proportion of people who reply) makes a survey useless, as you do not know if the small number of replies is representative of all who were sent the questionnaire. Those who reply might have strong opinions on an issue, for example, whereas the majority may have much less firm convictions. Without an adequate number of replies, you will never know.
- It is difficult to go into depth in a questionnaire, because the questions need to be as clear and simple as possible.

- You can never be sure that the correct person answers. If you mail a questionnaire to one member of a household, how do you know that that person answers it?
- You can never be sure that the person who replies to the questionnaire interprets the questions in the way that the researcher intended, so their replies might actually mean something different from what the researcher believes they mean.
- Lying is also a danger. People may simply not tell the truth when answering questionnaires. There is little that the researcher can do, apart from putting in 'check questions' – questions that ask for the same information, but are phrased differently.

Figure 6.6 Types of survey questions

1 Quantity or information
In which year did you enrol on the part-time degree? _____

2 Category
Have you ever been, or are you now, involved almost full-time in domestic duties (i.e. as a housewife/househusband)?
☐ yes (currently)   ☐ yes (in the past)   ☐ never

3 List or multiple choice
Do you view the money spent on your higher education as any of the following?
☐ a luxury   ☐ an investment   ☐ a necessity   ☐ a right
☐ a gamble   ☐ a burden   ☐ none of these

4 Scale
How would you describe your parents' attitude to higher education at that time? Please tick one of the options below:

very positive	positive	mixed/ neutral	very negative	negative	not sure
☐	☐	☐	☐	☐	☐

5 Ranking
What do you see as the main purpose(s) of your degree study? Please rank all those relevant in order from 1 downwards.
☐ personal development   ☐ career advancement
☐ subject interest   ☐ recreation
☐ fulfilling ambition   ☐ keeping stimulated
☐ other (please specify) _____

6 Complex grid or table
How would you rank the benefits of your degree study for each of the following?

for:	very positive	positive	mixed/ neutral	negative	very negative	not sure
you						
your family						
your employer						
the country						
your community						
your friends						

7 Open ended
Please note down any further comments about your degree:

_____

_____

Source: Blaxter, L., Hughes, C. and Tight, M. (1996) *How to Research*, Buckingham: Open University Press, p. 161

Questionnaires and scientific method

Questionnaires – particularly closed questionnaires – are a favourite method used by positivist sociologists (see Topic 2, p. 236), as they can be used in large numbers and the answers can be codified and subjected to statistical tests.

Interviews

An interview can either be a series of questions asked directly by the researcher to the respondent or it can be conducted as a discussion.

When to use interviews

- Sociologists generally use interviews if the subject of enquiry is complex, and a questionnaire would not allow the researcher to probe deeply.
- Interviews are also used when researchers want to compare their observations with the replies given by the respondents, to see if they appear true or not.

Advantages of interviews

- The interviewer can help explain questions to the respondent if necessary.
- Researchers are also sure that they are getting information from the right person.
- They can be organized virtually on the spot and so can be done immediately – as opposed to preparing a questionnaire, finding a sampling frame and posting the questionnaires out.
- There is a much higher response rate with interviews than with questionnaires, as the process is more personal and it is difficult to refuse a researcher when approached politely.

Types of interviews

Interviews fall between two extremes: **structured** and **unstructured**. At their most structured, they can be very tightly organized, with the interviewer simply reading out questions from a prepared questionnaire. At the other extreme they can be unstructured, where the interviewer simply has a basic area for discussion and asks any questions that seem relevant. Interviews that have fall between the two extremes are known as 'semi-structured' interviews.

There are also individual and group interviews. Most people assume that an interview is between just two people, but in sociological research a group of people may get together to discuss an issue, rather than simply giving an answer to a question. Group interviews are commonly used where the researcher wants to explore the dynamics of the group, believing that a 'truer' picture emerges when the group are all together, creating a 'group dynamic'. An example of this is Mairtin Mac an Ghaill's *The Making of Men: Masculinities, sexualities and schooling* (1994), in which a group of gay students discuss their experiences of school.

Issues in undertaking interviews

Influencing the replies

Interviews are a form of conversation between people and, as in any conversation, likes and dislikes emerge. The problem is to ensure that the interviewer does not influence the replies provided by the respondent in any way – known as **interviewer bias**. For example, respondents may want to please the interviewer and so give the replies they think the interviewer wants. Influences that can affect the outcome of the interview include manner of speech, ethnic origin, sex or personal habits.

Lying

There is no reason why people should tell the truth to researchers, and this is particularly true when a sensitive issue is being researched. When questioned about sexual activities or numbers of friends, for example, people may exaggerate in order to impress the interviewer.

Interview reliability

The aim of the research process is to conduct enough interviews for the researcher to be able to make an accurate generalization. However, if interviews are actually different from each other as a result of the interaction, then it is wrong to make generalizations.

Recording the information

Unstructured interviews are generally recorded and usually require **transcribing** (writing up), which is time-consuming. Tizard and Hughes (1991) recorded interviews with students to find out how they went about learning – every hour of interview took 17 hours to transcribe and check! However, writing down the replies at the time is slow and can disrupt the flow of an interview.

Operationalizing concepts

Ideas that are discussed in sociology, such as 'sexual deviance', 'educational failure', or 'ill health', are all pretty vague when you spend a few moments thinking about them. Take educational failure – does this mean not having A levels? Perhaps it means having 'low' grades at GCSE (whatever the concept 'low grades' means)? Or only having one or two GCSEs? You can see that a concept as apparently simple as 'educational failure' is actually capable of having different meanings to different people.

However, concepts such as educational failure or ill health are used all the time in sociological research, so sociologists have had to find a way around this problem when they ask people questions about the concepts. For example, if you were to ask somebody if they 'suffered from ill health', the reply would depend upon the individual definition of ill health and different people might (in fact we know they *do*) use very different definitions of ill health.

In research, we need to use concepts such as sexual deviance, educational failure and ill health, but in a way which is reliable (see p. 230) and valid (see p. 231). By this, we mean that the concepts are accurately measured (valid), and that each time we use them, we are sure that every respondent understands the concept in the same way (reliable).

When concepts are used in research, sociologists say that they are **operationalizing** them. So, if there is a piece of research to find out the levels of ill health amongst retired people, the concept 'ill health' will need to be operationalized. The problem when operationalizing' a concept is how to ensure that it is accurately and reliably measured.

Indicators

The answer is that sociologists use **indicators**. An indicator is something 'concrete' that stands in for the abstract concept, but which people can understand and sociologists can actually measure. Let us return to the example of 'ill health'. It is possible to ask people the following:

- whether they suffer from any specific diseases or any long-term disability
- whether they are receiving any specific medication
- how frequently they have attended a GP surgery or clinic in the last year.

Problems with indicators

An indicator then, is a short cut sociologists use to measure an abstract concept. Unfortunately, short cuts in any academic area of study bring problems. We need to remember **that what is actually being measured are the** *indicators, not the actual concept.* This may not be a problem if the indicators are a perfect reflection of the original concept, but this is rarely the case. Let's go back to ill health. One question used is how often

Questions about sex

A survey by the US National Opinion Research Center (Laumann *et al.* 1995) consisted of detailed questions about sexual behaviour. A sample of just under 3,500 people was used and methods consisted of a mixture of questionnaires, telephone and face-to-face interviews. In order to ensure a very high response rate, the researchers were prepared to pay some people up to $100 to 'bribe' them to reply to the questions.

The study sparked a very personal and heated debate in the *New York Review of Books* in which the sociologist Richard Lewontin heavily criticized the book. His main argument was that people simply lied to the interviewers and, in their replies to the questionnaires, male respondents were either engaged in wishful thinking or were lying to themselves. He points out, for example, that the total number of sexual partners claimed by the males added up to 75 per cent more than claimed by female respondents – he suggests that the numbers should more or less add up to the same totals. Furthermore, he expressed surprise that 45 per cent of males aged between 80 and 84 were still regularly engaging in sexual activity. Finally, he notes that people who belonged to organized religions had very much lower levels of homosexual and lesbian sex than those who were not religious. Lewontin suggests that they were simply 'hypocrites'.

The authors of the study replied that 'we went to great lengths to guarantee the privacy, confidentiality and anonymity of our respondents' answers'.

The issue that the debate raised was whether it is ever possible to get the truth about personal issues by asking people questions – whether through questionnaires or interviews.

1 Do you think that Lewontin's criticisms are correct and that people (males?) will lie about sexual activity?

2 What reasons could you suggest why people might lie?

3 If Lewontin is correct, what implications might this have for sociological research?

4 Can you suggest ways of 'getting around' the problems suggested by Lewontin?

KEY TERMS

Closed questions require a very specific reply, such as 'yes' or 'no'.

Indicator something easily measurable that can stand for a particular concept.

Interviewer bias the influence of the interviewer (e.g. their age, 'race', sex) on the way the respondent replies.

Open questions allow respondents to express themselves fully.

Operationalizing concepts the process of defining concepts in a way which makes them measurable.

Reliability quality achieved when all questionnaires and interviews have been completed consistently. This means that the data

gathered from each can be accurately compared.

Response rate the proportion of the questionnaires returned (could also refer to the number of people who agree to be interviewed).

Structured interview where the questions are delivered in a particular order and no explanation or elaboration of the questions is allowed by the interviewer.

Transcribing the process of writing up interviews that have been recorded.

Unstructured interview where the interviewer is allowed to explain and elaborate on questions.

Validity quality achieved when questions provide an accurate measurement of the concept being investigated.

Parker and his colleagues conducted a longitudinal study into drug use with school students in north west England. Here one respondent recalls the first questionnaire he was given.

<< The first time we had this questionnaire, I thought it was a bit of a laugh. That's my memory of it. I can't remember if I answered it truthfully or not... It had a list of drugs and some of them I'd never heard of, and just the names just cracked me up.>>

Youth quoted in Parker, H., Aldrige, J. and Measham, F. (1998) *Illegal Leisure*, London: Routledge, pp. 46–7

1 These questionnaires were used as part of a longitudinal study. Perhaps people learn about how to answer questionnaires and may change their responses over time. Would this have an impact on validity and reliability?

2 These comments suggest that the respondent did not answer truthfully – so this raises questions over validity. Would an interview have been better?

3 Sociologists often include fictional names of drugs in the list to check if people are answering truthfully. They also ask the same question in different ways. There is the possibility that the researchers thought the students more naïve than they really were and this might have affected the students' view of the research project. Could we safely generalize from this study?

people have visited the GP surgery in the last year. However, this does not necessarily tell us about *levels* of health, it may just tell us that some people tend to visit the GP (whether they need to or not) more than others. Someone might be very ill but refuse to visit a GP. For example, there is considerable evidence that older people visit GPs less often than their medical conditions warrant.

Furthermore, it is not the actual number of visits that could be considered important, but the reasons why they went. A younger person may see a GP for contraceptive advice, while an older person may be concerned about a heart condition.

Coding

Using clear indicators in research allows answers to be *coded* – that is broken down into simple, distinct answers that can be counted. The researchers can simply add up the numbers of people replying to each category of indicator and then make statements such as '82 per cent of people have seen a doctor on their own behalf in 2002' (Department of Health 2003).

Questions and values

Both questionnaires and interviews share the problem of the values of the researcher creeping into the questions asked. Two problems are particularly important – using leading questions and using loaded words.

Leading questions

Researchers write or ask questions that suggest what the appropriate answer is. For example, 'Wouldn't you agree that ...?'

Loaded words and phrases

Researchers use forms of language that either indicate a viewpoint or will generate a particular positive or negative response – for example, 'termination of pregnancy' (a positive view) or 'abortion' (a negative view); 'gay' or 'homosexual'.

Interviews and scientific methods

Interviews are used by all kinds of sociologists. The more structured the interviews, the more likely they are to be used in a quantitative way to produce statistics. The more unstructured the interviews (including group interviews), the more likely they are to be of use to interpretive sociologists.

Issues of validity and reliability

Validity

Questions asked should actually produce the information required. This is a crucial issue in sociological research and is known as the issue of **validity** (i.e. getting at the truth). The type of questions asked in the questionnaire or interview must allow the respondent to give a true and accurate reply.

Reliability

Researchers must ensure not only that the design of the question gets to the truth of the matter, but also that it does so consistently. If the question means different things to different people, or can be interpreted differently, then the research is not reliable. **Reliability**, then, refers to the fact that all completed questionnaires and interviews can be accurately compared.

web.tasks

1 Go to the website of the opinion polling organization Market and Opinion Research International (www.mori.com). Find out how MORI go about asking questions.

2 Search the world wide web for other examples of questionnaires. Assess the strengths and weaknesses of the question design.

Check your understanding

1 What are the three elements of a good questionnaire?

2 Why are response rates so important?

3 In what situations is it better to use self-completion questionnaires rather than interviews?

4 When would it be more appropriate to use open questions? Give an example of an open question.

5 Explain the difference between structured, semi-structured, unstructured and group interviews

6 What do we mean by 'transcribing'?

7 What do we mean when we talk about 'loaded questions' and 'leading questions'? Illustrate your answer with an example of each and show how the problem could be overcome by writing a 'correct' example of the same questions.

exploring questionnaires and interviews

Item A Gaining trust

≪ From my own experience in researching white British and Caribbean people with diabetes, I would argue that there is evidence suggesting that my own Caribbean background was a distinct advantage .... Rapport [a good relationship] with the Caribbeans developed fairly spontaneously ... We traded stories about how we ended up in England, what part of Jamaica or the Caribbean we are from and generally how we coped with the cold weather and lack of sunshine.

... The interviews with the white British sub-sample differed significantly. Initial conversations were polite and were confined to matters relating to the interview ....

Generally, there was no sharing of personal details and the interviewees did not elaborate on the issues of the research in the way that the Caribbean sample had. ≫

Scott, P. (1999) 'Black people's health: ethnic status and research issues' in S. Hod, B. Mayall and S. Oliver, *Critical Issues in Social Research*, Buckingham: Open University Press

Item B Finding out about the experiences of migrants

You have been asked to assess a research design in terms of its reliability, validity, representativeness and generalizability. The research is about the views of newly arrived migrants to Britain about their reception here and the help they have received in obtaining employment and housing.

The research design consists of the following steps:

- selecting a sample of newly arrived migrants living in one part of Britain

- carrying out five-minute unstructured interviews with the sample

- setting up a focus group with the help of a voluntary agency which campaigns for the rights of economic migrants, to discuss the migrants' main concerns.

a Briefly explain the concept of 'interviewer bias'. (6 marks)

b Using Item A, identify two differences in the interviews as a result of different levels of 'trust'. (8 marks)

c Using Item B, identify and explain two weaknesses of the research design. (16 marks)

d Outline and assess one sociological research method of collecting data on the opinions of young women on abortion. (30 marks)

Secondary sources of data

Lucy Moore, in *The Thieves' Opera*, wrote a social history about people living in London in the early to mid 18th century. One chapter is devoted to death by hanging – the penalty for any theft worth more than one shilling (equivalent in value to £10 today). Read the extract on the right and then answer the questions below.

1 List the aspects of 18th-century punishment noted in this extract that you didn't already know.

2 Do you think that the extract is true? How could you prove it?

3 If you wanted to find out more about public executions, what would you do?

4 If we told you that the person who wrote the book from which we took the extract was strongly against capital punishment, would that alter your view at all? (We don't actually know what the author's views are.)

<< According to Bleakely ... when the cart stopped at Tyburn and the hangman began his preparations, Jack held out a pamphlet called *A Narrative of All the Robberies, Escapes etc. of John Sheppard, written by himself* ... He declared that this should be published as his official confession. He agreed to publicize the account of his life in return for an assurance by the publisher that he would arrange his 'rescue', a common practice that involved waiting to collect the near-dead body once it had hung for the mandatory fifteen minutes, and taking it to the doctor who would try to revive it with warm blankets and wine.

Until the automatic drop was introduced in 1760, hanging more often resulted in unconsciousness than death. By tradition, if the first hanging was unsuccessful, a condemned man could go free because his survival was a sign of divine favour.

At last Jack was subdued and obedient. Once the noose was fastened around his neck, the cart moved out from beneath his feet and he was left dangling beneath the gibbet. Because he was so slight, it took several minutes for him to lose consciousness. He did not weigh enough to force his body to drop sharply and thus break his neck. He writhed and twisted on the end of the rope with people in the crowd pulling at his legs hoping to ease his pain by breaking his neck, until finally he grew limp and still.

After the allotted fifteen minutes were up, the hearse ordered by Defoe and Applebee to take Jack away and try to resuscitate him approached the dangling body. The crowd, fearing that the hearse was about to take him off to be dissected for anatomical research, pelted the driver with stones and surged forward to protect the body.

Being dissected was the overriding terror of men condemned to death.

Foremost in the minds of the crowd was the awareness that the dead man might just as easily have been them. They were compelled by a sense of solidarity with the victim as well as traditional religious beliefs in the sanctity of the corpse because of the soul's resurrection on Judgement Day.>>

Moore, L. (1997) *The Thieves' Opera*, Harmondsworth: Penguin

Not all research uses primary sources – that is, observing people in real life, sending out questionnaires or carrying out interviews. Many sociologists prefer to use material collected and published by other people. This material is known as **secondary data**.

Secondary data consist of a very wide range of material collected by organizations and individuals for their own purposes, and include sources as complex as official government statistics at one extreme and as personal as diaries at the other. These data include written material, sound and visual images. Such material can be from the present day or historical data. Finally, and most commonly, secondary sources include the work of sociologists, which is read, analysed and commented on by other sociologists.

Secondary sources are invaluable to sociologists, both on their own and in combination with primary sources. It is unheard of for a researcher not to refer to some secondary sources.

Why sociologists use secondary sources

Some of the main reasons for using secondary sources include:

- The information required already exists as secondary data.
- Historical information is needed, but the main participants are dead or too old to be interviewed.
- The researcher is unable for financial or other reasons to visit places to collect data at first hand.
- The subject of the research concerns illegal activities and it is unsafe for the researcher to collect primary data.
- Data need to be collected about groups who are unwilling to provide accounts of their activities – for instance, extreme religious sects who do not want their activities to be open to study.

Errors and biases

Whenever sociologists use a secondary source, they must be aware that the person who first created the source did so for a specific reason, and this could well create **bias**. A diary, for example, gives a very one-sided view of what happened and is bound to be sympathetic to the writer. Official statistics may have been constructed to shed a good light on the activities of the government – for example, so that they can claim they are 'winning the war against crime'. Even the work of previous sociologists may contain errors and biases.

Types of secondary data

The most common types of secondary data used by sociologists include:

- previous sociological research
- official publications, including statistics and reports

- diaries and letters
- novels and other works of fiction
- oral history and family histories
- the media.

Previous sociological research

Previous studies as a starting point

Whenever sociologists undertake a study, the first thing they do is to carry out a **literature search** – that is, go to the library or the internet and look up every available piece of sociological research on the topic of interest. The sociologist can then see the ways in which the topic has been researched before, the conclusions reached and the theoretical issues thrown up. Armed with this information, the researcher can then construct the new research study to explore a different 'angle' on the problem or simply avoid the mistakes made earlier.

However, there are sometimes methodological errors in published research, as well as possible bias in the research findings. There have been many examples of research that has formed the basis for succeeding work and that only many years later has been found to be faulty. A famous piece of anthropological research that was used for 40 years before it was found to be centrally flawed was Mead's *Coming of Age in Samoa* (1928). Mead made a number of mistakes in her interpretation of the behaviour of the people she was studying, but as no one knew this, many later studies used her (incorrect) findings in their work.

Reinterpreting previous studies

Often sociologists do not want to carry out a new research project, but prefer instead to examine previous research in great detail in order to find a new interpretation of the original research results. Secondary data then provides all the information that is needed.

Official publications

Statistics

Statistics compiled by governments and reputable research organizations are particularly heavily used by sociologists. These statistics often provide far greater scale and detail than a sociologist could manage. It is also much cheaper to work on statistics already collected than repeating the work.

The government will usually produce these statistics over a number of years (for example, the government statistical publication *Social Trends* has been published for 30 years), so comparisons can be made over a long period of time.

However, while these official statistics have many advantages, there are also some pitfalls that researchers have to be aware of. The statistics are collected for administrative reasons and the classifications used may omit crucial information for sociologists. For example, sociologists may be interested in exploring issues of 'race' or gender, but this information might be missing from the official statistics.

Official statistics may be affected by political considerations, such as when they are used to assist the image of the government of the day. They may also reflect a complex process of interaction and negotiation – as is the case with crime statistics – and may well need to be the focus of investigation themselves!

Reports and government inquiries

The civil service and other linked organizations will often produce official reports which investigate important problems or social issues. However, although they draw together much information on these issues, they are constrained by their 'remit', which states the limits of their investigations. The government and other powerful bodies are therefore able to exclude discussion of issues that they do not want to become the centre of public attention. Government discussions on issues related to drugs, for example, are usually carefully controlled so that legalization of drugs is simply not discussed.

Diaries and letters

It is difficult to understand a historical period or important social events if the researcher has no way of interviewing the people involved. Usually, only the official information or media accounts are available. Using such things as letters and diaries helps to provide an insight into how participants in the events felt at the time.

However, problems can occur, as the writers may have distorted views of what happened, or they may well be justifying or glorifying themselves in their accounts. Almost any politician's memoirs prove this.

Novels

Novels can give an insight into the attitudes and behaviour of particular groups, especially if the author is drawn from one of those groups. However, they are fiction and will exaggerate actions and values for the sake of the story. Also, writing books is typically a middle- or upper-class activity, which may limit the insight that can be gained about the particular group featured.

Oral history and family histories

The events to be studied may have taken place some considerable time ago, but there may be older people alive who can recall the events or who themselves were told about them. There may be recordings available of people (now dead) talking of their lives. People often have old cine-film or family photos of events of interest. All of these can be collected and used by the researcher to help understand past events. Of course, the best of all these methods is the interview, with the older person recalling events of long ago (although quite where the line can be drawn between this as secondary research and as a simple interview is rather unclear).

These approaches do all share the usual problems that events may be reinterpreted by older people or by families to throw a positive light on their actions and, of course, to hide any harm they did to others.

What are the advantages and disadvantage of using novels, such as those of Jane Austen, to understand life in the past?

The art(fulness) of letter-writing

1 Although letter-writing is a dying art, e-mails have grown in use and number, as has messaging on the internet. These are a new source of sociological inquiry.

<< Many insights can be gained from the study of letters, yet these materials are only rarely to be found in social science. And in good part this may simply be due to the obvious fact that such letters are increasingly hard to come by – letter-writing appears to be a dying art, and even when letters are sent they are most commonly thrown away rather than stored and collected. Nevertheless, even when such letters are available, social scientists are likely to remain suspicious of their value.

Every letter speaks not just of the writer's world, but also of the writer's perceptions of the recipient. The kind of story told shifts with the person and who will read it. The social scientist then should view a letter as an interactive product, always inquiring into the recipient's role ...>>

Plummer, K. (2001) *Documents of Life*, London: Sage p. 54

2 Quantitative sociologists are particularly suspicious of this sort of research data. They argue that the data fail tests such as representativeness, validity, generalizability and reliability!

3 Supporters of this qualitative approach argue that these insights can make up for all the weaknesses claimed by quantitative sociologists.

4 Sociologists who take the interpretive (or bottom-up perspectives, see p. 236) are most likely to use this form of research.

The media and content analysis

A huge amount of material is available from newspapers, the internet, magazines and television. This material is extremely useful for sociologists in their research, both as background material for other forms of research or as a focus of research itself. The importance of the media and their influence on our ways of thinking and acting has become one of the biggest areas of study within sociology in the last 20 years.

When sociologists study the contents of the media, it is known as '**content analysis**'. The process usually involves a researcher choosing a particular area of sociological interest, for example racism or the reporting of crime, and then searching through the chosen medium (newspapers or television, or both) and extracting all the relevant reports or programmes on these areas. This might be done, for example, using a search engine on the internet. The researcher then narrows down the search to the specific issues they are interested in. This is a very complex business and is usually done these days by using specially created software, such as NUmist, which searches for particular words or phrases.

One of the main problems of using the mass media as secondary data lies with the selection of material – on exactly what grounds are items included or excluded? Researchers have to be very careful to include all relevant material and not to be biased in their selection in order to 'prove' their point.

The Glasgow University Media Group's publications have explored a range of topics including television news, representations of mental illness in the media and the portrayal of the 1991 Iraq war; critics claim that they were selective in their choice of material and that they applied their own interpretations to the selections.

However, trying to understand and interpret accurately the printed and broadcast media is not just a matter of watching out for bias; there is also the issue of how to *interpret* the material. When we look at pictures or read a story in a magazine, different people find different meanings in the material. There are many factors influencing this, but one crucial factor is our own beliefs and attitudes towards the subject that we are reading about. The importance of this for research using secondary data is that we must not assume that what we read or see is the same as it was for the original readers or viewers.

Research based on secondary data discovered that differences in health between ethnic groups are closely linked to social class and income

George Davey Smith *et al.*

The health of ethnic minorities: a meta-study

George Davey Smith and his colleagues were concerned that there was relatively little information on the health of ethnic minorities in Great Britain. They therefore conducted a **meta-study** to try to provide an overall picture of health care. They looked at data from a range of surveys including official publications, small-scale surveys and earlier sociological studies. Putting all of this together, they provided a picture of standards of health for different ethnic groups in Britain, taking into account the impact of social class. In order to do this, they also had to review a wide range of theoretical and methodological books and articles. The study therefore includes secondary research, which is based upon both theoretical and statistical studies, from government as well as academic sources.

They found that, overall, the health standards of ethnic minorities in Britain were worse than those of the general population, and that these differences were most apparent in childhood and old age. They found that most previous studies tended to explain any differences in health between ethnic minorities and the majority population in terms of cultural, dietary or genetic differences. However, they concluded that ethnicity by itself does not explain these differences. They suggest instead that differences in health are closely linked to social class and income.

Davey Smith, G., Chaturverdi, N., Harding, S., Nazroo, J. and Williams, R. (2003) *Health Inequalities: Lifecourse approaches*, Bristol: Policy Press

1 Why did the researchers use a meta-study?

2 How did the use of secondary sources allow them to reach different conclusions from earlier research?

Check your understanding

1 What are secondary data?

2 Why do sociologists use secondary sources?

3 What are the disadvantages of using secondary sources?

4 What are the advantages and disadvantages of using official statistics and other government documents?

5 What are the advantages and disadvantages of using qualitative secondary data such as diaries?

web.task

1 Go to the government's National Statistics website (www.statistics.gov.uk) Find one set of statistics that you think is likely to be accurate and one set that you think is less likely to be accurate. What are they? Why should different official statistics be more or less accurate?

2 Find the website 'Corporate Watch' (www.corporatewatch.org.uk). Look up information about any two huge corporations (for example, Microsoft or Disney). Then go to the websites belonging to those corporations. What are the differences between the information given? Which do you think is more accurate? Why?

researchideas

● Watch *Eastenders*, *Coronation Street*, *Hollyoaks* or another 'soap' of your choosing. If sociologists were to watch this soap 50 years in the future, how accurate a picture of life today do you think it would give?

● Collect postcards sent to you, your friends and family. Look at their contents. Is there a pattern? Are they all positive? What sort of representation do postcards give of holidays? How accurate are they in representing holidays?

Bias where the material reflects a particular viewpoint to the exclusion of others. This may give a false impression of what happened. This is a particularly important problem for secondary sources.

Content analysis exploring the contents of the various media in order to find out how a particular issue is presented.

Literature search the process whereby a researcher finds as much published material as possible on the subject of interest. Usually done through library catalogues or the internet.

Meta-study a secondary analysis using all or most of the published information on a particular topic

Secondary data data already collected by someone else for their own purposes.

exploring secondary sources of data

Item A   Teachers' resignations

Destinations of teachers resigning from primary schools

Destination	% of full-time permanent teachers 2003
Supply teaching	5.1
Teaching abroad	5.9
Maternity	14.1
Family care	2.0
Travel	3.2
Early retirement	10.8
Redundancy	0.8
Normal age retirement	4.1

Note: Figures do not add up to 100% as full-table contents not included

Source: Smithers, A. and Robinson, P. (2004) *Teacher Turnover, Wastage and Destinations*, Department for Education and Skills, Research Report 553

Item B   Changing attitudes in the UK

You have been asked to assess a research design in terms of its reliability, validity, representativeness and generalizability. The research is about the changing attitudes to old age in the UK since 1800.

The research design consists of the following steps:

- a literature search to see what was written about old people in novels and other books since 1800
- obtaining a representative selection of diaries of people living since 1800 to find out what they wrote about old age
- searching out any previous research which has been undertaken on the subject
- conducting a search of newspaper archives since 1800, looking for articles on old age
- undertaking a survey of a sample of the population today to ask their views.

a Briefly explain the concept of 'content analysis'. (6 marks)

b Using Item A, identify the two most common reasons for primary-school teachers to leave teaching. (8 marks)

c Using Item B, identify and explain two weaknesses of the research design. (16 marks)

d Outline and assess one sociological research method of collecting information about the changing role of women in society. (30 marks)

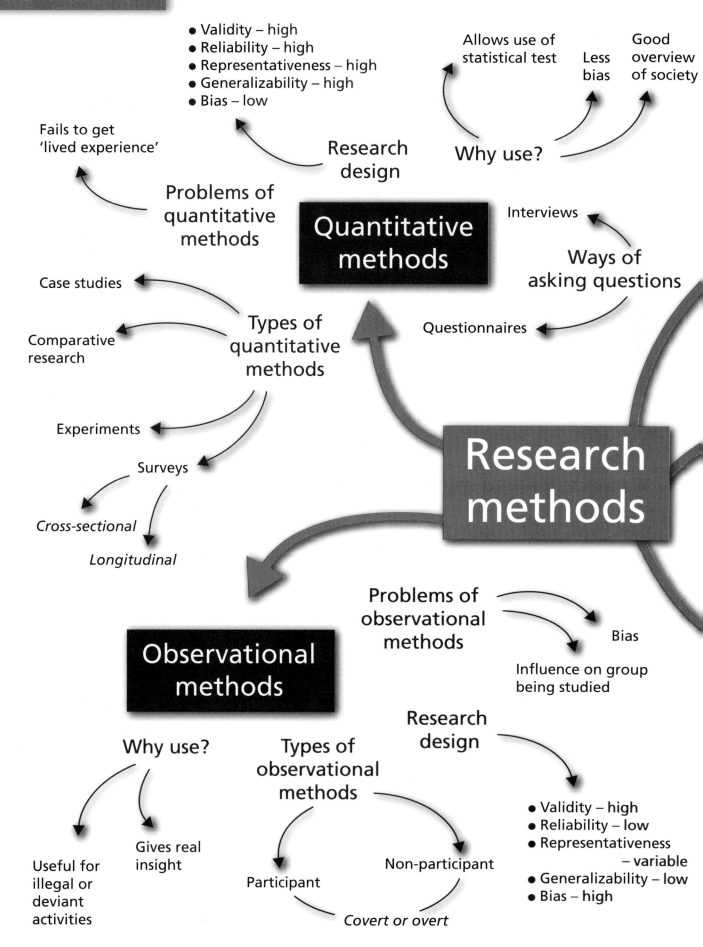

Good where
'primary methods'
not possible

Allows historical
research

Inaccuracy or bias
in original source

Censorship

Previous research

Official
publications

Why use?   Problems

Types of
secondary
data

Diaries
and letters

Secondary data

Research
design

- Validity – variable
- Reliability – variable
- Representativeness – variable
- Generalizability – variable
- Bias – variable

All depend on the original source

Novels
and fiction

Oral and
family history

The media

Research design

Validity

Reliability

Does it measure
what it is supposed to?

Generalizability   Representativeness

Bias

Are research sessions
comparable with each other?

Are researchers'
own values
interefering?

Are people selected
representative of group?

Are findings true
for wider society?

Theoretical and ethical issues

How theoretical
issues influence
research

Suggest one research area
rather than another

Influence research
method chosen

Influence
interpretation
of research
findings

How ethical issues
influence research

Influence choice
of research topic

Raise issue of whether
researcher may act
immorally/illegally
during research

Influence who is
chosen to be
researched

Ask researcher to
consider the effects
of the research

YES – YOU'VE ENJOYED STUDYING AS-LEVEL SOCIOLOGY. Yes – the issues you've covered have been interesting. Yes – you've learned a lot about society today. Yes – you feel more confident in discussions about social issues. But in the end, you know that your feelings about the course will probably depend on how well you get on in the exam board assessments that measure the standard of your work.

Your performance in the OCR AS-level course will be judged either totally by exams or through a combination of exams and coursework. Either way, you need to be completely confident about the organization of the exams: how long they last, how the questions are phrased and what knowledge and skills are being tested. You also need to be aware of the nature of the coursework task, how it is broken down and how marks are allocated.

This unit guides you through both OCR exams and OCR coursework. It provides essential information about the content and assessment of the course, including some really useful tips for both exams and coursework. After working through this unit, you should feel a lot more confident about the way your performance will be judged and be in a good position to get full value for all the work you've put in to your AS-level Sociology course.

Preparing for the AS exam

TOPIC 1 Preparing for the OCR AS-level exam **268**

Preparing for the OCR AS-level exam

What will I study?

Aims of the course

The OCR A-level specification aims to offer you an introduction to sociology, regardless of whether you are only interested in gaining the AS award or aiming for the full A-level. In particular, it aims to help you develop a knowledge and understanding of social processes, structures and theories which are both contemporary and relevant to your life. The AS course will help you to gain a critical understanding of the society in which you live. You are positively encouraged by this specification to reflect on your social identity and experience of the social world and to apply your knowledge and understanding of sociology to everyday life. The focus of this specification is on contemporary UK society. Your experience of this specification should equip you with the necessary skills to engage in sociological debate and to be able to interpret, apply and evaluate relevant evidence and to construct convincing sociological arguments.

Finally, this specification is designed to offer you choice and flexibility in terms of its content, its varied assessment system and its coursework options.

Themes of the course

The AS specification has three interlinked themes:

- examining how and to what extent individuals shape, and are shaped by, social structures – this underpins the entire specification and offers progression to the other AS units and to A2
- exploring the agencies that make up the cultural institutions of our society and especially those with which we have daily contact – a good deal of the sociology explored looks at how we are socialized into our identities and culture by such agencies
- examining how sociologists collect information about the social world and whether their views are truthful and worthwhile.

Modules

There are three modules at AS level:

- Module 2532 : The individual and society
- Module 2533 : Culture and socialization
- Module 2534 : Sociological research skills **or** Module 2535: Research report (sociology).

Topics

- The *individual and society* module involves a basic introduction to sociological theories aimed at understanding human behaviour, an examination of how culture is formed, the role of primary and secondary agents of socialization in the formation of identity, and debates about changing gender, ethnic, class and national identities.
- The *culture and socialization* module covers the family, mass media, religion, and youth and culture.
- The *sociological research skills* module involves basic concepts in research design such as reliability and validity, sampling, primary research methods, secondary data, and interpreting and evaluating different types of data.

How will I be assessed?

Skills

For AS-level sociology, you will be tested by the following assessment objectives.

Assessment objective 1 (AO1): Knowledge and understanding

After studying this specification, you should be able to demonstrate knowledge and understanding of sociological theories, methods, concepts and different types of evidence, how these are interlinked and how they relate to both social life and social problems. It is important to stress that you are not expected or required to have an advanced understanding of sociological theory. Rather, at this level, you should be 'conceptually confident', meaning that you will have to demonstrate that you understand important concepts and are able to apply these when constructing a sociological argument. It is also a good idea to know some sociological studies because these often count as evidence in support of a particular view.

Assessment objective 2 (AO2): Identification, interpretation and analysis, and evaluation

(a) **Interpretation and analysis**

This skill essentially involves showing the ability to select and analyse different types of evidence and data. In particular, it involves the ability to apply and link sociological evidence to specific sociological arguments. It also involves the ability to interpret quantitative and qualitative data, i.e. to work out what it is saying and/or put it into your own words.

(b) **Evaluation**

It is important to be able to evaluate specific sociological arguments. This normally involves assessing the available evidence or critically examining the methods used to collect that evidence.

Exams

See Table 7.1 below for details of the exam papers you will need to sit.

Coursework

Unit 2535 Research report is offered as an alternative to the written examination in Unit 2534 and represents 30 per cent of the AS level and 15 per cent of the full A level.

How can I do well in the written exams?

Timing

It is important that you use your time effectively in exams. All of the examined units at AS follow a 'mark a minute' rule. This means that where a paper is marked out of 60, you will have 60 minutes in which to complete it. Where a paper is marked out of 90, you will have 1 hour and 30 minutes (90 minutes) to complete it. This should help you in working out the timing for each subsection of the exam paper.

The individual and society

The examination lasts one hour. The data-response question is divided into four parts worth 60 marks in all. Ensure that you have studied the Item carefully. Questions (a) and (b) are worth 8 marks each and you are recommended to spend approximately 15 minutes in total on these two parts. Question (c) is worth 18 marks and you should spend approximately 18 minutes on this. Aim for about a page of writing. Finally, part (d) is worth 26 marks. Spend about 25 minutes on this – your response should aim for one to two sides of writing.

Table 7.1 Units of assessment

Unit code	Title	Exam	% of AS-level	% of full A-level
Unit 2532	**The individual and society**	You answer one from two four-part, structured questions in 1 hour	30	15
Unit 2533	**Culture and socialization**	You answer two two-part structured essay questions, chosen from the same or different options in 1 hour 30 minutes	40	20
Unit 2534	**Sociological research skills**	You answer one compulsory data-response question in 1 hour	30	15

Culture and socialization

You have to answer two questions in one hour and 30 minutes. These are organized into two parts: part (a) is worth 15 marks and part (b) is worth 30 marks. You should aim to spend about 15 minutes on the former and 30 minutes on the latter. Aim for about a half to two thirds of a side for part (a) and about two sides or more for part (b).

Sociological research skills

The examination lasts an hour and is a data-response, organized into four questions and worth 60 marks in all. It is recommended that you spend 30 minutes on parts (a), (b), and (c), and 30 minutes on part (d). Spend no longer than 5 minutes on part (a) – a short paragraph will be enough. Spend approximately 8 minutes on part (b) and 15 minutes on part (c). The last half of your time should be spend answering part (d), as this is worth 30 marks.

Style of questioning

OCR has decided to use the same action or trigger words and phrases for every examination session, so that you can respond in the most effective fashion to the question set.

The individual and society

- Question (a) will always be geared to asking about the data in the Item. This data may take a number of forms. It may be pictorial (e.g. a magazine cover, newspaper headline, cartoon), numerical (e.g. in the form of statistical tables, graphs or charts) or textual (e.g. an extract from a textbook). The trigger words are likely to be 'Identify and briefly explain two...' and these will be accompanied by an instruction to use the data.
- Question (b) also uses the trigger phrase 'Identify and briefly explain two...' and is likely to ask for two ways or examples.
- Question (c) will normally ask you to 'Outline and briefly evaluate ...' two ways that something happens. Note that the word outline means explain or describe.
- Question (d) will always begin 'Discuss the view that...' and most probably focus on a particular view (e.g. 'Discuss the view that gender identities have become confused in the 21st century'). You should be aware of two things when answering a question like this. First, you don't have to accept the view in the question. You can question it, but you should outline it before you do. Second, discuss implies both sides of an argument. In other words, it has an evaluative component because it should involve looking at both the strengths and weaknesses of the view.

Culture and socialization

- Part (a) of these questions will always ask you to 'Identify and explain' two ways or examples or aspects of a

sociological problem or issue. Part (b) will always begin 'Outline and discuss the view...' (see the discussion above).

Sociological research skills

- Question (a) will always ask you to define, in your own words, a sociological concept related to research design and is likely to use the action words, 'briefly explain'.
- Question (b) will always ask you to 'Identify two main differences/trends/patterns, etc.', from the data presented in Item A. You should carefully analyse the data to ensure that the findings which you are quoting are the main ones.
- Question (c) will ask you to 'Identify and explain' one strength and one weakness (or two strengths or two weaknesses) of the research design in Item B. To attain full marks on this question, you must use key research concepts when explaining the strength/weakness, and you need to address the specific context of the research given in Item B.
- Question (d) will always ask you to 'Outline and assess one sociological research method of collecting information about...' a specific sociological problem or issue. You must explain clearly and in detail what your chosen method is and how it relates to the given context. You also need to explain some aspects of the wider research process. The strengths and weaknesses of your chosen method must be discussed with specific reference to the basic concepts of research design.

The 'Exam tips' below will help you when it comes to sitting the exam.

Exam tips

- Do read the instructions on the front of the examination paper. Too many candidates waste time or throw away marks because they have answered too many questions or not enough, or they've answered from the wrong sections.

- Plan your response to any question worth over 20 marks.

- Try to avoid writing down all you know about a particular topic, regardless of the question asked. Think about how what you do know relates to the question set. Be prepared to think on your feet.

- Don't fall into the trap of mistaking your own opinion for sociology. Always support what you say with evidence.

- A coherent, logical presentation of argument and evidence is necessary to achieve a good A-level standard.

How do I do well in coursework?

Requirements

The Research Report requires you to choose and report on a short piece of sociological research (1000 words maximum). The research could be a well-known sociological study or a piece of research taken from the magazine, *Sociology Review*. You should aim to complete:

1 Section A: details of the research on which you are reporting
2 Section B: Outline of research objectives and design (210 to 300 words)
3 Section C: Reasons for selection of methodology (250 to 300 words)
4 Section D: Outline and evaluation of research findings (350 to 400 words).

What will the A2 course be like?

Modules and topics

If you decide to continue into A2, you can expect to study the following modules:

● Module 2536: power and control – this includes six topic areas: crime and deviance; education; health; protest and social movements; popular culture; and social policy and welfare
● Module 2537: applied sociological research skills.

Synoptic assessment

Unit 2539 is the synoptic unit, social inequality and difference. This involves looking at inequalities relating to social class, gender and ethnic minorities. Synoptic means being assessed on how well you understand the links between social inequality, sociological theory and research methods. You would also be expected to know how social inequality impacts on other units studied throughout AS and A2.

Coursework

OCR offers students the option of a personal study at A2. This is an extended piece of work (2500 words) on a sociological topic chosen by the candidate that involves practical research and the analysis of any primary and/or secondary data.

Ten coursework tips

1 Choose a study you can understand.

2 Choose a study that is relevant to one of the other topics you are studying – then it will be useful to you in the exam.

3 Make sure the study you choose includes enough information about its methods.

4 If you use a summary of a study, make sure the summary contains enough detail for you to write 1000 words of your own.

5 Make sure you use key concepts, such as quantitative, qualitative, sampling, reliability, validity and representativeness.

6 Stick to the word limit. If you exceed it, you will lose marks.

7 Wordprocess your research report – that makes it easier to improve, as you don't have to write it all out again.

8 If you do wordprocess your coursework, save it regularly and keep up-to-date back-up copies.

9 Be careful not to copy sentences straight out of the study – this is called 'plagiarism' and can have very serious consequences for you as it is a form of cheating.

10 Don't leave the research report until the last minute – the quality of your work will suffer and there will be less opportunity for feedback from your supervisor

Further information

This unit has, we hope, given you a good overview of how the course is assessed and how to approach the exam and coursework requirements. For up-to-date, definitive guidance on the latest OCR requirements, make sure you check the OCR website – **www.ocr.org.uk** – or ask your school or college for further information.

REFERENCES

Abercrombie, N., Ward, A., Soothill, K., Urry, J. and Walby, S. (2000) *Contemporary British Society* (3rd edition), Cambridge: Polity Press.

Abrams, M. (1959) *The Teenage Consumer*, London: Routledge & Kegan Paul

Ahmed, L. (1992) *Women and Gender in Islam: Historical Roots of a Modern Debate*, New Haven and London: Yale University Press

Ali, S. (2002) 'Interethnic Families', *Sociology Review*, 12(1)

Allan, G. (1985) *Family Life: Domestic Roles and Social Organization*, London: Blackwell

Althusser, L. (1971) 'Ideology and ideological state apparatuses', in *Lenin and Philosophy and Other Essays*, London: New Left Books

Anderson, C.A. and Dill, K.E. (2000) 'Video games and aggressive thoughts, feelings, and behavior in the laboratory and in life', *Journal of Personality and Social Psychology*, 78(4), pp. 772–90

Anderson, M. (1971) 'Family, household and the Industrial Revolution', in M. Anderson (ed.) *The Sociology of the Family*, Harmondsworth: Penguin

Anwar, M. (1981) *Between Two Cultures: A study of relationships between generations in the Asian community*, London: CRE

Aries, P. (1962) *Centuries of Childhood*, London: Random House

Armstrong, K. (1993) *The End of Silence: Women and the Priesthood*, London: Fourth Estate

Arnot, M., David, D. and Weiner, G. (1999) *Closing the Gender Gap*, Cambridge: Polity Press

Badawi, L. (1994) 'Islam' in J. Holm, and J. Bowker (eds) (1994) *Women in Religion*, London: Pinter

Bagdikian, B. (2000) *The Media Monopoly* (6th edn), Boston: Beacon Press

Bagdikian, B. (2004) *The New Media Monopoly*, Boston: Beacon Press

Bain. P. and Taylor, P. (2000) 'Entrapped by the "electronic panopticon"? Worker resistance in the call centre', *New Technology, Work and Employment*, 15(1)

Ball, S. (1981) *Beachside Comprehensive: a case study of secondary schooling*, Cambridge: Cambridge University Press

Bandura, A., Ross, D. and Ross, S.A. (1963) 'The imitation of film mediated aggressive models', *Journal of Abnormal and Social Psychology*, 66(1), pp. 3–11

Barker, E. (1984) *The Making of a Moonie*, Oxford: Blackwell

Barrett, M. and McIntosh, M. (1982) *The Anti-social Family*, London: Verso

Bauman, Z. (1990) *Thinking Sociologically*, Oxford: Blackwell

Bauman, Z. (1992) *Intimations of Postmodernity*, London: Routledge

Bauman, Z. (1993) *Postmodern Ethics*, Blackwell: Oxford

Bauman, Z. (1997) *Postmodernity and Its Discontents*, Cambridge: Polity Press

Beck, U. (1992) *Risk Society: Towards a new modernity*, London: Sage

Beck, U. and Beck-Gernsheim, E. (1995) *The Normal Chaos of Love*, Cambridge: Polity Press

Becker, H. (1950) *Through Values to Social Interpretation: Essays on Social Contexts, Actions, Types and Prospects*, California: Duke University Press

Becker, H. (1963) *Outsiders: Studies in the Sociology of Deviance*, London: Macmillan

Bell, N.W. and Vogel, E.F. (1968) *A Modern Introduction to the Family*, New York: the Free Press

Bellah, R. (1970) 'Civil religion in America' in *Beyond Belief: Essays in Religion in a Post-traditional World'*, New York: Harper & Row

Bennett, A. (1999) 'Rappin' on the Tyne: White hip hop culture in Northeast England – an ethnographic study', *Sociological Review*, 47(1), pp. 1–24

Bennett, T. and Holloway, K. (2004) 'Gang membership, drugs and crime in the UK', *British Journal of Criminology* 44(3), pp. 305–23

Benston, M. (1972) 'The political economy of women's liberation', in N. Glazer-Malbin and H.Y. Waehrer (eds) *Women in a Man-Made World*, Chicago: Rand McNally

Berger, A.L. (1997) *Children of Job: American Second Generation Witnesses to the Holocaust*, New York: New York State University Press

Berger, P. (1967) *The Sacred Canopy: Elements of a Sociological Theory of Religion*, New York: Anchor Books

Berger, P. (1973) *The Social Reality of Religion*, Harmondsworth: Penguin

Bernard, J. (1982, originally 1972) *The Future of Marriage*, Yale: Yale University Press

Bernstein, B. (1961) 'Social class and linguistic development : a theory of social learning', in A.H. Halsey, J. Floud and C.A. Anderson (eds), *Education, Economy and Society: a reader in the sociology of education*, New York: Collier-Macmillan

Bernstein, B. (1964) 'Elaborated and restricted codes: their social origins and some consequences', in J.J. Gumperz and D. Hymes (eds) *Ethnography of Communication*, American Anthropological Association

Bernstein, B. (1966) 'Elaborated and restricted codes: an outline', *Sociological Inquiry*, 36, pp. 254–61

Berthoud, R. (2000) 'Family formation in multi-cultural Britain: three patterns of diversity', *Working Paper of the Institute for Social and Economic Research*, Colchester: University of Essex

Berthoud, R. (2003) Lecture at ATSS Conference 2004, based on research conducted in 2003

Berthoud, R. and Gershuny, J. (2000) *Seven Years in the Lives of British Families: Evidence on the dynamics of social change from the British Household Panel Survey*, Bristol: The Policy Press

Billig, M. (1992) *Talking of the Royal Family*, London: Routledge

Billington, R., Hockey, J. and Strawbridge, S. (1998) *Exploring Self and Society*, Basingstoke: Macmillan

Bird, J. (1999) *Investigating Religion*, London: HarperCollins

Blumler, J.G. and McQuail, D. (1968) *Television in Politics: Its Uses and Influence*, London: Faber & Faber

Bourdieu, P. and Passeron, J. (1977) *Reproduction in Education, Society and Culture*, London: Sage

Bourgois, P. (2003) *In Search of Respect* (2nd edn), Cambridge: Cambridge University Press

Box, S. (1981) *Deviance, Reality and Society* (2nd edn), Eastbourne: Holt Rheinhart Wilson

Brake, M. (1984) *The Sociology of Youth and Youth Subcultures*, London: Routledge

Brannen, J. (2003) 'The age of beanpole families', *Sociology Review*, September 2003

Brierley, P. (2000) *Religious Trends 2000*, London: HarperCollins

Brierley, P. (ed.) (1979, 1989, 1999, 2001) *Christian Research Association, UK Christian Handbook, Religious Trends* 1979, 1989, 1999, 2001, London: HarperCollins

British Film Institute (2001) *The Stats*, British Film Institute

Broadcasters' Audience Research Board (2204) *see* www.barb.co.uk

Brooks, D. (2001) 'The next ruling class: meet the organization kid', *The Atlantic Monthly*, April

Brown, C. (1979) *Understanding Society*, Harlow: Longman

Brown, P. (1987) *Schooling Ordinary Kids: Inequality, unemployment and the new vocationalism*, London: Tavistock

Bruce, S. (1995) *Religion in Modern Britain*, Oxford: Oxford University Press

Bruce, S. (1996) *Religion in the Modern World: From cathedrals to cults*, Oxford: Oxford University Press

Bruce, S. (2001) 'The social process of secularisation' in R.K. Fenn *The Blackwell Companion to Sociology of Religion*, Oxford: Blackwell

Bruce, S. (2002) *God is Dead*, Oxford: Blackwell

Buckingham, D. (ed.) (1993) *Reading Audiences: Young People and the Media*, Manchester: Manchester University Press

Bullock, K. and Tilley, N. (2002) *Shootings, Gangs and Violent Incidents in Manchester*, London: Home

Burghes, L. (1997) *Fathers and Fatherhood in Britain*, London: Policy Studies Institute

Burghes, L. and Brown, M. (1995) *Single Lone Mothers: Problems, prospects and policies*, York: Family Policy Studies Centre with the support of the Joseph Rowntree Foundation

Butler, C. (1995) 'Religion and gender: young Muslim women in Britain', *Sociology Review*, 4(3)

Campbell, A. (1984) *The Girls in the Gang*, Oxford: Blackwell

Campbell, A. and Muncer, S. (1989) 'Them and Us: a comparison of the cultural context of American gangs and British subcultures', *Deviant Behavior*, 10, pp. 271–88

Campbell, B. (2000) *The Independent*, 20 November 2000

Caplan, L. (ed.) (1987) *Studies in Religious Fundamentalism*, London: Macmillan

Cashmore, E. (1997) *The Black Culture Industry*, London: Routledge

Chamberlain, M. and Goulbourne, H. (1999) *Caribbean Families in Britain and the Trans-Atlantic World*, Basingstoke: Macmillan

Chapman, S. (2001) 'Toffs and snobs: upper class identity in Britain', *Sociology Review*, 11(1)

Chapman, S. (2003) 'Nobody loves the middle class', *Sociology Review*, 12(3)

Charlesworth, S. (1999) *A Phenomenology of Working Class Experience*, Cambridge: Cambridge University Press

Charlton, T., Gunter, B. and Hannan, A. (2000) *Broadcast Television Effects in a Remote Community*, Hillsdale, NJ: Lawrence Erlbaum

Chatterton, P. and Hollands, R.G. (2001) *Changing Our 'Toon': Youth, nightlife and urban change in Newcastle*, Newcastle: University of Newcastle

Cloward, R. and Ohlin, L. (1960) *Delinquency and Opportunity*, London: Collier Macmillan

Cohen, A. (1955) *Delinquent Boys*, New York: The Free Press

Cohen, P. (1972) 'Subcultural conflict and working-class community', *Working Papers in Cultural Studies* 2, University of Birmingham: Centre for Contemporary Cultural Studies

Cohen, R. and Kennedy, P. (2000) *Global Sociology*, Basingstoke: Macmillan

Cohen, S. (1972) *Folk Devils and Moral Panics*, London: McKibbon & Kee

Coleman, J.C. (1980) *The Nature of Adolescence*, London: Methuen

Collison, M. (1996) 'In search of the high life: drugs, crime, masculinities and consumption', *British Journal of Criminology*

Connect Research (2003) *Connecting with Black and Asian Viewers*, Connect Research

Connell, R.W. (1995) *Masculinities*, Cambridge: Polity Press

Connolly, P. (1998) *Racism, Gender Identities and Young Children*, London: Routledge

Cooper, D. (1972) *The Death of the Family*, Harmondsworth: Penguin

Coté, J. and Allahar, A.L. (1996) *Generation on Hold: Coming of age in the late twentieth century*, London: New York University Press

Cumberbatch, G. (2004) *Video Violence: Villain or Victim?* Report for the Video Standards Council available at www.videostandards.org.uk/video_violence.htm

Curtice, J. and Heath, A. (2000) 'Is the English Lion about to roar? National Identity after devolution', in R. Jowell (eds) *British Social Attitudes, the 17th Report: Focusing on Diversity*, London: Sage

Daly, M. (1973) *Beyond God the Father*, Boston, MA: Beacon Press

Daly, M. (1978) *Gyn/Ecology: The Metaethics of Radical Feminism*, Boston, MA: Beacon Press

Davidman, L. (1991) *Religion in a Rootless World: Women turn to Orthodox Judaism*, Berkeley: University of California Press

Davidson, L. (2003) 'Men's advice line' quoted in I. Luckhurst, 'Violence in families: male victims', *Sociology Review*, 13(1)

Davie, G. (1994) *Religion in Britain 1945–1990, Believing Without Belonging*, Oxford: Blackwell

Davie, G. (1995) 'Competing fundamentalisms', *Sociology Review*, 4(4), Oxford: Philip Allan

Davis, M. (1990) *City of Quartz*, London: Verso

De Beauvoir, S. (1953) *The Second Sex*, London: Jonathan Cape

De'Ath, E. and Slater, D. (eds) (1992) *Parenting Threads: Caring for children when couples part*, Stepfamily Publications

Decker, S. (2001) 'The impact of organizational features on gangs activities and relationships', in M.W. Klein, H.J. Kerner, C.L. Maxson and E.G.M. Weitekamp (eds) *The Eurogang Paradox: Street Gangs and Youth Groups in the US and Europe*, London: Kluwer Academic Publishers

Delphy, C. (1984) *Close to Home*, London: Hutchinson

Dennis, N. and Erdos, G. (2000) *Families Without Fatherhood* (3rd edn), London: Civitas

Denscombe, M. (2001) *Sociology Update 2001*, Leicester: Olympus Books

Denscombe, M. (2004) *Sociology Update 2004*, Leicester: Olympus Books

Department of Health (2003) *National Survey of NHS Patients*, London: Department of Health

Dex, S. (2003) *Families and Work in the Twenty-first Century*, York: Joseph Rowntree Foundation

Dietz, T. (1998) 'An examination of violence and gender role portrayals in video games: Implications for gender socialization and aggressive behavior', *Sex Roles*, 38, pp. 425–42

Douglas, J.W.B. (1964) *The Home and the School*, London: MacGibbon & Kee

Drury, B. (1991) 'Sikh girls and the maintenance of an ethnic culture', *New Community*, 17(3), pp. 387–99

Dryden, C. (1999) *Being Married Doing Gender*, London: Routledge

Duncombe, J. and Marsden, D. (1995) 'Women's "triple shift": paid employment, domestic labour and "emotion work"', *Sociology Review* 4(4)

Dunne, G.A. (ed.) (1997) *Lesbian Lifestyles: Women's work and the politics of sexuality*, Basingstoke: Macmillan

Durkheim, E. (1897/1952) *Suicide: a Study in Sociology*, London: Routledge

Durkheim, E. (1912/1961) *The Elementary Forms of Religious Life*, London: Allen and Unwin

Edgell, S. (1980) *Middle-class Couples*, London: Allen & Unwin

Eisenstadt, S.N. (1956) *From Generation to Generation*, London: Routledge

El Sadaawi, N. (1980) *The Hidden Face of Eve: Women in the Arab World*, London: Zed Books.

Elias, N. (1978) *The Civilising Process*, Oxford: Blackwell

Equal Opportunities Commission (2005) *Sex and Power: Who Runs Britain? 2005*, Equal Opportunities Commission

Essex University Study (2000) *Family Formation in Multicultural Britain: Three Patterns of Diversity*, Institute for Social and Economic Research, Essex University (author: Richard Berthoud)

Ferguson, M. (1983) *Forever Feminine: Women's Magazines and the Cult of Femininity*, London: Heinemann

Fesbach, S. and Sanger, J.L. (1971) *Television and Aggression*, San Francisco: Jessey-Bass

Flowers, A. (1998) *The Fantasy Factory: An insider's view of the phone sex industry*, Philadelphia: University of Pennsylvania Press

Ford, R. and Millar, J. (eds) (1998) *Private Lives and Public Costs: Lone parents and the state*, London: Policy Studies Institute

Forest (2004) *Smoking in Public Places: An independent survey of public attitudes to smoking in pubs, bars and clubs*, www.forestonline.org

Foster, J. (1990) *Villains: Crime and community in the inner city*, London: Routledge

Fox Harding, L. (1996) *Family, State and Social Policy*, Basingstoke: Macmillan

Francis, B. (1997) 'Discussing discrimination: children's construction of sexism between pupils in primary school', *British Journal of Sociology of Education*, 18(4)

Francis, B. (1998) *Power Plays: Primary School Children's Constructions of Gender, Power and Adult Work*, Stoke-on-Trent: Trentham Books

Future Foundation Survey (2000) 'Complicated lives' (conducted by William Nelson)

Fyvel, T.R. (1961) *The Insecure Offender*, London: Chatto & Windus

Galtung, J. and Ruge, M. (1973) 'Structuring and selecting news', in S. Cohen and J. Young (eds) *The Manufacture of News, Social Problems, Deviance and the Mass Media*, London: Constable

Gauntlett, D. (2002) *Media, Gender and Identity: An Introduction*, London: Routledge

Gershuny, J. (2000) ISER, University of Essex with the Future Foundation for Abbey National

Ghate, D., Hazel, N., Creighton, S. J., Finch, S. and Field, J. (2003) *The National Study of Parents, Children and Discipline in Britain: Key Findings*, NSPCC

Ghuman, P.A.S. (1999) *Asian Adolescents in the West*, Leicester: BPS Books

Giddens, A. (2001) *Sociology* (4th edn), Cambridge: Polity Press

Gilroy, P. (1987) *There Ain't No Black in the Union Jack*, London: Hutchinson

Gilroy, P. (1993) *The Black Atlantic: Modernity and double consciousness*, London: Verso

Giroux, H.A. (1998) 'Teenage sexuality, body politics, and the pedagogy of display'. In J.S. Epstein (ed.) *Youth Culture: Identity in a postmodern world*, Oxford: Blackwell

Glaser, B. and Strauss. A. (1967) *The Discovery of Grounded Theory*, Chicago: Aldine

Glasgow Media Group (2000) *Viewing the World: News Content and Audience Studies*, DFID: London (web site: www.dfid.gov.uk)

Glasgow University Media Group and Eldridge, G. (ed.) (1993) *Getting the Message: News, truth and power*, London: Routledge

Glock, C.Y. and Stark, R. (1969) 'Dimensions in religious commitment', in R. Robertson (ed.) (1969) *The Sociology of Religion*, Harmondsworth: Penguin

Goffman, E. (1961, reissued 1984) *Asylums*, Harmondsworth: Penguin

Gottman, J.S. (1990) 'Children of gay and lesbian parents', in F.W. Bozett and M.B. Sussman (eds) *Homosexuality and Family Relations*, New York: Harrington Press

Greeley, A. (1972) *Unsecular Man*, New York: Schocken Books, Inc.

Greeley, A. (1992) *Sociology and Religion: A Collection of Readings*, New York: HarperCollins Publishers

Grieshaber, S. (1977) 'Mealtime rituals: power and resistance in the construction of mealtime rules', *British Journal of Sociology*, 48(4)

Griffin, C. (1985) *Typical Girls: Young Women from School to the Job Market*, London: Routledge & Kegan Paul

Gross, R.M. (1994) 'Buddhism' in J. Holm, and J. Bowker (eds), (1994) *Women in Religion*, London: Pinter

Guibernau, M. and Goldblatt, D. (2000) 'Identity and nation', in K. Woodward (ed.) *Questioning Identity: Gender, Class, Nation*, London: Routledge

Haddon, J.K. and Long, T.E. (eds) (1993) *Religion and Religiosity in America*, US: Crossroad Publishing Company

Hakim, C. (1996) *Key Issues in Women's Work*, London: Athlone

Halevy, E. (1927) *A History of the English People in 1815*, London: Unwin

Hall, S. (1985) 'Religious ideologies and social movements in Jamaica', in R. Bocock and K. Thompson (eds) *Religion and Ideology*, Manchester: Manchester University Press

Hall, S. and Jefferson, T. (1976) *Resistance through Rituals: Youth subcultures in post-war Britain*, London: Hutchinson

Hall, S., Critcher, C., Jefferson, T., Clarke, J. and Robert, B. (1978) *Policing the Crisis: Mugging, the State and Law and Order*, London: Palgrave Macmillan

Hamilton, M. (2001) *The Sociology of Religion* (2nd edn) London: Routledge

Hanson, E. (1997) *Decadence and Catholicism*, Cambridge, Mass: Harvard University Press

Haralambos, M. and Holborn, M. (2004) *Sociology: Themes and Perspectives* (6th edn), London: Collins Education

Hargreaves, D.H. (1967) *Social Relations in a Secondary School*, London: Routledge & Kegan Paul

Hart, N. (1976) *When Marriage Ends*, London: Tavistock

Haskey, J. (2002) Report for the Office for National Statistics, London: ONS

Hayward, K.J. (2004) *City Limits: Crime, consumer culture and the urban experience*, London: Glasshouse Press

Haywood, C. (2003) *Men and Masculinities: Theory, research and social practice*, Buckingham: Open University Press

Hebdige, D. (1979) *Subculture: The meaning of style*, London: Methuen

Hebdige, D. (1988) *On Hiding in the Light*, London: Comedia

Heelas, P. (1996) *The New Age Movement*, Cambridge: Polity Press

Heelas, P., Woodhead, W., Seel, B., Tusting, K. and Szerszynski, B. (2004) *The Spiritual Revolution: Why Religion Is Giving Way to Spirituality*, Oxford: Blackwell

Herberg, W. (1960) *Protestant – Catholic – Jew* (revised edn), New York: Anchor Books

Hervieu Leger, D. (1993) *The Religion of Memory*, Paris: Stag

Himmelweit, H. (1958) *TV and the Child*, Oxford: Oxford University Press

Holden, A. (2002) *Jehovah's Witnesses: Portrait of a contemporary religious movement*, London/New York: Routledge

Holloway, K., Bennett, T. and Lower, C (2003) *Trends in Drug Use and Offending: the results of the N E W-ADAM Programme 1999–2002* (Research Findings 214), London: Home Office

Holm, J. and Bowker, J. (eds) (1994) *Women in Religion*, London: Pinter

Hook, S. (1990) *Convictions*, New York: Prometheus Books

Humphreys, L. (1975) *Tearoom Trade: Impersonal sex in public places*, New York: Aldine De Gruyter.

Humphries, S. (1981) *Hooligans or Rebels: An oral history of working class childhood and youth, 1889–1939*, Oxford: Blackwell

Hunt, S. (2001) 'Dying to be thin: a sociology of eating disorders', *Sociology Review,* 10(4)

Hunter, J.D. (1987) *Evangelism: The Coming Generation*, Chicago, University of Chicago Press

Jackson, M. (2000) 'From South Fork to South Park', The Fleming Lecture 2000, 10 May

Jackson, M. (2001) 'Channel 4: The Fourth Way', New Statesman Media Lecture 2001, 31 October

Jacobson, J. (1997) 'Religion and ethnicity: dual and alternative sources of identity among young British Pakistanis', *Ethnic and Racial Studies*, 20(2)

Jefferis, B., Power, C. and Hertzman, C. (2002) 'Birth weight, childhood socioeconomic environment, and cognitive development in the 1958 British birth cohort study', *British Medical Journal,* 325, p. 305

Jhally, S. and Lewis, J. (1992) *Enlightened Racism. The Cosby Show, Audiences and the Myth of the American Dream*, Oxford: Westview Press

Johal, S. (1998) 'Brimful of Brasia', *Sociology Review,* 8(1)

Jones, E. and Jones, M. (1999) *Mass Media*, Basingstoke: MacMillan

Jordan, B. (1992) *Trapped in Poverty? Labour market decisions in low income households*, London: Routledge

Jowell, R., Curtice, J., Park, A., Brook, L. and Ahrendt, A. (eds) (1995) *British Social Attitudes: the 12th Report*, Aldershot: Dartmouth

Kahane, R. with Rapoport, T. (1997) *The Origins of Postmodern Youth: Informal youth movements in a comparative perspective*, Berlin/New York: Walter de Gruyter

Katz, J. (1988) *Seductions of Crime: Moral and sensual attractions in doing evil*, New York: Basic Books

Katz, J. (2000) 'The gang myth', in S. Karstedt and K.D. Bussman (eds) *Social Dynamics of Crime and Control,* Oxford: Hart

Kaur-Singh, K. (1994) 'Sikhism' in J. Holm, and J. Bowker (eds), (1994) *Women in Religion*, London: Pinter

Kautsky, K. (1953) *Foundations of Christianity*, New York: Russell

Kinder, M. (1999) *Kid's Media Culture*, Durham, North Carolina: Duke University Press.

King, R. and Raynor, J. (1981) *The Middle Class*, Harlow: Longman

Klapper, J.T. (1960) *The Effects of Mass Communication*, New York: The Free Press

Lacey, C. (1970) *Hightown Grammar,* Manchester: Manchester University Press

Laidler, K. and Hunt, G. (2001) 'Accomplishing femininity among the girls in the gang', *British Journal of Criminology*, 41, p. 658

Laslett, P. (1972) 'Mean household size in England since the sixteenth century', in P. Laslett (ed.) *Household and Family in Past Time*, Cambridge: Cambridge University Press

Laumann, E.O., Gagnon, J.H., Michael, R.T. and Michaels, S. (1995) *The Social Organization of Sexuality: Sexual Practices in the United States*, Chicago: University of Chicago Press

Lea, J. and Young, J. (1984) *What Is to be Done about Law and Order?* Harmondsworth: Penguin

Leach, E. (1967) *A Runaway World?*, London: BBC Publications

Leach, E. (1988) *Culture and Communication*, Cambridge: Cambridge University Press

Lees, S. (1986) *Losing Out: Sexuality and adolescent girls*, London: Hutchinson

Legal & General Survey (2000) 'The value of a mum'

Leighton, G. (1992) 'Wives' paid and unpaid work and husbands' unemployment', *Sociology Review*, 1(3)

Liddiment, D. (2001) The McTaggart Lecture, Guardian Edinburgh International Television Festival

Luke, A. and Luke, C. (2000) 'A situated perspective on cultural globalisation', in N. Burbules and C. Torres (eds) *Globalisation and Education,* New York: Routledge

Lyng, S. (1998) 'Dangerous methods: risk taking and the research process', in J Ferrell and M.S. Hamm (eds) *Ethnography at the Edge: Crime, deviance and field research*, Boston: Northeastern University Press

Lyng, S. (1990) 'Edgework: a social psychological analysis of voluntary risk taking', *American Journal of Sociology,* 95(4), pp. 851–6

Lyotard, J.-F. (1984) *The Post-Modern Condition: A Report on Knowledge*, Manchester: University of Manchester Press

Mac an Ghaill, M. (1988) *Young, Gifted and Black*, Milton Keynes: Open University Press

Mac an Ghaill, M. (1994) *The Making of Men: masculinities, sexualities and schooling*, Milton Keynes: Open University Press

Mac An Ghaill, M. (ed.) (1996) *Understanding Masculinities: Social relations and cultural arenas*, Buckingham: Open University Press

McAllister, F. with Clarke, L. (1998) *Choosing Childlessness*, York: Family Policy Studies Centre and Joseph Rowntree Foundation

McGlone, F., Park, A. and Smith, K. (1998) *Families and Kinship*, York: Family Policy Studies Centre in association with the Joseph Rowntree Foundation

MacGuire, M.B. (1981) *Religion: The Social Context*, California: Wadsworth Publishing

McKay, G. (1996) *Senseless Acts of Beauty: Cultures of Resistance since the Sixties*, London: Verso

Mackintosh, M. and Mooney, G. (2000) 'Identity, inequality and social class', in K. Woodward (ed.) *Questioning Identity: Gender, class, nation*, London: Routledge/Open University

McNamara, R.P. (1994) *The Times Square Hustler: Male prostitution in New York City*, Westport: Praeger

McRobbie, A. (1991) 'Romantic individualism and the teenage girl' in A. McRobbie (ed.) *Feminism and Youth Culture*, Basingstoke: Macmillan

McRobbie, A. and Garber, J. (1976) 'Girls and subcultures', in S. Hall, and T. Jefferson, *Resistance through Rituals*, London: Hutchinson

McRobbie, A. and Nava, M. (1984) *Gender and Generation*, London: Macmillan

Maffesoli, M. (1998) 'The future and postmodern youth', in J.S. Epstein (ed.) *Youth Culture: Identity in a postmodern world*, Oxford: Blackwell

Malinowski, B. (1954) *Magic, Science and Religion and Other Essays*, New York: Anchor Books

Marcuse, H. (1964) *One Dimensional Man,* London: Routledge & Keegan Paul

Mares, D. (2001) 'Gangstas or Lager Louts? Working class street gangs in Manchester', in M.W. Klein, H.J. Kerner, C.L. Maxson and E.G.M. Weitekamp (eds) *The Eurogang Paradox: Street Gangs and Youth Groups in the US and Europe,* London: Kluwer Academic

Marshall, G. (1982) *In Search of the Spirit of Capitalism: Max Weber and the Protestant Ethic Thesis*, London: Hutchison

Marshall, G., Newby, H., Rose, D. and Vogler, C. (1988) *Social Class in Modern Britain*, London: Hutchinson

Martin, D. (1978) *A General Theory of Secularisation*, Blackwell: Oxford

Marx, K. and Engels, F. (1957) *On Religion*, Moscow: Progress Publishers

Mason, D. (2000) *Race and Ethnicity in Modern Britain*, Oxford: Oxford University Press

Matza, D. (1964) *Delinquency and Drift*, New York: Wiley

Mead, M. (1928) *Coming of Age in Samoa*, New York: Morrow

Metcalf, H., Modood, T. and Virdee, S. (1996) *Asian Self-Employment*, London: Policy Studies Institute

Miller, A.S. and Hoffman, J.P. (1995) 'Risk and religion: an explanation of gender differences in religiosity', *Journal for the Scientific Study of Religion* 34, pp. 63–75

Miller, W.B. (1962) 'Lower class culture as a generating milieu of gang delinquency', in M.E. Wolfgang, L. Savitz and N. Johnston (eds) *The Sociology of Crime and Delinquency*, New York: Wiley

Miller, W.B. (1975) *Violence by Youth Gangs and Youth Groups as a Crime Problem in Major American Cities*, Washington: Government Printing Office

Mirrlees-Black, C. (1999) 'Domestic violence: findings from a new British Crime Survey self-completion questionnaire', *Home Office Research Study* 191

Mirza, H. (1992) *Young, Female and Black*, London: Routledge

Modood, T. (1997) *Ethnic Minorities in Britain: Diversity and disadvantage*, London: Policy Studies Institute

Modood, T. (2001) 'British Asian Identities: Something old, something borrowed, something new', in Morley, D. and Robins, K. (eds) *British Cultural Identities*, Oxford: Oxford University Press

Modood, T., Beishon, S. and Virdee, S. (1994) *Changing Ethnic Identities*, London: Policy Studies Institute

Moore. S. (2004) 'Hanging around: the politics of the busstop', *Youth and Policy*, 82, pp. 47–59

Morgan, P. (2000) *Marriage-Lite: The rise of cohabitation and its consequences,* London: Civitas

Morley, D. (1980) *The Nationwide Audience*, London: BFI

Morrison, D.E. (1999) *Defining Violence: The Search for Understanding*, Luton: University of Luton Press

Morrow, V. (1998) *Understanding Families: Children's perspectives,* York: National Children's Bureau in association with the Joseph Rowntree Foundation

Mount, F. (2004) *Mind the Gap: Class in Britain now*, London: Short Books

Mulvey, L. (1975) 'Visual pleasures and narrative cinema', *Screen*, 16(3)

Muncie, J. (1984) *The Trouble with Kids Today: Youth and Crime in Post-War Britain*, London: Hutchinson

Muncie, J. (2004) *Youth and Crime*, London: Sage

Murdock, G. and McCron, R. (1976) 'Consciousness of class and consciousness of generation', in S. Hall and T. Jefferson (eds) *Resistance through Rituals*, London: Hutchinson

Murdock, G.P. (1949) *Social Structure,* New York: Macmillan

Murphy, P. And Elwood, J. (1998) 'Gendered experiences, choices and achievement – exploring the links', *International Journal of Inclusive Education*, 2(2), pp. 95–118

Murray, C. (1990) *The Emerging British Underclass*, London: Institute of Economic Affairs, Health and Welfare Unit

National Centre for Social Research (1998) *British Social Attitudes Survey* (15th Report), London: Sage Publications

Nazroo, J. (1999) *The Sociology of the Family: A Reader*, edited by Graham Allan, Blackwell, Oxford

Nelson, G.K. (1986) 'Religion' in M. Haralambos (ed.) *Developments in Sociology*, Vol. 2, Ormskirk: Causeway Press

Newbold, C., Boyd-Barrett, O. and Van Den Bulk, H. (2002) *The Media Book*, London: Arnold

Newsom, E. (1994) 'Video violence and the protection of children', *The Psychologist*, June

Newson, J. and Newson, E. (1963) *Patterns of Infant Care in an Urban Community*, Harmondsworth: Penguin

Newson, J. and Newson, E. (1965) *Cultural Aspects of Child Rearing,* Harmondsworth: Penguin

Niebuhr, H.R. (1929) *The Social Sources of Denominationalism*, New York: The World Publishing Company

O'Donnell, M. and Sharpe, S. (2000) *Youth, Ethnicity and Class in Contemporary Britain*, London: Routledge

Oakley, A. (1982) *Subject Women*, London: Fontana

Oakley, A. (1986) 'Feminism, motherhood and medicine – Who cares?', in J. Mitchell and A. Oakley (eds) *What is Feminism?*, Oxford: Blackwell

Orbach, S. (1991) *Fat is a Feminist Issue*, London: Hamlyn

Packard, V. (1957) *The Hidden Persuaders*, Harlow: Longman

Parkin, F. (1972) *Class Inequality and Political Order*, St Albans: Paladin

Parsons, T. (1955) 'The social structure of the family' in T. Parsons and R.F. Bales (eds) *Family, Socialization and Interaction Process*, New York: The Free Press

Parsons, T. (1965) 'Religious perspectives in sociology and social psychology', in W.A. Lessa and E.Z. Vogt (1965) *Reader in Comparative Religion: An Anthropological Approach* (2nd edn), New York: Harper & Row

Parton, N. (1989) *The Politics of Child Abuse*, Basingstoke: Palgrave

Pearson, G. (1983) *Hooligan: A history of respectable fears,* London: Macmillan

Phillips, M. (1997) *All Must Have Prizes* London: Little Brown

Philo, G. and Berry, M. (2004) *Bad News from Israel*, London: Pluto Press

Plummer, K. (1995) *Telling Sexual Stories: Power, change and social worlds,* London: Routledge

Postman, N. (1982) *The Disappearance of Childhood*, New York: Delacorte Press

Pritchard, D. (2005) 'Nobody loves the working class', *Sociology Review*, 14(3)

Pryce K. (1979) *Endless Pressure*, Harmondsworth: Penguin.

Pudney, S. (2002) *The Road to Ruin? Sequences of initiation into drug use and offending by young people in Britain*, Home Office Research Study 253, London: Home Office

Rapoport, R.N., Fogarty, M.P. and Rapoport, R. (eds) (1982) *Families in Britain*, London: Routledge

Reynolds, T., Callender, C. and Edwards, R. (2003) *Caring and Counting: The impact of mothers' employment on family relationships,* Bristol: The Policy Press

Riddell, S. (1992) *Polities and the Gender of the Curriculum*, London: Routledge

Riseborough, G. (1993) 'The gobbo barmy army: one day in the life of YTS boys', in I. Bates (ed.) *Youth and Inequality*, Milton Keynes: Open University Press

Robbins, T. and Palmer, S. (eds) (1997) *Millennium, Messiahs and Mayhem*, New York: Routledge Press

Roberts, K. (1997) 'Same activities, different meanings: British youth cultures in the 1990s', *Leisure Studies*, 16, pp. 1–15

Roberts, M. (2004) 'Crack down on Gin Lane', *Criminal Justice Matters*, 55

Rosenhan, D.L. (1973) 'On being sane in insane places', *Science*, 179, pp. 250–8

Roszak, T. (1970) *The Making of a Counter Culture*, London: Faber & Faber

Rutherford, J. (1988) 'Who's that man?', in R. Chapman and J. Rutherford (eds) *Male Order: Unwrapping Masculinity*, London: Laurence & Wishart

Said, E. (1985) *Orientalism*, Harmondsworth: Penguin

Sanders, W.B. (1994) *Gangbangs and Drive-Bys: Grounded Culture and Juvenile Gang Violence*, New York: Aldine De Gruyter

Saraga, E. (1993) 'The abuse of children', in R. Dallos and E. McLaughlin (eds) *Social Problems and the Family*, London: Sage

Saunders, P. (1990) *Social Class and Stratification*, Routledge: London

Savage, M. (1995) 'The Middle Classes in Modern Britain', *Sociology Review*, 5(2)

Schlesinger, P. (1978) *Putting Reality Together*, London: Constable

Schudsen, M. (1994) 'Culture and integration of national societies' in D. Crane (ed.) *The Sociology of Culture*, Oxford: Blackwell

Sclater, S.D. (2000) *Access to Sociology: Families*, London: Hodder Arnold

Sclater, S.D. (2001) 'Domestic violence', *Sociology Review*, 10(4)

Scott, S. (2003) 'Symbolic interactionism and shyness', *Sociology Review*, 12(4)

Sewell, T. (2000) 'Identifying the pastoral needs of African-Caribbean students: A case of "critical antiracism"', *Education and Social Justice*, 3(1)

Sewell, T. (2004) Lecture at annual conference of the Association for the Teaching of the Social Sciences, September 2004

Sharpe, S. (1976) *Just Like a Girl*, Harmondsworth: Penguin.

Sharpe, S. (1994) *Sugar and Spice*, Harmondsworth: Penguin

Shropshire, S. and McFarquhar, M. (2002) *Developing Multi-Agency Strategies to Address the Street Gang Culture and Reduce Gun Violence among Young People Briefing No. 4,* Manchester: Shropshire & McFarquhar Consultancy Group

Sivananden, A. (1981) 'From resistance to rebellion', *Journal of Race and Class*, 23(2/3)

Skelton, C. (2001) *Schooling the Boys: Masculinites and Primary Education*, Buckingham: Open University Press

Smart, C. and Stevens, P. (2000) *Cohabitation Breakdown*, London: The Family Policy Studies Centre

Smith, J. (1989) *Mysogenies*, London: Faber & Faber

Smith, J. (2001) *Moralities, Sex, Money and Power in the 21st century*, Allen Lane

Spender, D. (1982) *Invisible Women*, London: Writers & Readers

Stanko, E. (2000) 'The day to count: a snapshot of the impact of domestic violence in the UK', *Criminal Justice,* 1(2)

Stark, R. and Bainbridge, W. (1985) *The Future of Religion: Secularisation, Revival and Cult Formation*, Berkeley: California University Press

Statham, J. (1986) *Daughters and Sons: Experiences of non-sexist child-raising*, Oxford: Blackwell

Stopes-Roe, M. and Cochrane, R. (1990) *Citizens of this Country: The Asian British*, Clevedon: Multilingual Matters

Strinati, D. (1995) *An Introduction to Theories of Popular Culture*, London: Routledge

Swale, J. (2001) 'Researching British Asians', *Sociology Review*, 11(2)

Swingewood, A. (2000) *A Short History of Sociological Thought*, Basingstoke: Macmillan

Taylor, S. (1991) 'Measuring child abuse', *Sociology Review*, 1(3)

Taylor, S. (1999) 'Postmodernism: a challenge to sociology', *'S' Magazine*, 4

Thompson, D. (1996) *The End of Time: Faith and Fear in the Shadow of the Millennium*, London: Sinclair Stevenson

Thornes, B. and Collard, J. (1979) *Who Divorces?* London : Routledge & Kegan Paul

Thornton, S. (1995) *Club Cultures: Music, media and subcultural capital*, Cambridge: Polity

Thrasher, F. (1927) *The Gang,* Chicago: University of Chicago Press

Tizard, B. and Hughes, M. (1991) 'Reflections on young people learning', in G. Walford (ed.) *Doing Educational Research*, London: Routledge

Tizard, B. and Phoenix, A. (1993) *Black, White or Mixed Race*, London: Routledge

Troeltsch, E. (1931/1976) *The Social Teachings of the Christian Churches*, Chicago: University of Chicago Press

Tuchman, G., Kaplan Daniels, A. and Benit, J. (eds) (1978) *Hearth and Home: Images of Women in the Mass Media*, New York: Oxford University Press

Tunnell, K.D. (1998) 'Honesty, secrecy, and deception in the sociology of crime: confessions and reflections from the backstage', in J. Ferrell and M.S. Hamm (eds) *Ethnography at the Edge* (1998), Boston: Northeastern University Press

Turner, B. (1983) *Religion and Social Theory*, London: Sage

Urban, M. (1999) 'Which is the true face of England?', *The Guardian*, 5 May 1999

van Dijk, T. (1991) *Racism and the Press*, London: Routledge

Vertovec, S. (1993) *Local Contexts and the Development of Muslim Communities in Britain: Observations in Keighley, West Yorkshire*, unpublished

Viewing the World (2000) Department for International Development

Wallis, R. (1984) *The Elementary Forms of New Religious Life*, London: Routledge

Walter, N. (1999) *The New Feminism*, London: Virago

Warin, J., Solomon, Y., Lewis, C. and Langford, W. (1999) *Fathers, Work and Family Life,* York: Joseph Rowntree Foundation

Waters, M. (1995) *Globalization*, London: Routledge

Watson, H. (1994) 'Women and the veil: personal responses to global process', in A. Ahmed and H. Donnan (eds) *Islam, Globalisation and Postmodernity*, London: Routledge

Weber, M. (1905/1958) *The Protestant Ethic and the Spirit of Capitalism*, London: Unwin

Weber, M. (1920/1963) *The Sociology of Religion*, Boston, Mass: Beacon Press

Whannel, G. (2002) 'David Beckham: Identity and masculinity', *Sociology Review*, 11(3)

Whyte, W.F. (1943) *Street Corner Society: The social structure of an Italian slum*, Chicago: University of Chicago Press.

Widdicombe, S. and Wooffitt, R. (1995) *The Language of Youth Subcultures*, Hemel Hempstead: Harvester

Wilkinson, H. (1994) *No Turning Back: Generations and the gender quake*, London: Demos

Williams, J. (1996) 'Football's coming home?', *Sociology Review*, November 1996

Willis, P. (1977) *Learning to Labour*, Aldershot: Ashgate

Wilson, B. (1982) *Religion in Sociological Perspective*, Oxford: Oxford University Press

Wilson, B. (1966) *Religion in a Secular Society*, London: B.A. Watts

Winship, J. (1987) *Inside Women's Magazines*, London: Pandora Press

Wolf, N. (1990) *The Beauty Myth*, London: Vintage

Wood, J. (1993) 'Repeatable pleasures: notes on young people's use of video', in D. Buckingham (ed.) *Reading Audiences: Young People and the Media*, Manchester: Manchester University Press

Woodhead, L. and Heelas, P. (2000) *Religion in Modern Times: An Interpretive Anthology*, Oxford: Blackwell

Young, M. and Willmott, P. (1957) *Family and Kinship in East London*, Harmondsworth: Penguin

Young, M. and Willmott, P. (1973) *The Symmetrical Family*, Harmondsworth: Penguin

INDEX

Note: page numbers in **bold** refer to definitions/explanations of key terms.

Abrams, M. 187
abuse 58, 78, 88–91
achieved statuses 3, 193, **196**
active audience approaches 113–14, **114**, 118
advertising 102, 103, 108, 112–13
African-Caribbean populations 36, 37, 216, 219
age differences 113, 130–1, 187
agenda-setting 99, **100**
Alpha course 157
Althusser, Louis 11
ambiguity **23**, 168, **168**
Americanism 143
anomie 144, **146**, 205, **208**
anticult movement 160
antisocial behaviour 205, **208**
Anwar, M. 36
argot 189, **190**
Aries, Philippe 75–6, 190
Armstrong, K. 165
arranged marriages 83
asceticism 149, **150**, 165, **168**
ascribed statuses 3, 193, **196**
Asian populations 36–8, 203, 220
assimilation 171, **174**
audience cults 161

Badawi, Leila 167
Bagdikian, Ben 97, 98
Bainbridge, W. 179
Bandura, A. 117
Barrett, M. 59
Bauman, Zygmunt 5, 200
Beck, U. 65, 72
Beck-Gernsheim, E. 65, 72
Becker, Howard 16
Beckham, David 33
Bellah, R. 143, 180
Berger, P. 148, 178
Berthoud, R. 63, 70, 71
bias **232**, **263**
    news 106, 108
    personal experience 228
    research 248, 259, 261
Big Brother 228
'big stories' 21, **23**
Billig, M. 42
binuclear families 70
biological determination 31, **32**
biology 3–4
birth rate 64, 188
births outside marriage 63–4
blasphemy **168**
body 17, 18
bottom-up theories 236, **237**
Bourdieu, Pierre 28
bourgeoisie 11, **12**
Bourgois, Philippe 229, 249
Box, S. 206
Brake, M. 195–6
Brannen, J. 70
Brierley, P. 159, 170, 177, 178, 179
British Crime Survey 87–8, 240
British Empire 42
British identity 41–5

British Social Attitudes Survey 11–12, 63, 241
British Sociological Association 237
broadcasting regulators 103, **104**, 108
Brown, P. 217–18
Bruce, S. 156, 161, 164, 167, 178, 179
Buckingham, D. 117, 118, 124
bureaucracy 153, **156**
bureaucratic government 21, **23**

Calvinists 149, **150**
Campbell, A. 211, 214
canalization 31, **32**
capitalism **12**
    family 83, 87
    Marx 11–12
    Marxist-feminists 13
    media 98–9, 108
    religion 149
case studies 243, **244**
Cashmore, E. 201
caste system 12, **39**
catharsis 117, **120**
causal relationships 229, 230, **232**
The Celestine Prophecy 158
celibacy 165, **168**
Celtic identity 43, **45**
charismatic religion 149, **150**, 173, **174**
Charlesworth, S. 12, 26–7
'chav' culture 26
child abuse 58, 78, 88–91
child-centredness 27, **29**, 76, **78**
childhood 74–9
childlessness 64
children
    families 51, 53, 58
    family diversity 69–70, 71–2
    media 105, 117–19
    power and control 81, 82
    representations 132
Christian Right **146**, 147
Church of England 145, 157, 164, 165, 171, 173, 177, 178
Church of Scientology 160
churches 152, 153
civil religion 143, **146**
class *see* social class
classic realist narrative 108, **110**
classic working-class extended family 70, **72**
clergy 178
clerical workers 27, **29**
client cults 161
close-knit communities 65, **66**
closed questions 253, **255**
Cloward, R. 205–6
cluster sampling 242, **244**
cohabitation 51, 52, **53**, 63, 64, 66
Cohen, Albert 205, 212
Cohen, Phil 194
Cohen, Stan 196, 197
co-parenting 70
Collard, J. 64, 65
collective conscience 143, **146**
commercial television 102, **104**
common sense 228–9
community solidarity 171
comparative method 243, **244**
compartmentalism 38, **39**
complicit masculinity 32, **32**
computer-assisted interviewing 88
conflict 10–13
conjugal relationships 80, **84**

Connell, R.W. 32, 218
Connolly, P. 219, 220
consensus 6–9, **8**, 52
conservative 143, **146**
conspicuous consumption **29**
consumption **23**, **190**
    family 52, 87
    gender 32
    mass media 97
    postmodernity 21, 22
    youth culture 187, 189, 199–200
consumption cleavage 26, **29**
content analysis 109, **110**, 123–4, 261, **263**
conversionist 167, **168**
coping strategies 193
'copycat' violence 117, **120**
correlation **120**, 229, 230, **232**
countercultures 199
covert observation 247, 248, 249, **251**
crime
    lone-parent families 69
    media violence 121
    researchers 235
    surveys 240
crisis of masculinity **32**, 33, 88, **90**
critical sociology *see* Marxist sociology
cross-media ownership 99, **100**
cross promotion 97, **100**
cross-sectional surveys 241, **244**
crystals 161, **162**
cult apologists 160, **162**
cultic milieu 161, **162**
cults 153, 167
cultural capital 27, 28, **29**
cultural diversity 3, **4**
cultural effects model 113, **114**, 118
cultural hierarchy 135, **136**
cultural hybridity 173, **174**
cultural tendency 221
culture **4**, 193, **196**
    conflict 10–13
    consensus 6–9
    religion 150
    social action theory 14–19
    socialization 2–5
Cumberbatch, Guy 119
customs 3, **4**
cybersex 231

data 229–32, **232**, 258–63
Davie, Grace 156, 165, 178
Davis, M. 212, 215
decoding 194, **196**
decontextualization 135, **136**
defensive patriotism 44, **45**
Dennis, N. 81
denominations 152–3
dependent variables 230
deprogrammers 160, **162**
deregulation 103, **104**
desensitization 117, **120**
deviance 3, **4**
    family 57
    labelling theory 16, 19
    participant observational studies 248
deviance amplification **131**
Diana, Princess of Wales 42
diaries 260
differentiation 6–11
discourses 190, **190**
discrimination 35–6

disease model of child abuse 89
disengagement 178, **179**
disneyfication 104
diversification 97, **100**
diversity 21, **23**, 68–73, **72**
division of labour 7, 53, **53**, 59, 80
divorce 58, 62, 64–5, **66**, 70, 81–2
divorce petition 64, **66**
domestic violence 58–9, 69–70, 86–91
dominant reading *see* preferred reading
drug use 212–13, 229–30
Dryden, C. 81
dual burden 81, **84**
dual heritage *see* mixed-race
dumbing down 103, **104**
Duncome, J. 81
Durkheim, Emile 9, 143–5, 171, 177, 192, 203, 229, 243
dysfunctional **90**

eating disorders 17, 31, 124
eclecticism 201, **202**
economic asset **78**
economic capital 28
ecstatic trances 173, **174**
ecumenical movement 178, **179**
Edgell, S. 81
edgework 207, **208**
education
    ethnicity 37–8
    family 53
    gender 31
    labelling theory 16
    Marxism 12
    national identity 42
    role 162–7
    social class 27–8
effects approach 117–18, **120**
effigies 165, **168**
egalitarianism 80, **84**
Eisenstadt, S.N. 193
El Sadaawi, N. 166
Elias, Norbert 4
elite 70, **72**
emotional abuse 89
employment *see* work
empowerment 173, **174**
empty-shell marriages 64, **66**
Engels, F. 145
'English disease' 44, **45**
English identity 43, 44
entrepreneurialism 27, **29**, 149, **150**
Erdos, G. 81
ethical issues 234–8, **237**, 243, 248
ethnicity 35, **39**
    childhood 77
    families 53, 70–1
    identity 34–9
    marriage 63
    media 110, 113, 128–30
    meta-study 273
    national identity 43–4, 45
    postmodernity 22
    religion 170–5
    schooling 219–21
    subculture 195
ethnocentrism 3, **4**
ethnographic research **39**, **214**, 247, **251**
    ethnic identity 37
    gangs 212
    methods 248–50

evaluating data 230–2
evangelical goals 167, **168**
experience 228
experimenter effects 243
experiments 235, 242–3, **244**
extended kinship networks **53**
    diversity 70
    divorce 65
    ethnicity 71
    working class 70, **72**

facts 228–9
false class consciousness 11–12, **12**
familial ideology 57–61, **59**, 69
family
    childhood 74–9
    definitions 50–5
    diversity 68–73
    division of labour 53, 59, 80
    ethnic identity 36–7
    functionalism 8
    history 260
    marriage 62–7
    middle class 27
    morality and the state 56–61
    power and control 80–5
    radical feminists 13
    violence and abuse 86–91
fate 149
fatherhood 81–2, 85
female subcultures 219
femininity 30, 31, 123–4, 213–14, 219, **222**
feminism **32**, **237**
    child abuse 90
    conflict 12–13
    divorce 64
    domestic violence 88
    family 53, 58, 69, 81–4
    femininity 30
    marriage 63
    media 112–15, 123–4, 125
    religion 164–9
    research 236, 242
    subcultures 208
feminization of masculinity 124, **126**
feral children 2, 3, **4**
Ferguson, M. 123–4
feudalism 145, **146**
fidelity 51, **53**
field diaries 249, **251**
field experiments 243, **244**
folk devils 130–1, **131**
Fox Harding, L. 58
fragmentation 26, **29**
Francis, B. 31
functionalism **8**, **237**
    child abuse 89
    childhood 76–7
    consensus 6–9
    family 52–5, 68, 83
    religion 143–4
    research 236
    socialization 6–9
fundamentalism 146, **146**, 155–6, 168
funding for research 236–7

Galtung, J. 107
gangs 210–15
gatekeepers 107–8, **110**, 249, **251**
gathering data 229
Gauntlett, David 120, 125, 126

gender 31, **32**
    childhood 77
    divorce 64–5
    domestic violence 88
    eating disorders 17
    family 57–61, 69–70, 72, 80–5
    fatherhood 81–2
    feminism 12–13
    identity 8, 30–3
    marriage 63
    media 110, 113, 122–7
    postmodernism 22, 32
    religion 164–9
    social status 8
    subcultures 207–8
    victimization 124
gender-role socialization 31–2, **32**, 88, 90
generalizability 231, **232**, 248, **251**
'generation gap' 193
Gershuny, J. 60, 71
Gilroy, P. 36, 201
girls' culture 208, **208**
Glaser, B. 242
Glasgow University Media Group (GUMG) 109–10, 111, 261
global village 135, **136**
globalization **45**, **156**, **190**, **202**
    national identity 43
    postmodernism 22
    religion 155
    resistance 136
    youth culture 187, 201
Goffman, Erving 15–18, 90–2
government policy
    children 76
    divorce 64
    family 52, 56–61
    modernity 21
    research 237
    statistics 259–60
grand narrative 161, **162**
Griffin, C. 219
GUMG *see* Glasgow University Media Group

Hakim, Catherine 84
halal food 172, **174**
Halevy, E. 145
Hall, S. 12, 193, 194, 195
health 52
Hebdige, D. 190, 194–5
Heelas, P. 154, 161, 168, 169, 180, 181
hegemony **100**, 193, **196**
    Marxism 98–9, 109
    masculinity 32, **32**, 218, **222**
Herberg, W. 155
heterosexuality 51, **53**
hidden curriculum **222**
high culture 103, 135, **136**
hippies 199
holistic milieu 161, **162**, 180
Holmes, Kelly 40, 41
home ownership 27
homosexuality
    family 52, 55, 57, 71–2
    media 133
    representations 130
    schooling 218–19
house church movement 173, **174**
housewife role 30, 82, 83
hybridization 38, **39**, 201, **202**
hypodermic syringe model 112–13, **114**, 117

'I' 15, 17–18
idealization 58, **59**
identity **4**, 8, **8**
   conflict 10–13
   consensus 6–9
   cultural influences 5
   ethnicity 34–9
   gender 30–3
   labelling theory 16–18
   media 135
   mixed-race families 38, 71
   national 35, 40–5
   postmodernity 21, 22, 135
   social action theory 14–19
   social class 24–9
   socialization 2–5
ideological apparatus 145, **146**
ideology **12**, **100**
Ik tribe 50–1
illegitimate opportunity structure 205–6, **208**, 212
inarticulate 194, **196**
inclusivity **179**
income 10
indicators 255, **255**
individualism 26, **90**
industrialization 20–1, **23**, 75–6
inequality
   families 57, 83–4
   feminism 12–13
   Marxism 11–12
   media 122–7
   religion 145
   Weber 12
infant mortality rate 76, **78**
instinct 3, **4**
institutional racism 35, **39**
instrumental working class 26
interactionism **18**, 236
   see also social action theory
internalization **4**
interpretations 15, **18**
interpretive sociology 236, **237**
interviewer bias 254, **255**
interviews 242, 252–7
intra-corporate self-promotion 97, **100**
introversionist sect 167, **168**
investigative journalism 100, **100**
invisible girl 196, **196**
irretrievability **66**
Islamic Revolution 157
Islamophobia 35, **39**, 172, **174**

Jacobson, J. 36
Jefferson, Tony 12, 193, 194, 195
Jordan, B. 26

Katz, J. 207, 213
Kendal project 154

labelling theory 16–18, **18**, 69
landed classes 145, **146**
language 42
late modernity 198–203
Lawrence, Stephen 35, 129
Lees, S. 31
legitimacy **12**
leisure 188, 199–200
letters 260, 261
liberal feminists 13, 83, 125
liberalism 155, **156**

liberation theology 149, **150**
licence fees 102, 104, **104**
life-changing events 144
literature search 259, **263**
lone households 71
lone parent families 52, 57, 58, 63, 69–70, 73
longitudinal surveys 241, **244**
Lyng, S. 207
Lyotard, J.-F. 155

Mac an Ghaill, Mairtin 33, 218–19, 222, 254
McDonaldization **136**
macho 218, 219, **222**
McIntosh, M. 59
McRobbie, A. 196, 208
Maffesoli, Michel 200, 201
magazines 123–4, 125
Malinowski, B. 144
manipulation 31
mantra 160, **162**
manual work 25
Marcuse, H. 87, 199
marginalization **110**, 123, **126**, 161
marginalized masculinity 32–3, **32**
market research 242
marriage 62–7
   ethnicity 70–1
   family and morality 57–61
   nuclear family 51
   power and control 80–5
   procreation 52
Marsden, D. 81
Marshall, G. 11–12, 149
Martin, D. 178
Marx, Karl 11, 12, 21, 145, 146, 166, 174, 175
Marxism 11–12, **12**, **237**
   family 87
   media 98–9, 108–9, 112–15
   religion 145–6
   research 236
   social action theory 18
   youth offending 207
Marxist-feminists 13, 83, 87, 125
masculinity 32–3, **208**, **222**
   crisis of **32**, 33, 88, **90**
   ethnic identity 37
   feminization of 124, 125, **126**
   gangs 215
   schooling 217, 218–19
   youth culture 207–8, 209
master status 16, **18**, 19
maternal deprivation 57, **59**
maternal instinct 58
Matza, D. 206, 207, 209
'me' 15, 17–18
Mead, Margaret 259
means of production 11, **12**
media concentration **100**
media conglomerates 97, 99, **100**
media consumption **136**
media literate **120**
media regulation **114**
media-saturated society **136**
media texts 113, **114**
media
   content analysis 261
   effects 112–15
   femininity 31
   gangs 213
   gender 122–7

growth 187–8
Marxism 11
national identity 41, 43
news 106–11
ownership and control 96–101
postmodernism 21, 134–7
public service broadcasting 102–5
representations **126**, 128–33, **131**
social class 28
violence 116–21
youth culture 200–1
meritocratic system 11, **12**
meta-narratives 21, **23**, 155, **156**
meta-study 263, 273
middle class 27–8, 218–19
millennarian religions 160, **162**
Miller, Walter 206, 210
minority groups 35–6
   see also ethnicity
Mirza, H. 219–20
mixed-race families 38, 71
modernity 21, **23**, 178, **179**, 199, **202**
Modood, T. 36, 37, 38, 44, 45
monarchy 42
monogamy 63, **66**
monopoly of truth 153, **156**
monotheism 165, **168**
moral consensus **8**
moral panics **66**, **131**, **156**
   child abuse 89
   ethnic minorities 129
   religion 153
   teenage pregnancy 63–4
   youth culture 130–1
morality 8, 52, 56–61, 112–15
Morley, D. 114
mortification 16–17
mother role 82, 83
Mount, F. 26
multicultural society 43–4, **45**
multinational companies **45**
Muncie, J. 199, 209, 213
Murdoch, Rupert 98, 99, 108, 136
Murdock, G.P. 53
Murray, C. 26
music 188
Muslims
   British 172, 175
   dress 166, 175
   education 38
   ethnic identity 35–6, 38, 45
   marriage 83
   power and control 83
   women 39

narrativization 108, **110**
Nation of Islam 168, **168**
nation-state 41, **45**
national identity 35, 40–5
nationalism 22, **23**
nationality 41, **45**
Nazroo, J. 88
negative labelling 69, **72**
neglect 89
negotiated reading 114, **114**
neo-tribes 200, 201, **202**
neutralization 206–7
New Age movements 158–63, 168
'new man' 32, **32**, 80, 84, 125
New Media **100**
new religious movements (NRMs) 158–63, 167

New Right **59**
 childhood 76–7
 family 57–9, 68, 69–70, 71–2
 fatherhood 81–2
 marital breakdown 63–4, 65
 power and control 82
news 106–11
news diary 106–7, **110**
news values 107, **110**
niche audiences 103, **104**
Niebuhr, H.R. 153
non-participant observation 247, **251**
norms 3, **4**, 8–9, 52
NRMs *see* new religious movements
nuclear family 51–2, **53**, 55, 67
 diversity 68, 69
 divorce 65
 familial ideology 57–61
 functionalism 52–3
 power and control 80–1
nurturing 51, **53**

Oakley, A. 31
objectivity 232, **232**
observation 246–51
O'Donnell, M. 219, 221
offending 204–9
Office for Communications (OFCOM) 103
official statistics 89, **90**
Ohlin, L. 205–6
one-parent families *see* lone parent families
open questions 253, **255**
operationalizing concepts 254–6, **255**
oppositional reading 114, **114**
oppositional subcultures 12, **12**, 195, **196**
oral history 260
Orbach, Susie 124
organized religion 152–7
overt observation 247, 248, **251**

Packard, Vance 112
parenting
 conventional approach 76–7
 fatherhood 81–2
 reconstituted families 70
 standards 60
 state policy 58
Parsons, Talcott 8, 52, 53, 83, 144, 179
participant observational studies 236, 247–8, **251**
passive audience approaches 112–13
patriarchal rationale 165, **168**
patriarchy **32**, **237**
 child abuse 90
 domestic violence 88
 family 58, 82, 83, 91
 feminism 12–13
 media 125
 power and control 82
 religion 165, 166–7
Pearson, G. 190, 211
peer group 37, 189, **190**, 217
Pentecostalism 173–4
personal experience 228
personality stabilization 52, 54
Phillips, Melanie 76, 82
Philo, Greg 109, 115
physical abuse 89
pilot surveys 240, **244**
pluralism 99–100, **100**, 102, 109, 125
polytheism 165, **168**

popular culture 103, 135, **136**
pornography 124
positivism 21, **23**, 236, **237**, 254
Postman, Neil 77
postmodernism 20–3, **23**, **202**
 ethnicity 201
 family diversity 72
 gangs 213
 gender 32
 marriage 63–4
 media 114, 134–7
 religion 153, 155, 156, 180
 social class 28
 youth culture 198–203, 207
poverty 69, 71, 77
power
 family 80–5
 gender 32
 media 98, 113, 123
 research 234, 248
 social action theory 18
pragmatic motives 161, **162**
pre-industrial society 75
predestination 149, **150**
preferred (dominant) reading 113, **114**
presenting culture 108
primary data 230, **232**
primary socialization **4**
private institutions 57, 58, **59**
privatized nuclear family 65, **66**, **78**, 80–1
procreation 52, **53**, 54
production
 industrialization 21
 means of 11, **12**
 national identity 43
profane 143, **146**
proletariat 11, **12**
Protestant ethic 149, 151
public service broadcasting 102–5, **104**
punk 194–5

qualitative research 230, **232**, 236, 246–51, **251**
quantitative research 230, **232**, 236, 240–5
questionnaires 252–7
quota sampling 241, 242, **244**

racism 35–6
radical change 149
radical feminists 13, 83, 87, 125
random sampling 241–2, **244**
rap music 201, 215
Rapoport, R.N. 68, 71
Rastafarianism 37, **39**, 173, **174**
rationality 21, **23**, **179**
rationalization 178, **179**
reception analysis 113
reconstituted families 70, **72**
reflexology 161, **162**
regulators for broadcasting 103, **104**, 108
reincarnation 148, **150**
relativity **23**
reliability **179**, 230–1, **232**, **251**, **255**
 participant observation 248
 questionnaires and interviews 256
 secularization data 178
religio-political events **179**, 180
religion
 conservative influence 142–7
 ethnic identity 37, 170–5
 family 53

feminism 164–9
gender 164–9
institutions 152–7
national identity 42
new religious movements 158–63
organized 152–7
secularization 176–81
social change 148–51
social class 28
religiosity 155, **156**
religious compensators 179, **179**
religious dogma 173, **174**
religious pluralism 155, **156**, 173, **174**, 178
remasculinization 222, **222**
representation by media 122–33, **126**, **131**
representativeness 231, **232**, 241, **244**
resacrilization 158, **162**
research
 advantages 229
 diaries 249
 interviews 252–7
 methods 234–8
 observation 246–51
 quantitative 240–5
 questionnaires 252–7
 secondary sources of data 258–63
resistance 36, 194, **196**
response rates 253, **255**
retributive man 125
rites 170, **174**
rituals 42
roles 3, **4**
 gender 31–2
 media 123, 125
 social identity 15
Roman Catholic church 150, 152, 164, 165–6
Roszak, T. 193, 199
Ruge, M. 107

sacred 143, **146**
sacred canopy 148, **150**
Said, E. 35
same-sex couples *see* homosexuality
sampling 241–2
sampling frame 241, **244**
sanctions **4**
satellite TV 102, 103, **104**
Savage, M. 27
scapegoating 69–70, **72**
schooling 216–23
Schudsen, M. 42
science 21, 256
screening programmes 102, **104**
second-generation 35, 38, **39**, 172–3
secondary data 230, **232**, 258–63, **263**
secondary socialization **4**
sects 152, 153, 167
secularization 42, **45**, 146, **146**, 176–81, **179**
seductive 207, **208**
segregated division of labour 80, **84**
selective exposure 113, **114**
selective filter model 113, **114**
selective perception 113, **114**
selective retention 113, **114**
self 15–16, **18**, 27
self-fulfilling prophecies 16, **18**
semiotic analysis 194, **196**
sensationalization 124, **126**
separation 64
September 11th 151
serial monogamy 65, **66**

service sector 21, **23**
Sewell, T. 37, 219
sex 30, **32**
sex education 56
sexual abuse 89
sexuality
    family diversity 71–2
    gender 31
    media 124, 130
    religion 165
    see also heterosexuality; homosexuality
Sharpe, Sue 31, 32, 219, 221
Shirbit culture 2, 3
shyness 17–18
single-faith schools 172–3
single-parent families *see* lone parent families
skateboarding 195
skinheads 194
snapshot survey *see* cross-sectional surveys
snowball sampling 241, 242, **244**
social action theory 14–19, **18**
social capital 28, 96
social change 148–51, 187
social class
    childhood 75–6, 77
    family 71, 81
    identity 24–9
    late modernity 199
    Marxism 11–12
    media 113, 130
    modernity 199
    postmodernity 21, 22
    schooling 217–18
    subcultures 193–4
    Weber 12
social closure 28, **29**
social construction **32, 78**
    age categories 187
    childhood 75, 79
    gender roles 31, **32**
social control 52, 54
social identity 15, **18**
social institutions 7, 8, **8**, 9
social integration 8, **8**, 52, **53**, 143
social order 7, **8**, 52
social policy 52, **53**
social solidarity 7, **8**
social status 52
social structure 6, **8**
social surveys *see* cross-sectional surveys
socialism 22, **23**
socialization 2–5, **4**
    domestic violence 88
    ethnic identity 36
    family 52, 53, 54
    fatherhood 81–2
    feminism 13
    functionalism 6–9
    gender 31–2
    labelling theory 16–18
    Marxism 11–12
    middle class 27
    national identity 42–3
    religion 143, 167
    social action theory 15–16
    working class 25
society **4**
sociobiology 3–4, **4**
sociological method 234–8
sociological theory 230, **232**
speaking in tongues 160, **162**, 173, **174**

spiritual revolution 154
spiritual shoppers 156, **156**, 178, **179**
sporting contests 41, 43
statistics 259–60
status 3, **4**
    labelling theory 16–18
    Weber 12
status frustration 205, **208**, 212, **214**
status quo 148, **150**
stereotypes 128–33, **152**
strain theory 205, **208**, 212
stratified sampling 242, **244**
Strauss, A. 242
Strinati, D. 135
structuralist theories **8**
    child abuse 90
    functionalism 6
    health 96–7
    Marxism 11
structured interpretation model 113–14, **114**
structured interviews 254, **255**
style 188–9, 194, 200, 203
subcultures 3, **4**, 193, **196, 208**
    functionalism 8–9
    gangs 212–13
    labelling theory 16
    Marxism 12
    offending 204–9
    social class 27
    see also youth culture
subject choice 221–2
subjectivization 15, **18**, 154, **156**
subordinate masculinity 32, **32**
subterranean values 206
suburban lifestyle 6, 27
suicide 229
surrogacy 161, **162**
surveys 240–1, **244**, 252–7
Swingewood, A. 22
symbolic annihilation 123, **126**
symbols of identity 41, 43, 44
symmetry **84**
synergy 97, **100**
systematic sampling 242, **244**

tarot readings 161, **162**
Taylor, Steve 21, 22, 23
technological convergence **100**
teddy boys 194
teenage pregnancy 57, 63–4, 69
television 97, 102–5, 106–7
terrestrial TV 103, **104**
theodicy 148–9, **150**
theoretical sampling 241, 242, **244**
theories 234–8
theorizing 228
third-generation 35, 38, **39**
Thornes, B. 64, 65
Thornton, S. 201, 203
Thrasher, F. 205, 211, 212, **214**
TM *see* transcendental meditation
top-down theories 236, **237**
totemism 143, **146**
trade sanctions 149, **150**
transcendental meditation (TM) 160
transcribing 254, **255**
transition 188, **190**, 192–3
transnational companies 22, **23**, 43, **45**, 97
Troeltsch, E. 152

underclass 26–7, **29**, 57
unstructured interviews 254, **255**
upper class 28
upward social mobility 52, **222**
Urban, M. 44
urbanization 20–1, **23**
uses and gratifications model 113, **114**, 118

validity 178, **179**, 231, **232, 255**
value consensus 7, 8, **8**
values 3, 4, **4**
    family 52
    functionalism 8–9
    middle class 27–8
    questionnaires and interviews 256
van Dijk, T. 128
vertical integration 97, 99, **100**
victim surveys 89, **90**
violence 86–91, 116–21, 124, 125
vocationalism 218, **222**

Waco siege 163
Wallis, R. 153, 159, 161, 178, 179
Walter, Natasha 12
war 42
watchdogs **100**
Waters, M. 43
wealth 11
Weber, Max 12, 143, 149, 151, 152, 161, 162, 171, 174, 178
welfare benefits 52, 54, 57, 69
Welsh identity 43
white-collar workers 27, **29**
Whyte, W.F. 205, 212
Willis, P. 217–19
Willmott, P. 80
Wilson, Bryan 153, 177, 178, 179
women priests 164, 165
Woodhead, L. 154, 168, 169, 181
work
    childhood 75–6, 77
    conflict of interest 10
    division of labour 7
    family 81, 82
    fatherhood 82
    gender 31
    identity 25
    Marxism 11–12
    mothers 82
    postmodernity 21, 22
working class 25–6
    child abuse 89
    schooling 217–18
    subcultures 193–5
    values 206
working class extended family 70, **72**
working mothers 57, 58, 63, 64–5, 81, 85
world-accommodating religious groups 160
world-affirming religious groups 159–60, 162
world-rejecting religious groups 160, 161

xenophobia 41, **45**

Young, M. 80, 81
youth culture 186–91
    conflict theories 192–7
    functionalism 192–7
    gangs 210–15
    late-modern theories 198–203
    offending 204–9
    postmodern theories 198–203
    schooling 216–23

Sociology AS for OCR